Drug War Facts

DISCARD

Compiled and Maintained by
Common Sense for Drug Policy

© Copyright 2007
ISBN 978-0-615-16429-8
Printed in Canada
November 2007

D0168865

Drug Prohibition Timeline

875: First anti-drug law in US enacted: San Francisco Opium Den Ordinance passed Nov. 15.

906: Congress passes Pure Food and Drug Act.

914: Harrison Narcotics Act enacted; federal control of narcotics established; nonmedical use of heroin and cocaine made illegal.

919: Congress passes Eighteenth Amendment to US Constitution, establishing national alcohol prohibition. Nine months later, on Oct. 28, Congress passes the Volstead Act providing for the law's enforcement.

933: Congress repeals national alcohol prohibition.

937: Marihuana (sic) Tax Act enacted. Objections were raised during hearings from the American Medical Association as well as from hemp producers.

970: Comprehensive Drug Abuse Prevention and Control Act passed into law, containing Controlled Substances Act (which lists marijuana in Schedule 1, prohibiting any legitimate medical uses).

970: The National Organization for Reform of Marijuana Laws (NORML) is founded.

971: President Richard M. Nixon declares "war on drugs" at press conference on June 17; announces creation of Special Action Office for Drug Abuse Prevention to be headed by Dr. Jerome Jaffe.

978: Federal forfeiture introduced via amendment to Comprehensive Drug Abuse Prevention and Control Act.

984: Comprehensive Crime Control Act of 1984 enacted: broadened criminal and civil asset forfeiture laws, increased federal penalties for drug offenses.

986: Anti-Drug Abuse Act of 1986 enacted; creates mandatory minimum sentences, establishes disparity in sentences involving equivalent weights of crack vs. powder cocaine.

988: Anti-Drug Abuse Amendment Act of 1988 enacted, increasing penalties for drug offenses and creating new federal offenses.

988: First needle exchange in United States established in Tacoma, WA.

989: US Office of National Drug Control Policy established. William S. Bennett, former Education Secretary, is named first "Drug Czar."

995: US Sentencing Commission recommends revising mandatory minimum sentencing guidelines to resolve crack/powder cocaine sentencing disparity. Congress overrides their recommendation.

996: California passes Proposition 215, legalizing sale and possession of medical marijuana by patients in need. Over the following decade, 10 more states legalize possession and cultivation of medical marijuana.

000: California voters pass Proposition 36, allowing people convicted of first or second time, no-violent drug possession to receive drug treatment instead of prison.

003: Seattle, WA voters approve Initiative 75, to make "the investigation, arrest and prosecution of marijuana offenses, where the marijuana was intended for adult personal use, the City's lowest law enforcement priority."

Facts by Topic

Facts by Topic

Introduction

Drug War Facts provides reliable information with applicable citations on important public health and criminal justice issues. It appears in longer form at *www.drugwarfacts.org* where it is updated regularly by Editor Douglas A. McVay.

Most charts, facts, and figures are from government sources, government-sponsored sources, peer-reviewed journals, and occasionally newspapers. In all cases the source is cited so that journalists and students can verify, check context, and obtain additional information.

For the Sixth Edition, data has been added from a variety of sources, statistical material which appeared in earlier editions has been updated, and the number of topics has increased.

Our mission is to offer useful facts, cited from authoritative sources, for a debate that is too often characterized by myths, error, emotion, and dissembling. We believe that in time an informed society will correct its errors and adopt wiser policies.

Drug War Facts is sponsored by Common Sense for Drug Policy, *www.CSDP.org*. Its directors are Kevin B. Zeese, President; H. Michael Gray, Chair; Robert E. Field, Co-Chair; and Melvin R. Allen.

To the extent of its copyrights, Common Sense for Drug Policy authorizes and encourages the use and republication of some or all portions of this book. Questions, comments, or suggestions for additions and modifications are most welcome and may be addressed to Doug McVay at *dmcvay@drugwarfacts.org*.

Addictive Qualities of Popular Drugs

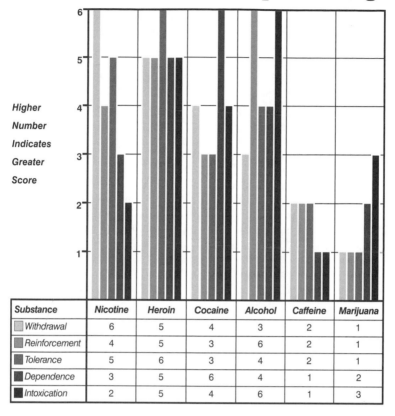

Higher Number Indicates Greater Score

Substance	Nicotine	Heroin	Cocaine	Alcohol	Caffeine	Marijuana
Withdrawal	6	5	4	3	2	1
Reinforcement	4	5	3	6	2	1
Tolerance	5	6	3	4	2	1
Dependence	3	5	6	4	1	2
Intoxication	2	5	4	6	1	3

Withdrawal: Presence and severity of characteristic withdrawal symptoms.

Reinforcement: A measure of the substance's ability, in human and animal tests, to get users to take it again and again, and in preference to other substances.

Tolerance: How much of the substance is needed to satisfy increasing cravings for it, and the level of stable need that is eventually reached.

Dependence: How difficult it is for the user to quit, the relapse rate, the percentage of people who eventually become dependent, the rating users give their own need for the substance and the degree to which the substance will be used in the face of evidence that it causes harm.

Intoxication: Though not usually counted as a measure of addiction in itself, the level of intoxication is associated with addiction and increases the personal and social damage a substance may do.

Source: Dr. Jack E. Henningfield, Ph.D. for NIDA. Reported by: Philip J. Hilts, New York Times, Aug. 2, 1994 "Is Nicotine Addictive? It Depends on Whose Criteria You Use."

Adolescents

1. The Monitoring the Future survey reports that from 1996 through 2005 more than half of the students in the United States tried an illegal drug before they graduated from high school. In 2006, that figure dropped to 48.2% lifetime prevalence.

   Source: Johnston, L. D., P.M. O'Malley, J.G. Bachman & J.E. Schulenberg, Monitoring the Future National Results on Adolescent Drug Use: Overview of Key Findings 2006, (Washington, DC: NIDA, April 2007), Table 1, p. 47.

2. In 2006, 5.0 percent of 12th graders reported daily use of marijuana, unchanged from the previous year. This compares with 6.0% in 1999 and 4.9% in 1996. Also in 2006, 25.4% of twelfth graders reported having had 5 or more drinks in a row in the last two weeks, compared with 27.1% the previous year. This compares with 30.8% in 1999 and 30.2% in 1996. And finally in 2006, 5.9% of twelfth graders reported smoking 1/2 pack or more of cigarettes daily, compared with 6.9% in 2005. This compares with 13.2% in 1999 and 13.0% in 1996.

   Source: Johnston, L. D., P.M. O'Malley, J.G. Bachman & J.E. Schulenberg, Monitoring the Future National Results on Adolescent Drug Use: Overview of Key Findings 2006, (Washington, DC: NIDA, April 2007), Table 4, p. 59.

3. "Since the study began in 1975, between 83% and 90% of every senior class have said that they could get marijuana fairly easily or very easily if they wanted some; therefore, it seems clear that this has remained a highly accessible drug. Since 1991, when data were also available for 8th and 10th graders, we have seen that marijuana is considerably less accessible to younger adolescents. Still, in 2006 two fifths of 8th graders (40%) and almost three quarters of all 10th graders (71%) reported it as being accessible. This compares to 85% for seniors."

   Source: Johnston, L. D., P.M. O'Malley, J.G. Bachman & J.E. Schulenberg, Monitoring the Future National Results on Adolescent Drug Use: Overview of Key Findings 2006, (Washington, DC: NIDA, April 2007), p. 13.

4. "What is most noteworthy, however, is how little change has occurred in the proportion of 12th graders who say that marijuana is 'fairly' or 'very' easy to get. By this measure, marijuana has been almost universally available to American 12th graders (from 83% to 90%) over at least the past 31 years."

   Source: Johnston, L. D., O'Malley, P. M., Bachman, J. G., & Schulenberg, J. E., Monitoring the Future national survey results on drug use, 1975-2005: Volume I, Secondary school students (NIH Publication No. 06-5883) (Bethesda, MD: National Institute on Drug Abuse), August 2006, p. 402.

5. "Overall, it is important to note that supply reduction — that is, reducing the availability of drugs — does not appear to have played as major a role as many had assumed in three of the most important downturns in illicit drug use that have occurred to date, namely, those for marijuana, cocaine, and ecstasy."

   Source: Johnston, L. D., O'Malley, P. M., Bachman, J. G., & Schulenberg, J. E., Monitoring the Future national survey results on drug use, 1975-2005: Volume I, Secondary school students (NIH Publication No. 06-5883) (Bethesda, MD: National Institute on Drug Abuse), August 2006, p. 407.

Adolescents

6. "As shown in Table 8-8, three of every ten (30%) 12th graders in the Class of 2005 believed that marijuana use should be treated as a crime. Similar proportions thought it should be entirely legal (28%), and another 28% felt it should be treated as a minor violation — like a parking ticket — but not as a crime. (The remaining 15% said they 'don't know.')

"Asked whether they thought it should be legal to sell marijuana if it were legal to use it, just over half (54%) said 'yes.' However, about four fifths of those answering 'yes' (43% of all respondents) would permit the sale only to adults. A small minority (11%) favored the sale to anyone, regardless of age, while 32% said that sale should not be legal even if use were made legal, and 14% said they 'don't know.'"

   Source: Johnston, L. D., O'Malley, P. M., Bachman, J. G., & Schulenberg, J. E., Monitoring the Future national survey results on drug use, 1975-2005: Volume I, Secondary school students (NIH Publication No. 06-5883) (Bethesda, MD: National Institute on Drug Abuse), August 2006, p. 354.

7. "Most 12th graders felt that they would be little affected personally by the legalization of either the sale or the use of marijuana. Three fifths (60%) of the respondents said that they would not use the drug even if it were legal to buy and use, and another 17% indicated they would use it about as often as they do now or less often. Only 6.1% said they would use it more often than they do at present while another 8.9% thought they would try it. (Eight percent said they did not know how their behavior would be affected if marijuana were legalized.)"

   Source: Johnston, L. D., O'Malley, P. M., Bachman, J. G., & Schulenberg, J. E., Monitoring the Future national survey results on drug use, 1975-2005: Volume I, Secondary school students (NIH Publication No. 06-5883) (Bethesda, MD: National Institute on Drug Abuse), August 2006, p. 354.

8. "A study of the effects of decriminalization by several states during the late 1970s found no evidence of any impact on the use of marijuana among young people, nor on attitudes and beliefs concerning its use. However, it should be noted that decriminalization falls well short of the full legalization posited in the questions here. Moreover, the situation today is very different than it was in the late 1970s, with much more peer disapproval and more rigorous enforcement of drug laws. More recent studies suggest that there may be an impact of decriminalization, such that 'youths living in decriminalized states are significantly more likely to report currently using marijuana.'"

   Source: Johnston, L. D., O'Malley, P. M., Bachman, J. G., & Schulenberg, J. E., Monitoring the Future national survey results on drug use, 1975-2005: Volume I, Secondary school students (NIH Publication No. 06-5883) (Bethesda, MD: National Institute on Drug Abuse), August 2006, pp. 354-5.

9. "Marijuana continues to be easier for teens to purchase than beer: 21 percent of teens ranked marijuana easiest to buy, compared to 14 percent for beer. As we have observed in the past, more teens rank cigarettes easiest to buy (28 percent) than the other substances. Eleven percent of teens say prescription drugs are easiest to buy."

   Source: QEV Analytics, "National Survey of American Attitudes on Substance Abuse XI: Teens and Parents" (New York, NY: National Center on Addiction and Substance Abuse at Columbia University, August 2006), p. 14.

Adolescents

10. "Most teens who use alcohol, cigarettes and marijuana do so before they are 14. Among teens who have tried alcohol, tobacco or marijuana, the average age of first use is a little more than 12 for alcohol, 12½ for cigarettes, and 13 years 11 months for marijuana."

   Source: QEV Analytics, "National Survey of American Attitudes on Substance Abuse VIII: Teens and Parents" (New York, NY: National Center on Addiction and Substance Abuse at Columbia University, August 2003), p. 2.

11. The US has higher rates of illegal drug use by young people than European nations, as noted by the Monitoring The Future survey: "The MTF study found that in 1999 41% of tenth grade students in the United States had used marijuana or cannabis at least once in their lifetimes. All the participating European countries had a considerably lower rate of lifetime use, averaging 17%. This proportion varied among European countries from 1% in Romania to a high of 35% in France, the United Kingdom, and the Czech Republic. The US also had one of the lowest proportions of students seeing marijuana use as carrying a risk of harm to the user, and one of the lowest proportions saying that they personally disapprove of marijuana use (pp. 345 and 348).... The US also had the highest rates of use of most of the other illicit drugs studied, as well as marijuana, with the important exception of heroin. These included amphetamines, hallucinogens, cocaine, crack, and ecstasy."

   Source: Johnston, Lloyd D., PhD, Patrick M. O'Malley, PhD, and Jerald G. Bachman, PhD, "Monitoring The Future: National Survey Results on Drug Use, 1975-2000, Volume 1: Secondary School Students" (Bethesda, MD: National Institute on Drug Abuse, August 2001), p. 363.

12. "In 1980, there were an estimated 1,476 arrests of persons ages 10–12 for every 100,000 persons in this age group in the U.S. population. By 2003, this arrest rate had fallen to 1,296, a decline of 12%. In 1980, 9.5% of all juvenile arrests were arrests of persons under age 13; in 2003, this percentage had decreased to 8.5%—with the majority of the decrease occurring during the mid-1990s."

   Source: Snyder, Howard N., and Sickmund, Melissa, "Juvenile Offenders and Victims: 2006 National Report," (Washington, DC: U.S. Department of Justice, Office of Justice Programs, Office of Juvenile Justice and Delinquency Prevention, March 2006), p. 130.

13. "In contrast to the 1980–1993 period, the overall juvenile drug arrest rate increased by 77% in the short period between 1993 and 1997. Large increases were also seen in the rates of juvenile subgroups: male (72%), female (119%), white (109%), American Indian (160%), and Asian (105%). The black juvenile arrest rate for drug abuse violations, which had increased dramatically in the earlier period, increased an additional 25% between 1993 and 1997. Between 1997 and 2003, the juvenile drug arrest rate fell marginally (22%), with most of the overall decline attributable to a drop in arrests of blacks (41%) and males (24%)."

   Source: Snyder, Howard N., and Sickmund, Melissa, "Juvenile Offenders and Victims: 2006 National Report" (Washington, DC: U.S. Department of Justice, Office of Justice Programs, Office of Juvenile Justice and Delinquency Prevention, March 2006), p. 144.

Adolescents

14. The Office of Juvenile Justice and Delinquency Prevention estimated that in 2004 there were 193,900 arrests of juveniles for drug abuse violations out of a total 2,202,000 juvenile arrests. By comparison, there were 91,100 violent crime index offense arrests and 452,300 property crime index offense arrests of juveniles that year.

    Source: Snyder, Howard N., "Juvenile Arrests 2004" (Washington, DC: US Department of Justice, Office of Justice Programs, Office of Juvenile Justice and Delinquency Prevention, March 2006), p. 3.

15. "Juveniles using drugs or alcohol committed 1 in 10 of the nonfatal violent victimizations against older teens. This was 2-1/2 times higher than the percentage of victimizations against younger teens perceived to be committed by a juvenile who was using drugs or alcohol.

    "Younger teens were more likely than older teens to report that their juvenile offender was not using drugs or alcohol. In about 4 in 10 victimizations against younger and older teens committed by juveniles, the victim could not ascertain whether or not the offender was using drugs or alcohol."

    Source: Baum, Katrina, PhD, "Juvenile Victimization and Offending, 1993-2003" (Washington, DC: US Dept. of Justice, Bureau of Justice Statistics, Aug. 2005), p. 8.

16. Even after controlling for other factors (e.g., age, gender, family structure, income, past month marijuana use, etc.), there is "a relationship between past month alcohol use and emotional and behavioral problems. The relationships were particularly strong among heavy and binge alcohol use and delinquent, aggressive, and criminal behaviors."

    Source: Greenblatt, Janet C., US Department of Justice, Bureau of Justice Statistics, Patterns of Alcohol Use Among Adolescents and Associations with Emotional and Behavioral Problems (Washington, DC: US Department of Justice, March 2000), p. 9.

17. Of the Nation's 72.3 million minor children in 1999, 2.1% had a parent in State or Federal prison. Black children (7.0%) were nearly 9 times more likely to have a parent in prison than white children (0.8%). Hispanic children (2.6%) were 3 times as likely as white children to have an inmate parent."

    Source: Mumola, Christopher J., US Department of Justice Bureau of Justice Statistics, Incarcerated Parents and Their Children (Washington, DC: US Department of Justice, August 2000), p. 2.

18. "A majority of parents in both State (62%) and Federal (84%) prison were held more than 100 miles from their last place of residence."

    Source: Mumola, Christopher J., US Department of Justice Bureau of Justice Statistics, Incarcerated Parents and Their Children (Washington, DC: US Department of Justice, August 2000), p. 5.

19. The Bureau of Justice Statistics estimates that 2.8% of all children under age 18 have at least one parent in a local jail or a State or Federal prison — a total of 1,941,796 kids. One in 40 have an incarcerated father, and 1 in 359 have an incarcerated mother.

    Source: Greenfield, Lawrence A., and Snell, Tracy L., US Department of Justice, Bureau of Justice Statistics, Women Offenders (Washington, DC: US Department of Justice, December 1999), p. 8, Table 18.

Adolescents

20. "The number of offenders under age 18 admitted to prison for drug offenses increased twelvefold (from 70 to 840) between 1985 to 1997. By 1997 drug offenders made up 11% of admissions among persons under 18 compared to 2% in 1985."

   Source: Strom, Kevin J., US Department of Justice, Bureau of Justice Statistics, Profile of State Prisoners Under Age 18, 1985-1997 (Washington, DC: US Department of Justice, February 2000), p. 4.

21. "During 1985, an estimated 20 white males and 30 black males under age 18 were admitted to State prison for drug offenses. In 1997 black males under age 18 outnumbered white males of the same age by more than 5 to 1 (640 to 120 admissions for drug offenses)."

   Source: Strom, Kevin J., US Department of Justice, Bureau of Justice Statistics, Profile of State Prisoners Under Age 18, 1985-1997 (Washington, DC: US Department of Justice, February 2000), p. 5.

22. "Fifty-eight percent of offenders admitted under 18 in 1997 were black and 25% were white, representing a gradual change from 1990, when blacks comprised 61% of admissions and whites 21% (table 6). The racial characteristics of persons admitted under 18 had shifted more dramatically between 1985 and 1990. During this period the percentage of black admissions increased from 53% to 62%, and the percentage of whites fell from 32% to 21%. Hispanic admissions, as a proportion of all persons under age 18 entering State prison, have remained stable from 1985 to 1997."

   Source: Strom, Kevin J., US Department of Justice, Bureau of Justice Statistics, Profile of State Prisoners Under Age 18, 1985-1997 (Washington, DC: US Department of Justice, February 2000), p. 6 & Table 6.

23. "Adolescence is a period in which youth reject conventionality and traditional authority figures in an effort to establish their own independence. For a significant number of adolescents, this rejection consists of engaging in a number of 'risky' behaviors, including drug and alcohol use. Within the past few years, researchers and practitioners have begun to focus on this tendency, suggesting that drug use may be a 'default' activity engaged in when youth have few or no opportunities to assert their independence in a constructive manner."

   Source: Maria Carmona and Kathryn Stewart, A Review of Alternative Activities and Alternatives Programs in Youth-Oriented Prevention (National Center for the Advancement of Prevention, under contract for the Substance Abuse Mental Health Services Administration(SAMHSA), Center for Substance Abuse Prevention, 1996), p. 5.

Alcohol and Crime

1. "Slightly more than half of Americans aged 12 or older reported being current drinkers of alcohol in the 2005 survey (51.8 percent). This translates to an estimated 126 million people, which is higher than the 2004 estimate of 121 million people (50.3 percent).

   "More than one fifth (22.7 percent) of persons aged 12 or older participated in binge drinking at least once in the 30 days prior to the survey in 2005. This translates to about 55 million people, comparable with the estimates reported since 2002.

   "In 2005, heavy drinking was reported by 6.6 percent of the population aged 12 or older, or 16 million people. This percentage is similar to the rates of heavy drinking in 2002 (6.7 percent), 2003 (6.8 percent), and 2004 (6.9 percent)."

   These categories are defined thus:

   "Current (past month) use - At least one drink in the past 30 days (includes binge and heavy use).

   "Binge use - Five or more drinks on the same occasion (i.e., at the same time or within a couple of hours of each other) on at least 1 day in the past 30 days (includes heavy use).

   "Heavy use - Five or more drinks on the same occasion on each of 5 or more days in the past 30 days."

   Source: Substance Abuse and Mental Health Services Administration, US Department of Health and Human Services, Results from the 2005 National Survey on Drug Use and Health: National Findings (Rockville, MD: Office of Applied Studies, Sept. 2006), p. 27.

2. "When an alcoholic beverage is consumed, approximately 20% of the alcohol is absorbed in the stomach and 80% is absorbed in the small intestine (Freudenrich, 2001). After absorption, alcohol enters the bloodstream and dissolves in the water of the blood where it is quickly distributed to body tissues. When alcohol reaches the brain, it affects the cerebral cortex first, followed by the limbic system (hippocampus and septal area), cerebellum, hypothalamus, pituitary gland, and lastly, the medulla, or brain stem. Some of these regions are similar to those affected by cannabis, but alcohol also affects sexual arousal/function and increases urinary output. When BAC is near toxic levels, lower order brain regions are affected, which is often followed by sleepiness, lack of consciousness, coma, or death."

   Source: Laberge, Jason C., Nicholas J. Ward, "Research Note: Cannabis and Driving — Research Needs and Issues for Transportation Policy," Journal of Drug Issues, Dec. 2004, pp. 973.

3. On an average day in 1996, an estimated 5.3 million convicted offenders were under the supervision of criminal justice authorities. Nearly 40% of these offenders, about 2 million, had been using alcohol at the time of the offense for which they were convicted.

   Source: Greenfield, Lawrence A., US Department of Justice, Bureau of Justice Statistics, Alcohol and Crime: An Analysis of National Data on the Prevalence of Alcohol Involvement in Crime (Washington, DC: US Department of Justice, April, 1998), p. 20.

C

4. About 6 in 10 convicted jail inmates said that they had been drinking on a regular basis during the year before the offense for which they were serving time. Nearly 2 out of 3 of these inmates, regardless of whether they drank daily or less often, reported having previously been in a treatment program for an alcohol dependency problem.

   Source: Greenfield, Lawrence A., US Department of Justice, Bureau of Justice Statistics, Alcohol and Crime: An Analysis of National Data on the Prevalence of Alcohol Involvement in Crime (Washington, DC: US Department of Justice, April, 1998), p. 27.

5. About a quarter of the women on probation nationwide had been drinking at the time of their offense compared to more than 40% of male probationers (figure 30). For those convicted of public-order crimes, nearly two-thirds of women and three-quarters of men had been drinking at the time of the offense.

   Source: Greenfield, Lawrence A., US Department of Justice, Bureau of Justice Statistics, Alcohol and Crime: An Analysis of National Data on the Prevalence of Alcohol Involvement in Crime (Washington, DC: US Department of Justice, April, 1998), p. 24.

6. For more than 4 in 10 convicted murderers being held either in jail or in state prison, alcohol use is reported to have been a factor in the crime. Nearly half of those convicted of assault and sentenced to probation had been drinking when the offense occurred.

   Source: Greenfield, Lawrence A., US Department of Justice, Bureau of Justice Statistics, Alcohol and Crime: An Analysis of National Data on the Prevalence of Alcohol Involvement in Crime (Washington, DC: US Department of Justice, April, 1998), p. 21.

7. According to a literature review of the effects of alcohol on driving, "As with cannabis, alcohol use increased variability in lane position and headway (Casswell, 1979; Ramaekers et al., 2000; Smiley et al., 1981; Stein et al., 1983) but caused faster speeds (Casswell, 1977; Krueger & Vollrath, 2000; Peck et al., 1986; Smiley et al., 1987; Stein et al., 1983). Some studies also showed that alcohol use alone and in combination with cannabis affected visual search behavior (Lamers & Ramaekers, 2001; Moskowitz, Ziedman, & Sharma, 1976). Alcohol consumption combined with cannabis use also worsened driver performance relative to use of either substance alone. Lane position and headway variability were more exaggerated (Attwood et al., 1981; Ramaekers et al., 2000; Robbe, 1998) and speeds were faster (Peck et al., 1986).

   "Both simulator and road studies showed that relative to alcohol use alone, participants who used cannabis alone or in combination with alcohol were more aware of their intoxication. Robbe (1998) found that participants who consumed 100 g/kg of cannabis rated their performance worse and the amount of effort required greater compared to those who consumed alcohol (0.05 BAC). Ramaekers et al.(2000) showed that cannabis use alone and in combination with alcohol consumption increased self-ratings of intoxication and decreased self-ratings of performance. Lamers and Ramaekers (2001) found that cannabis use alone (100 g/kg) and in combination with alcohol consumption resulted in lower ratings of alertness, greater perceptions of effort, and worse ratings of performance."

   Source: Laberge, Jason C., Nicholas J. Ward, "Research Note: Cannabis and Driving — Research Needs and Issues for Transportation Policy," Journal of Drug Issues, Dec. 2004, pp. 978.

Alcohol and Crime

8. "When compared to alcohol, cannabis is detected far less often in accident-involved drivers. Drummer et al. (2003) cited several studies and found that alcohol was detected in 12.5% to 79% of drivers involved in accidents. With regard to crash risk, a large study conducted by Borkenstein, Crowther, Shumate, Zeil and Zylman (1964) compared BAC in approximately 6,000 accident-involved drivers and 7,600 nonaccident controls. They determined the crash risk for each BAC by comparing the number of accident-involved drivers with detected levels of alcohol at each BAC to the number of nonaccident control drivers with the same BAC. They found that crash risk increased sharply as BAC increased. More specifically, at a BAC of 0.10, drivers were approximately five times more likely to be involved in an accident.

"Similar crash risk results were obtained when data for culpable drivers were evaluated. Drummer (1995) found that drivers with detected levels of alcohol were 7.6 times more likely to be culpable. Longo et al. (2000) showed that drivers who tested positive for alcohol were 8.0 times more culpable, and alcohol consumption in combination with cannabis use produced an odds ratio of 5.4. Similar results were also noted by Swann (2000) and Drummer et al. (2003)."

Source: Laberge, Jason C., Nicholas J. Ward, "Research Note: Cannabis and Driving — Research Needs and Issues for Transportation Policy," Journal of Drug Issues, Dec. 2004, pp. 981.

9. "In 2002 and 2003, an estimated 88.2 percent of persons aged 21 or older (175.6 million) were lifetime alcohol users, whereas an estimated 11.8 percent (23.5 million) were lifetime nondrinkers. Over half of lifetime alcohol users (52.7 percent) had used one or more illicit drugs at some time in their life, compared to 8.0 percent of lifetime nondrinkers. Among persons who had used an illicit drug in their lifetime, the average age at first illicit drug use was 19 years for lifetime alcohol users, versus 23 years for lifetime nondrinkers."

Source: "The NSDUH Report: Illicit Drug Use Among Lifetime Nondrinkers and Lifetime Alcohol Users," Office of Applied Programs, Substance Abuse & Mental Health Services Administration, US Dept. of Health and Human Services, June 14, 2005, p. 2.

10. "Lifetime alcohol users aged 21 or older had a significantly higher rate of past year illicit drug use (13.7 percent) compared with lifetime nondrinkers (2.7 percent). In addition, lifetime alcohol users had significantly higher rates of past year use across all illicit drug categories, with the exception of inhalants (Table 1). Nonmedical use of pain relievers was the illicit drug used most often by lifetime nondrinkers, whereas lifetime alcohol users reported using marijuana most frequently."

Source: "The NSDUH Report: Illicit Drug Use Among Lifetime Nondrinkers and Lifetime Alcohol Users," Office of Applied Programs, Substance Abuse & Mental Health Services Administration, US Dept. of Health and Human Services, June 14, 2005, p. 2.

Annual Causes of Death in the United States

Tobacco:	435,000	(see #1)
Poor Diet and Physical Inactivity:	365,000	(see #1)
Alcohol:	85,000	(see #1)
Microbial Agents:	75,000	(see #1)
Toxic Agents:	55,000	(see #1)
Motor Vehicle Crashes:	26,347	(see #1)
Adverse Reactions to Prescription Drugs:	32,000	(see #2)
Suicide:	30,622	(see #3)
Incidents Involving Firearms:	29,000	(see #1)
Homicide:	20,308	(see #4)
Sexual Behaviors:	20,000	(see #1)
Illicit Use of Drugs:	17,000	(see #1 & #5)
Anti-Inflammatory Drugs Such As Aspirin:	7,600	(see #6)
Marijuana:	0	(see #7)

1. "The leading causes of death in 2000 were tobacco (435,000 deaths; 18.1% of total US deaths), poor diet and physical inactivity (400,000 deaths; 16.6%), and alcohol consumption (85,000 deaths; 3.5%). Other actual causes of death were microbial agents (75,000), toxic agents (55,000), motor vehicle crashes (43,000), incidents involving firearms (29,000), sexual behaviors (20,000), and illicit use of drugs (17,000)."
(Note: According to a correction published by the Journal on Jan. 19, 2005, "On page 1240, in Table 2, '400,000 (16.6)' deaths for 'poor diet and physical inactivity' in 2000 should be '365,000 (15.2).' A dagger symbol should be added to 'alcohol consumption' in the body of the table and a dagger footnote should be added with 'in 1990 data, deaths from alcohol-related crashes are included in alcohol consumption deaths, but not in motor vehicle deaths. In 2000 data, 16,653 deaths from alcohol-related crashes are included in both alcohol consumption and motor vehicle death categories." Journal of the American Medical Association, Jan. 19, 2005, Vol. 293, No. 3, p. 298.)

   Source: Mokdad, Ali H., PhD, James S. Marks, MD, MPH, Donna F. Stroup, PhD, MSc, Julie L. Gerberding, MD, MPH, "Actual Causes of Death in the United States, 2000," Journal of the American Medical Association, March 10, 2004, Vol. 291, No. 10, pp. 1238, 1241. A copy of the report is at http://www.csdp.org/research/1238.pdf

2. "Illicit drug use is associated with suicide, homicide, motor-vehicle injury, HIV infection, pneumonia, violence, mental illness, and hepatitis. An estimated 3 million individuals in the United States have serious drug problems. Several studies have reported an undercount of the number of deaths attributed to drugs by vital statistics; however, improved medical treatments have reduced mortality from many

Annual Causes of Death in the United States

diseases associated with illicit drug use. In keeping with the report by McGinnis and Foege, we included deaths caused indirectly by illicit drug use in this category. We used attributable fractions to compute the number of deaths due to illicit drug use. Overall, we estimate that illicit drug use resulted in approximately 17,000 deaths in 2000, a reduction of 3000 deaths from the 1990 report."

Source: Mokdad, Ali H., PhD, James S. Marks, MD, MPH, Donna F. Stroup, PhD, MSc, Julie L. Gerberding, MD, MPH, "Actual Causes of Death in the United States, 2000," Journal of the American Medical Association, March 10, 2004, Vol. 291, No. 10, p. 1242.

3. According to Canadian researchers, approximately 32,000 hospitalized patients (and possibly as many as 106,000) in the USA die each year because of adverse reactions to their prescribed medications.

    Source: Lazarou, J, Pomeranz, BH, Corey, PN, "Incidence of adverse drug reactions in hospitalized patients: a meta-analysis of prospective studies," Journal of the American Medical Association (Chicago, IL: American Medical Association, 1998), 1998;279:1200-1205, also letters column, "Adverse Drug Reactions in Hospitalized Patients," JAMA (Chicago, IL: AMA, 1998), Nov. 25, 1998, Vol. 280, No. 20, from the web at http://jama.ama-assn.org/issues/ v280n20/ffull/ jlt1125-1.html, last accessed Feb. 12, 2001.

4. The US Centers for Disease Control reports that in 2003, there were a total of 31,484 deaths from suicide in the US.

    Source: Hoyert, Donna L., PhD, Heron, Melonie P., PhD, Murphy, Sherry L., BS, Kung, Hsiang-Ching, PhD; Division of Vital Statistics, "Deaths: Final Data for 2003," National Vital Statistics Reports, Vol. 54, No. 13 (Hyattsville, MD: National Center for Health Statistics, April 19, 2006), p. 5, Table C.

5. The US Centers for Disease Control reports that in 2003, there were a total of 17,732 deaths from homicide in the US.

    Source: Hoyert, Donna L., PhD, Heron, Melonie P., PhD, Murphy, Sherry L., BS, Kung, Hsiang-Ching, PhD; Division of Vital Statistics, "Deaths: Final Data for 2003," National Vital Statistics Reports, Vol. 54, No. 13 (Hyattsville, MD: National Center for Health Statistics, April 19, 2006), p. 5, Table C.

6. "In 2003, a total of 28,723 persons died of drug-induced causes in the United States (Tables 21 and 22). The category 'drug-induced causes' includes not only deaths from dependent and nondependent use of drugs (legal and illegal use), but also poisoning from medically prescribed and other drugs. It excludes unintentional injuries, homicides, and other causes indirectly related to drug use. Also excluded are newborn deaths due to mother's drug use."

    Source: Hoyert, Donna L., PhD, Heron, Melonie P., PhD, Murphy, Sherry L., BS, Kung, Hsiang-Ching, PhD; Division of Vital Statistics, "Deaths: Final Data for 2003," National Vital Statistics Reports, Vol. 54, No. 13 (Hyattsville, MD: National Center for Health Statistics, April 19, 2006), p. 10.

7. "In 2003, a total of 20,687 persons died of alcohol-induced causes in the United States (Tables 23 and 24). The category 'alcohol-induced causes' includes not only deaths from dependent and nondependent use of alcohol, but also accidental poisoning by alcohol. It excludes unintentional injuries, homicides, and other causes indirectly related to alcohol use as well as deaths due to fetal alcohol syndrome."

Annual Causes of Death in the United States

Source: Hoyert, Donna L., PhD, Heron, Melonie P., PhD, Murphy, Sherry L., BS, Kung, Hsiang-Ching, PhD; Division of Vital Statistics, "Deaths: Final Data for 2003," National Vital Statistics Reports, Vol. 54, No. 13 (Hyattsville, MD: National Center for Health Statistics, April 19, 2006), p. 10.

8. "Each year, use of NSAIDs (Non-Steroidal Anti-Inflammatory Drugs) accounts for an estimated 7,600 deaths and 76,000 ospitalizations in the United States." (NSAIDs include aspirin, ibuprofen, naproxen, diclofenac, ketoprofen, and tiaprofenic acid.)

Source: Robyn Tamblyn, PhD; Laeora Berkson, MD, MHPE, FRCPC; W. Dale Jauphinee, MD, FRCPC; David Gayton, MD, PhD, FRCPC; Roland Grad, MD, MSc; Allen Huang, MD, FRCPC; Lisa Isaac, PhD; Peter McLeod, MD, FRCPC; and Linda Snell, MD, MHPE, FRCPC, "Unnecessary Prescribing of NSAIDs and the Management of NSAID-Related Gastropathy in Medical Practice," Annals of Internal Medicine (Washington, DC: American College of Physicians, 1997), September 15, 1997, 127:429-438, from the web at http://www.acponline.org/journals/annals/15sep97/nsaid.htm , last accessed Feb. 14, 2001, citing Fries, JF, "Assessing and understanding patient risk," Scandinavian Journal of Rheumatology Supplement, 1992;92:21-4.

9. An exhaustive search of the literature finds no credible reports of deaths induced by marijuana. The US Drug Abuse Warning Network (DAWN) records instances of drug mentions in medical examiners' reports, and though marijuana is mentioned, it is usually in combination with alcohol or other drugs. Marijuana alone has not been conclusively shown to cause an overdose death.

Source: Drug Abuse Warning Network (DAWN), available on the web at http://www.samhsa.gov/ ; also see Janet E. Joy, Stanley J. Watson, Jr., and John A. Benson, Jr., "Marijuana and Medicine: Assessing the Science Base," Division of Neuroscience and Behavioral Research, Institute of Medicine (Washington, DC: National Academy Press, 1999), available on the web at http://www.nap.edu/html/marimed/ ; and US Department of Justice, Drug Enforcement Administration, "In the Matter of Marijuana Rescheduling Petition" (Docket #86-22), September 6, 1988, p. 57.

Civil and Human Rights

1. "Black and Hispanic Americans, and other minority groups as well, are victimized by disproportionate targeting and unfair treatment by police and other front-line law enforcement officials; by racially skewed charging and plea bargaining decisions of prosecutors; by discriminatory sentencing practices; and by the failure of judges, elected officials and other criminal justice policy makers to redress the inequities that become more glaring every day."

   Source: Welch, Ronald H., and Angulo, Carlos T., Leadership Conference on Civil Rights, Justice on Trial: Racial Disparities in the American Criminal Justice System (Washington, DC: Leadership Conference on Civil Rights, May 2000), p. vi.

2. "In both 2002 and 2005, white, black, and Hispanic drivers were stopped by police at similar rates, while blacks and Hispanics were more likely than whites to be searched by police. About 5% of all stopped drivers were searched by police during a traffic stop. Police found evidence of criminal wrong-doing (such as drugs, illegal weapons, or other evidence of a possible crime) in 11.6% of searches in 2005."

   Source: Durose, Matthew R., Smith, Erica L., and Langan, Patrick A., PhD, "Contacts Between Police and the Public, 2005," (NCJ215243) (Washington, DC: Bureau of Justice Statistics, April 2007), p. 1.

3. "Police issued tickets to more than half of all stopped drivers and arrested about 2.4% of drivers. Male drivers were 3 times more likely than female drivers to be arrested, and black drivers were twice as likely as white drivers to be arrested."

   Source: Durose, Matthew R., Smith, Erica L., and Langan, Patrick A., PhD, "Contacts Between Police and the Public, 2005," (NCJ215243) (Washington, DC: Bureau of Justice Statistics, April 2007), p. 1.

4. "Of the 43.5 million persons who had contact with police in 2005, an estimated 1.6% had force used or threatened against them during their most recent contact, a rate relatively unchanged from 2002 (1.5%). In both 2002 and 2005, blacks and Hispanics experienced police use of force at higher rates than whites. Of persons who had force used against them in 2005, an estimated 83% felt the force was excessive."

   Source: Durose, Matthew R., Smith, Erica L., and Langan, Patrick A., PhD, "Contacts Between Police and the Public, 2005," (NCJ215243) (Washington, DC: Bureau of Justice Statistics, April 2007), p. 1.

5. "In 11.6% of searches conducted during a traffic stop in 2005, police found drugs, an illegal weapon, open containers of alcohol, or other illegal items. Consent and nonconsent searches turned up evidence of criminal wrong-doing at similar rates."

   Source: Durose, Matthew R., Smith, Erica L., and Langan, Patrick A., PhD, "Contacts Between Police and the Public, 2005," (NCJ215243) (Washington, DC: Bureau of Justice Statistics, April 2007), p. 7.

6. "The number of wiretaps reported increased by 4 percent in 2006. A total of 1,839 applications were reported as authorized in 2006,

Civil and Human Rights

including 461 submitted to federal judges and 1,378 to state judges. No applications were denied. Compared to the number approved during 2005, the number of applications reported as approved by federal judges in 2006 fell 26 percent (see sidebar on page 8). The number of applications approved by state judges rose 20 percent. Wiretap applications in California (430 applications), New York (377 applications), New Jersey (189 applications), and Florida (98 applications) accounted for 79 percent of all applications approved by state judges."

Source: Administrative Office of the United States Courts, 2006 Wiretap Report (Washington, DC: USGPO, April 2007), p. 7.

7. "Violations of drug laws and homicide/assault were the two most prevalent types of offenses investigated through communications intercepts. Racketeering was the third most frequently recorded offense category, and gambling the fourth. Table 3 indicates that 80 percent of all applications for intercepts (1,473 wiretaps) authorized in 2006 cited a drug offense as the most serious offense under investigation."

Source: Administrative Office of the United States Courts, 2006 Wiretap Report (Washington, DC: USGPO, April 2007), p. 9.

8. "The average cost of intercept devices installed in 2006 was $52,551, down 5 percent from the average cost in 2005. For federal wiretaps for which expenses were reported in 2006, the average cost was $67,044, a 5 percent decrease from the average cost in 2005. The average cost of a state wiretap increased 3 percent to $46,687 in 2006."

Source: Administrative Office of the United States Courts, 2006 Wiretap Report (Washington, DC: USGPO, April 2007), p. 12.

9. Contrary to international standards, prisons and jails in the USA employ men to guard women and place relatively few restrictions on the duties of male staff. As a consequence, much of the touching and viewing their bodies by staff that women experience as shocking and humiliating is permitted by law.

Source: Amnesty International, "Not Part of My Sentence": Violations of the Human Rights of Women in Custody" (Washington, DC: Amnesty International, March 1999), p. 39.

10. Retaliation for reports of abuse impedes women's access to protection of their human rights. One woman who won a lawsuit against the Federal Bureau of Prisons for sexual abuse reported that she was beaten, raped and sodomized by three men who in the course of the attack told her that they were attacking her in retaliation for providing a statement to investigators.

Source: Amnesty International, "Not Part of My Sentence:" Violations of the Human Rights of Women in Custody (Washington, DC: Amnesty International, March 1999), p. 59.

11. "In December 2000, the Prison Journal published a study based on a survey of inmates in seven men's prison facilities in four states. The results showed that 21 percent of the inmates had experienced at least one episode of pressured or forced sexual contact since being incarcerated,

Civil and Human Rights

and at least 7 percent had been raped in their facility. A 1996 study of the Nebraska prison system produced similar findings, with 22 percent of male inmates reporting that they had been pressured or forced to have sexual contact against their will while incarcerated. Of these, over 50 percent had submitted to forced anal sex at least once. Extrapolating these findings to the national level gives a total of at least 140,000 inmates who have been raped."

Source: Human Rights Watch, "No Escape: Male Rape in US Prisons - Summary and Recommendations," 2001, from the web at http://www.hrw.org/reports/2001/prison/report.html last accessed May 18, 2004.

12. "Reports of sexual violence varied across systems and sampled facilities, with every State prison system except New Mexico reporting at least one allegation of sexual violence. Among the 347 sampled local jails, 131 (38%) reported an allegation. About 42% of the 36 sampled privately operated prisons and jails reported at least one allegation.
"Combined, the 2005 survey recorded 5,247 allegations of sexual violence. Taking into account weights for sampled facilities, the estimated total number of allegations for the Nation was 6,241. Expressed in terms of rates, there were 2.83 allegations of sexual violence per 1,000 inmates held in 2005, up from 2.43 per 1,000 inmates held in prisons, jails, and other adult correctional facilities in 2004. Prison systems reported 74% of all allegations; local jails, 22%; private prisons and jails, 3%; and other adult facilities, 1%."

Source: Beck, Allen J., PhD, and Harrison, Paige M., Sexual Violence Reported by Correctional Authorities, 2005 (NCJ214646) (Washington, DC: Bureau of Justice Statistics, July 2006), p. 4.

13. Nationwide, one in every 20 black men over the age of 18 is in prison. In five states, between one in 13 and one in 14 black men is in prison. This compares to one in 180 white men.

Source: Human Rights Watch, Racial Disparities in the War on Drugs (Washington, DC: Human Rights Watch, 2000), from their website at http://www.hrw.org/campaigns/drugs/war/key-facts.htm

14. At the start of the 1990s, the U.S. had more Black men (between the ages of 20 and 29) under the control of the nation's criminal justice system than the total number in college. This and other factors have led some scholars to conclude that, "crime control policies are a major contributor to the disruption of the family, the prevalence of single parent families, and children raised without a father in the ghetto, and the 'inability of people to get the jobs still available.'"

Source: Craig Haney, Ph.D., and Philip Zimbardo, Ph.D., "The Past and Future of U.S. Prison Policy: Twenty-five Years After the Stanford Prison Experiment," American Psychologist, Vol. 53, No. 7 (July 1998), p. 716.

15. "Since 1997, 16 states have implemented reforms to their felony disenfranchisement policies
"These reforms have resulted in the restoration of voting rights to an estimated 621,400 persons

Civil and Human Rights

"By 2004, the total number of people disenfranchised due to a felony conviction had risen to 5.3 million

"Among those disenfranchised, 74% are currently living in the community

"In 2004, 1 in 12 African Americans was disenfranchised because of a felony conviction, a rate nearly five times that of non-African Americans

"Voting is linked with reduced recidivism; one study shows that 27 percent of non-voters were rearrested, compared with 12 percent of voters"

Source: King, Ryan S., "A Decade of Reform: Felony Disenfranchisement Policy in the United States" (Washington, DC: Sentencing Project, 2006), p. 2.

16. "Thirteen percent of all adult black men — 1.4 million — are disenfranchised, representing one-third of the total disenfranchised population and reflecting a rate of disenfranchisement that is seven times the national average. Election voting statistics offer an approximation of the political importance of black disenfranchisement: 1.4 million black men are disenfranchised compared to 4.6 million black men who voted in 1996."

Source: Jamie Fellner and Mark Mauer, Losing the Vote: The Impact of Felony Disenfranchisement Laws in the United States (Washington, DC: Human Rights Watch & The Sentencing Project, 1998), p. 8. Election data cited comes from the US Census Bureau, Voting and Registration in the Election of November 1996 (P20-504) (Washington, DC: US Census Bureau, July 1998).

17. In his book No Equal Justice, Georgetown Law Professor David Cole notes "The (Supreme) Court's removal of meaningful Fourth Amendment review allows the police to rely on unparticularized discretion, unsubstantiated hunches, and nonindividualized suspicion. Racial prejudice and stereotypes linking racial minorities to crime rush to fill the void."

Source: Cole, David, No Equal Justice: Race and Class in the American Criminal Justice System (New York: The New Press, 1999), p. 53.

18. The report "Justice on Trial" from the Leadership Conference on Civil Rights notes that though "blacks are just 12 percent of the population and 13 percent of the drug users, and despite the fact that traffic stops and similar enforcement yield equal arrest rates for minorities and whites alike, blacks are 38 percent of those arrested for drug offenses and 59 percent of those convicted of drug offenses. Moreover, more frequent stops, and therefore arrests, of minorities will also result in longer average prison terms for minorities because patterns of disproportionate arrests generate more extensive criminal histories for minorities, which in turn influence sentencing outcomes."

Source: Welch, Ronald H., and Angulo, Carlos T., Leadership Conference on Civil Rights, "Justice on Trial: Racial Disparities in the American Criminal Justice System" (Washington, DC: Leadership Conference on Civil Rights, May 2000), p. 7.

Cocaine and Crack

1. "Most cocaine users are episodic recreational users who voluntarily curtail their use. However, cocaine use and the development of addictive behavior in some users has increased in North America, although recent declines are recorded. Availability of highly biologically active forms, such as crack cocaine, has worsened the problem of cocaine dependence."

   Source: "Cocaine," The Merck Manual, Section 15. Psychiatric Disorders, Chapter 198. Drug Use and Dependence, Merck & Co. Inc., from the web at http://www.merck.com/ mmpe/sec15/ch198/ch198f.html last accessed June 11, 2007.

2. "Although most cocaine in the US is snorted, smoking crack cocaine has become widely publicized. The hydrochloride salt is converted to a more volatile form, usually by adding NaHCO3, water, and heat. The converted material is combusted and the resultant smoke inhaled. Onset of effect is quicker, and intensity of the high is magnified."

   Source: "Cocaine," The Merck Manual, Section 15. Psychiatric Disorders, Chapter 198. Drug Use and Dependence, Merck & Co. Inc., from the web at http://www.merck.com/ mmpe/sec15/ch198/ch198f.html last accessed June 11, 2007.

3. "Tolerance to cocaine occurs, and withdrawal from heavy use is characterized by somnolence, increased appetite, and depression. The tendency to continue taking the drug is strong after a period of withdrawal."

   Source: "Cocaine," The Merck Manual, Section 15. Psychiatric Disorders, Chapter 198. Drug Use and Dependence, Merck & Co. Inc., from the web at http://www.merck.com/ mmpe/sec15/ch198/ch198f.html last accessed June 11, 2007.

4. " Effects differ with different modes of use. When injected or smoked, cocaine produces hyperstimulation, alertness, euphoria, and feelings of competence and power. The excitation and high are similar to those produced by injecting amphetamine. These feelings are less intense and disruptive in users who snort cocaine powder.
   "An overdose may produce tremors, seizures, and delirium. Death may result from MI, arrhythmias, and heart failure. Patients with extreme clinical toxicity may, on a genetic basis, have decreased (atypical) serum cholinesterase, an enzyme needed for clearance of cocaine. The concurrent use of cocaine and alcohol produces a condensation product, cocaethylene, which has stimulant properties and may contribute to toxicity."

   Source: "Cocaine," The Merck Manual, Section 15. Psychiatric Disorders, Chapter 198. Drug Use and Dependence, Merck & Co. Inc., from the web at http://www.merck.com/ mmpe/sec15/ch198/ch198f.html last accessed June 11, 2007.

5. "Some users of cocaine report feelings of restlessness, irritability, and anxiety. A tolerance to the 'high' may develop—many addicts report that they seek but fail to achieve as much pleasure as they did from their first exposure. Some users will increase their doses to intensify and prolong the euphoric effects. While tolerance to the high can occur, users can also become more sensitive to cocaine's anesthetic and convulsant effects without increasing the dose taken. This increased sensitivity may explain some deaths occurring after apparently low doses of cocaine."

Cocaine and Crack

Source: National Institute on Drug Abuse, InfoFacts: Crack and Cocaine (Rockville, MD: US Department of Health and Human Services), from the web at http://www.nida.nih.gov/infofacts/cocaine.html last accessed January 9, 2006.

6. "Because cocaine is a very short-acting drug, heavy users may inject it or smoke it q 10 to 15 min. This repetition produces toxic effects, such as tachycardia, hypertension, mydriasis, muscle twitching, sleeplessness, and extreme nervousness. Hallucinations, paranoid delusions, and aggressive behavior may develop, which can make the person dangerous. Pupils are maximally dilated, and the drug's sympathomimetic effect increases heart and respiration rates and BP.

    "Severe toxic effects occur in the compulsive heavy user. Rarely, repeated snorting causes nasal septal perforation due to local ischemia. Repeatedly smoking volatile crack cocaine in high doses can have serious toxic cardiovascular and behavioral consequences."

    Source: "Cocaine," The Merck Manual, Section 15. Psychiatric Disorders, Chapter 198. Drug Use and Dependence, Merck & Co. Inc., from the web at http://www.merck.com/mmpe/sec15/ch198/ch198f.html last accessed June 11, 2007.

7. "In 2003, 34.9 million Americans age 12 and over reported lifetime use of cocaine, and 7.9 million reported using crack. About 5.9 million reported annual use of cocaine, and 1.4 million reported using crack. About 2.3 million reported 30-day use of cocaine, and 604,000 reported using crack.

    "The percentage of youth ages 12 to 17 reporting lifetime use of cocaine was 2.6 percent in 2003. Among young adults ages 18 to 25, the rate was 15 percent, showing no significant difference from the previous year. However, there was a statistically significant decrease in the rate of lifetime crack use among females in the 12 to 17 age bracket."

    Source: National Institute on Drug Abuse, InfoFacts: Crack and Cocaine (Rockville, MD: US Department of Health and Human Services), from the web at http://www.nida.nih.gov/infofacts/cocaine.html last accessed January 9, 2006.

8. "Stopping sustained use requires considerable assistance, and the depression that may result requires close supervision and treatment. Many nonspecific therapies, including support and self-help groups and cocaine hotlines, exist. Extremely expensive inpatient therapy is available."

    Source: "Cocaine," The Merck Manual, Section 15. Psychiatric Disorders, Chapter 198. Drug Use and Dependence, Merck & Co. Inc., from the web at http://www.merck.com/mmpe/sec15/ch198/ch198f.html last accessed June 11, 2007.

Corruption of Law Enforcement Officers & Public Officials

1. A report by the General Accounting Office noted, "...several studies and investigations of drug-related police corruption found on-duty police officers engaged in serious criminal activities, such as (1) conducting unconstitutional searches and seizures; (2) stealing money and/or drugs from drug dealers; (3) selling stolen drugs; (4) protecting drug operations; (5) providing false testimony; and (6) submitting false crime reports."

   Source: General Accounting Office, Report to the Honorable Charles B. Rangel, House of Representatives, Law Enforcement: Information on Drug-Related Police Corruption (Washington, DC: USGPO, May 1998), p. 8.

2. On average, half of all police officers convicted as a result of FBI-led corruption cases between 1993 and 1997 were convicted for drug-related offenses.

   Source: General Accounting Office, Report to the Honorable Charles B. Rangel, House of Representatives, Law Enforcement: Information on Drug-Related Police Corruption (Washington, DC: USGPO, May 1998), p. 35.

3. "Although profit was found to be a motive common to traditional and drug-related police corruption, New York City's Mollen Commission identified power and vigilante justice as two additional motives for drug-related police corruption."

   Source: General Accounting Office, Report to the Honorable Charles B. Rangel, House of Representatives, Law Enforcement: Information on Drug-Related Police Corruption (Washington, DC: USGPO, May 1998), p. 3.

4. "The most commonly identified pattern of drug-related police corruption involved small groups of officers who protected and assisted each other in criminal activities, rather than the traditional patterns of non-drug-related police corruption that involved just a few isolated individuals or systemic corruption pervading an entire police department or precinct."

   Source: General Accounting Office, Report to the Honorable Charles B. Rangel, House of Representatives, Law Enforcement: Information on Drug-Related Police Corruption (Washington, DC: USGPO, May 1998), p. 3.

5. "In systems where a member of the legislature or judiciary, earning only a modest income, can easily gain the equivalent of some 20 months' salary from a trafficker by making one "favourable" decision, the dangers of corruption are obvious."

   Source: United Nations International Drug Control Program, Technical Series Report #6: Economic and Social Consequences of Drug Abuse and Illicit Trafficking (New York, NY: UNDCP, 1998), p. 39.

6. "Colombia has suffered the tragic consequences of endemic theft by politicians and public officials for decades. Entwined with the production and trafficking of illegal drugs, this behaviour exacerbated underdevelopment and lawlessness in the countryside, where a brutal war continues to claim the lives of some 3,500 civilians a year. A World Bank survey released in February 2002 found that bribes are paid in 50 per cent of all state contracts. Another World Bank report estimates the cost of corruption in Colombia at US $2.6 billion annually, the equivalent of 60 per cent of the country's debt."

Corruption of Law Enforcement Officers & Public Officials

Source: Hodess, Robin (ed.), Transparency International, Global Corruption Report 2003 (Berlin, Germany: Transparency International, 2003), p. 108.

G

7. "The Presidential Programme Against Corruption in Colombia specifically addresses 'narco-corruption'. Colombia, with a capacity to produce 580 tonnes of pure cocaine in 2000, is particularly poisoned by the interplay of narcotics and violence, with an estimated one million people internally displaced as a result of battles for territorial control by rebel groups and paramilitary forces. 'The corruptive effect of this kind of profit is devastating, since it has penetrated to perverse levels in the judiciary and the political system,' the official report of the Presidential Programme concluded, adding that the rapid accumulation of wealth from illegal drugs 'has fostered codes and behaviours which promote corruption, fast money and the predominance of private welfare over general interest'."

Source: Hodess, Robin (ed.), Transparency International, Global Corruption Report 2001 (Berlin, Germany: Transparency International, 2001), p. 176.

8. "Mexico's police and armed services are known to be contaminated by multimillion dollar bribes from the transnational narco-trafficking business. Though the problem is not as pervasive in the military as it is in the police, it is widely considered to have attained the status of a national security threat."

Source: Hodess, Robin (ed.), Transparency International, Global Corruption Report 2001 (Berlin, Germany: Transparency International, 2001), p. 158.

9. "Another problem occurs when officials turn a blind eye to a narcotics trade that looms large in the region. 'Central America has become the meat in the sandwich' - as a trans-shipment point, storehouse and money laundering centre - in the drug traffic from Colombia to the US, said Costa Rican parliamentarian Belisario Solano. The Costa Rican Defence Ministry estimates that between 50 and 70 tonnes of cocaine travel through Costa Rica to the US every year."

Source: Hodess, Robin (ed.), Transparency International, Global Corruption Report 2001 (Berlin, Germany: Transparency International, 2001), p. 160.

10. The United Nations Drug Control Program noted the inevitable risk of drug-related police corruption, when it reported that "wherever there is a well-organized, illicit drug industry, there is also the danger of police corruption."

Source: United Nations International Drug Control Program, Technical Series Report #6: Economic and Social Consequences of Drug Abuse and Illicit Trafficking (New York, NY: UNDCP, 1998), p. 38.

Crime

1. It is important to note that each of the most violent episodes in this century coincide with the prohibition on alcohol and the escalation of the modern-day war on drugs. In 1933 the homicide rate peaked at 9.7 per 100,000 people, which was the year that alcohol prohibition was finally repealed. In 1980, the homicide rate peaked again at 10 per 100,000.

    Source: US Census Data and FBI Uniform Crime Reports.

Murder in America
Homicides per 100,000 population
1900-1997 (FBI Uniform Crime Reports)

2. "The data are quite consistent with the view that Prohibition at the state level inhibited alcohol consumption, and an attempt to explain correlated residuals by including omitted variables revealed that enforcement of Prohibitionist legislation had a significant inhibiting effect as well. Moreover, both hypotheses about the effects of alcohol and Prohibition are supported by the analysis. Despite the fact that alcohol consumption is a positive correlate of homicide (as expected), Prohibition and its enforcement increased the homicide rate."

    Source: Jensen, Gary F., "Prohibition, Alcohol, and Murder: Untangling Countervailing Mechanisms," Homicide Studies, Vol. 4, No. 1 (Sage Publications: Thousand Oaks, CA, February 2000), p. 31.

3. "Generalizing from the findings on Prohibition, we can hypothesize that decriminalization would increase the use of the previously criminalized drug, but would decrease violence associated with attempts to control illicit markets and as resolutions to disputes between buyers and sellers. Moreover, because the perception of violence associated with the drug market can lead people who are not directly involved to be prepared for violent self-defense, there could be additional reductions in peripheral settings when disputes arise (see Blumstein & Cork, 1997; Sheley & Wright, 1996)."

    Source: Jensen, Gary F., "Prohibition, Alcohol, and Murder: Untangling Countervailing Mechanisms," Homicide Studies, Vol. 4, No. 1 (Sage Publications: Thousand Oaks, CA, February 2000), pp. 33-4.

4. "Since the definition of homicide is similar in most countries, absolute comparisons of rates are possible. For the period 1999 to 2001, the average rate (the number of homicides per 100,000 population) was 1.6 in the EU with the highest rates in Finland (2.9), Northern Ireland (2.7) and Scotland (2.2). For the other countries, the highest rates were found in Russia (22.1), Estonia (10.6), Lithuania (10.6) and the USA (5.6)."

Crime

Source: Barclay, Gordon & Cynthia Tavares, "International Comparisons of Criminal Justice Statistics 2001," Home Office Bulletin 12/03 (London, England, UK: Home Office Research, Development, and Statistics Directorate, October 24, 2003), p. 3.

H

5. The Canadian Medical Association Journal published research on the impact of a police crackdown on a public illicit drug market in the Downtown Eastside (DTES) section of Vancouver, British Columbia, Canada. The researchers found that: "We detected no reduction in drug use frequency or drug price in response to a large-scale police crackdown on drug users in Vancouver's DTES. The evidence that drugs became more difficult to obtain was consistent with reports of displacement of drug dealers and was supported by the significantly higher rates of reporting that police presence had affected where drugs were used, including changes in neighbourhood and increases in use in public places. These observations were validated by examination of needle-exchange statistics.

"Our findings are consistent with those showing that demand for illicit drugs enables the illicit drug market to adapt to and overcome enforcement-related constraints. Although evidence suggested that police presence made it more difficult to obtain drugs, this appeared to be explained by displacement of drug dealers."

Source: Wood, Evan, Patricia M. Spittal, Will Small, Thomas Kerr, Kathy Li, Robert S. Hogg, Mark W. Tyndall, Julio S.G. Montaner, Martin T. Schechter, "Displacement of Canada's Largest Public Illicit Drug Market In Response To A Police Crackdown," Canadian Medical Association Journal, May 11, 2004: 170(10), p. 1554.

6. "Our results probably explain reports of increased injection drug use, drug-related crime and other public-order concerns in neighbourhoods where activities related to illicit drug use and the sex trade emerged or intensified in the wake of the crackdown. Such displacement has profound public-health implications if it 'normalizes' injection drug use among previously unexposed at-risk youth. Furthermore, since difficulty in obtaining syringes has been shown to be a significant factor in promoting syringe sharing among IDUs in Vancouver, displacement away from sources of sterile syringes may increase the rates of bloodborne diseases. Escalated police presence may also explain the observed reduction in willingness to use a safer injection facility. It is unlikely that the lack of benefit of the crackdown was due to insufficient police resources. Larger crackdowns in the United States, which often involved helicopters to supplement foot and car patrols, have not had measurable benefits and have instead been associated with substantial health and social harms."

Source: Wood, Evan, Patricia M. Spittal, Will Small, Thomas Kerr, Kathy Li, Robert S. Hogg, Mark W. Tyndall, Julio S.G. Montaner, Martin T. Schechter, "Displacement of Canada's Largest Public Illicit Drug Market In Response To A Police Crackdown," Canadian Medical Association Journal, May 11, 2004: 170(10), pp. 1554-1555.

7. In 1988 in New York City, 85% of crack-related crimes were caused by the market culture associated with illicit crack sales, primarily territorial disputes between rival crack dealers.

Source: Goldstein, P.J., Brownstein, H.H., Ryan, P.J. & Bellucci, P.A., "Crack and Homicide in New York City: A Case Study in the Epidemiology of Violence," in Reinarman, C. and Levine, H. (eds.), Crack in America: Demon Drugs and Social Justice (Berkeley, CA: University of California Press, 1997), pp. 113-130.

8. The average "dealer" holds a low-wage job and sells part-time to obtain drugs for his or her own use.

Source: Reuter, P., MacCoun, R., & Murphy, P., Money from Crime: A Study of the Economics of Drug Dealing in Washington, DC (Santa Monica, CA: The RAND Corporation, 1990), pp. 49-50.

Crime

9. In 1973, there were 328,670 arrests logged in the FBI's Uniform Crime Reports (UCR) for drug law violations. In 2005, that number rose to 1,846,351 arrests for drug law violations logged in the UCR. Also in 2005, there were a reported 603,503 arrests for all violent crimes and 1,609,327 arrests for all property crimes, out of a total 14,094,186 arrests for all offenses.

Source: FBI Uniform Crime Reports 1973 (Note: 1973 data supplied by the National Criminal Justice Reference Service); Crime in America: FBI Uniform Crime Reports 2005 (Washington, DC: US Dept. of Justice, 2006), Table 29, from the web at http://www.fbi.gov/ucr/05cius/data/table_29.html last accessed Sept. 20, 2006.

10. Of the 1,846,351 arrests for drug law violations in 2005, 81.7% (1,508,469) were for possession of a controlled substance. Only 18.3% (337,882) were for the sale or manufacture of a drug.

Source: Crime in America: FBI Uniform Crime Reports 2005 (Washington, DC: US Dept. of Justice, 2006), Table 29, from the web at http://www.fbi.gov/ucr/05cius/data/ table_29.html and Arrest Table: Arrests for Drug Abuse Violations, from the web http://www.fbi.gov/ucr/05cius/arrests/index.htm last accessed Sept. 20, 2006.

11. Although people may think that the Drug War targets drug smugglers and 'King Pins,' in 2005, 42.6 percent of the 1,846,351 total arrests for drug abuse violations in the US were for marijuana — a total of 786,545. Of those, 696,074 people were arrested for possession alone. By contrast in 2000, a total of 734,497 Americans were arrested for marijuana offenses, of which 646,042 were for possession alone.

Marijuana Arrests and Total Drug Arrests in the US						
Year	Total Drug Arrests	Total MJ Arrests	MJ Trafficking/ Sale Arrests	MJ Possession Arrests	Total Violent Crime Arrests	Total Property Crime Arrests	Total Arrests (excluding simple traffic violations)
2005	1,846,351	786,545	90,471	696,074	603,503	1,609,327	14,094,186
2004	1,745,712	771,605	87,286	684,319	590,258	1,649,825	14,004,327
2003	1,678,192	755,186	92,300	662,886	597,026	1,605,127	13,639,479
2002	1,538.813	697,082	83,096	613,986	620,510	1,613,954	13,741,438
2001	1,586,902	723,628	82,519	641,109	627,132	1,618,465	13,699,254
2000	1,579,566	734,497	88,455	646,042	625,132	1,620,928	13,980,297
1999	1,532,200	704,812	84,271	620,541	644,770	1,627,100	14,355,600
1998	1,559,100	682,885	84,191	598,694	675,900	1,805,600	14,528,300
1997	1,583,600	695,201	88,682	606,519	717,750	2,015,600	15,284,300
1996	1,506,200	641,642	94,891	546,751	729,900	2,045,600	15,168,100
1995	1,476,100	588,964	85,614	503,350	796,250	2,128,600	15,119,800
1990	1,089,500	326,850	66,460	260,390	705,500	2,128,600	14,195,100
1980	580,900	401,982	63,318	338,664	475,160	1,863,300	10,441,000

Crime

Sources: Crime in America: FBI Uniform Crime Reports 2005 (Washington, DC: US Dept. of Justice, 2006), Table 29, from the web at http://www.fbi.gov/ucr/05cius/ data/table_29.html and Arrest Table: Arrests for Drug Abuse Violations, from the web http://www.fbi.gov/ucr/05cius/arrests/index.htm last accessed Sept. 20, 2006; Crime in the United States: FBI Uniform Crime Reports 2004 (Washington, DC: US Government Printing Office, 2005), p. 278, Table 4.1 & p. 280, Table 29; Crime in America: FBI Uniform Crime Reports 2003 (Washington, DC: US Government Printing Office, 2004), p. 269, Table 4.1 & p. 270, Table 29; Crime in America: FBI Uniform Crime Reports 2002 (Washington, DC: US Government Printing Office, 2003), p. 234, Table 4.1 & p. 233, Table 29; Crime in America: FBI Uniform Crime Reports 2001 (Washington, DC: US Government Printing Office, 2002), p. 232, Table 4.1 & p. 233, Table 29; Federal Bureau of Investigation, Uniform Crime Reports for the United States 2000 (Washington, DC: US Government Printing Office, 2001), pp. 215-216, Tables 4.1 and 29; Federal Bureau of Investigation, Uniform Crime Reports for the United States 1999 (Washington DC: US Government Printing Office, 2000), pp. 211-212; Federal Bureau of Investigation, Uniform Crime Reports for the United States 1998 (Washington, DC: US Government Printing Office, 1999), pp. 209-210; Crime in America: FBI Uniform Crime Reports 1997 (Washington, DC: US Government Printing Office, 1998), p. 221, Table 4.1 & p. 222, Table 29; Crime in America: FBI Uniform Crime Reports 1996 (Washington, DC: US Government Printing Office, 1997), p. 213, Table 4.1 & p. 214, Table 29; FBI, UCR for the US 1995 (Washington, DC: US Government Printing Office, 1996), pp. 207-208; FBI, UCR for the US 1990 (Washington, DC: US Government Printing Office, 1991), pp. 173-174; FBI, UCR for the US 1980 (Washington, DC: US Government Printing Office, 1981), pp. 189-191; Bureau of Justice Statistics, Chart of arrests by age group, number and rates for total offenses, violent offenses, and property offenses, 1970-2003, Dec. 2004.

12. The FBI's Uniform Crime Report for 2005 reported that: "Nationwide in 2005, 45.5 percent of violent crimes and 16.3 percent of property crimes were cleared by arrest or exceptional means.

"Of the violent crimes of murder and nonnegligent manslaughter, forcible rape, robbery, and aggravated assault, murder had the highest percentage—62.1 percent—of offenses cleared.

"Of the property crimes of burglary, larceny-theft, and motor vehicle theft, burglary was the offense least often cleared with 12.7 percent cleared by arrest or exceptional means.

"Nationwide in 2005, 42.2 percent of arson offenses cleared by arrest or exceptional means involved juveniles, the highest percentage of all offense clearances involving only juveniles."

According to the FBI:

"In the UCR Program, a law enforcement agency reports that an offense is cleared by arrest, or solved for crime reporting purposes, when all of the following three conditions have been met for at least one person: Arrested. Charged with the commission of the offense. Turned over to the court for prosecution (whether following arrest, court summons, or police notice).

"In its calculations, the UCR Program counts the number of offenses that are cleared, not the number of arrestees. The arrest of one person may clear several crimes, and the arrest of many persons may clear only one offense. In addition, some clearances that an agency records in a particular calendar year, such as 2005, may pertain to offenses that occurred in previous years.

Crime

"Cleared by Exceptional Means
"In certain situations, elements beyond law enforcement's control prevent the agency from arresting and formally charging the offender. When this occurs, the agency can clear the offense exceptionally. Law enforcement agencies must meet the following four conditions in order to clear an offense by exceptional means. The agency must have: Identified the offender. Gathered enough evidence to support an arrest, make a charge, and turn over the offender to the court for prosecution. Identified the offender's exact location so that the suspect could be taken into custody immediately. Encountered a circumstance outside the control of law enforcement that prohibits the agency from arresting, charging, and prosecuting the offender."

> *Source: Crime in America: FBI Uniform Crime Reports 2004 (Washington, DC: US Government Printing Office, 2005), p. 263; Crime in America: FBI Uniform Crime Reports 2005 (Washington, DC: US Dept. of Justice, 2006), from the web at http://www.fbi.gov/ucr/05cius/offenses/clearances/index.html and http://www.fbi.gov/ucr/05cius/offenses/clearances/clearances.htm last accessed Sept. 20, 2006.*

13. South Bank University's Criminal Policy Research Unit conducted a detailed study of the policing of cannabis in England. The study found that: "One in seven of all known offenders in England and Wales were arrested for the possession of cannabis.

"There has been a tenfold increase in the number of possession offences since the mid-1970s. There is no evidence that this increase has been an intended consequence of specific policy.

"Possession offences most often come to light as a by-product of other investigations.

"A minority of patrol officers 'specialise' in cannabis offences: 3 per cent of officers who had made any arrests for possession accounted for 20 per cent of all arrests.

"Arrests for possession very rarely lead to the discovery of serious crimes.

"Officers often turn a blind eye to possession offences, or give informal warnings.

"Of the 69,000 offenders who were cautioned or convicted in 1999, just over half (58 per cent) were cautioned.

"The financial costs of policing cannabis amount to at least £50 million a year (including sentencing costs), and absorb the equivalent of 500 full-time police officers.

"The researchers conclude that:

"- re-classification of cannabis to a Class C drug will yield some financial savings, allowing patrol officers to respond more effectively to other calls on their time;

"- the main benefits of reclassification would be non-financial, in removing a source of friction between the police and young people;

"- there would be a very small decline in detection of serious offences, but this should readily be offset by the savings in police time."

> *Source: "Findings: The Policing of Cannabis as a Class B Drug," (London, England: Joseph Rowntree Foundation, March 2002), p. 1.*

Crime

14. Law enforcement authorities in the UK conducted an experiment in policing in the London borough of Lambeth, wherein cannabis violations were given a low priority. Researchers for PRS Consultancy Group undertook an evaluation of the program at the request of the Borough Police Commander. The researchers found that: "The measures of police activity demonstrate that the policy has succeeded in releasing resources, and that activity against more serious offences has increased.

"During the 6 months of the evaluation, Lambeth officers issued 450 warnings. This released at least 1350 hours of officer time (by avoiding custody procedures and interviewing time), equivalent to 1.8 full-time officers. A further 1150 hours of CJU staff time was released by avoiding case file preparation.

"In comparison with the same 6 months in 2000, Lambeth officers recorded 35% more cannabis possession offences and 11% more for trafficking. In adjoining Boroughs possession offences fell by 4% and trafficking fell by 34%.

"Lambeth also increased its activity against Class A drugs relative to adjoining Boroughs."

Source: PRS Consultancy Group, "Evaluation of Lambeth's pilot of warnings for possession of cannabis - summary of final report," March 2002, p. 1.

15. A study by the National Center on Addiction and Substance Abuse at Columbia University confirms what many criminologists have long known: alcohol is associated with more violent crime than any illegal drug, including crack, cocaine, and heroin. Twenty-one percent of violent felons in state prisons committed their crimes while under the influence of alcohol alone. Only 3% were high on crack or powder cocaine alone and only 1% were using heroin alone.

Source: Califano, Joseph, Behind Bars: Substance Abuse and America's Prison Population, Forward by Joseph Califano, The National Center on Addiction and Substance Abuse at Columbia University (1998).

16. Federal statistics show that a large percentage of criminal offenders were under the influence of alcohol alone when they committed their crimes (36.3%, or a total of 1,919,251 offenders). Federal research also shows for more than 40% of convicted murderers being held in either jail or State prison, alcohol use was a factor in the crime.

Source: Greenfield, Lawrence A., Alcohol and Crime: An Analysis of National Data on the Prevalence of Alcohol Involvement in Crime (Washington, DC: US Department of Justice, April 1998), pp. 20-21.

Diversion of Pharmaceuticals

1. "In 2004, 6.0 million persons were current users of psychotherapeutic drugs taken nonmedically (2.5 percent). These include 4.4 million who used pain relievers, 1.6 million who used tranquilizers, 1.2 million who used stimulants, and 0.3 million who used sedatives. These estimates are all similar to the corresponding estimates for 2003.
   "There were significant increases in the lifetime prevalence of use from 2003 to 2004 in several categories of pain relievers among those aged 18 to 25. Specific pain relievers with statistically significant increases in lifetime use were Vicodin®, Lortab®, or Lorcet® (from 15.0 to 16.5 percent); Percocet®, Percodan®, or Tylox® (from 7.8 to 8.7 percent); hydrocodone products (from 16.3 to 17.4 percent); OxyContin® (from 3.6 to 4.3 percent); and oxycodone products (from 8.9 to 10.1 percent)."

   Source: Substance Abuse and Mental Health Services Administration, Results from the 2004 National Survey on Drug Use and Health: National Findings (Rockville, MD: US Dept. of Health and Human Services, Office of Applied Studies, 2005), p. 1.

2. "Lifetime nonmedical pain reliever prevalence among youths aged 12 to 17 increased from 2001 (9.6 percent) to 2002 (11.2 percent), continuing an increasing trend from 1989 (1.2 percent). Among young adults aged 18 to 25, the rate increased from 19.4 percent in 2001 to 22.1 percent in 2002. The young adult rate had been 6.8 percent in 1992.
   "Lifetime nonmedical use of stimulants increased steadily from 1990 to 2002 for youths aged 12 to 17 (0.7 to 4.3 percent). For young adults aged 18 to 25, rates declined from 1981 to 1994 (from 10.9 to 5.9 percent), then increased to 10.8 percent in 2002. Rates increased between 2001 and 2002 for both youths (3.8 to 4.3 percent) and young adults (10.2 to 10.8 percent)."

   Source: Substance Abuse and Mental Health Services Administration. (2003). Results from the 2002 National Survey on Drug Use and Health: National Findings (Office of Applied Studies, NHSDA Series H-22, DHHS Publication No. SMA 03-3836), Rockville, MD, p. 39.

3. "In 2004, an estimated 2.8 million persons used psychotherapeutics nonmedically for the first time within the past year. The numbers of new users of psychotherapeutics in 2004 were 2.4 million for pain relievers, 1.2 million for tranquilizers, 793,000 for stimulants, and 240,000 for sedatives. These estimates are similar to the corresponding estimates for 2002 and 2003.
   "The average age of first nonmedical use of psychotherapeutics among recent initiates was 24.7 years. For specific drug classes, the average ages were 23.3 years for pain relievers, 25.2 years for tranquilizers, 24.1 years for stimulants, and 29.3 years for sedatives.
   "In 2004, the number of new nonmedical users of OxyContin® was 615,000, with an average age at first use of 24.5 years. Comparable data on past year OxyContin® initiation are not available for prior years, but calendar year estimates of OxyContin® initiation show a steady increase in the number of initiates from 1995, the year this drug was first available, through 2003 (Figure 5.5).

Diversion of Pharmaceuticals

"The number of recent new users of methamphetamine nonmedically was 318,000 in 2004. Between 2002 and 2004, the number of methamphetamine initiates remained level at around 300,000 per year. The average age of new users was 18.9 years in 2002, 20.4 years in 2003, and 22.1 years in 2004."

Source: Substance Abuse and Mental Health Services Administration, Results from the 2004 National Survey on Drug Use and Health: National Findings (Rockville, MD: US Dept. of Health and Human Services, Office of Applied Studies, 2005), p. 50.

4. The General Accounting Office reported in 2003 that "DEA officials told us that it is difficult to obtain reliable data on what controlled substances are being abused by individuals and diverted from pharmacies because available drug abuse and diversion tracking systems do not capture data on a specific brand-name product or indicate where a drug product is being abused and diverted on a state and local level. Because of the time lags in reporting information, the data reflect a delayed response to any emerging drug abuse and diversion problem."

Source: General Accounting Office, "Prescription Drugs: Oxycontin Abuse and Diversion and Efforts to Address the Problem," GAO-04-110 (Washington, DC: Government Printing Office, December 2003), p. 32.

5. The Journal of Pain and Symptom Management published a research letter by scientists from the Pain & Policy Studies Group at the University of Wisconsin-Madison on drug crime as a source of diverted pharmaceuticals. The researchers examined data maintained by the US Drug Enforcement Administration on thefts and other incidents of loss of controlled substances by DEA registrants including pharmacists, manufacturers, and distributors. The data was complete for the years 2000-2003 for 22 Eastern states representing 53% of the US population. According to the researchers, "A total of 12,894 theft/loss incidents were reported in these states between 2000 and 2003. Theft/losses were primarily from pharmacies (89.3%), with smaller portions from medical practitioners, manufacturers, distributors, and some addiction treatment programs that reported theft/losses of methadone.

"Over the 4-year period, almost 28 million dosage units of all controlled substances were diverted. The total number of dosage units for the six opioids is as follows: 4,434,731 for oxycodone; 1,026,184 for morphine; 454,503 for methadone; 325,921 for hydromorphone; 132,950 for meperidine; 81,371 for fentanyl."

Source: Joranson, David E. MSSW & Aaron M. Gilson, PhD, Pain & Policy Studies Group, University of Wisconsin-Madison, "Drug Crime is a Source of Abuse Pain Medication in the United States," Letters, Journal of Pain & Symptom Management, Vol. 30, No. 4, Oct. 2005, p. 299.

6. "According to IMS Health data, the annual number of OxyContin prescriptions for noncancer pain increased nearly tenfold, from about 670,000 in 1997 to about 6.2 million in 2002. In contrast, during the same 6 years, the annual number of OxyContin prescriptions for cancer pain increased about fourfold, from about 250,000 in 1997 to just over

Diversion of Pharmaceuticals

1 million in 2002. The noncancer prescriptions therefore increased from about 73 percent of total OxyContin prescriptions to about 85 percent during that period, while the cancer prescriptions decreased from about 27 percent of the total to about 15 percent. IMS Health data indicated that prescriptions for other schedule II opioid drugs, such as Duragesic and morphine products, for noncancer pain also increased during this period. Duragesic prescriptions for noncancer pain were about 46 percent of its total prescriptions in 1997, and increased to about 72 percent of its total in 2002. Morphine products, including, for example, Purdue's MSContin, also experienced an increase in their noncancer prescriptions during the same period. Their noncancer prescriptions were about 42 percent of total prescriptions in 1997, and increased to about 65 percent in 2002."

> Source: General Accounting Office, "Prescription Drugs: Oxycontin Abuse and Diversion and Efforts to Address the Problem," GAO-04-110 (Washington, DC: Government Printing Office, December 2003), p. 18.

7. "From fiscal year 1996 through fiscal year 2002, DEA initiated 313 investigations involving OxyContin, resulting in 401 arrests. Most of the investigations and arrests occurred after the initiation of the action plan. Since the plan was enacted, DEA initiated 257 investigations and made 302 arrests in fiscal years 2001 and 2002. Among those arrested were several physicians and pharmacists. Fifteen health care professionals either voluntarily surrendered their controlled substance registrations or were immediately suspended from registration by DEA. In addition, DEA reported that $1,077,500 in fines was assessed and $742,678 in cash was seized by law enforcement agencies in OxyContin-related cases in 2001 and 2002."

> Source: General Accounting Office, "Prescription Drugs: Oxycontin Abuse and Diversion and Efforts to Address the Problem," GAO-04-110 (Washington, DC: Government Printing Office, December 2003), p. 37.

8. "There are several factors that may have contributed to the abuse and diversion of OxyContin. OxyContin's formulation as a controlled-release opioid that is twice as potent as morphine may have made it an attractive target for abuse and diversion. In addition, the original label's safety warning advising patients not to crush the tablets because of the possible rapid release of a potentially toxic amount of oxycodone may have inadvertently alerted abusers to possible methods for misuse. Further, the rapid growth in OxyContin sales increased the drug's availability in the marketplace and may have contributed to opportunities to obtain the drug illicitly. The history of abuse and diversion of prescription drugs in some geographic areas, such as those within the Appalachian region, may have predisposed some states to problems with OxyContin. However, we could not assess the relationship between the growth in OxyContin prescriptions or increased availability with the drug's abuse and diversion because the data on abuse and diversion are not reliable, comprehensive, or timely."

Diversion of Pharmaceuticals

Source: General Accounting Office, "Prescription Drugs: Oxycontin Abuse and Diversion and Efforts to Address the Problem," GAO-04-110 (Washington, DC: Government Printing Office, December 2003), p. 29.

9. "The large amount of OxyContin available in the marketplace may have increased opportunities for abuse and diversion. Both DEA and Purdue have stated that an increase in a drug's availability in the marketplace may be a factor that attracts interest by those who abuse and divert drugs."

Source: General Accounting Office, "Prescription Drugs: Oxycontin Abuse and Diversion and Efforts to Address the Problem," GAO-04-110 (Washington, DC: Government Printing Office, December 2003), p. 30.

10. "According to a 2001 HIDTA [High Intensity Drug Trafficking Area] report, the Appalachian region, which encompasses parts of Kentucky, Tennessee, Virginia, and West Virginia, has been severely affected by prescription drug abuse, particularly pain relievers, including oxycodone, for many years. Three of the four states — Kentucky, Virginia, and West Virginia — were among the initial states to report OxyContin abuse and diversion. Historically, oxycodone, manufactured under brand names such as Percocet, Percodan, and Tylox, was among the most diverted prescription drugs in Appalachia. According to the report, OxyContin has become the drug of choice of abusers in several areas within the region. The report indicates that many areas of the Appalachian region are rural and poverty-stricken, and the profit potential resulting from the illicit sale of OxyContin may have contributed to its diversion and abuse. In some parts of Kentucky, a 20-milligram OxyContin tablet, which can be purchased by legitimate patients for about $2, can be sold illicitly for as much as $25. The potential to supplement their incomes can lure legitimate patients into selling some of their OxyContin to street dealers, according to the HIDTA report."

Source: General Accounting Office, "Prescription Drugs: Oxycontin Abuse and Diversion and Efforts to Address the Problem," GAO-04-110 (Washington, DC: Government Printing Office, December 2003), pp. 31-32.

11. According to a report on prescription drug monitoring programs in the US, of the 24 state programs listed, 17 allow law enforcement to use data to support investigations of prescription abuse, and 8 allow law enforcement to use the data to initiate investigations of prescription abuse.

Source: "Prescription Monitoring Programs: Current Practices and Consideration of Their Effectiveness," Abt Associates, Presented to the National Institute of Justice Annual Conference on Criminal Justice Research & Evaluation, Washington, DC, July 2005.

Drug Courts and Treatment as an Alternative to Incarceration

Drug Courts and Treatment Alternatives to Incarceration programs are popular, widely praised and rapidly expanding alternative approaches of dealing with drug offenders and people charged with nonviolent crimes who are drug users. Drug Courts substitute mandatory treatment for incarceration. Because they are relatively new, much of the research on their effectiveness is recent, incomplete and inconclusive. Drug Courts have been much applauded, however some concerns about their fairness and effectiveness have been expressed. These include:

- Providing coerced treatment at a time when the needs for voluntary treatment are not being met creates the strange circumstance of someone needing to get arrested to get treatment.
- People who are forced into treatment may not actually need it. They may just be people who use drugs in a non-problematic way who happened to get arrested. Arrest may not be the best way to determine who should get treatment services.
- Drug Courts are a much less expensive way of handling drug cases in the criminal justice system, thus they may result in more people being arrested and processed, many of whom would not have been arrested or would have been diverted. And it is true that the number of drug arrests has grown dramatically since the early 1990s. Thus, drug courts may be expanding the number of people hurt by the drug war.
- Drug Courts are creating a separate system of justice for drug offenders, a system that does not rely on the key traditions of an adversary system of justice and due process, a system where the defense, prosecution and judge work as a team to force the offender into a treatment program.
- Drug Courts typically rely on abstinence-based treatment. For example, methadone is sometimes not available to heroin addicts. In addition, Drug Courts rely heavily on urine testing rather than focusing on whether the person is succeeding in employment, education or family relationships, and in avoiding re-arrest.
- Drug Courts also sometimes mandate twelve-step treatment programs which some believe to be an infringement on religious freedom.
- Drug Courts invade the confidentiality of patient and health-care provider. The health-care provider's client is really the court, prosecutor and probation officer, rather than the person who is getting drug treatment.

1. "Of the 1,700 drug court programs operating or planned as of September 2004, about 1,040 — nearly 770 operating and about 270 being planned— were adult drug court programs, according to data collected by the Office of Justice Programs' Drug Court Clearinghouse and Technical Assistance Project. The primary purpose of these programs is to use a court's authority to reduce crime by changing defendants' substance abuse behavior. In exchange for the possibility of dismissed charges or reduced sentences, eligible defendants who agree to participate are diverted to drug court programs in various ways and at various stages in the judicial process. These programs are typically offered to defendants as an alternative to probation or short-term incarceration."

Drug Courts and Treatment as an Alternative to Incarceration

Source: "Adult Drug Courts: Evidence Indicates Recidivism Reductions and Mixed Results for Other Outcomes," Government Accountability Office, GAO-05-219, Feb. 2005, p. 3.

2. The Drug Court Clearinghouse & Technical Assistance Project at the American University in Washington, DC, released the results of a survey of drug courts in 2001. Based on information reported by 372 of the 420 adult family drug court programs which were in operation as of January 1, 2001, DCC/TAP estimated:

Total number of individuals who have enrolled in adult drug court programs:	226,000
Number of participants as of 6/1/01:	77,000
Number of graduates as of 6/1/01:	74,000
Participants retention rates (overall):	67% +
Jail/prison days saved, average reported:	9,980 days
Jail/Prison days saved, median reported:	4,015 days
Costs saved, average reported:	$697,652
Costs saved, median reported:	$330,000

"Summary Information on All Drug Court Programs and Detailed Information on Adult Drug Courts," Office of Justice Programs Drug Court Clearinghouse and Technical Assistance Project (Washington, DC: American University, June 25, 2001), pp. 2, 6.

3. Drug courts offer court-supervised treatment as an alternative to incarceration for low-level drug offenders. Most target first-time drug offenders, while others target habitual offenders.

Source: Marc Pearce, National Center for State Courts Information Service, "Drug Courts: A Criminal Justice Revolution", Report on Trends in the State Courts 1998-1999 Final Report (Williamsburg, VA: National Center for State Courts, 1999), pp. 8-12.

4. "Drug courts do not always target users of 'hard' drugs. In several adult drug courts a substantial proportion of clients reported that marijuana was the primary drug used: Chester County (PA) (47%), Lackawanna County (NY) (22%) and Syracuse (NY) (25%). A majority of participants in the Cumberland County (ME) drug court reported alcohol as their primary drug (58%)."

Source: Belenko, Steven, PhD, "Research on Drug Courts: A Critical Review 2001 Update" (New York, NY: National Center on Addiction and Substance Abuse (CASA) at Columbia University, June 2001), p. 20.

5. "In most of the evaluations we reviewed, adult drug court programs led to recidivism reductions during periods of time that generally corresponded to the length of the drug court program -— that is, within-program. Our analysis of evaluations reporting recidivism data for 23 programs showed that lower percentages of drug court program participants than comparison group members were rearrested or reconvicted. Program participants also had fewer incidents of rearrests or reconvictions and a longer time until rearrest or reconviction than

Drug Courts and Treatment as an Alternative to Incarceration

comparison group members. These recidivism reductions were observed for any felony offense and for drug offenses, whether they were felonies or misdemeanors. However, we were unable to find conclusive evidence that specific drug court program components, such as the behavior of the judge, the amount of treatment received, the level of supervision provided, and the sanctions for not complying with program requirements, affect participants' within-program recidivism. Post-program recidivism reductions were measured for up to 1 year after participants completed the drug court program in several evaluations, and in these the evidence suggests that the recidivism differences observed during the program endured."

Source: "Adult Drug Courts: Evidence Indicates Recidivism Reductions and Mixed Results for Other Outcomes," Government Accountability Office, GAO-05-219, Feb. 2005, pp. 5-6.

6. "Completion rates, which refer to the number of individuals who successfully completed a drug court program as a percentage of the total number admitted, in the programs we reviewed that assessed completion ranged from 27 to 66 percent. As might be expected, program completion was associated with participants' compliance with program requirements. Specifically, evaluations of 16 adult drug court programs that assessed completion found that participants' compliance with procedures was consistently associated with completion. These program procedures include attending treatment sessions, engaging in treatment early in the program, and appearing at status hearings. No other program factor, such as the severity of the sanction that would be invoked if participants failed to complete the program and the manner in which judges conducted status hearings, predicted participants' program completion. Several characteristics of the drug court program participants themselves were also associated with an increased likelihood of program completion. These characteristics include lower levels of prior involvement in the criminal justice system and age, as older participants were more likely to complete drug court programs than younger ones."

Source: "Adult Drug Courts: Evidence Indicates Recidivism Reductions and Mixed Results for Other Outcomes," Government Accountability Office, GAO-05-219, Feb. 2005, p. 6.

7. "A limited number of evaluations in our review discussed the costs and benefits of adult drug court programs. Four evaluations of seven drug court programs provided sufficient cost and benefit data to estimate their net benefits (that is, the benefits minus costs). The cost per drug court program participant was greater than the cost per comparison group member in six of these drug court programs. However, all seven programs yielded positive net benefits, primarily from reductions in recidivism affecting both judicial system costs and avoided costs to potential victims. Net benefits ranged from about $1,000 per participant to about $15,000 in the seven programs. These benefits may underestimate drug court programs' true benefits because the evaluations did not include indirect benefits (such as reduced medical costs of treated participants). Financial cost savings for the criminal justice system (taking into account recidivism reductions) were found in two of the seven programs."

Drug Courts and Treatment as an Alternative to Incarceration

Source: "Adult Drug Courts: Evidence Indicates Recidivism Reductions and Mixed Results for Other Outcomes," Government Accountability Office, GAO-05-219, Feb. 2005, pp. 6-7.

8. "Carey and Finigan (2004) estimated the benefits and costs of the Multnomah County Drug Court in Portland, Oregon. They evaluated a sample of 1,173 individuals to determine the cost and criminal justice outcome differences between the drug court and the business-as-usual process over a 30-month period following the initial court appearance. Based on their cost and benefit estimates, the benefit-cost ratio associated with Multnomah County Drug Court was 2.5.

   "In an unpublished report, Harrell, Cavanaugh, & Roman (1999) estimated benefit-cost ratio of about 2 for the sanctions docket program that was part of the D.C. Superior Court Drug Intervention Program. Similarly, in an evaluation the Multnomah County, Oregon, S.T.O.P. (Sanction Treatment Opportunity Progress) Drug Court Diversion Program, Finigan (1998) estimated a benefitcost ratio of 2.5 from the taxpayer perspective. In these studies, benefits were calculated as the dollar value of averted crime costs (Harrell et al.) or averted CJS [criminal justice system] costs (Finigan) due to decreased criminal activity."

Source: Zarkin, Gary A., Laura J. Dunlap, Steven Belenko & Paul A. Dynia, "A Benefit-Cost Analysis of the Kings County District Attorney's Office Drug Treatment Alternative to Prison (DTAP) Program," Justice Research and Policy, Vol. 7, No. 1 (Washington, DC: Justice Research and Statistics Association, 2005), p. 3.

9. "Importantly, Belenko et al. (2005) have shown just the opposite result for DTAP [Drug Treatment Alternative to Prison]: 57% of DTAP participants were rearrested for any offense at least once in the follow-up period compared with 75% of the comparison group. Similarly, only 42% of DTAP participants were reconvicted of any offense compared with 65% of the prison comparison group. Finally, only 30% of the DTAP participants had a new jail sentence (compared with 51% of prison comparisons) and only 7% had a new prison sentence (compared with 18% of prison comparisons).

   "When these outcomes are monetized, our study shows that the DTAP program is cost beneficial from the CJS perspective; it is less costly to divert drugabusing offenders to treatment instead of prison. In addition, the findings suggest that a long-term perspective is important in evaluating treatment diversion or other criminal justice-based treatment programs. We find that benefits increase in each subsequent year of analysis. Findings from this analysis provide an economic justification for the DTAP program. In addition, our unit cost estimates for the CJS and diversion expenses for New York City may be used by policymakers and researchers to evaluate other diversion programs."

Source: Zarkin, Gary A., Laura J. Dunlap, Steven Belenko & Paul A. Dynia, "A Benefit-Cost Analysis of the Kings County District Attorney's Office Drug Treatment Alternative to Prison (DTAP) Program," Justice Research and Policy, Vol. 7, No. 1 (Washington, DC: Justice Research and Statistics Association, 2005), p. 20.

Drug Courts and Treatment as an Alternative to Incarceration

10. "All six drug courts (Bronx, Brooklyn, Queens, Suffolk, Syracuse, and Rochester) produced recidivism reductions compared with conventional case processing. The six courts represent a mix of geographic areas and policies (e.g., regarding eligibility criteria, screening and assessment protocols, graduation requirements, approach to sanctions, and supplemental services). Since the measurement periods tracked defendants at least three years after the initial arrest and at least one year after program completion, the results indicate that positive drug court impacts are durable over time.

"The six drug courts generated an average 29% recidivism reduction over the three-year postarrest period and an average 32% reduction over the one-year post-program period."

Source: Rempel, Michael, Dana Fox-Kralstein, Amanda Cissner, Robyn Cohen, Melissa Labriola, Donald Farole, Ann Bader and Michael Magnani, "The New York State Adult Drug Court Evaluation: Policies, Participants and Impacts" (New York, NY: Center for Court Innovation, Oct. 2003), p. x.

11. "When in-program participation time was included in the calculation, processing time for participants was far longer than for comparison defendants (due to the length of the drug court program). Hence to achieve positive impacts such as lower recidivism, drug courts require a significant up-front investment of court resources."

Source: Rempel, Michael, Dana Fox-Kralstein, Amanda Cissner, Robyn Cohen, Melissa Labriola, Donald Farole, Ann Bader and Michael Magnani, "The New York State Adult Drug Court Evaluation: Policies, Participants and Impacts" (New York, NY: Center for Court Innovation, Oct. 2003), p. xi.

12. "Graduation is itself a powerful predictor of avoiding postprogram recidivism; those who failed drug court were far more likely to recidivate in the post-program period. Further, contrary to previous research with non-drug court populations, no benefit was found to spending more total time in treatment only to fail in the end. Among those who failed, more time in the drug court program (measured in four courts) or more days specifically attending treatment (measured in one court) had no impact on post-program recidivism. These results strongly point to drug court graduation as the pivotal indicator of long-term outcomes."

Source: Rempel, Michael, Dana Fox-Kralstein, Amanda Cissner, Robyn Cohen, Melissa Labriola, Donald Farole, Ann Bader and Michael Magnani, "The New York State Adult Drug Court Evaluation: Policies, Participants and Impacts" (New York, NY: Center for Court Innovation, Oct. 2003), p. xiii.

13. Recidivism Rates Compared

City	Traditional Court	Drug Court
Denver, CO	58.0%	53.0%
Multnomath County, OR *(Portland)*	1.53 a	0.59 a
Oakland, CA	1.33 a	0.75 a
Riverside, CA	33.0%	13.4%
Travis County, RX *(Austin)*	41.0%	38.0%
Wilmington, DE	51.1%	33.3%

"(a) Expressed not as a percentage, but rather as the average number of arrests suffered during the follow-up period."

35

Drug Courts and Treatment as an Alternative to Incarceration

Source: Belenko, Steven & Dumanovsky, Tamara, Bureau of Justice Assistance, US Depart of Justice, "Special Drug Courts: Program Brief 2," (Washington, DC: US Department of Justice, 1993), and Granfield, Robert & Eby, Cindy, "An Evaluation of the Denver Drug Court: The Impact of a Treatment-Oriented Drug Offender System 10" (1997), as cited by District Judge Morris B. Hoffman, Second Judicial District (Denver), State of Colorado, "The Drug Court Scandal," North Carolina Law Review (Chapel Hill, NC: North Carolina Law Review Association, June 2000), Vol. 78, No. 5, p. 1496.

14. "Despite their ongoing popularity and rapid spread, historically there has been a relative paucity of empirically sound and comprehensive research on drug court operations and impacts. Most evaluations have been relatively small-scale local process evaluations mandated for DCPO grantees, which include program and client descriptions, with some retention and outcome data."

Source: Belenko, Steven, PhD, "Research on Drug Courts: A Critical Review 2001 Update" (New York, NY: National Center on Addiction and Substance Abuse (CASA) at Columbia University, June 2001), p. 6.

15. "More generally, few evaluations presented data on recidivism during program participation (in several cases, anecdotal data were presented or the number of drug cases was too small to draw any conclusions)."

Source: Belenko, Steven, PhD, "Research on Drug Courts: A Critical Review 2001 Update" (New York, NY: National Center on Addiction and Substance Abuse (CASA) at Columbia University, June 2001), p. 6.

16. According to the US General Accounting Office in 2002, the data on drug courts collected by the Justice Department is inadequate for evaluating drug court effectiveness. "In 1998, DCPO required its implementation and enhancement grantees to collect and provide performance and outcome data on program participants, including data on participants' criminal recidivism and substance abuse relapse after they have left the program. However, in 2000, DCPO revised its survey and eliminated the questions that were intended to collect post-program outcome data. The DCPO Director said that DCPO's decision was based on, among other things, drug court program grantees indicating that they were not able to provide post-program outcome data and that they lacked sufficient resources to collect such data. DCPO, however, was unable to produce specific evidence from grantees (i.e., written correspondence) that cited difficulties with providing post-program outcome data. The Director said that difficulties have generally been conveyed by grantees, in person, through telephone conversations, or are evidenced by the lack of responses to the post-program questions on the survey. Contrary to DCPO's position, evidence exists that supports the feasibility of collecting post-program performance and outcome data. During our 1997 survey of the drug court programs, 53 percent of the respondents said that they maintained follow-up data on participants' rearrest or conviction for a nondrug crime. Thirty-three percent said that they maintained follow-up data on participants' substance abuse relapse."

Drug Courts and Treatment as an Alternative to Incarceration

Source: US General Accounting Office, "Drug Courts: Better DOJ Data Collection and Evaluation Efforts Needed To Measure Impact of Drug Court Programs," (GAO-02-434: Government Printing Office, April 2002), pp. 12-13.

17. "One of the Drug Court Clearinghouse's functions has been to identify DCPO-funded drug court programs. However, the Drug Court Clearinghouse has only been tasked since 1998 with following up with a segment of DCPO grantees to determine their implementation date. Thus, the information provided to DCPO on the universe of DCPO-funded drug court programs is at best an estimate and not a precise count of DCPO drug court program grantees. Noting that its current grant information system was not intended to readily identify and track the number of DCPO-funded drug court programs, DCPO officials said that they plan to develop a new management information system that will enable DOJ to do so. Without an accurate universe of DCPO-funded drug court programs, DCPO is unable to readily determine the actual number of programs or participants it has funded or, as discussed below, the drug court programs that should have responded to its semiannual data collection survey."

Source: US General Accounting Office, "Drug Courts: Better DOJ Data Collection and Evaluation Efforts Needed To Measure Impact of Drug Court Programs," (GAO-02-434: Government Printing Office, April 2002), p. 9.

18. In a 2003 report, New York's Center for Court Innovation examined eleven different adult drug courts in New York state. They found that "Relapse and noncompliance are common, even among those who ultimately succeed. In seven of eight courts examined, at least half of all graduates had at least one positive drug test, and many had several positives – usually in the earlier stages of participation. This highlights the value of drug courts according multiple chances to participants experiencing early problems."

Source: Rempel, Michael, Dana Fox-Kralstein, Amanda Cissner, Robyn Cohen, Melissa Labriola, Donald Farole, Ann Bader and Michael Magnani, "The New York State Adult Drug Court Evaluation: Policies, Participants and Impacts" (New York, NY: Center for Court Innovation, Oct. 2003), p. xiv.

19. "Drug courts are experiencing a variety of difficulties engaging and retaining clients in treatment and clients who are deemed 'unmotivated.' Fifty-nine percent of drug courts indicate that 'lack of motivation for treatment' is used as a criterion to exclude people from drug court admission. Fifty-six percent of drug courts report that participants are discharged early from treatment because they have a poor attitude or lack motivation. Other reasons for early discharge from treatment include failure to appear in court (59 percent), failure to engage in treatment (70 percent), and missing too many treatment appointments (64 percent)."

Drug Courts and Treatment as an Alternative to Incarceration

Source: Peyton, Elizabeth A., and Robert Gossweiler, PhD, "Treatment Services in Adult Drug Courts: Report on the 1999 National Drug Court Treatment Survey, Executive Summary", Drug Courts Program Office, Office of Justice Programs, US Dept. of Justice, and the Substance Abuse and Mental Health Services Administration, Center for Substance Abuse Treatment, US Dept. of Health and Human Services (Washington, DC: US Dept. of Justice and US Dept. of Health and Human Services, May 2001), p. 10.

J

20. "Even offenders who do not succeed in drug court appear to be less criminally active than they were previously. This may be due to the benefits of treatment or the supervision, sanctions, intensive surveillance, and specific deterrence of the drug court."

    Source: Gebelein, Richard S., National Institute of Justice, "The Rebirth of Rehabilitation: Promise and Perils of Drug Courts" (Washington, DC: US Department of Justice, May 2000), p. 5.

21. "To facilitate an individual's progress in treatment, the prosecutor and defense counsel must shed their traditional adversarial courtroom relationship and work together as a team. Once a defendant is accepted into the drug court program, the team's focus is on the participant's recovery and law-abiding behavior — not on the merits of the pending case."

    Source: National Association of Drug Court Professionals Drug Court Standards Committee, "Defining Drug Courts: The Key Components" (Washington, DC: US Department of Justice), January 1997, on the web at http://www.ojp.usdoj.gov/dcpo/Define/key2.htm, last accessed August 9, 2000.

22. Judge Morris Hoffman of the Second Judicial District (Denver), State of Colorado, wrote in a recent North Carolina Law Review article "As with drugs themselves, however, the promises of drug courts to not measure up to their harsh reality. They are compromising deep-seated legal values, including the doctrine of separation of powers, the idea that truth is best discovered in the fires of advocacy, and the traditional role of judges as quiet, rational arbiters of the truth-finding process."

    Source: District Judge Morris B. Hoffman, Second Judicial District (Denver), State of Colorado, "The Drug Court Scandal", North Carolina Law Review (Chapel Hill, NC: North Carolina Law Review Association, June 2000), Vol. 78, No. 5, p. 1533.

23. Treatment options must be carefully considered by the courts. Various federal court rulings have determined that offering only AA and NA programs, because of their religious basis, violates the establishment clause of the US Constitution. Ruling in the case of Kerr v. Farrey in the 7th Circuit Federal Court of Appeals, Judge Diane P. Wood wrote, "We find, to the contrary, that the state has impermissibly coerced inmates to participate in a religious program." Judge Wood further notes that "the Court of Appeals of New York has recently come to the same conclusion we reach today in Matter of David Griffin v. Coughlin," and that "Our conclusion is thus in harmony with that of other courts that have considered similar questions."

Drug Courts and Treatment as an Alternative to Incarceration

Source: Ruling in the United States Court of Appeals for the Seventh Circuit No. 95-1843 James W. Kerr, Plaintiff-Appellant, v. Catherine J. Farrey and Lloyd Lind, Defendants-Appellees, Judge Diane P. Wood, decided August 27, 1996, from the web at http://www.kentlaw.edu/7circuit/1996/aug/95-1843.html

24. "The greatest frustrations described by drug courts include limited access to residential treatment, treatment for mental health disorders, and specialized services for women, racial and ethnic minorities, and the mentally ill. Problems with client engagement and retention in treatment are also identified. Followup interviews with a sample of respondents suggest that, while services may be available, they may be limited in quantity or otherwise very difficult to access."

Source: Peyton, Elizabeth A., and Robert Gossweiler, PhD, "Treatment Services in Adult Drug Courts: Report on the 1999 National Drug Court Treatment Survey, Executive Summary," Drug Courts Program Office, Office of Justice Programs, US Dept. of Justice, and the Substance Abuse and Mental Health Services Administration, Center for Substance Abuse Treatment, US Dept. of Health and Human Services (Washington, DC: US Dept. of Justice and US Dept. of Health and Human Services, May 2001), p. 9.

25. "Drug courts report that screening, assessing, and determining drug court eligibility occur quickly, and most participants are able to enter treatment less than 2 weeks after drug court admission. However, not all drug courts use screening or assessment instruments that have proved reliable and valid, and some do not appear to use appropriate clinically trained staff to conduct assessments."

Source: Peyton, Elizabeth A., and Robert Gossweiler, PhD, "Treatment Services in Adult Drug Courts: Report on the 1999 National Drug Court Treatment Survey, Executive Summary," Drug Courts Program Office, Office of Justice Programs, US Dept. of Justice, and the Substance Abuse and Mental Health Services Administration, Center for Substance Abuse Treatment, US Dept. of Health and Human Services (Washington, DC: US Dept. of Justice and US Dept. of Health and Human Services, May 2001), p. 9.

26. The US Dept. of Justice and US Dept. of Health and Human Services reported on treatment services available to drug courts around the US. The government found the following types of dedicated and external treatment programs available to drug courts:

(Type of Treatment/Percent of drug courts making specific form of treatment available)

Residential Treatment: 92%

Intensive Outpatient: 93%

Outpatient: 85%

Detoxification: 82%

Alcohol and Other Drug Education: 82%

Methadone Maintenance: 39%

Other Pharmacological Interventions: 25%

Drug Courts and Treatment as an Alternative to Incarceration

Prison- or Jail-Based Therapeutic Community: 39%
Community-Based Therapeutic Community: 51%
Acupuncture: 32%
Self-Help: 93%
Relapse Prevention: 85%
Other: 17%

Source: Peyton, Elizabeth A., and Robert Gossweiler, PhD, "Treatment Services in Adult Drug Courts: Report on the 1999 National Drug Court Treatment Survey, Executive Summary," Drug Courts Program Office, Office of Justice Programs, US Dept. of Justice, and the Substance Abuse and Mental Health Services Administration, Center for Substance Abuse Treatment, US Dept. of Health and Human Services (Washington, DC: US Dept. of Justice and US Dept. of Health and Huma Services, May 2001), p. 7, Figure A.

27. The US Dept. of Justice and US Dept. of Health and Human Services reported on treatment services available to drug courts around the US. The government found the following types of support services available to program participants:

    (Type of Service/Percent of drug courts making specific service available)

    Mental Health Treatment: 91%
    Mental Health Referral: 96%
    Vocational Training: 86%
    Job Placement: 77%
    Housing Assistance: 59%
    Housing Referral: 72%
    Parenting Education: 84%
    Educational Remediation/GED: 92%
    Domestic Violence Intervention Services: 73%
    Transportation Assistance: 59%
    Anger Management: 87%
    Life Skills Management: 79%
    Stress Management: 72%
    Relapse Prevention: 93%
    Childcare: 32%

Source: Peyton, Elizabeth A., and Robert Gossweiler, PhD, "Treatment Services in Adult Drug Courts: Report on the 1999 National Drug Court Treatment Survey, Executive Summary," Drug Courts Program Office, Office of Justice Programs, US Dept. of Justice, and the Substance Abuse and Mental Health Services Administration, Center for Substance Abuse Treatment, US Dept. of Health and Human Services (Washington, DC: US Dept. of Justice and US Dept. of Health and Human Services, May 2001), p. 8, Figure B.

28. It is possible that managed care will become a barrier to the success of drug courts and treatment as alternative to incarceration. The National

Drug Courts and Treatment as an Alternative to Incarceration

Institute of Justice notes, "The premise of managed care, increasingly the norm, is that the least treatment required should be provided. This is at odds with research on substance abuse treatment, which has shown that the longer a person remains in treatment, the more successful treatment will be. Furthermore, managed care assumes the patient will aggressively pursue the treatment he or she deems necessary. Because most drug court clients initially prefer not to be treated, they are likely to welcome a ruling by the health care provider or the managed care insurer that treatment is not needed. Finally, drug court clients frequently encounter delays in obtaining treatment funding or must cobble together bits and pieces of various programs because the 'exhaustion' rules of health care plans limit treatment."

Source: Gebelein, Richard S., National Institute of Justice, "The Rebirth of Rehabilitation: Promise and Perils of Drug Courts" (Washington, DC: US Department of Justice, May 2000), p. 6.

29. "It is unlikely that the level and intensity of services required for drug court participants will be supported by managed care. Pressures to reduce treatment expenditures and manage costs associated with Medicaid are driving States to shorten length of stay in treatment and increasing the thresholds for admission to intensive treatment."

Source: Peyton, Elizabeth A., and Robert Gossweiler, PhD, "Treatment Services in Adult Drug Courts: Report on the 1999 National Drug Court Treatment Survey, Executive Summary," Drug Courts Program Office, Office of Justice Programs, US Dept. of Justice, and the Substance Abuse and Mental Health Services Administration, Center for Substance Abuse Treatment, US Dept. of Health and Human Services (Washington, DC: US Dept. of Justice and US Dept. of Health and Human Services, May 2001), p. 13.

30. In a law review article, Colorado Judge Morris B. Hoffman writes "Reductions in recidivism are so small that if they exist at all they are statistically meaningless. Net-widening is so large that, even if drug courts truly were effective in reducing recidivism, more drug defendants would continue to jam our prisons than ever before."

Source: District Judge Morris B. Hoffman, Second Judicial District (Denver), State of Colorado, "The Drug Court Scandal," North Carolina Law Review (Chapel Hill, NC: North Carolina Law Review Association, June 2000), Vol. 78, No. 5, p. 1533-4.

31. "As the results of more sophisticated evaluations become available, preliminary success rates will not be sustained. As less tractable groups participate, rates of compliance and graduation will decline and recidivism will rise."

Source: Gebelein, Richard S., National Institute of Justice, "The Rebirth of Rehabilitation: Promise and Perils of Drug Courts" (Washington, DC: US Department of Justice, May 2000), p. 5.

32. James L. Nolan Jr., an assistant professor of sociology at Williams College, notes "Likewise, in a study conducted by W. Clinton Terry, professor of criminal justice at Florida International University, no real differences were found between the recidivism rates of those who completed and those who dropped out of Broward County's Drug

Drug Courts and Treatment as an Alternative to Incarceration

Court treatment program. Only a 4 percent difference in the number of felony rearrests and a 1 percent difference in the number of misdemeanor rearrests were found between the two groups."

Source: Nolan, James L., "The Therapeutic State," (New York, NY: New York University Press, 1998), p. 104.

33. James L. Nolan Jr. discusses the 1993 American Bar Association study of drug courts in his book "The Therapeutic State." The study found that among offenders who were sent to the Drug Court, 20% were rearrested for a drug offense and 32% were rearrested for any felony offense within one year of the sampled arrest. Among pre-Drug Court defendants, 23% were rearrested for a narcotics offense and 33% for any felony offense within one year. He further notes, "Again, they found little difference between the samples. Drug offenders sent through the Drug Court were rearrested, on average, 324 days after their first court appearance, whereas drug offenders sentenced prior to the Drug Court were rearrested, on average, 319 days after their first court appearance."

Source: Nolan, James L., "The Therapeutic State," (New York, NY: New York University Press, 1998), p. 105.

34. "In identifying target populations, drug courts need to be sensitive to class and race bias. Unless care is taken, diversion courts may tend disproportionately to work with white and middle-class substance abusers."

Source: Gebelein, Richard S., National Institute of Justice, "The Rebirth of Rehabilitation: Promise and Perils of Drug Courts" (Washington, DC: US Department of Justice, May 2000), p. 5.

35. "According to the most recent American University survey of 237 responding adult drug courts (out of 438 operational adult drug courts; American University, 2001), an estimated 72% of drug court clients are male; 38% are African American, 42% white non-Hispanic, and 17% Hispanic; 49% are unemployed; 76% had prior substance abuse treatment; 74% had at least one prior felony conviction; and 56% had been previously incarcerated."

Source: Belenko, Steven, PhD, "Research on Drug Courts: A Critical Review 2001 Update" (New York, NY: National Center on Addiction and Substance Abuse (CASA) at Columbia University, June 2001), p. 19.

37. David Rottman of the National Center for State Courts noted in an article for the American Judges Association's Court Review, "Specialized forums like drug or domestic violence courts require a judicial temperament in interacting directly with litigants and an openness to insights from fields like mental health.
"It is unclear that legal training is the best preparation for judging in specialized contexts."

Drug Courts and Treatment as an Alternative to Incarceration

Source: Rottman, David B., "Does Effective Therapeutic Jurisprudence Require Specialized Courts (and do Specialized Courts Require Specialist Judges?)," Court Review (Williamsburg, VA: American Judges Association, Spring 2000), pp. 25-26.

38. "When a drug court judge steps down, it is not always possible to find a sufficiently motivated replacement. Without a highly motivated judge, the drug court approach simply does not work."

Source: Gebelein, Richard S., National Institute of Justice, "The Rebirth of Rehabilitation: Promise and Perils of Drug Courts" (Washington, DC: US Department of Justice, May 2000), p. 6.

39. "Drug court judges and coordinators ranked improving staff skills to engage and retain drug court participants in treatment as the most needed improvement in the court's treatment component."

Source: Peyton, Elizabeth A., and Robert Gossweiler, PhD, "Treatment Services in Adult Drug Courts: Report on the 1999 National Drug Court Treatment Survey, Executive Summary," Drug Courts Program Office, Office of Justice Programs, US Dept. of Justice, and the Substance Abuse and Mental Health Services Administration, Center for Substance Abuse Treatment, US Dept. of Health and Human Services (Washington, DC: US Dept. of Justice and US Dept. of Health and Human Services, May 2001), p. 11.

40. In a law review article, Colorado Judge Morris B. Hoffman writes "By existing simply to appease two so diametric and irreconcilable sets of principles, drug courts are fundamentally unprincipled. By simultaneously treating drug use as a crime and as a disease, without coming to grips with the inherent contradictions of those two approaches, drug courts are not satisfying either the legitimate and compassionate interests of the treatment community or the legitimate and rational interests of the law enforcement community. They are, instead, simply enabling our continued national schizophrenia about drugs."

Source: District Judge Morris B. Hoffman, Second Judicial District (Denver), State of Colorado, "The Drug Court Scandal," North Carolina Law Review (Chapel Hill, NC: North Carolina Law Review Association, June 2000), Vol. 78, No. 5, p. 1477.

Drug Testing —
Employment, Schools, and Benefits

1. Companies which use Factor 1000, an impairment testing system, find that drug and alcohol use are not the most common reasons for accidents; rather, severe fatigue and illness are more common.

   Source: Hamilton, "A Video Game That Tells if Employees Are Fit To Work," Businessweek, (June 3, 1991).

2. "Few employers have used impairment testing, and information concerning that experience is very limited and extremely difficult to obtain. The available information, however, indicates that impairment testing is not just a better answer on paper, but in practice as well. Employers who have used impairment testing consistently found that it reduced accidents and was accepted by employees. Moreover, these employers consistently found that it was superior to urine testing in achieving both of these objectives."

   Source: National Workrights Institute, "Impairment Testing: Does It Work?" (Princeton, NJ: NWI, undated), from the web at http://www.workrights.org/issue_drugtest/dt_impairment_testing.html last accessed March 17, 2004.

3. "Drug testing of athletes was not a significant predictor of marijuana use by male athletes in high school."

   Source: Yamaguchi, Ryoko, Lloyd D. Johnston & Patrick M. O'Malley, "Relationship Between Student Illicit Drug Use and School Drug-Testing Policies," Journal of School Health, April 2003, Vol. 73, No. 4, p. 163.

4. "Drug testing of any kind, including for cause or suspicion, was not a significant predictor of marijuana use. These results remained for all samples, even after controlling for student demographic characteristics."

   Source: Yamaguchi, Ryoko, Lloyd D. Johnston & Patrick M. O'Malley, "Relationship Between Student Illicit Drug Use and School Drug-Testing Policies," Journal of School Health, April 2003, Vol. 73, No. 4, p. 163.

5. "Similar to results for marijuana use, drug testing of any kind and drug testing for cause and suspicion were not significant predictors for use of other illicit drugs among students in grades eight, 10, and 12. Within the high school subsamples, use of illicit drugs among high school male athletes and current marijuana users was not significantly different based on drug testing at the school. Even after controlling for student demographic characteristics, drug testing was not a significant predictor for other illicit drug use in any of the samples."

   Source: Yamaguchi, Ryoko, Lloyd D. Johnston & Patrick M. O'Malley, "Relationship Between Student Illicit Drug Use and School Drug-Testing Policies," Journal of School Health, April 2003, Vol. 73, No. 4, p. 163.

6. "Does drug testing prevent or inhibit student drug use? Members of the Supreme Court appear to believe it does. However, among the eighth-, 10th-, and 12-grade students surveyed in this study, school drug testing was not associated with either the prevalence or the frequency of student marijuana use, or of other illicit drug use. Nor was drug testing of athletes associated with lower-than-average marijuana and other illicit drug use by high school male athletes. Even among those

Drug Testing —
Employment, Schools, and Benefits

who identified themselves as fairly experienced marijuana users, drug testing also was not associated with either the prevalence or the frequency of marijuana or other illicit drug use."

Source: Yamaguchi, Ryoko, Lloyd D. Johnston & Patrick M. O'Malley, "Relationship Between Student Illicit Drug Use and School Drug-Testing Policies," Journal of School Health, April 2003, Vol. 73, No. 4, p. 164.

7. The American Management Association surveys US employers on various policies including testing for illegal substance use. According to their 2004 survey, in 1995 78% of companies did some sort of testing for illegal drugs, with 63% of companies testing applicants and 68% testing current employees. By 2004, the number dropped to just 62% of all companies testing for illegal drugs, with 55% testing applicants and 44% testing current employees.

Source: American Management Association, "AMA 2004 Workplace Testing Survey: Medical Testing" (New York, NY: American Management Association, 2004), p. 3.

8. The American Management Association in its survey of companies on workplace surveillance and medical testing reports the following percentages of companies who conduct drug tests:

Business Category	Testing of New Hires	Testing of All Employees
Financial Services	35.8%	18.8%
Business & Professional Services	36.0%	18.4%
Other Services	60.3%	34.7%
Wholesale & Retail	63.0%	36.8%
Manufacturing	78.5%	42.2%

Source: American Management Association, "A 2000 AMA Survey: Workplace Testing: Medical Testing: Summary of Key Findings" (New York, NY: American Management Association, 2000), p. 1.

9. The Bureau of Labor Statistics noted the downward trend in drug testing after a large survey of 145,000 businesses. It found that "overall about 1 of 3 establishments that reported having a drug testing program in 1988 said they did not have one in 1990." 46% of the companies with under 50 employees dropped drug testing programs.

Source: Bureau of Labor Statistics, "Anti-Drug Programs in the Workplace: Are They Here to Stay?" Monthly Labor Review, Washington D.C.: US Bureau of Labor Statistics (April 1991), pp. 26-28.

10. In a study of high tech industries, researchers found that "drug testing programs do not succeed in improving productivity. Surprisingly, companies adopting drug testing programs are found to exhibit lower levels of productivity than their counterparts that do not... Both pre-employment and random testing of workers are found to be associated with lower levels of productivity."

Drug Testing —
Employment, Schools, and Benefits

Source: Shepard, Edward M., and Thomas J. Clifton, "Drug Testing and Labor Productivity: Estimates Applying a Production Function Model," Institute of Industrial Relations, Research Paper No. 18, Le Moyne University, Syracuse, NY (1998), p. 1.

11. It has been estimated that the United States spends $1 billion annually to drug test about 20 million workers.

Source: Shepard, Edward M., and Thomas J. Clifton, "Drug Testing and Labor Productivity: Estimates Applying a Production Function Model," Institute of Industrial Relations, Research Paper No. 18, Le Moyne University, Syracuse, NY (1998), p. 8.

K

12. One reason drug testing is not used by some employers is the cost. One electronics manufacturer estimated that the cost of finding each positive result was $20,000. After testing 10,000 employees he only found 49 positive results. A congressional committee estimated that the cost of each positive in government testing was $77,000 because the positive rate was only 0.5%.

Source: "Workplace Substance Abuse Testing, Drug Testing: Cost and Effect," Cornell/Smithers Report, Utica, New York: Cornell University (January 1992).

13. "Nonchronic drug use was not statistically related to either of the labor supply measures, indicating that light or casual drug use did not lead to negative effects on the labor supply."

Source: French, Michael T., M. Christopher Roebuck, and Pierre Kebreau Alexandre, "Illicit Drug Use, Employment, and Labor Force Participation," Southern Economic Journal (Southern Economic Association: Oklahoma State University, Stillwater, OK, 2001), 68(2), p. 366.

14. According to a study funded by the Robert Wood Johnson Foundation and published by the Southern Economic Journal in 2001, "In conclusion, this study found that chronic drug use was significantly related to employment status for men and women. On the other hand, male chronic drug users were less likely to participate in the labor force, but no significant relationship existed between chronic drug use and labor force participation for females. Perhaps the most important finding of this study, however, was the lack of any significant relationships between nonchronic drug use, employment, and labor force participation. An implication of this finding is that employers and policy makers should focus on problematic drug users in the same way that they focus on problematic alcohol users."

Source: French, Michael T., M. Christopher Roebuck, and Pierre Kebreau Alexandre, "Illicit Drug Use, Employment, and Labor Force Participation," Southern Economic Journal (Southern Economic Association: Oklahoma State University, Stillwater, OK, 2001), 68(2), p. 366.

15. "Before saliva can become an accepted specimen for illegal drug testing, several problems have to be resolved. For one, current testing methods usually measure the chemical breakdown products of illegal drugs rather than the parent drugs themselves. Usually, those parent drugs are found in saliva more often than the breakdown products. Eventually, however, this may be helpful because the parent drugs often can be extracted from a saliva sample more easily than the metabolites.

Drug Testing —
Employment, Schools, and Benefits

"Also, if an inmate being tested has recently smoked, say, a marijuana joint, saliva concentrations of tetrahydrocannabinol will likely be elevated. Tetrahydrocannabinol, or THC, is the active ingredient in marijuana. That would make saliva, at least temporarily, a poor predictor of how much THC is in the blood or other specimens. Several hours would have to pass and repeat tests would be needed before saliva concentrations will actually correlate with those in the blood. The same is true for other drugs.

"Further, the methods used to stimulate the flow of saliva and collect it can affect the results. Collection by an absorbent dental swab placed in the mouth, for example, requires an additional testing step of separating the saliva from the swab that spitting into a container does not."

Source: Fatah, Alim and Jeffrey P. Cohn, "Developments in Drug Testing: Saliva as an Alternative to Urine and Blood," National Institute of Justice, reprinted from the Oct. 2003 issue of Corrections Today, Vol. 65, No. 6.

Drug Use Estimates

1. An estimated 112,085,000 Americans aged 12 or over (46.1% of the US population aged 12 and over) report having used an illicit drug at least once in their lifetimes.

   Source: Substance Abuse and Mental Health Services Administration, US Department of Health and Human Services, 2005 National Survey on Drug Use and Health: Tables (Rockville, MD: Office of Applied Studies, Sept. 2006), Tables 1.1A and 1.1B.

2. An estimated 35,041,000 Americans aged 12 or over (14.4% of the US population aged 12 and over) used an illicit drug during the previous year.

   Source: Substance Abuse and Mental Health Services Administration, US Department of Health and Human Services, 2005 National Survey on Drug Use and Health: Tables (Rockville, MD: Office of Applied Studies, Sept. 2006), Tables 1.1A and 1.1B.

3. Below are the results of the National Survey on Drug Use and Health 2005, showing estimates of the US population aged 12 and over who admit to using substances. It is important to note that the Survey finds very slight use of 'hard drugs' like cocaine, heroin and crack. (Note: Numbers of users are in millions.)

Substance	Ever Used	Past Year	Past Month	Frequent Users
Alcohol	201.67 82.9%	161.63 66.5%	126.03 51.8%	16.04 *(Heavey users)* 6.6%
Tobacco	172.28 70.8%	84.96 34.9%	71.52 29.4%	N/A
Marijuana	97.55 40.1%	25.38 10.4%	14.63 6.0%	N/A
Cocaine	33.67 13.8%	5.52 2.3%	2.34 1.0%	N/A
Crack	7.93 3.3%	1.38 0.6%	0.68 0.3%	N/A
Heroin	3.53 1.5%	0.38 0.2%	0.14 0.1%	N/A

Source: Substance Abuse and Mental Health Services Administration, US Department of Health and Human Services, 2005 National Survey on Drug Use and Health: Tables (Rockville, MD: Office of Applied Studies, Sept. 2006), Tables 1.1A, 1.1B, 2.1A, and 2.1B.

4. An estimated 971 thousand Americans used crack cocaine in 1998. Of those, 462 thousand were White, 324 thousand were Black, and 157 thousand were Hispanic.

   Source: Substance Abuse and Mental Health Services Administration, US Department of Health and Human Services, National Household Survey on Drug Abuse: Population Estimates 1998 (Washington DC: US Department of Health and Human Services, 1999), pp. 37-39.

5. "The total number of drug users in the world is now estimated at some 200 million people, equivalent to about 5 per cent of the global population age 15-64. Cannabis remains by far the most widely used drug (some 162 million people), followed by amphetamine-type stimulants (some 35 million people), which include amphetamines (used by 25 million people) and ecstasy (almost 10 million people). The number of opiate abusers is estimated at some 16 million people, of which 11 million are heroin abusers. Some 13 million people are cocaine users."

Drug Use Estimates

Source: United Nations Office on Drugs and Crime (UNODC), World Drug Report 2006 Vol. 1: Analysis (Vienna, Austria: UNODC, June 2006), p. 9.

6. "Of these 5 per cent of the population (age 15-64), who use illicit drugs at least once a year (annual prevalence), only about half of them (2.7 per cent of the population age 15-64) use drugs regularly, that is, at least once per month. The number of what are commonly understood to be drug addicts or problem drug users is some 25 million persons worldwide, equivalent to 0.6 per cent of the population age 15-64. This estimate does not seem to have changed much in recent years at the global level as increases in some countries were offset by declines in others."

Source: United Nations Office on Drugs and Crime (UNODC), World Drug Report 2006 Vol. 1: Analysis (Vienna, Austria: UNODC, June 2006), p. 8.

7. "Tobacco, a particularly addictive substance, is a case in point. About 28 per cent of the world's adult population is estimated to use tobacco, which exceeds, by far, the number of people using illicit drugs (4 per cent for cannabis and 1 per cent for ATS, cocaine and opiates combined)."

Source: United Nations Office on Drugs and Crime (UNODC), World Drug Report 2006 Vol. 1: Analysis (Vienna, Austria: UNODC, June 2006), p. 7.

8. According to the United Nations Office on Drugs and Crime (UNODC), "Unsurprisingly, the main problem drugs at the global level continue to be the opiates (notably heroin) followed by cocaine. For most of Europe and Asia, opiates continued to be the main problem drug, accounting for 62% of all treatment demand in 2003. In South-America, drug related treatment demand continued to be mainly linked to the abuse of cocaine (59% of all treatment demand). In Africa, the bulk of all treatment demand – as in the past – is linked to cannabis (64%). Analysis of these responses suggests that overall drug consumption continues to spread at the global level."

Source: United Nations Office on Drugs and Crime (UNODC), World Drug Report 2005 (Vienna, Austria: UNODC, June 2005), pp. 5-6.

9. "The paucity of the data on which the annual prevalence estimates are based does not allow for the identification of clear global trends in the short term. As an imperfect complement, UNODC relies on the perception of the trends in their countries by national experts. A global analysis of these perceptions suggest that the strongest increase over the last decade was for cannabis use and ATS, and at lower levels for opiates and cocaine. After some stabilization in 2003, ATS drug use was perceived as having increased again, reflecting the prevailing view in East and South-East Asia that methamphetamine use has started rising again.
    "Opiate abuse trends flattened in recent years. However, by 2004, opiate abuse perceptions again went upwards, as many countries around Afghanistan experienced a renewed supply-push following Afghanistan's good opium harvests of 2003 and 2004. In other parts of the world, including North America and Western Europe, abuse levels remained constant for opiates. After years of increases, cocaine use is perceived as declining slightly, notably in the Americas. In Europe, by contrast, cocaine use continues to expand."

Drug Use Estimates

Source: United Nations Office on Drugs and Crime (UNODC), World Drug Report 2006 Vol. 1: Analysis (Vienna, Austria: UNODC, June 2006), p. 9.

10. Below are results from a survey of drug use in The Netherlands published in 1999. Note the difference in drug use prevalence. For more information check out the Netherlands section of Drug War Facts.

Substance	Ever Used	Past Year	Past Month	Frequent Users
Alcohol	90.2%	82.5%	73.3%	24.3% *(of past month users)*
Cigarettes	67.9%	38.1%	34.3%	N/A
Marijuana	15.6%	4.5%	2.5%	25.6% *(of past month users)*
Cocaine	2.1%	0.6%	0.2%	1.8% *(of past month users)*
Crack	*not tracked separately			
Heroin	0.3%	0.1%	N/A	N/A

Source: University of Amsterdam, Centre for Drug Research, Licit and Illicit Drug Use in the Netherlands, 1997 (Amsterdam: University of Amsterdam, September 1999), pp. 45, 46, 47, 55

For Further Research:

The NSDUH survey (formerly called the National Household Survey), issued, is available online at http://www.oas.samhsa.gov/p0000016.htm#Standard

An online version of the National Household Survey on Drug Abuse: Population Estimates 1998 is available at http://www.oas.samhsa.gov/nhsda/Pe1998/TOC.htm.

Downloadable PDF versions of the Population Estimates, the Main Findings, and a Summary Report on the findings from the 1998 Survey are available at http://www.oas.samhsa.gov/p0000016.htm

To order a free copy of the Survey call the National Clearinghouse for Alcohol and Drug Information at 1-800-729-6686.

Economics

1. According to the United Nations Office on Drugs and Crime, "[T]he value of the global illicit drug market for the year 2003 was estimated at US$13 bn [billion] at the production level, at $94 bn at the wholesale level (taking seizures into account), and at US$322bn based on retail prices and taking seizures and other losses into account. This indicates that despite seizures and losses, the value of the drugs increase substantially as they move from producer to consumer."

   Source: United Nations Office on Drugs and Crime (UNODC), World Drug Report 2005 (Vienna, Austria: UNODC, June 2005), p. 127.

2. "If compared to global licit exports (US$7,503 bn in 2003) or compared to global GDP (US$35,765 bn in 2003) the estimated size [of] the global illicit drug market may not appear to be particularly high (0.9% of global GDP at retail level or 1.3% of global exports measures at wholesale level).

   "Nonetheless, the size of the global illicit drug market is substantial. The value, measured at retail prices, is higher than the GDP of 88% of the countries in the world (163 out of 184 for which the World Bank has GDP data) and equivalent to about three quarters of Sub-Saharan Africa's combined GDP (US$439 bn in 2003). The sale of drugs, measured at wholesale prices, was equivalent to 12% of global export of chemicals (US$794 bn), 14% of global agricultural exports (US$674 bn) and exceeded global exports of ores and other minerals (US$79 bn) in 2003. Such sales of drugs were also higher than the combined total licit agricultural exports from Latin America (US$75 bn) and the Middle East (US$10 bn) in 2003."

   Source: United Nations Office on Drugs and Crime (UNODC), World Drug Report 2005 (Vienna, Austria: UNODC, June 2005), p. 127.

3. "It is also worth noting that by 1999, the UNDCP had not attempted to follow up its efforts to estimate the size of the world illegal drug market. That year, the Financial Action Task Force (FATF) [an inter-governmental body focusing on anti-money laundering activities and legislation] decided to begin work to assess the size of the world illegal economy and found it convenient to start with an estimate of the illegal drug market, a task that was considered easier than estimating other illegal activities, given the large work on drugs already available. FATF hired Peter Reuter, a well-known economist who has done extensive work on illegal drug markets, and produced an estimate. This job had the full cooperation of the UNDCP, which opened its data bank to the researcher. The resulting study is probably the most serious attempt to ascertain the size of the world illegal drug market and resulted in an estimated range between $45 and $280 billion."

   Source: Francisco E. Thoumi, PhD, "The Numbers Game: Let's All Guess the Size of the Illegal Drug Industry!" Journal of Drug Issues, Vol. 35, No. 1, Winter 2005, p. 191.

Economics

4. "The most recent figures available from the Office of National Drug Control Policy (ONDCP) indicate that, in 1999, federal expenditures on control of illegal drugs surpassed $17 billion; combined expenditures by federal, state, and local governments exceeded $30 billion. What is more, the nation's so-called 'drug war' is a protracted one. The country has spent roughly this amount annually throughout the 1990s."

   Source: National Research Council, National Academy of Sciences, "Informing America's Policy on Illegal Drugs: What We Don't Know Keeps Hurting Us" (Washington, DC: National Academy Press, 2001), p. 1.

5. "The long-run elasticities provide a basis for estimating potential benefits from changing the current policy mix away from enforcement and interdiction and towards education and treatment. Applying the estimated coefficients, a 10 percent reduction in expenditures on enforcement (about 1 billion dollars by the late 1990s) would be associated with a long-run reduction of over 20% in both the number of deaths and the age-adjusted death rate. This would imply that close to 3,000 deaths a year might be avoided with a shift away from enforcement approaches to drug control. Adding the billion dollars to education and treatment would represent an 18% increase in 1998. The estimated elasticity of 1.59 implies a reduction of close to 5,000 drug-induced deaths per year as a result. Thus, the underlying estimates suggest that very substantial improvements in public health may be achieved by emphasizing education and treatment over enforcement and interdiction."

   Source: Shepard, Edward & Paul R. Blackley, "US Drug Control Policies: Federal Spending on Law Enforcement Versus Treatment in Public Health Outcomes," Journal of Drug Issues, Vol. 34, No. 4, Fall 2004, pp. 781-782.

6. According to the United Nations, profits in illegal drugs are so inflated that three-quarters of all drug shipments would have to be intercepted to seriously reduce the profitability of the business. Current efforts only intercept 13% of heroin shipments and 28%-40%* of cocaine shipments. (*At most; the UN Office for Drug Control and Crime Prevention notes that estimates of production and total supply are probably understated by reporting governments.)

   Source: United Nations Office for Drug Control and Crime Prevention, Global Illicit Drug Trends 1999 (New York, NY: UNODCCP, 1999), p. 51.

7. In 2004 a kilogram of heroin no. 3 in Pakistan typically sold for an average of $2,520; a kilogram of heroin no. 4 typically sold for $4,076 that year. In Afghanistan, a kilogram of heroin no. 3 typically sold for $1,600 and a kilogram of heroin no. 4 typically sold for $4,000. In Colombia, a kilogram of heroin no. 4 typically sold for $10,149. In the US in 2004, a kilogram of heroin no. 4 cost an average of $66,250.

   Source: United Nations Office on Drugs and Crime, World Drug Report 2006 Volume 2: Statistics (Vienna, Austria: UNODC, 2006), pp. 365-366.

Economics

8. According to the US Office of National Drug Control Policy, the cost of heroin at the retail level declined from an average estimated $1,974.49 per gram in 1981 to $361.95 per gram in 2003. At the wholesale level, the drop went from $1,007.60 per gram in 1981 to $139.22 per gram in 2003. The average purity of heroin on the US market increased in that time as well, going at the retail level from an average of 11% in 1981 to an average 32% in 2003, and at the wholesale level from an average 12% in 1981 to an average 46% in 2003.

   Source: Office of National Drug Control Policy, "The Price and Purity of Illicit Drugs: 1981 Through the Second Quarter of 2003" (Washington DC: Executive Office of the President, November 2004), Publication Number NCJ 207768, p. 62, Table 5 & p. 63, Table 6.

9. In 2004, a kilogram of cocaine base in Colombia typically sold for $810 and a kilogram of cocaine typically sold for $1,713. In Peru in 2004, a kilogram of cocaine base typically sold for $700 and a kilogram of cocaine typically sold for $1,000. In Mexico in 2004, a kilogram of cocaine typically sold for $7,880. In the United States in 2001, a kilogram of cocaine typically sold for $23,500.

   Source: United Nations Office on Drugs and Crime, World Drug Report 2006 Volume 2: Statistics (Vienna, Austria: UNODC, 2006), pp. 369-370.

10. According to the US Office of National Drug Control Policy, the cost of cocaine at the retail level declined from an average estimated $544.59 per gram in 1981 to $106.54 per gram in 2003. At the wholesale level, the drop went from $201.18 per gram in 1981 to $37.96 per gram in 2003. The purity of cocaine also went up during that time. At the retail level, it averaged 40% purity in 1981 and 70% purity in 2003, while at the wholesale level cocaine averaged 56% purity in 1981 and 63% purity in 2003.

    Source: Office of National Drug Control Policy, "The Price and Purity of Illicit Drugs: 1981 Through the Second Quarter of 2003" (Washington DC: Executive Office of the President, November 2004), Publication Number NCJ 207768, p. 58, Table 1 & p. 59, Table 2.

11. "In summary, prices for powder cocaine, crack, and heroin declined sharply in the 1980s and have declined more gradually since then, with periodic interruptions by modest price spikes that have usually persisted for a year or less. For d-methamphetamine, the pattern is broadly similar, but the price spikes appear to be larger and longer-lasting, particularly for 1989-1991. Marijuana prices have followed a very different pattern, increasing from 1981 to 1991, then declining through 2000 and increasing over the past three years.
    "The average purities of these drugs have varied substantially by drug, occasionally with divergent trends. Trends over time suggest that cutting, or diluting, across quantity levels occurs today primarily in the case of heroin. The data also show that the average purity of drugs obtained through seizures is generally higher than that of drugs observed through purchases, particularly at higher quantity levels."

Economics

Source: Office of National Drug Control Policy, "The Price and Purity of Illicit Drugs: 1981 Through the Second Quarter of 2003" (Washington DC: Executive Office of the President, November 2004), Publication Number NCJ 207768, p. vii.

12. "Between 1989 and 1998, American users spent $39 billion to $77 billion yearly on cocaine and $10 billion to $22 billion yearly on heroin. To arrive at these estimates, we multiplied the number of users by their typical expenditures, and then converted the resulting estimates to 1998-dollar equivalents. Most of the downward trend results from changes in the consumer price index."

Source: Abt Associates, "What America's Users Spend on Illegal Drugs 1988-1998" (Washington, DC: ONDCP, Dec. 2000), p. 5.

13. According to the US Office of National Drug Control Policy, federal spending on the drug war in 2001 totaled $18.095 Billion, rising to $18.822 Billion in 2002 and $19.179 Billion for 2003. ONDCP estimates of federal drug control budgets released since publication of the 2002 national strategy utilize a much different methodology and exclude several billion dollars in costs including spending by the federal Bureau of Prisons to incarcerate drug offenders, so comparisons with ONDCP's budgets from 2003 onward are impossible.

Source: Office of National Drug Control Policy, "National Drug Control Strategy: FY 2003 Budget Summary" (Washington, DC: Office of the President, February 2002), Table 2, p. 6, pp. 16-23.

14. According to ONDCP, the $18.822 Billion spent by the federal government on the drug war in 2002 breaks down as follows:
    Treatment (with Research): $3.587 Billion (19.1% of total)
    Prevention (with Research): $2.548 Billion (13.5% of total)
    Domestic Law Enforcement: $9.513 Billion (50.5% of total)
    Interdiction: $2.074 Billion (11.0% of total)
    International: $1.098 Billion (5.8% of total)
In other words, $12.686 Billion in 2002 was directed to supply reduction, i.e. law enforcement (67.4% of total), and $6.136 Billion to demand reduction, i.e. treatment, prevention and education (32.6% of total).

Source: Office of National Drug Control Policy, "National Drug Control Strategy: FY 2003 Budget Summary" (Washington, DC: Office of the President, February 2002), Table 2, p. 6.

15. "In 2003 the United States spent a record $185 billion for police protection, corrections, and judicial and legal activities. Expenditures for operating the Nation's justice system increased from almost $36 billion in 1982 to over $185 billion in 2003, an increase of 418%"

Source: Hughes, Kristen A., "Justice Expenditure and Employment in the United States, 2003" (Washington, DC: US Dept. of Justice, Bureau of Justice Statistics, April 2006), NCJ212260, p. 2.

Economics

16. "- Overall, local police spending represented 45% of the Nation's total justice expenditure, and State corrections accounted for the second largest portion, 33%.
"- Police protection is primarily a local responsibility; accordingly, local governments spent 69% of the total police protection expenditure in the country in 2003.
"- Corrections is primarily a State responsibility; as such State governments accounted for 64% of the Nation's corrections expenditure.
"- Judicial and legal services in the United States were funded primarily by local (43%) and State (38%) governments."

Source: Bauer, Lynn & Steven D. Owens, "Justice Expenditure and Employment in the United States, 2001" (Washington, DC: US Dept. of Justice, Bureau of Justice Statistics, May 2004), NCJ202792, p. 4.

17. "The increase in justice expenditures over nearly 20 years reflects the expansion of the Nation's justice system. For example, in 1982 the justice system employed approximately 1.27 million persons; in 2003 it reached over 2.3 million.
"Police protection
"One indicator of police workload, the FBI's arrest estimates for State and local police agencies, grew from 12 million in 1982 to an estimated 13.6 million in 2003. The number of employees in police protection increased from approximately 724,000 to over 1.1 million.
"Judicial and legal
"The judicial and legal workload, including civil and criminal cases, prosecutor functions, and public defender services, also expanded during this period. Cases of all kinds (criminal, civil, domestic, juvenile, and traffic) filed in the nearly 16,000 general and limited jurisdiction State courts went from about 86 million to 100 million in the 16-year period, 1987-2003. The total of judicial and legal employees grew about 101% to over 494,000 persons in 2003.
"Corrections
"The total number of State and Federal inmates grew from 403,000 in 1982 to over 1.4 million in 2003. The number of local jail inmates more than tripled from approximately 207,000 in 1982 to over 691,000 in 2003. Adults on probation increased from over 1.4 million to about 4.1 million persons. Overall, corrections employment more than doubled from nearly 300,000 to over 748,000 during this same period."

Source: Bauer, Lynn & Steven D. Owens, "Justice Expenditure and Employment in the United States, 2001" (Washington, DC: US Dept. of Justice, Bureau of Justice Statistics, May 2004), NCJ202792, p. 7.

18. "In 2003, 7.2% of total State and local expenditures was for justice activities – 3% for police protection, 2.6% for corrections, and 1.5% for judicial and legal services (figure 3).
"By comparison, 29% of State and local government spending went to education, 14% to public welfare, 7% to health and hospitals, and 4% to interest on debt."

Economics

Source: Bauer, Lynn & Steven D. Owens, "Justice Expenditure and Employment in the United States, 2001" (Washington, DC: US Dept. of Justice, Bureau of Justice Statistics, May 2004), NCJ202792, p. 4.

19. "The few studies on the local economic impacts of prisons to date have not found significant positive impacts. For example, a study by the Sentencing Project challenges the notion that a new prison brings economic benefits to smaller communities. Using 25 years of data from New York State rural counties, the authors looked at employment rates and per capita income and found 'no significant difference or discernible pattern of economic trends' between counties that were home to a prison and counties that were not home to a prison (King, Mauer, and Huling 2003). According to a recent study by Iowa State University, many towns that made sizeable investments in prisons did not reap the economic gains that were predicted (Besser 2003). Another analysis in Texas found no impacts as measured by consumer spending in nearly three-fourths of the areas examined (Chuang 1998)."

Source: Lawrence, Sarah and Jeremy Travis, "The New Landscape of Imprisonment: Mapping America's Prison Expansion" (Washington, DC: Urban Institute, April 2004), p. 3.

20. "The economic benefits of new prisons may come from the flow of additional state and federal dollars. In the decennial census, prisoners are counted where they are incarcerated, and many federal and state funding streams are tied to census population counts. According to the U.S. General Accounting Office (2003), the federal government distributes over $140 billion in grant money to state and local governments through formula-based grants. Formula grant money is in part based on census data and covers programs such as Medicaid, Foster Care, Adoption Assistance, and Social Services Block Grant (U.S. General Accounting Office 2003). Within a state, funding for community health services, road construction and repair, public housing, local law enforcement, and public libraries are all driven by population counts from the census."

Source: Lawrence, Sarah and Jeremy Travis, "The New Landscape of Imprisonment: Mapping America's Prison Expansion" (Washington, DC: Urban Institute, April 2004), p. 3.

21. "Every dollar transferred to a 'prison community' is a dollar that is not given to the home community of a prisoner, which is often among the country's most disadvantaged urban areas. According to one account, Cook County Illinois will lose nearly $88 million in federal benefits over the next decade because residents were counted in the 2000 Census in their county of incarceration rather than their county of origin (Duggan 2000). Losing funds from the 'relocation' of prisoners is also an issue for New York City, as two-thirds of state prisoners are from the city, while 91 percent of prisoners are incarcerated in upstate counties (Wagner 2002a)."

Source: Lawrence, Sarah and Jeremy Travis, "The New Landscape of Imprisonment: Mapping America's Prison Expansion" (Washington, DC: Urban Institute, April 2004), p. 3.

Economics

22. "A qualitative analysis, featuring in-depth interviews with 101, nonrandomly selected former recipients revealed that disability benefits promoted housing autonomy, successful cohabitation, and overall housing stability. The termination of benefits, at a time of diminishing social services (e.g., cash and housing assistance) and a housing market explosion, increased various types of homelessness for respondents and dependency on family and friends. Such negative living outcomes, in turn, further escalated the risk of drug and alcohol use, criminal participation, and victimization."

Source: Anderson, Tammy L., Caitlin Shannon, Igor Schyb, and Paul Goldstein, "Welfare Reform and Housing: Assessing the Impact to Substance Abusers," Journal of Drug Issues (Tallahassee, FL: Florida State University, Winter 2002), Vol. 32, No. 1, p. 265.

M

23. Research assessing the impact of the Personal Responsibility and Work Opportunity Reconciliation Act of 1996 (PRWORA) found that the termination of addiction disability payments has had a negative effect. According to the study,
"First, PRWORA of 1996 has destabilized the housing situations of the respondents and has placed them at greater risk for various types of housing problems and homelessness. Second, these housing complications have exacerbated numerous social problems (drug and alcohol abuse, crime, and victimization). It is important to consider, however, that changes in the housing market, decreased housing subsidies, and individual characteristics and behaviors also played a role in these negative outcomes.
"More specifically, we found considerable housing dependency, at some level, for all respondents, albeit most often among those who currently had no SSI benefits. Problematic dependence on family, friends, and significant others (doubling up or sharing housing with other adults) was most common, followed by dependence on state-funded program. Independent living (e.g., having one's own place and paying one's own rent), which we would hope for most by middle-age, was an uncommon occurrence."

Source: Anderson, Tammy L., Caitlin Shannon, Igor Schyb, and Paul Goldstein, "Welfare Reform and Housing: Assessing the Impact to Substance Abusers," Journal of Drug Issues (Tallahassee, FL: Florida State University, Winter 2002), Vol. 32, No. 1, p. 289.

24. "While the aim of SSI addiction disability termination was, for conservatives, to force individuals to take greater responsibility in their lives and to decrease dependence on governmentally funded programs, this goal appears nearly impossible to achieve given the lack of resources had by this under-skilled and poor population. Nor did the policy change necessarily decrease their risk of continued involvement in drugs and crime. We estimate that losing a stable housing situation has placed respondents at greater risk for continued drug and alcohol use, something not considered by extant etiological work on individual substance abuse. These consequences could mean a greater dependence of this population on state and federally funded programs."

Economics

Source: Anderson, Tammy L., Caitlin Shannon, Igor Schyb, and Paul Goldstein, "Welfare Reform and Housing: Assessing the Impact to Substance Abusers," Journal of Drug Issues (Tallahassee, FL: Florida State University, Winter 2002), Vol. 32, No. 1, p. 290.

25. In January 2001, the National Center on Addiction and Substance Abuse at Columbia University published an analysis of costs to states from tobacco, alcohol and other drug addiction. According to the report, "CASA's analysis revealed a few cost categories where only a single category of substances is implicated. (Figure 2.B) For instance, CASA identified $1.1 billion in state spending linked to illicit drug use only: $574 million for public safety costs for drug enforcement programs; $114 million for drug courts; and $412 million linked to illegal drugs in state spending on Medicaid.

"CASA estimates that $7.4 billion in state spending is linked exclusively to tobacco through state Medicaid spending.

"The single drug linked to the largest percentage of state costs is alcohol. We were able to identify $9.2 billion in state spending linked to only to alcohol in addition to the costs associated with abuse of both alcohol and illegal drugs: $915 million on highway safety and local law enforcement associated with drunk driving; $837 million in state costs for the developmentally disabled as a result of fetal alcohol syndrome; and, $7.4 billion in state Medicaid costs."

Source: National Center on Addiction and Substance Abuse at Columbia University, Shoveling Up: The Impact of Substance Abuse on State Budgets (New York, NY: CASA, Jan. 2001), p. 11.

26. "Of the $81.3 billion states spent on substance abuse in 1998, $77.9 billion were spent shoveling the wreckage of this enormous health and social problem. These clean-up costs equal 12.6 percent of the total $620 billion in state spending for 1998. (Table 3.1)

"Almost ninety-six (95.8) cents of every state dollar spent on substance abuse goes to carry its burden in state programs such as criminal justice, school aid, Medicaid, child welfare, developmental disabilities and mental illness because of our failure to prevent substance abuse and treat those who are abusers and addicts."

Source: National Center on Addiction and Substance Abuse at Columbia University, Shoveling Up: The Impact of Substance Abuse on State Budgets (New York, NY: CASA, Jan. 2001), p. 13.

27. "In 1998, states spent a total of $39.7 billion for justice-related programs in adult corrections, juvenile justice and the judiciary amounting to 6.3 percent of their budgets. Of this amount, $30.7 billion (77 percent) was linked to substance abuse."

Source: National Center on Addiction and Substance Abuse at Columbia University, Shoveling Up: The Impact of Substance Abuse on State Budgets (New York, NY: CASA, Jan. 2001), p. 15.

28. "State spending for substance abuse in the justice system amounts to over one-third (39.4 percent) of the $77.9 billion states spend on the burden of substance abuse to state programs – 10 times the amount states spend on all substance abuse prevention, treatment and research."

Economics

Source: National Center on Addiction and Substance Abuse at Columbia University, Shoveling Up: The Impact of Substance Abuse on State Budgets (New York, NY: CASA, Jan. 2001), p. 15.

29. "States spent $29.8 billion in 1998 for adult corrections including incarceration, probation and parole. Eighty-one percent of this amount ($24.1 billion) was spent on substance-involved offenders. Of the $24.1 billion, $21.4 billion went to run and build prisons to house substance-involved offenders, $1.1 billion for parole and $695 million for probation for substance-involved offenders. An additional $899 million was spent on state aid to localities for substance-involved offenders (Figure 3.A)".

Source: National Center on Addiction and Substance Abuse at Columbia University, Shoveling Up: The Impact of Substance Abuse on State Budgets (New York, NY: CASA, Jan. 2001), p. 15.

30. "Only $513.3 million in state funds is spent nationwide on substance abuse prevention. This includes $223 million through the department of health, $210 million through the department of substance abuse and $80 million in prevention in elementary and secondary education. Most spending for prevention through the schools is federally funded and that amount is not included here."

Source: National Center on Addiction and Substance Abuse at Columbia University, Shoveling Up: The Impact of Substance Abuse on State Budgets (New York, NY: CASA, Jan. 2001), p. 22.

31. "Of the $3 billion states spend on prevention, treatment and research, $920 million (30.7 percent) is spent by state health agencies; $843 million (27.9 percent) by state alcohol and drug abuse offices; $433 million (14.3 percent) by the justice system."

Source: National Center on Addiction and Substance Abuse at Columbia University, Shoveling Up: The Impact of Substance Abuse on State Budgets (New York, NY: CASA, Jan. 2001), p. 22.

32. "States report spending $2.5 billion a year on treatment. States did not distinguish whether the treatment was for alcohol, illicit drug abuse or nicotine addiction. Of the $2.5 billion total, $695 million is spent through the departments of health and $633 million through the state substance abuse agencies. We believe that virtually all of these funds are spent on alcohol and illegal drug treatment."

Source: National Center on Addiction and Substance Abuse at Columbia University, Shoveling Up: The Impact of Substance Abuse on State Budgets (New York, NY: CASA, Jan. 2001), p. 24.

33. "The justice system spends $433 million on treatment: $149 million for state prison inmates; $103 million for those on probation and parole; $133 million for juvenile offenders; $46 million to help localities treat offenders; $1 million on drug courts. Treatment provided by mental health institutions for co-morbid patients totals $241 million. The remaining $492 million is for the substance abuse portion of state employee assistance programs ($97 million), treatment programs for adults involved in child welfare services ($4.5 million) and capital spending for the construction of treatment facilities ($391 million). (Figure 4.B)"

Economics

Source: National Center on Addiction and Substance Abuse at Columbia University, Shoveling Up: The Impact of Substance Abuse on State Budgets (New York, NY: CASA, Jan. 2001), p. 24.

34. "The final component of state substance abuse spending is the $433 million states spent in 1998 to regulate the sale of alcohol and tobacco and to collect alcohol and tobacco taxes (Table 5.1) Tax rates vary significantly from state to state and revenues generally are not dedicated to prevent, treat or cope with the burden substance abuse and addiction places on many state programs.
 "In 1998, states collected $4.0 billion in alcohol and $7.4 billion in tobacco taxes for a total of $11.4 billion. For every dollar of such tax revenues, states spent $7.13 on substance abuse and addiction — $6.83 to shoulder the burden on public programs, $0.26 for prevention and treatment, and $0.04 to collect alcohol and tobacco taxes and run licensing boards."

Source: National Center on Addiction and Substance Abuse at Columbia University, Shoveling Up: The Impact of Substance Abuse on State Budgets (New York, NY: CASA, Jan. 2001), p. 27.

35. According to the American Corrections Association, the average daily cost per state prison inmate per day in the US in 2005 was $67.55. States held an estimated 250,900 drug offenders in 2003. That means it costs states approximately $16,948,295 per day to imprison drug offenders, or $6,186,127,675 per year.

Sources: American Correctional Association, 2006 Directory of Adult and Juvenile Correctional Departments, Institutions, Agencies and Probation and Parole Authorities, 67th Edition (Alexandria, VA: ACA, 2006), p. 16; Harrison, Paige M. & Allen J. Beck, PhD, US Department of Justice, Bureau of Justice Statistics, Prisoners in 2005 (Washington, DC: US Department of Justice, November 2006), p. 9.

36. A study by the RAND Corporation found that every additional dollar invested in substance abuse treatment saves taxpayers $7.46 in societal costs.

Source: Rydell, C.P. & Everingham, S.S., Controlling Cocaine, Prepared for the Office of National Drug Control Policy and the United States Army (Santa Monica, CA: Drug Policy Research Center, RAND Corporation, 1994), p. xvi.

37. The RAND Corporation study found that additional domestic law enforcement efforts cost 15 times as much as treatment to achieve the same reduction in societal costs.

Source: Rydell, C.P. & Everingham, S.S., Controlling Cocaine, Prepared for the Office of National Drug Control Policy and the United States Army (Santa Monica, CA: Drug Policy Research Center, RAND Corporation, 1994), p. xvi.

38. "The heavy toll drug abuse exacts on the United States is reflected in related criminal and medical costs totaling over $67 billion. Almost 70 percent of this figure is attributable to the cost of crime."

Source: Office of National Drug Control Policy, National Drug Control Strategy 2000 Annual Report (Washington, DC: US Government Printing Office, 2000), p. 66.

Economics

39. In 1969, $65 million was spent by the Nixon administration on the drug war; in 1982 the Reagan administration spent $1.65 billion; in 2000 the Clinton administration spent more than $17.9 billion; and in 2002, the Bush administration spent more than $18.8 billion.

    Sources: U.S. Congress, Hearings on Federal Drug Enforcement before the Senate Committee on Investigations, 1975 and 1976 (1976); Office of National Drug Control Policy, National Drug Control Strategy, 1992: Budget Summary (Washington DC: US Government Printing Office, 1992), p. 214; Office of National Drug Control Policy, National Drug Control Budget Executive Summary, Fiscal Year 2002 (Washington, DC: US Government Printing Office, April 9, 2001), p. 2, Table 1; Office of National Drug Control Policy, "National Drug Control Strategy: FY 2003 Budget Summary" (Washington, DC: Office of the President, February 2002), Table 2, p. 6.

40. "The value of illegal drug exports from the Caribbean during the past two decades has fallen into two very well differentiated periods. The first period, from 1981 to 1990, was an epoch of impressive depression in the total value of the Caribbean drugs exports — from an income over US$20bn at its peak in 1983 to US$5bn in 1991. Since 1991, the value of Caribbean exports of illegal drugs has stabilised around US$5bn."

    Source: "The Value Of Illegal Drug Exports Transiting The Caribbean - 1981-2000," United Nations Office on Drugs and Crime, Caribbean Regional Office, February 2004, p. 39.

41. In a report funded by the Wisconsin Policy Research Institute, researchers concluded that "drug sales in poor neighborhoods are part of a growing informal economy which has expanded and innovatively organized in response to the loss of good jobs." The report characterizes drug dealing as "fundamentally a lower class response [to the information economy] by men and women with little formal education and few formal skills," and the report notes "If the jobs won't be created by either the public or private sector, then poor people will have to create the jobs themselves."

    Source: Hagedorn, John M., Ph.D., The Business of Drug Dealing in Milwaukee (Milwaukee, WI: Wisconsin Policy Research Institute, 1998), p. 3.

42. In a report funded by the Wisconsin Policy Research Institute, researchers concluded that drug-dealing plays a substantial role in the local economies of poorer urban neighborhoods. "At least 10% of all male Latinos and African- Americans aged 18-29 living in these two [surveyed] neighborhoods are supported to some extent by the drug economy." The report also concluded that "most drug entrepreneurs are hard working, but not super rich" and that "most drug entrepreneurs aren't particularly violent." One-fourth of all drug-dealers surveyed said they encountered no violence at all in their work, and two-thirds reported that violence occurred less than once per month.

    Source: Hagedorn, John M., PhD, The Business of Drug Dealing in Milwaukee (Milwaukee, WI: Wisconsin Policy Research Institute, 1998), p. 1.

Economics

43. "Although residents of disadvantaged neighborhoods, neighborhoods with high concentrations of minorities, and neighborhoods with high population densities reported much higher levels of visible drug sales, they reported only slightly higher levels of drug use, along with somewhat higher levels of drug dependency. This finding indicates that conflating drug sales with use, so that poor and minority areas are assumed to be the focus of the problem of drug use, is plainly wrong. The finding is based on the data collected across 41 sites, including city and suburban (but not rural) areas in all regions."

Source: Saxe, Leonard, PhD, Charles Kadushin, PhD, Andrew Beveridge, PhD, et al., "The Visibility of Illicit Drugs: Implications for Community-Based Drug Control Strategies," American Journal of Public Health (Washington, DC: American Public Health Association, Dec. 2001), Vol. 91, No. 12, p. 1991.

44. "Although serious drug use is slightly more prevalent in poor minority neighborhoods than elsewhere, the major problem for disadvantaged neighborhoods is drug distribution. These communities are victims not only of their own drug abuse but also of a criminal drug market that serves the entire society. The market establishes itself in disadvantaged communities in part because of the low social capital in these neighborhoods.The drug economy further erodes that social capital."

Source: Saxe, Leonard, PhD, Charles Kadushin, PhD, Andrew Beveridge, PhD, et al., "The Visibility of Illicit Drugs: Implications for Community-Based Drug Control Strategies," American Journal of Public Health (Washington, DC: American Public Health Association, Dec. 2001), Vol. 91, No. 12, p. 1992.

45. The French organization OGD points out the deeper economic impact from the eventual release of American drug felons: "(A)ccording to some estimates some 3.5 million prisoners will be released between now and 2010, and an additional 500,000 each year thereafter.
"Such a large-scale release of unskilled people - most of them cannot even read and write - will have a negative impact on wages, which are already low in deprived urban areas, due to a massive influx of men desperate to get a job; especially, since the reform of the welfare system in 1996 severely reduced felons' access to welfare money."

Source: Observatoire Geopolitique des Drogues, The World Geopolitics of Drugs 1998/1999 (Paris, France: OGD, April, 2000), p. 133.

Ecstasy: What the Evidence Shows

1. Ecstasy (MDMA) is a semi-synthetic drug patented by Merck Pharmaceutical Company in 1914 and abandoned for 60 years. In the late 1970s and early 1980s psychiatrists and psychotherapists in the US used it to facilitate psychotherapy.

   Source: Greer G and Tolbert R. A Method of Conducting Therapeutic Sessions with MDMA. in Journal of Psychoactive Drugs 30 (1998) 4:371.379. For research on the therapeutic use of MDMA see: www.maps.org

2. Ecstasy's effects last 3 to 6 hours. It is a mood elevator that produces feelings of empathy, openness and well-being. People who take it at all night "rave" dances say they enjoy dancing and feeling close to others. It does not produce violence or physical addiction.

   Source: Beck J and Rosenbaum M. Pursuit of Ecstasy: The MDMA Experience. Albany: State University of New York Press, 1994.

3. The Drug Abuse Warning Network estimated that ecstasy was involved in — though not necessarily the cause of — nine deaths in 1998. According to DAWN's 2002 mortality report:
   "The DAWN metropolitan area profiles include information on 'club drugs' as a group, combining all mentions of methylenedioxymethamphetamine (MDMA or Ecstasy), Ketamine, gamma hydroxy butyrate (GHB) and its precursor gamma butyrolactone (GBL), and flunitrazepam (Rohypnol). As in prior years, these substances accounted for very few deaths in any of the DAWN metropolitan areas. Seven metropolitan areas reported no deaths involving these drugs, and only 7 metropolitan areas reported more than 5 mentions of club drugs. The areas with the highest numbers in 2002 were New York (19 mentions), Miami (9), Chicago (7), New Orleans (7), Philadelphia (9), Boston (6), and San Diego (6). Club drugs were rarely reported alone."

   Source: "Club Drugs," The DAWN Report, Drug Abuse Warning Network, Office of Applied Studies, Substance Abuse and Mental health Services Administration (Washington, DC: SAMHSA, December 2000), p. 4; and Substance Abuse and Mental Health Services Administration, Office of Applied Studies, "Mortality Data From the Drug Abuse Warning Network, 2002," DAWN Series D25, DHHS Publication No. (SMA) 043875 (Rockville, MD), 2004, pp. 9-10.

4. Some of these deaths are related to overheating. MDMA slightly raises body temperature. This is potentially lethal in hot environments where there is vigorous dancing and the lack of adequate fluid replacement. Many of these tragic deaths are preventable with simple harm reduction techniques such as having free water available and rooms where people can rest and relax.

   Source: C.M. Milroy; J.C. Clark; A.R.W. Forrest, Pathology of deaths associated with "ecstasy" and "eve" misuse, Journal of Clinical Pathology Vol 49 (1996) 149-153.

5. One of the recent risks associated with Ecstasy is the possibility of obtaining adulterated drugs that may be more toxic than MDMA. Some of the reported deaths attributed to Ecstasy are likely caused by other, more dangerous drugs.

Ecstasy: What the Evidence Shows

Source: Laboratory Pill Analysis Program, DanceSafe. For results visit www.DanceSafe.org. See also, Byard RW et al., Amphetamine derivative fatalities in South Australia — is "Ecstasy" the culprit?, American Journal of Forensic Medical Pathology, 1998 (Sep) 19(3): 261-5.

6. Deaths from adulterated drugs are another consequence of a zero tolerance approach. The drug should be tested for purity to minimize the risk from adulterated drugs by those who consume it.

   Source: DanceSafe provides testing equipment and a testing service which can be used to determine what a substance is. See www.DanceSafe.org.

7. MDMA raises blood pressure and heart rate. Persons with known cardiovascular or heart disease should not take MDMA.

8. Studies have indicated that individuals who have used MDMA may have decreased performance in memory tests compared to nonusers. These studies are presently controversial because they involved people who used a variety of other drugs. Furthermore, it is difficult to rule out possible pre-existing differences between research subjects and controls.

   Source: E. Gouzoulis-Mayfrank; J. Daumann; F. Tuchtenhagen; S. Pelz; S. Becker; H.J. Kunert; B. Fimm; H. Sass; Impaired cognitive performance in drug free users of recreational ecstasy (MDMA), by Journal Neurol Neurosurg Psychiatry Vol 68, June 2000, 719-725; K.I. Bolla; U.D.; McCann; G.A. Ricaurte; Memory impairment in abstinent MDMA ('Ecstasy') users, by Neurology Vol 51, Dec 1998, 1532-1537.

9. Some assertions about the negative health affects of MDMA use are exaggerated, and researchers have been forced to retract their more extreme claims. Dr. George Ricuarte wrote the journal Science on Sept. 12, 2003: "We write to retract our report "Severe dopaminergic neurotoxicity in primates after a common recreational dose regimen of MDMA ("ecstasy")" (1), following our recent discovery that the drug used to treat all but one animal in that report came from a bottle that contained (+)-methamphetamine instead of the intended drug, (±)MDMA. Notably, (+)-methamphetamine would be expected to produce the same pattern of combined dopaminergic/serotonergic neurotoxicity (2) as that seen in the animals reported in our paper (1)."

   Source: Ricuarte, George A., Jie Yuan, George Hatzidimitriou, Branden J. Cord, Una D. McCann, "Retraction," Letter to Science Magazine, Sept. 12, 2003, Vol. 31, p. 1479.

10. In 2004, the Drug Enforcement Administration gave permission for the first US trial of MDMA for use in treating trauma.

    Source: "DEA Approves Trial Use Of Ecstasy In Trauma Cases," Washington Post, March 2, 2004.

11. "Pill testing interventions are important measures to enter into contact with hard-to-reach populations and to raise their interest in preventive and harm reduction messages."

    Source: Kriener, Harald, Renate Billeth, Christoph Gollner, Sophie Lachout, Paul Neubauer, Rainer Schmid, "An Inventory of On-Site Pill-Testing Interventions in the EU" (Lisbon, Portugal: European Monitoring Centre for Drugs and Drug Addiction, 2001), p. 60.

Ecstasy: What the Evidence Shows

12. In an evaluation of on-site pill testing, a European Monitoring Centre for Drugs and Drug Addiction scientific report concluded that "Despite the lack of empirical data – for health systems in general and information and prevention projects in particular – it is crucial to know about new substances and consumption trends, otherwise there is a high risk of loosing credibility with well-informed users of psychoactive substances. Pill-testing projects can be an important source of information on new substances and consumption trends as they are in closest possible contact with the relevant scenes, more so than other organisations within the prevention system. They have, furthermore, an insight into most substances that are actually being consumed, and know who and where, in which manner, and why these substances are being consumed.

"Pill-testing interventions have to be part of a global strategy for prevention and harm reduction in recreational settings.

"By using the information from on-site pill-testing interventions, a national warning system could deepen its data pool in terms of social contexts: who are the people consuming these substances, how, where and why are they consuming these substances in this and that particular way and which information can be passed on to potential consumers in a meaningful and successful manner?

"Due to the lack and difficulties of evaluation, on one hand there is still no strict scientific proof for the protective impact of on-site pill testing interventions, but on the other hand there is also no scientific evidence to conclude that such interventions would rather promote drug use or might be used by dealers for marketing purposes. Bringing together pieces of evidence is however often a first step for deciding on new intervention models."

Source: Kriener, Harald, Renate Billeth, Christoph Gollner, Sophie Lachout, Paul Neubauer, Rainer Schmid, "An Inventory of On-Site Pill-Testing Interventions in the EU" (Lisbon, Portugal: European Monitoring Centre for Drugs and Drug Addiction, 2001), pp. 60-61.

Environment

1. "Illicit production of methamphetamine may involve hazardous materials that are toxic, corrosive, flammable, or explosive. Such materials include anhydrous ammonia, sulfuric acid, hydrochloric acid, red phosphorous, lithium metal, sodium metal, iodine, and toluene. Upon discovery, the hazardous materials contained at clandestine drug laboratory locations are classified and managed as hazardous wastes."

   Source: "Methamphetamine Initiative: Final Environmental Assessment," US Dept. of Justice Office of Community Oriented Policing Services, May 13, 2003, p. 4.

2. "The incidence of clandestine drug laboratories has grown dramatically in the past 10 years. For example, in Fiscal Year 1992, the DEA's National Clandestine Laboratory Cleanup Program funded approximately 400 removal actions and by fiscal year 2001, the DEA Program funded more than 6,400 removal actions."

   Source: "Methamphetamine Initiative: Final Environmental Assessment," US Dept. of Justice Office of Community Oriented Policing Services, May 13, 2003, p. 6.

3. "Further contributing to the threat posed by the trafficking and abuse of methamphetamine, some chemicals used to produce methamphetamine are flammable, and improper storage, use, or disposal of such chemicals often leads to clandestine laboratory fires and explosions. National Clandestine Laboratory Seizure System (NCLSS) 2003 data show that there were 529 reported methamphetamine laboratory fires or explosions nationwide, a slight decrease from 654 reported fires or explosions in 2002."

   Source: National Drug Threat Assessment 2004 (Johnstown, PA: National Drug Intelligence Center, April 2004), pp. 17-18.

4. "Toxic chemicals used to produce methamphetamine often are discarded in rivers, fields, and forests, causing environmental damage that results in high cleanup costs. For example, DEA's annual cost for cleanup of clandestine laboratories (almost entirely methamphetamine laboratories) in the United States has increased steadily from FY1995 ($2 million), to FY1999 ($12.2 million), to FY 2002 ($23.8 million). Moreover, the Los Angeles County Regional Criminal Information Clearinghouse, a component of the Los Angeles HIDTA, reports that in 2002 methamphetamine laboratory cleanup costs in the combined Central Valley and Los Angeles HIDTA areas alone reached $3,909,809. Statewide, California spent $4,974,517 to remediate methamphetamine laboratories and dumpsites in 2002."

   Source: National Drug Threat Assessment 2004 (Johnstown, PA: National Drug Intelligence Center, April 2004), p. 18.

5. "Guio (2003), in his study in Samaniego, NariZo (Colombia), reports that aerial fumigation of poppy crops also affect household crops and alternative crops promoted by UNODC. Intensification of fumigation has lead to an increase in complaints to the Defensoria del Pueblo regarding impacts on farmers' health, domestic animals, fishes and

Environment

legal crops. Ortiz et al. (2004), in an essay about agriculture, illicit crops and the environment for the National Environmental Forum (Colombia), mentions that recent studies in Putumayo have concluded that more than 2,700 hectares of licit crops, including fruits, and more than 200,000 fish, were lost because of fumigations. These figures are for people that submitted their cases to local authorities."

Source: United Nations Office on Drugs and Crime, "Coca Cultivation in the Andean Region: A Survey of Bolivia, Colombia and Peru" (Vienna, Austria: June 2006), p. 44.

6. "Velaidez (2001) visited the Municipality of Cartagena de Chaira in the Department of Caquetá between November 1998 and February 1999 to investigate the impact of aerial fumigation on farmers and their crops. This study reported unintended effects of aerial glyphosate spraying but no quantitative data, with affects on rubber and cocoa plantations and food crops such as plantain, maize, yucca, rice, vegetables and fruits. Cattle were reported to lose hair after eating pastures previously affected by the fumigation. The death of young chickens and farmed fish was reported as a result of related water contamination."

Source: United Nations Office on Drugs and Crime, "Coca Cultivation in the Andean Region: A Survey of Bolivia, Colombia and Peru" (Vienna, Austria: June 2006), p. 44.

7. "The chemicals used in the processing of coca leaf to cocaine, and of opium latex to heroin, are thought to have a much greater impact on the environment than the agrochemicals used in their production. Each year millions of tons and litres of processing chemicals and materials are released into the environment, both as wastes from processing laboratories and from the destruction of confiscated chemicals. However, only one specific study on the environmental effects of these chemicals has been identified, that conducted in the Chapare region of Bolivia in 1992 (Southwest Research Associates, 1993, cited by Henkel, 1995). Here, chemical spills were quickly diluted by the high rainfall received in the region. Some loss of soil microorganisms was noted, but no damage to wildlife, vegetation, fish species or bird life was detected in areas near the processing laboratories. "The discharge of chemicals from illicit drug processing undoubtedly has some environmental impact, but it is impossible to assess the scale of this impact due to the lack of data of almost any kind on soils, water supplies or biodiversity or the health of local people."

Source: United Nations Office on Drugs and Crime, "Coca Cultivation in the Andean Region: A Survey of Bolivia, Colombia and Peru" (Vienna, Austria: June 2006), p. 45.

8. "These data (Figure 11) estimate that over the four years from 2000 to 2004, a total of 97,622 hectares of primary forest was converted to coca cultivations in Colombia. The annual loss of primary forest was similar in 2000-2001 and 2001-2002 at about 34,000 hectares, but decreased by over 50% to 16,017 hectares converted in 2002-2003. This decrease continued in 2003-2004 to 13 202 hectares, which is only 39% of the area in 2000-2001. The high percentage of 20% of the converted land area that was classified as 'uncertain changes and corrections' in 2002-2003 should be noted.

Environment

"Over the four year period of 2000 to 2004 the annual percentages of coca cultivation on land cleared from primary forest were 25%, 37%, 20% and 20%, with an average of 26%. The percentage of coca cultivation on land cleared from secondary forest, grassland and crops was 43%, 38%, 45% and 37% respectively over the same period. Thus, the ratio of new coca plots established from primary forest compared to plots established from other land uses varied from 1:1.7 to 1:1.0 to 1:2.2 to 1:1.9 over these four years. New coca plots were as least as likely to be established on areas other than primary forest in 2001-2002, and much more likely to be on land other than primary forest in the other three years."

Source: United Nations Office on Drugs and Crime, "Coca Cultivation in the Andean Region: A Survey of Bolivia, Colombia and Peru" (Vienna, Austria: June 2006), pp. 23-24.

9. "The data on total reduction of forest cover over Colombia and that on losses resulting from coca cultivation span different periods of time, so only rough comparisons of the two can be made. It is likely that several hundred thousand hectares of forest were cleared due to the direct and indirect effects of coca cultivation prior to 2000, before UNODC estimates from remote sensed data were available. Forest cover change in Colombia for the period 1990 – 2000 is estimated at –190,470 hectares per year. If this rate was assumed to have continued from 2000 to 2004, the total area deforested in those four years would have been 761,880 hectares, of which the 97,622 hectares of primary forest identified as converted to coca cultivations in this period would form 13%. As already noted, the actual of primary forest cleared due to coca cultivation is greater than the area being directly cultivated for this purpose, because of the other crops and activities of the farmers including the opening of roads and airstrips for transport of coca products."

Source: United Nations Office on Drugs and Crime, "Coca Cultivation in the Andean Region: A Survey of Bolivia, Colombia and Peru" (Vienna, Austria: June 2006), pp. 24-25.

10. "Damage to soils resulting from cultivation and elimination of the natural vegetation is widely reported in reference to the environmental impacts of illicit drug cultivation, as are the likely effects of the discharge of the chemical wastes from coca processing to soils and waterways. However, very little field assessment on the quantity of discharges and their effects on the environment (soils, fauna, flora or water) has been carried out by government agencies or universities. The only analysis found by this study was conducted in Chapare (Bolivia) in 1992 (Southwest Research Associates, 1993, quoted by Henkel, 1995). Here, a study of three cocaine processing laboratories found that pollution was concentrated in a small area at the processing site. Most chemicals were disposed of in holding ponds constructed for the purpose and were not dumped into nearby streams. Chemical spills at the site were quickly diluted by the high rainfall received in the region. Because coca processing sites are widely scattered in the Chapare, pollution is widely dispersed rather than concentrated at a

Environment

few large sites. Some loss of soil microorganisms was noted, but no damage to wildlife, vegetation, fish species or bird life was detected near the processing laboratories. However, the study did not assess the long-term effects of pollution.

"For Colombia, DNE (2002) states that the agrochemicals used in coca processing are capable of polluting freshwater sources for human consumption, but no specific cases of this are given."

Source: United Nations Office on Drugs and Crime, "Coca Cultivation in the Andean Region: A Survey of Bolivia, Colombia and Peru" (Vienna, Austria: June 2006), p. 31.

11. "Aerial fumigation and forced eradication of coca crops is one factor in the dynamics of coca cultivation and deforestation. Several studies report that in response to coca eradication measures farmers have been deforesting new plots in more remote areas. These new plots can be in the local region or in other parts of the country, since migration and displacement of people is widespread, especially in Colombia. It has also been suggested that farmers create more scattered plots of smaller size in response to fumigation. This further fragments the forest and increases the impact on biodiversity. The relative importance of this phenomenon compared to the other drivers of coca cultivation and deforestation have not been determined."

Source: United Nations Office on Drugs and Crime, "Coca Cultivation in the Andean Region: A Survey of Bolivia, Colombia and Peru" (Vienna, Austria: June 2006), p. 46.

12. "Solomon et al. (2005) conducted a study on the effects on human health and the environment of aerial spraying of glyphosate herbicide for the illicit crops eradication programme in Colombia, based on a review of literature. It was found the formulation of glyphosate used could produce temporary irritation in eyes and skin, but no effects on reproduction were observed. No ecological field data were collected from the region, but a review found that glyphosate had low toxicity to non-target organisms other than plants. The formulation used in the eradication programme in Colombia is of low toxicity for mammals and vertebrates, although some temporary impacts may occur. Amphibians are the group most sensitive to this formulation, and it has been suggested that other formulations be tested when eradication is conducted near to water bodies, in order to minimise impacts on amphibian populations (Solomon et al., 2005). Relyea (2005) tested the impacts of glyphosate on amphibians and concluded that it could cause high rates of mortality in larval stages and lead to population decline.

"There appear to have been no systematic field studies on the possibility of loss of forest from unintended drift of glyphosate during aerial spraying."

Source: United Nations Office on Drugs and Crime, "Coca Cultivation in the Andean Region: A Survey of Bolivia, Colombia and Peru" (Vienna, Austria: June 2006), p. 44.

13. "From December 2000 to February 2001, US-backed antidrug drives resulted in the destruction of more than 29,000 hectares of coca fields (enough to produce 200-250 tons of cocaine annually)."

Environment

Source: Rabasa, Angel & Peter Chalk, "Colombian Labyrinth: The Synergy of Drugs and Insurgency and Its Implications for Regional Instability" (Santa Monica, CA: RAND Corporation, 2001), p. 69, from the web at http://www.rand.org/publications/ MR/MR1339/ last accessed May 21, 2007.

14. "Aerial spraying of a marijuana field near a Rarámuri village carried out by the Federal Attorney General's Office Procuraduría General de la República, PGR) left 300 sick and injured and may have killed a two-year old girl according to the Chihuahua State Human Rights Office (Comisión Estatal de Derechos Humanos, CEDH)."

    Source: Macias Medina, Silvia, "PGR Allegedly Sprays Marijuana Field, Killing Child and Injuring 300", reprinted in Frontera NorteSur, originally published in El Diaro, August 5, 2000. Available on the web at http://www.nmsu.edu/~frontera/jul_ aug00/today.html, accessed May 21, 2007.

15. In July 2000, the Colombian government agreed to work with the UN Drug Control Program on research into the use of a fungicide called fusarium oxysporum. Tests have yet to show that use of the fungus is feasible, and methods to produce the fungicide in sufficient quantities as well as a delivery mechanism have yet to be developed.

    Source: George Gedda, Associated Press, "Colombia Tries New Drug Eradication", July 7, 2000.

16. The US Department of Agriculture reports "A pathogenic strain of Fusarium oxysporum, causes Fusarium wilt, a disease that afflicts many crops such as watermelon, muskmelon, and basil but is a bigger problem for tomato growers."

    Source: "USDA, Canada Collaborate on Fusarium Wilt", Methyl Bromide Alternatives Newsletter (Beltsville, MD: USDA Agricultural Research Service, April 2000), Vol. 6, No. 2.

17. When aerially sprayed, the herbicide Glyphosate can drift for up to about half of a mile. In Colombia, where the herbicide Glyphosate is sprayed from airplanes, children have lost hair and suffered diarrhea as a result of its application.

    Sources: Cox, C., "Glyphosate, Part 2: Human Exposure and Ecological Effects," Journal of Pesticide Reform, Vol. 15 (Eugene, OR: Northwest Coalition for Alternatives to Pesticides, 1995); Lloyd, R., "Publisher Warns about Impacts of Drug War," World Rainforest Report 37, (Lismore, NSW: Australia, 1997); Drug Enforcement Agency, Draft Supplement to the Environmental Impact Statements for Cannabis Eradication in the Contiguous United States and Hawaii (Washington DC: U.S. Government Printing Office, April 1998).

Families, Impact of the Drug War on

1. "In 1999 State and Federal prisons held an estimated 721,500 parents of minor children. A majority of State (55%) and Federal (63%) prisoners reported having a child under the age of 18. Forty-six percent of the parents reported living with their children prior to admission. As a result, there were an estimated 336,300 US households with minor children affected by the imprisonment of a resident parent."

   Source: Mumola, Christopher J., US Department of Justice Bureau of Justice Statistics, Incarcerated Parents and Their Children (Washington, DC: US Department of Justice, August 2000), p. 1.

2. The Bureau of Justice Statistics estimates that 2.8% of all children under age 18 have at least one parent in a local jail or a State or Federal prison – a total of 1,941,796 kids. One in 40 have an incarcerated father, and 1 in 359 have an incarcerated mother.

   Source: Greenfield, Lawrence A., and Snell, Tracy L., US Department of Justice, Bureau of Justice Statistics, Women Offenders (Washington, DC: US Department of Justice, December 1999), p. 8, Table 18.

3. "Black children (7.0%) were nearly 9 times more likely to have a parent in prison than white children (0.8%). Hispanic children (2.6%) were 3 times as likely as white children to have an inmate parent."

   Source: Mumola, Christopher J., US Department of Justice Bureau of Justice Statistics, Incarcerated Parents and Their Children (Washington, DC: US Department of Justice, August 2000), p. 2.

4. "Within the family domain, higher levels of parental communication about substances were significantly associated with lower odds of past year marijuana use among Hispanic youths (OR = 0.67), but not among youths of other racial/ethnic groups (Table 3.8). Within the peer/individual domain, participation in two or more extracurricular activities was significantly associated with lower odds of past year marijuana use among whites (OR = 0.45), blacks (OR = 0.64), and Hispanics (OR = 0.70), but not for youths in the 'other' category (Table 3.9). Within the school domain, strong sanctions against illegal drug use were significantly associated with lower odds of past year marijuana use among whites (OR = 0.48), Hispanics (OR = 0.61), and youths in the 'other' category (OR = 0.31), but not for blacks (Table 3.10). Finally, exposure to prevention messages in school was associated with lower odds of past year marijuana use for whites (OR = 0.60) and Hispanics (OR = 0.55), but not for blacks or youths in the 'other' category."

   Source: Wright, Douglas & Michael Pemberton, "Risk and Protective Factors for Adolescent Drug Use: Findings from the 1999 National Household Survey on Drug Abuse," DHHS Publication No. SMA 04-3874, Analytic Series A-19 (Rockville, MD: Substance Abuse and Mental Health Services Administration, Office of Applied Studies, January 2004), p. 60.

Families, Impact of the Drug War on

5. In its evaluation of ONDCP's Antidrug Media Campaign, researchers from Westat and the Annenberg School of Communication in 2003 concluded: "In sum, the analysis of the NSPY data does not support a claim that use among the target audience of 14- to 16-year-olds has declined with the initiation of the Marijuana Initiative. Contrarily, it appears to have increased in the past year compared to prior measurement, although the increase appears to have occurred before the start of the Marijuana Initiative and was only maintained during the first half of 2003. The MTF [Monitoring the Future] data does show declines, particularly for 8th and 10th graders. However, these declines cannot be confidently attributed to the operation of the Campaign."

   Source: Hornik, Robert, David Maklan, Diane Cadell, Carlin Henry Barmada, Lela Jacobsohn, Vani R. Henderson, Anca Romantan, Jeffrey Niederdeppe, Robert Orwin, Sanjeev Sridharan, Adam Chu, Carol Morin, Kristie Taylor, Diane Steele, "Evaluation of the National Youth Anti-Drug Media Campaign: 2003 Report of Findings," Delivered to National Institute on Drug Abuse, National Institutes of Health, Department of Health and Human Services By Westat & the Annenberg School for Communication, Contract No. N01DA-8-5063, December 22, 2003, p. 4-15.

6. In its evaluation of ONDCP's Antidrug Media Campaign, researchers from Westat and the Annenberg School of Communication in 2003 concluded: "In the previous reports, based on both favorable trends over time and cross-sectional associations, there was evidence supportive of Campaign effects on talking with children; on beliefs and attitudes regarding monitoring of children; and, in the case of the cross-sectional associations, on doing fun activities with them. These results still hold when Wave 7 parent reports are added, although youth reports of monitoring and talking behaviors are not consistent with parent reports and thus call into question the favorable changes in behavior that may be associated with the Campaign."

   Source: Hornik, Robert, David Maklan, Diane Cadell, Carlin Henry Barmada, Lela Jacobsohn, Vani R. Henderson, Anca Romantan, Jeffrey Niederdeppe, Robert Orwin, Sanjeev Sridharan, Adam Chu, Carol Morin, Kristie Taylor, Diane Steele, "Evaluation of the National Youth Anti-Drug Media Campaign: 2003 Report of Findings," Delivered to National Institute on Drug Abuse, National Institutes of Health, Department of Health and Human Services By Westat & the Annenberg School for Communication, Contract No. N01DA-8-5063, December 22, 2003, p. 6-1.

7. Public Housing Authorities (PHAs) in the US operate under a "One Strike" policy regarding drug use that is so over-reaching that even drug use by a guest can be grounds for eviction. According to the Department of Housing and Urban Development, "The 1998 amendments of the 1996 Extension Act provisions on ineligibility of illegal drug users and alcohol abusers confirm that a PHA or owner may deny admission or terminate assistance for the whole household that includes a person involved in the proscribed activity. With respect to a PHA or owner's discretion to consider rehabilitation for a household member with the offending substance abuse problem, the rule would permit a PHA or owner to hold the whole household responsible for that member's successful rehabilitation as a condition for continued occupancy and avoidance of eviction."

Families, Impact of the Drug War on

Source: Federal Record, Vol. 64, No. 141, Friday, July 23, 1999, p. 40266.

8. "Research and clinical experience teach that when, as here, the personal risks of seeking medical care are raised to intolerably high levels, it is more likely that prenatal care and patient candor - and not drug use - will be what is deterred, often with tragic health consequences."

Source: American Public Health Association, along with South Carolina Medical Association, American College of Obstetricians and Gynecologists, American Nurses Association, et al., Amicus Curiae brief in support of plaintiff in case of Ferguson v. City of Charleston, et al., Docket Number 99-0936, from the web at http://supreme.lp.findlaw.com/supreme_court/briefs/99-936/99-936fo4/brief/brief01.html last accessed May 23, 2007.

P

Forfeiture

1. "Criminal forfeiture is an action brought as a part of the criminal prosecution of a defendant. It is an in personam (against the person) action and requires that the government indict (charge) the property used or derived from the crime along with the defendant. If the jury finds the property forfeitable, the court issues an order of forfeiture.

   "For forfeitures pursuant to the Controlled Substances Act (CSA), Racketeer Influenced and Corrupt Organizations (RICO), as well as money laundering and obscenity statutes, there is an ancillary hearing for third parties to assert their interest in the property. Once the interests of third parties are addressed, the court issues a final forfeiture order.

   "Civil judicial forfeiture is an in rem (against the property) action brought in court against the property. The property is the defendant and no criminal charge against the owner is necessary.

   "Administrative forfeiture is an in rem action that permits the federal seizing agency to forfeit the property without judicial involvement. The authority for a seizing agency to start an administrative forfeiture action is found in the Tariff Act of 1930, 19 U.S.C. § 1607. Property that can be administratively forfeited is: merchandise the importation of which is prohibited; a conveyance used to import, transport, or store a controlled substance; a monetary instrument; or other property that does not exceed $500,000 in value."

   Source: A Guide to Equitable Sharing of Federally Forfeited Property for State and Local Law Enforcement Agencies, U.S. Department of Justice, March 1994, from the web at http://www.usdoj.gov/jmd/afp/07federalforfeiture/index.htm last accessed May 23, 2007.

2. According to a 1998 article published in the University of Chicago Law Review, the ability of law enforcement agencies to financially benefit from forfeited assets, and the provision of large block grants from Congress to fight the drug trade "have distorted governmental policy making and law enforcement." The authors believe that "the law enforcement agenda that targets assets rather than crime, the 80 percent of seizures that are unaccompanied by any criminal prosecution, the plea bargains that favor drug kingpins and penalize the 'mules' without assets to trade, the reverse stings that target drug buyers rather than drug sellers, the overkill in agencies involved in even minor arrests, the massive shift in resources towards federal jurisdiction over local law enforcement - is largely the unplanned by-product of this economic incentive structure."

   Source: Blumenson, E. & and Nilsen, E., "Policing for Profit: The Drug War's Hidden Economic Agenda," University of Chicago Law Review, 65: 35-114 (1998, Winter).

3. On April 25, 2000, HR 1658, the Civil Forfeiture Reform Act of 2000, was signed by President Clinton and became Public Law 106-185. The Act significantly reformed the Federal civil forfeiture law, including: safeguarding an innocent owner's interest in property, and placing the burden of proof on the Government to establish by a preponderance of evidence that the property is subject to forfeiture, among others.

Forfeiture

Source: Text of H.R. 1658 (enrolled and sent to President) and Congressional Research Service bill summary, Library of Congress THOMAS Federal Legislative Information Service, on the web at http://thomas.loc.gov/ and the Government Printing Office website at http://www.gpo.gov/

4. "In Fiscal Year (FY) 2006, monies were available under a permanent indefinite appropriation to finance the following:
   "(1) The operational costs of the forfeiture program, including handling and disposal of seized and forfeited assets, and the execution of legal forfeiture proceedings to perfect the title of the United States in that property.
   "(2) The payment of innocent third party claims.
   "(3) The payment of equitable shares to participating foreign governments and state and local law enforcement agencies.
   "(4) The costs of ADP equipment and ADP support for the program.
   "(5) Contract services in support of the program.
   "(6) Training and printing associated with the program.
   "(7) Other management expenses of the program.
   "(8) Awards for information leading to forfeiture.
   "(9) Joint Federal, state, and local law enforcement operations.
   "(10) Investigative expenses leading to seizure."

   Source: Office of the Inspector General, Audit Division, US Dept. of Justice, "Assets Forfeiture Fund and Seized Asset Deposit Fund Annual Financial Statement Fiscal Year 2006" (Audit Report 07-15, January 2007), p. 5.

5. "Total assets, which presents as of a specific time, the amounts of future economic benefits owned or managed by the AFF/SADF [Assets Forfeiture Fund/Seized Asset Deposit Fund] increased in FY 2006 to $2,053.4 million, from $1,370.4 million in FY 2005, an increase of 49.8 percent. If seized assets, which are not yet owned by the government, are backed out, the adjusted assets of the Fund increased to $1,256.2 million in FY 2006 from $659.2 million in FY 2005, an increase of 90.6 percent. This is attributable to an increase in both forfeited assets and seized assets in FY 2006 from FY 2005, indicating a strong current and future potential stream of assets flowing into the AFF."

   Source: Source: Office of the Inspector General, Audit Division, US Dept. of Justice, "Assets Forfeiture Fund and Seized Asset Deposit Fund Annual Financial Statement Fiscal Year 2006" (Audit Report 07-15, January 2007), p. 6.

6. During a 10-month national survey, it was discovered that 80% of people who had property forfeited were never charged with a crime.

   Source: Schneider, A. & Flaherty, M.P., "Presumed Guilty: The Law's Victims in the War on Drugs," The Pittsburgh Press, (1991, August 11).

Gateway Theory

1. "The gateway hypothesis holds that abusable drugs occupy distinct ranks in a hierarchy as well as definite positions in a temporal sequence. Accordingly, substance use is theorized to progress through a sequence of stages, beginning with legal, socially acceptable compounds that are low in the hierarchy, followed by use of illegal 'soft' and later 'hard' drugs ranked higher in the hierarchy. One of the main findings of this study is that there is a high rate of nonconformance with this temporal order. In a neighborhood where there is high drug availability, youths who have low parental supervision are likely to regularly consume marijuana before alcohol and/or tobacco. Consumption of marijuana prior to use of licit drugs thus appears to be related to contextual factors rather than to any unique characteristics of the individual. Moreover, this reverse pattern is not rare; it was observed in over 20% of our sample."

   Source: Tarter, Ralph E., PhD, Vanyukov, Michael, PhD, Kirisci, Levent, PhD, Reynolds, Maureen, PhD, Clark, Duncan B., MD, PhD, "Predictors of Marijuana Use in Adolescents Before and After Licit Drug Use: Examination of the Gateway Hypothesis," American Journal of Psychiatry, Vol. 63, No. 12, December 2006, p. 2138.

2. "There is no conclusive evidence that the drug effects of marijuana are causally linked to the subsequent abuse of other illicit drugs."

   Source: Janet E. Joy, Stanley J. Watson, Jr., and John A Benson, Jr. Division of Neuroscience and Behavioral Research, Institute of Medicine, Marijuana and Medicine: Assessing the Science Base (Washington, DC: National Academy Press, 1999).

3. "Our key findings were that 1) there are no unique factors distinguishing the gateway sequence and the reverse sequence — that is, the sequence is opportunistic; 2) the gateway sequence and the reverse sequence have the same prognostic accuracy; and 3) a sizable proportion of substance users begin regular consumption with an illicit drug. These results, considered in the aggregate, indicate that the gateway sequence is not an invariant pathway and, when manifest, is not related to specific risk factors and does not have prognostic utility. The results of this study as well as other studies demonstrate that abusable drugs occupy neither a specific place in a hierarchy nor a discrete position in a temporal sequence. These latter presumptions of the gateway hypothesis constitute what Whitehead referred to as the 'fallacy of misplaced connectedness,' namely, asserting 'assumptions about categories that do not correspond with the empirical world.'"

   Source: Tarter, Ralph E., PhD, Vanyukov, Michael, PhD, Kirisci, Levent, PhD, Reynolds, Maureen, PhD, Clark, Duncan B., MD, PhD, "Predictors of Marijuana Use in Adolescents Before and After Licit Drug Use: Examination of the Gateway Hypothesis," American Journal of Psychiatry, Vol. 63, No. 12, December 2006, p. 2139.

4. "The results of this study suggest that general behavioral deviancy and not specific risk factors accounts for illicit drug use. When illicit drug use occurs first, it is very likely due to the opportunity afforded by the neighborhood environment in context of low parental supervision. The

Gateway Theory

probability and rate of development of a diagnosis of marijuana use disorder and alcohol use disorder were the same whether or not there was conformance with the gateway sequence. Evidence supporting 'causal linkages between stages,' as specified by the gateway hypothesis, was not obtained. Nor were specific risk factors identified that were related to consumption of each drug. Our results indicate that efforts to prevent marijuana use should utilize strategies directed at averting the development of the characteristics prodromal to the manifestation of behavior problems."

Source: Tarter, Ralph E., PhD, Vanyukov, Michael, PhD, Kirisci, Levent, PhD, Reynolds, Maureen, PhD, Clark, Duncan B., MD, PhD, "Predictors of Marijuana Use in Adolescents Before and After Licit Drug Use: Examination of the Gateway Hypothesis," American Journal of Psychiatry, Vol. 63, No. 12, December 2006, p. 2139.

5. The Institute of Medicine's 1999 report on marijuana explained that marijuana has been mistaken for a gateway drug in the past because "Patterns in progression of drug use from adolescence to adulthood are strikingly regular. Because it is the most widely used illicit drug, marijuana is predictably the first illicit drug most people encounter. Not surprisingly, most users of other illicit drugs have used marijuana first. In fact, most drug users begin with alcohol and nicotine before marijuana — usually before they are of legal age."

Source: Janet E. Joy, Stanley J. Watson, Jr., and John A Benson, Jr. Division of Neuroscience and Behavioral Research, Institute of Medicine, Marijuana and Medicine: Assessing the Science Base (Washington, DC: National Academy Press, 1999).

6. The 2005 federal National Survey on Drug Use and Health provides an estimate of the age of first use of drugs among past year initiates. According to the Survey, the mean age of first use of marijuana in the US in 2005 was 15.1 years. The mean age of first use of alcohol in 2005 was 14.8 years, and the mean age of first use of cigarettes that year was 14.9 years old.

Source: Substance Abuse and Mental Health Services Administration, Results from the 2005 National Survey on Drug Use and Health: National Findings (Office of Applied Studies, NSDUH Series H-30, DHHS Publication No. SMA 06-4194), Rockville, MD, Sept. 2006, Table 4.14B.

7. "In 2005, the rate of current illicit drug use was approximately 8 times higher among youths aged 12 to 17 who smoked cigarettes in the past month (46.7 percent) than it was among youths who did not smoke cigarettes in the past month (5.5 percent).
"Past month illicit drug use also was associated with the level of past month alcohol use. Among youths aged 12 to 17 in 2005 who were heavy drinkers (i.e., drank five or more drinks on the same occasion [i.e., at the same time or within a couple of hours of each other] on each of 5 or more days in the past 30 days), 59.9 percent also were current illicit drug users, which was higher than among nondrinkers (5.0 percent).

Gateway Theory

"Among youths aged 12 to 17 who were both smokers and heavy drinkers in the past month in 2005, 70.9 percent used illicit drugs in the past month, higher than the 3.5 percent among youths who did not drink or smoke in the past month."

Source: Substance Abuse and Mental Health Services Administration, Results from the 2005 National Survey on Drug Use and Health: National Findings (Office of Applied Studies, NSDUH Series H-30, DHHS Publication No. SMA 06-4194), Rockville, MD, Sept. 2006, p. 25.

8. Over 97 million Americans have tried marijuana; 19.7 million Americans are estimated to be "past-month" users. There are only an estimated 2,397,000 "past-month" users of cocaine and 136,000 "past-month" users of heroin.

Source: Substance Abuse and Mental Health Services Administration, Results from the 2005 National Survey on Drug Use and Health: National Findings (Office of Applied Studies, NSDUH Series H-30, DHHS Publication No. SMA 06-4194), Rockville, MD, Sept. 2006, Table 1.1A.

R 9. "While covariates differed between equations, early regular use of tobacco and alcohol emerged as the 2 factors most consistently associated with later illicit drug use and abuse/dependence. While early regular alcohol use did not emerge as a significant independent predictor of alcohol dependence, this finding should be treated with considerable caution, as our study did not provide an optimal strategy for assessing the effects of early alcohol use."

Source: Lynskey, Michael T., PhD, et al., "Escalation of Drug Use in Early-Onset Cannabis Users vs Co-twin Controls," Journal of the American Medical Association, Vol. 289 No. 4, January 22/29, 2003, online at http://jama.ama-assn.org/issues/v289n4/rfull/joc21156.html last accessed Jan. 31, 2003.

10. "While the findings of this study indicate that early cannabis use is associated with increased risks of progression to other illicit drug use and drug abuse/dependence, it is not possible to draw strong causal conclusions solely on the basis of the associations shown in this study."

Source: Lynskey, Michael T., PhD, et al., "Escalation of Drug Use in Early-Onset Cannabis Users vs Co-twin Controls," Journal of the American Medical Association, Vol. 289 No. 4, January 22/29, 2003, online at http://jama.ama-assn.org/issues/v289n4/rfull/joc21156.html last accessed Jan. 31, 2003.

11. "Other mechanisms that might mediate a causal association between early cannabis use and subsequent drug use and drug abuse/dependence include the following:

"1. Initial experiences with cannabis, which are frequently rated as pleasurable, may encourage continued use of cannabis and also broader experimentation.

"2. Seemingly safe early experiences with cannabis may reduce the perceived risk of, and therefore barriers to, the use of other drugs. For example, as the vast majority of those who use cannabis do not experience any legal consequences of their use, such use may act to diminish the strength of legal sanctions against the use of all drugs.

Gateway Theory

"3. Alternatively, experience with and subsequent access to cannabis use may provide individuals with access to other drugs as they come into contact with drug dealers. This argument provided a strong impetus for the Netherlands to effectively decriminalize cannabis use in an attempt to separate cannabis from the hard drug market. This strategy may have been partially successful as rates of cocaine use among those who have used cannabis are lower in the Netherlands than in the United States."

Source: Lynskey, Michael T., PhD, et al., "Escalation of Drug Use in Early-Onset Cannabis Users vs Co-twin Controls," Journal of the American Medical Association, Vol. 289 No. 4, January 22/29, 2003, online at http://jama.ama-assn.org/issues/v289n4/rfull/joc21156.html last accessed Jan. 31, 2003.

12. In 2002 the English government published research on the initiation of drug use and criminal offending by young people in Britain. According to the study, "After applying these methods, there is very little remaining evidence of any causal gateway effect. For example, even if soft/medium drugs (cannabis, amphetamines, LSD, magic mushrooms, amyl nitrite) could somehow be abolished completely, the true causal link with hard drugs (crack, heroin, methadone) is found to be very small. For the sort of reduction in soft drug use that might be achievable in practice, the predicted causal effect on the demand for hard drugs would be negligible. Although there is stronger evidence of a gateway between soft drugs and ecstasy/cocaine, it remains small for practical purposes. My interpretation of the results of this study is that true gateway effects are probably very small and that the association between soft and hard drugs found in survey data is largely the result of our inability to observe all the personal characteristics underlying individual drug use. From this viewpoint, the decision to reclassify cannabis seems unlikely to have damaging future consequences."

Source: Pudney, Stephen, "Home Office Research Study 253: The road to ruin? Sequences of initiation into drug use and offending by young people in Britain" (London, England: Home Office Research, Development, and Statistics Directorate, December 2002), p. vi.

13. The World Health Organization's investigation into the gateway effect of marijuana stated emphatically that the theory that marijuana use by adolescents leads to heroin use is the least likely of all hypotheses.

Source: Hall, W., Room, R. & Bondy, S., WHO Project on Health Implications of Cannabis Use: A Comparative Appraisal of the Health and Psychological Consequences of Alcohol, Cannabis, Nicotine and Opiate Use, August 28, 1995 (Geneva, Switzerland: World Health Organization, March 1998).

14. The World Health Organization noted the effects of prohibition in its March 1998 study, when it stated that "exposure to other drugs when purchasing cannabis on the black market, increases the opportunity to use other illicit drugs."

Source: Hall, W., Room, R. & Bondy, S., WHO Project on Health Implications of Cannabis Use: A Comparative Appraisal of the Health and Psychological Consequences of Alcohol, Cannabis, Nicotine and Opiate Use, August 28, 1995 (Geneva, Switzerland: World Health Organization, March 1998).

Hemp

1. "Approximately 30 countries in Europe, Asia, and North America currently permit farmers to grow hemp, although most banned production for certain periods of time in the past. The United States is the only developed nation in which industrial hemp is not an established crop. Great Britain lifted its ban in 1993 and Germany followed suit in 1996. In order to help reestablish a hemp industry, the European Union administered a subsidy program in the 1990s for hemp fiber production.

   "In 1998, Canada authorized production for commercial purposes, following a three-year experimental period and a 50-year prohibition. As a condition of receiving a license to grow industrial hemp, Canadian farmers are required to register the GPS coordinates of their fields, use certified low-THC hemp seed, allow government testing of their crop for THC levels, and meet or beat a 10ppm standard for maximum allowable THC residue in hemp grain products. Agriculture Canada (the Canadian department of agriculture) estimates that more than 100 farmers nationwide are growing hemp, with the majority in central and western Canada.

   "Despite the number of nations where industrial hemp production is permissible, the number of acres worldwide devoted to hemp production in 2004 was estimated to be 250,000."

   Source: Rawson, Jean M., Congressional Research Service, "Hemp as an Agricultural Commodity (updated)" (Washington, DC: Library of Congress, July 8, 2005), pp. 3-4.

2. "Strictly speaking, the CSA does not make Cannabis illegal; rather, it places the strictest controls on its production, making it illegal to grow the crop without a DEA permit. DEA officials confirm issuing a permit for an experimental plot in Hawaii in the 1990s (now expired), and they confirm that DEA still has not ruled on an application submitted in 1999 by a North Dakota researcher. Hemp industry officials assert that the security measures the DEA requires are substantial and costly, and deter both public and private interests from initiating research projects requiring growing plots. All hemp products sold in the United States are imported or manufactured from imported hemp materials."

   Source: Rawson, Jean M., Congressional Research Service, "Hemp as an Agricultural Commodity (updated)" (Washington, DC: Library of Congress, July 8, 2005), p. CRS-3.

3. According to David West, PhD, "The THC levels in industrial hemp are so low that no one could ever get high from smoking it. Moreover, hemp contains a relatively high percentage of another cannabinoid, CBD, that actually blocks the marijuana high. Hemp, it turns out, is not only not marijuana; it could be called 'antimarijuana.'"

   Source: West, David P, Hemp and Marijuana: Myths and Realities (Madison, WI: North American Industrial Hemp Council, 1998), p. 3

4. Although opponents of hemp production claim that hemp fields will be used to hide marijuana fields, this is unlikely because cross-pollination between hemp and marijuana plants would significantly reduce the potency of the marijuana plant. On March 12, 1998, Canada legalized hemp production and set a limit of 0.3% THC content that may be present in the plants and requires that all seeds be certified for THC content.

Hemp

Source: West, David P, Hemp and Marijuana: Myths and Realities (Madison, WI: North American Industrial Hemp Council, 1998)., pp. 4, 21.

5. In a July 1998 study issued by the Center for Business and Economic Research at the University of Kentucky, researchers concluded that Kentucky hemp farmers could earn a net profit of $600 per acre for raising certified seeds, $320 net profit per acre for straw only or straw and grain production, and $220 net profit per acre for grain only production. The only crop found to be more profitable was tobacco.

   Source: Tompson, Eric C., PhD, Berger, Mark C., PhD, and Allen, Steven N., Economic Impacts of Industrial Hemp in Kentucky (Lexington, KY: University of Kentucky, Center for Business and Economic Research, 1998), p. 21.

6. In a July 1998 study issued by the Center for Business and Economic Research at the University of Kentucky, researchers estimated that if Kentucky again became the main source for industrial hemp seed (as it was in the past), the state could earn the following economic benefits:

Scenario	Full time jobs created	Workers Earnings
Main source for certified industrial seeds only	69 jobs	$1,300,000.00
Certified seeds, plus one processing facility	303 jobs	$6,700,000.00
Certified seeds, plus two processing facilities	537 jobs	$12,000.000.00
Certified seeds, one processing facility, one industrial hemp paper-pulp plant	771 jobs	$17,600,000.00

   Source: Tompson, Eric C., PhD, Berger, Mark C., PhD, and Allen, Steven N., Economic Impacts of Industrial Hemp in Kentucky (Lexington, KY: University of Kentucky, Center for Business and Economic Research, 1998), p. iv.

7. In February 2004, the 9th Circuit Court of Appeals ruled that the Drug Enforcement Administration cannot ban hemp products. The Associated Press reported that "On Friday, the court said that though the DEA has regulatory authority over marijuana and synthetically derived tetrahydrocannabinol, or THC, the agency did not follow the law in asserting authority over all hemp food products as well. 'They cannot regulate naturally-occuring THC not contained within or derived from marijuana,' the court ruled, noting it's not possible to get high from products with only trace amounts of the mind-altering chemical. Hemp is an industrial plant related to marijuana. Fiber from the plant long has been used to make paper, clothing, rope and other products. Its oil is found in body-care products such as lotion, soap and cosmetics and in a host of foods, including energy bars, waffles, milk-free cheese, veggie burgers and bread." The case is *Hemp Industries Association v. Drug Enforcemen Administration*, number 01-71662.

   Source: Terence Chea, Associated Press, "Appeals Court Rejects DEA Bid To Outlaw Hemp Foods," Feb. 6, 2004.

Hepatitis C & Drug Use

1. "HCV [Hepatitis C Virus], also transmitted parenterally, is the most prevalent bloodborne infection in the United States; approximately 3.2 million persons are chronically infected with HCV (4). No vaccine for this infection is available."

   Source: Centers for Disease Control and Prevention, "Surveillance for Acute Viral Hepatitis — United States, 2005," Surveillance Summaries, March 16, 2007, MMWR 2007;56(No. SS-3), p. 2.

2. "Of the cases reported in 2005 for which information concerning exposures during the incubation period was available, the most common risk factor identified for hepatitis C was injection-drug use (50%). During 1995–2005, injection-drug use was reported for an average of 39% of persons (range: 31%–50%). In 2005, 14% of persons with hepatitis C reported having had surgery, and 23% of persons reported having had multiple sex partners during the incubation period. A total of 8% of persons reported occupational exposure to blood."

   Source: Centers for Disease Control and Prevention, "Surveillance for Acute Viral Hepatitis — United States, 2005," Surveillance Summaries, March 16, 2007, MMWR 2007;56(No. SS-3), pp. 5-6.

3. "In the United States, chronic HCV infection accounts for 8,000 to 10,000 related deaths annually. It has become the leading cause of liver transplantation, accounting for 30% of all liver transplants. The Centers for Disease Control and Prevention (CDC) conservatively estimates expenditures devoted to HCV to be more than $600 million annually."

   Source: Wong, John B., MD, McQuillan, Geraldine M., PhD, McHutchison, John G., MD, and Poynard, Thierry, MD, "Estimating Future Hepatitis C Morbidity, Mortality, and Costs in the United States," American Journal of Public Health, Vol. 90, No. 10, Oct. 2000, p. 1562.

4. "Injection drug users (IDUs) account for more than 60% of all new hepatitis C virus (HCV) infections in the United States. Fifty to eighty percent of new IDUs are infected within 6 to 12 months of initial injection. Current treatment regimens are not highly effective, and no vaccine against HCV is available."

   Source: Udeagu Pratt, Chi-Chi N., MPH, Paone, Denise, EdD, Carter, Rosalind J., PhD, and Layton, Marcelle C., MD, "Hepatitis C Screening and Management Practices: A Survey of Drug Treatment and Syringe Exchange Programs in New York City," American Journal of Public Health, Vol. 92, No. 8, Aug. 2002, p. 1254.

5. "Hepatitis C virus (HCV) infection is very common among injection drug users. Studies of injection drug users in regions with a longstanding pattern of endemic injection drug use have reported prevalences of HCV antibody in the range of 65% to 90%, even where HIV prevalence is quite low. The majority of HCV infections become chronic, resulting in a large reservoir of HCV infection among injection drug users. Incidence of HCV infection in previously uninfected injection drug users ranges from 10 to 30 per 100 person-years at risk."

Hepatitis C & Drug Use

Source: Hagan, Holly, PhD, Thiede, Hanne, DVM, MPH, Weiss, Noel S., MD, DrPH, Hopkins, Sharon G., DVM, MPH, Duchin, Jeffrey S., MD, and Alexander, E. Russell, MD, "Sharing of Drug Preparation Equipment as a Risk Factor for Hepatitis C," American Journal of Public Health, Vol. 91, No. 1, Jan. 2001, p. 42.

6. "The potential for blood-borne viral transmission via injection equipment other than syringes was reported in an earlier study of equipment collected in a Miami shooting gallery, where HIV-1 DNA was detected in rinses from cottons and cookers and in water used to clean paraphernalia and to dissolve drugs. A sterile syringe may become contaminated when the tip of the needle is inserted into a contaminated cooker or when the drug is drawn up through contaminated filtration cotton. This type of injection risk behavior appears to be quite common, and fewer injection drug users may recognize the hazard of sharing drug preparation equipment than recognize the hazard of sharing syringes. The present study suggests that HCV may be transmitted via the shared use of drug cookers and filtration cotton even without injection with a contaminated syringe."

Source: Hagan, Holly, PhD, Thiede, Hanne, DVM, MPH, Weiss, Noel S., MD, DrPH, Hopkins, Sharon G., DVM, MPH, Duchin, Jeffrey S., MD, and Alexander, E. Russell, MD, "Sharing of Drug Preparation Equipment as a Risk Factor for Hepatitis C," American Journal of Public Health, Vol. 91, No. 1, Jan. 2001, p. 43.

T

Heroin

1. "Heroin is processed from morphine, a naturally occurring substance extracted from the seedpod of the Asian poppy plant. Heroin usually appears as a white or brown powder. Street names for heroin include 'smack,' 'H,' 'skag,' and 'junk.' Other names may refer to types of heroin produced in a specific geographical area, such as 'Mexican black tar.'"

    Source: National Institute on Drug Abuse, InfoFacts: Heroin (Rockville, MD: US Department of Health and Human Services), from the web at http://www.nida.nih.gov/ infofacts/heroin.html last accessed May 24, 2007.

2. "Acute intoxication (overdose) is characterized by euphoria, flushing, itching (particularly with morphine), miosis, drowsiness, decreased respiratory rate and depth, hypotension, bradycardia, and decreased body temperature."

    Source: "Opioids," The Merck Manual, Section 15: Psychiatric Disorders, Chapter 198: Drug Use and Dependence, Merck & Co. Inc., from the web at http://www.merck.com/mmpe/ sec15/ch198/ch198l.html last accessed May 24, 2007.

3. "Complications of heroin addiction may be related to the unsanitary administration of the drug or to the drug's inherent properties, overdose, or intoxicated behavior accompanying drug use. Common complications are pulmonary, bone, and neurologic disorders; hepatitis; and immunologic changes."

    Source: "Opioids," The Merck Manual, Section 15: Psychiatric Disorders, Chapter 198: Drug Use and Dependence, Merck & Co. Inc., from the web at http://www.merck.com/mmpe/ sec15/ch198/ch198l.html last accessed May 24, 2007.

4. "The short-term effects of heroin abuse appear soon after a single dose and disappear in a few hours. After an injection of heroin, the user reports feeling a surge of euphoria ('rush') accompanied by a warm flushing of the skin, a dry mouth, and heavy extremities. Following this initial euphoria, the user goes 'on the nod,' an alternately wakeful and drowsy state. Mental functioning becomes clouded due to the depression of the central nervous system. Long-term effects of heroin appear after repeated use for some period of time. Chronic users may develop collapsed veins, infection of the heart lining and valves, abscesses, cellulitis, and liver disease. Pulmonary complications, including various types of pneumonia, may result from the poor health condition of the abuser, as well as from heroin's depressing effects on respiration.
    "Heroin abuse during pregnancy and its many associated environmental factors (e.g., lack of prenatal care) have been associated with adverse consequences including low birth weight, an important risk factor for later developmental delay."

    Source: National Institute on Drug Abuse, InfoFacts: Heroin (Rockville, MD: US Department of Health and Human Services), from the web at http://www.nida.nih.gov/ infofacts/heroin.html last accessed January 9, 2006.

5. "In addition to the effects of the drug itself, street heroin may have additives that do not readily dissolve and result in clogging the blood vessels that lead to the lungs, liver, kidneys, or brain. This can cause infection or even death of small patches of cells in vital organs."

Heroin

Source: National Institute on Drug Abuse, InfoFacts: Heroin (Rockville, MD: US Department of Health and Human Services), from the web at http://www.nida.nih.gov /infofacts/heroin.html last accessed January 9, 2006.

6. "A striking finding from the toxicological data was the relatively small number of subjects in whom morphine only was detected. Most died with more drugs than heroin alone 'on board', with alcohol detected in 45% of subjects and benzodiazepines in just over a quarter. Both of these drugs act as central nervous system depressants and can enhance and prolong the depressant effects of heroin."

Source: Zador, Deborah, Sunjic, Sandra, and Darke, Shane, "Heroin-related deaths in New South Wales, 1992: toxicological findings and circumstances," The Medical Journal of Australia, (MJA 1996; 164:204) published on the web at http://www.mja. com.au/public/issues/feb19/zador/zador.html last accessed on May 24, 2007.

7. "Our findings that an ambulance was called while the subject was still alive in only 10% of cases, and that a substantial minority of heroin users died alone, strongly suggest that education campaigns should also emphasise that it is safer to inject heroin in the company of others, and important to call for an ambulance early in the event of an overdose. Consideration should also be given to trialling the distribution of the opioid antagonist naloxone to users to reduce mortality from heroin use."

Source: Zador, Deborah, Sunjic, Sandra, and Darke, Shane, "Heroin-related deaths in New South Wales, 1992: toxicological findings and circumstances," The Medical Journal of Australia, (MJA 1996; 164:204) published on the web at http://www.mja. com.au/public/issues/feb19/zador/zador.html last accessed on May 24, 2007.

8. "This pilot trial is the first in North America to prospectively evaluate a program of naloxone distribution to IDUs to prevent heroin overdose death. After an 8-hour training, our study participants' knowledge of heroin overdose prevention and management increased, and they reported successful resuscitations during 20 heroin overdose events. All victims were reported to have been unresponsive, cyanotic, or not breathing, but all survived. These findings suggest that IDUs can be trained to respond to heroin overdose by using CPR and naloxone, as others have reported. Moreover, we found no evidence of increases in drug use or heroin overdose in study participants. These data corroborate the findings of several feasibility studies recommending the prescription and distribution of naloxone to drug users to prevent fatal heroin overdose."

Source: Seal, Karen H., Robert Thawley, Lauren Gee, Joshua Bamberger, Alex H. Kral, Dan Ciccarone, Moher Downing, and Brian R. Edlin, "Naloxone Distribution and Cardiopulmonary Resuscitation Training for Injection Drug Users to Prevent Heroin Overdose Death: A Pilot Intervention Study," Journal of Urban Medicine (New York, NY: New York Academy of Medicine, 2005), Vol. 82, No. 2, p. 308.

9. "The disadvantage of continuing to describe heroin-related fatalities as 'overdoses' is that it attributes the cause of death solely to heroin and detracts attention from the contribution of other drugs to the cause of death. Heroin users need to be educated about the potentially dangerous practice of concurrent polydrug and heroin use."

Heroin

Source: Zador, Deborah, Sunjic, Sandra, and Darke, Shane, "Heroin-related deaths in New South Wales, 1992: toxicological findings and circumstances," The Medical Journal of Australia, (MJA 1996; 164:204) published on the web at http://www.mja. com.au/public/issues/feb19/zador/zador.html last accessed on May 24, 2007.

10. "A first priority for prevention must be to reduce the frequency of drug overdoses. We should inform heroin users about the risks of combining heroin with alcohol and other depressant drugs. Not all users will act on such information, but if there are similar behavioral changes to those that occurred with needle-sharing overdose deaths could be substantially reduced. Heroin users should also be discouraged from injecting alone and thereby denying themselves assistance in the event of an overdose."

Source: Dr. W.D. Hall, "How can we reduce heroin 'overdose' deaths?" The Medical Journal of Australia (MJA 1996; 164:197), from the web at http://www.mja.com.au/public/issues/feb19/hall/hall.html last accessed on May 24, 2007.

11. "Physical dependence necessitates continued use of the same opioid or a related one to prevent withdrawal. Withdrawal of the drug or administration of an antagonist precipitates a characteristic, self-limited withdrawal syndrome.

    "Therapeutic doses taken regularly over 2 to 3 days can lead to some tolerance and dependence, and when the drug is stopped, the user may have mild withdrawal symptoms which are scarcely noticed or are flu-like."

Source: "Opioids," The Merck Manual, Section 15: Psychiatric Disorders, Chapter 198: Drug Use and Dependence, Merck & Co. Inc., from the web at http://www.merck.com/mmpe/sec15/ch198/ch198l.html last accessed May 24, 2007.

12. "Withdrawal, which in regular abusers may occur as early as a few hours after the last administration, produces drug craving, restlessness, muscle and bone pain, insomnia, diarrhea and vomiting, cold flashes with goose bumps ('cold turkey'), kicking movements ('kicking the habit'), and other symptoms. Major withdrawal symptoms peak between 48 and 72 hours after the last dose and subside after about a week. Sudden withdrawal by heavily dependent users who are in poor health is occasionally fatal, although heroin withdrawal is considered less dangerous than alcohol or barbiturate withdrawal."

Source: National Institute on Drug Abuse, InfoFacts: Heroin (Rockville, MD: US Department of Health and Human Services), from the web at http://www.nida.nih.gov/infofacts/heroin.html last accessed January 9, 2006.

13. "There is a broad range of treatment options for heroin addiction, including medications as well as behavioral therapies. Science has taught us that when medication treatment is integrated with other supportive services, patients are often able to stop heroin (or other opiate) use and return to more stable and productive lives."

Source: National Institute on Drug Abuse, InfoFacts: Heroin (Rockville, MD: US Department of Health and Human Services), from the web at http://www.nida.nih.gov/infofacts/heroin.html last accessed January 9, 2006.

Heroin

14. "The 2003 NSDUH reports stability at low levels for heroin use among young people. In 2002, 13,000 youth between the ages of 12 and 17 had used heroin at least once in the past year ("annual" use), compared with 12,000 in 2003. Among the general population age 12 and older, 404,000 had used annually in 2002, compared with 314,000 in 2003."

Source: National Institute on Drug Abuse, InfoFacts: Heroin (Rockville, MD: US Department of Health and Human Services), from the web at http://www.nida.nih.gov/infofacts/heroin.html last accessed January 9, 2006.

PERSPECTIVES FROM EXPERTS IN THE FIELD OF NARCOTICS TREATMENT

1. "Unlike alcohol or tobacco, heroin causes no ongoing toxicity to the tissues or organs of the body. Apart from causing some constipation, it appears to have no side effects in most who take it. When administered safely, its use may be consistent with a long and productive life. The principal harm comes from the risk of overdose, problems with injecting, drug impurities and adverse legal or financial consequences."

Source: Byrne, Andrew, MD, "Addict in the Family: How to Cope with the Long Haul" (Redfern, NSW, Australia: Tosca Press, 1996), pp. 33-34, available on the web at http://www.csdp.org/addict/.

2. "People rarely die from heroin overdoses - meaning pure concentrations of the drug which simply overwhelm the body's responses."

Source: Peele, Stanton, MD, "The Persistent, Dangerous Myth of Heroin Overdose," from the web at http://www.peele.net/lib/heroinoverdose.html last accessed on May 24, 2007.

3. "The majority of drug deaths in an Australian study, conducted by the National Alcohol and Drug Research Centre, involved heroin in combination with either alcohol (40 percent) or tranquilizers (30 percent)."

Source: Peele, Stanton, MD, "The Persistent, Dangerous Myth of Heroin Overdose," from the web at http://www.peele.net/lib/heroinoverdose.html last accessed on May 24, 2007.

4. "If it is not pure drugs that kill, but impure drugs and the mixture of drugs, then the myth of the heroin overdose can be dangerous. If users had a guaranteed pure supply of heroin which they relied on, there would be little more likelihood of toxic doses than occur with narcotics administered in a hospital.

Source: Peele, Stanton, MD, "The Persistent, Dangerous Myth of Heroin Overdose," from the web at http://www.peele.net/lib/heroinoverdose.html last accessed on May 24, 2007.

4. "But when people take whatever they can off the street, they have no way of knowing how the drug is adulterated. And when they decide to augment heroin's effects, possibly because they do not want to take too much heroin, they may place themselves in the greatest danger."

Source: Peele, Stanton, MD, "The Persistent, Dangerous Myth of Heroin Overdose," from the web at http://www.peele.net/lib/heroinoverdose.html last accessed on May 24, 2007.

Heroin-Assisted Therapy/Heroin Maintenance

1. A study of the Swiss heroin prescription program found: "With respect to the group of those treated uninterruptedly during four years, a strong decrease in the incidence and prevalence rates of overall criminal implication for both intense and moderate offenders was found. As to the type of offense, similar diminutions were observed for all types of offenses related to the use or acquisition of drugs. Not surprisingly, the most pronounced drop was found for use/possession of heroin. In accordance with self-reported and clinical data (Blaettler, Dobler-Mikola, Steffen, & Uchtenhagen, 2002; Uchtenhagen et al., 1999), the analysis of police records suggests that program participants also tend strongly to reduce cocaine and cannabis use probably because program participants dramatically reduced their contacts with the drug scene when entering the program (Uchtenhagen et al., 1999) and were thus less exposed to opportunities to buy drugs. Consequently, their need for money is not only reduced with regard to heroin but also to other substances. Accordingly, the drop in acquisitive crime, such as drug selling or property crime, is also remarkable and related to all kinds of thefts like shoplifting, vehicle theft, burglary, etc. Detailed analyses indicated that the drop found is related to a true diminution in criminal activity rather than a more lenient recording practice of police officers towards program participants.

   "On average, males had higher overall rates than females in the pretreatment period. However, no marked gender differences were found with regard to intreatment rates. Taken as a whole, this suggests that the treatment had a somewhat more beneficial effect on men than women. This result is corroborated by selfreport data (Killias et al., 2002). With respect to age and cocaine use, no relevant in-treatment differences were observed. As to program dropout, after one year, about a quarter of the patients had left the program, and after four years, about 50% had left. Considering the high-risk profile of the treated addicts, this retention rate is, at least, promising."

   Source: Ribeaud, Denis, "Long-term Impacts of the Swiss Heroin Prescription Trials on Crime of Treated Heroin Users," Journal of Drug Issues (Talahassee, FL: University of Florida, Winter 2004), p. 187.

2. A study of the Swiss heroin prescription program found: "Finally, the analysis of the reasons for interrupting treatment revealed that, even in the group of those treated for less than one year, the majority did not actually drop out of the program but rather changed the type of treatment, mostly either methadone maintenance or abstinence treatment. Knowing that methadone maintenance treatment – and a fortiori abstinence treatment – is able to substantially reduce acquisitive crime, the redirection of heroin maintenance patients toward alternative treatments is probably the main cause for the ongoing reduction or at least stabilization of criminal involvement of most patients after treatment interruption. Thus the principal post-treatment benefit of heroin maintenance seems to be its ability to redirect even briefly treated high-risk patients towards alternative treatments rather than back 'on the street'."

Heroin-Assisted Therapy/Heroin Maintenance

Source: Ribeaud, Denis, "Long-term Impacts of the Swiss Heroin Prescription Trials on Crime of Treated Heroin Users," Journal of Drug Issues (Talahassee, FL: University of Florida, Winter 2004), p. 188.

3. "Overall, results indicate that heroin prescription is a very promising approach in reducing any type of drug related crime across all relevant groups analyzed. It affects property crime as well as drug dealing and even use/possession of drugs other than heroin. These results suggest that heroin maintenance does not only have an impact by reducing the acquisitive pressure of treated patients, but also seems to have a broader effect on their entire life-style by stabilizing their daily routine through the commitment to attend the prescription center twice or three times a day, by giving them the opportunity for psychosocial support, and by keeping them away from open drug scenes."

Source: Ribeaud, Denis, "Long-term Impacts of the Swiss Heroin Prescription Trials on Crime of Treated Heroin Users," Journal of Drug Issues (Talahassee, FL: University of Florida, Winter 2004), p. 188.

4. "The harm reduction policy of Switzerland and its emphasis on the medicalisation of the heroin problem seems to have contributed to the image of heroin as unattractive for young people."

Source: Nordt, Carlos, and Rudolf Stohler, "Incidence of Heroin Use in Zurich, Switzerland: A Treatment Case Register Analysis," The Lancet, Vol. 367, June 3, 2006, p. 1830.

5. "Heroin misuse in Switzerland was characterised by a substantial decline in heroin incidence and by heroin users entering substitution treatment after a short time, but with a low cessation rate. There are different explanations for the sharp decline in incidence of problematic heroin use. According to Ditton and Frischer, such a steep decline in incidence of heroin use is caused by the quick slow down of the number of non-using friends who are prepared to become users in friendship chains. Musto's generational theory regards the decline in incidence more as a social learning effect whereby the next generation will not use heroin because they have seen the former generation go from pleasant early experiences to devastating circumstances for addicts, families, and communities later on."

Source: Nordt, Carlos, and Rudolf Stohler, "Incidence of Heroin Use in Zurich, Switzerland: A Treatment Case Register Analysis," The Lancet, Vol. 367, June 3, 2006, p. 1833.

6. "The incidence of regular heroin use in the canton of Zurich started with about 80 new users in 1975, increased to 850 in 1990, and declined to 150 in 2002, and was thus reduced by 82%. Incidence peaked in 1990 at a similar high level to that ever reported in New South Wales, Australia, or in Italy. But only in Zurich has a decline by a factor of four in the number of new users of heroin been observed within a decade. This decline in incidence probably pertains to the whole of Switzerland because the number of patients in substitution treatment is stable, the age of the substituted population is rising, the mortality caused by drugs is declining, and confiscation of heroin is falling. Furthermore, incidence trends did not differ between urban and rural regions of Zurich. This finding is suggestive of a more similar spatial dynamic of heroin use for Switzerland than for other countries."

Heroin-Assisted Therapy/Heroin Maintenance

Source: Nordt, Carlos, and Rudolf Stohler, "Incidence of Heroin Use in Zurich, Switzerland: A Treatment Case Register Analysis," The Lancet, Vol. 367, June 3, 2006, p. 1833.

7. "The central result of the German model project shows a significant superiority of heroin over methadone treatment for both primary outcome measures. Heroin treatment has significantly higher response rates both in the field of health and the reduction of illicit drug use. According to the study protocol, evidence of the greater efficacy of heroin treatment compared to methadone maintenance treatment has thus been produced. Heroin treatment is also clearly superior to methadone treatment when focusing on patients, who fulfill the two primary outcome measures."

Source: Naber, Dieter, and Haasen, Christian, Centre for Interdisciplinary Addiction Research of Hamburg University, "The German Model Project for Heroin Assisted Treatment of Opioid Dependent Patients — A Multi-Centre, Randomised, Controlled Treatment Study: Clinical Study Report of the First Study Phase," January 2006, p. 117.

8. "The German model project for heroin-assisted treatment of opioid dependent patients is so far the largest randomised control group study that investigated the effects of heroin treatment. This fact alone lends particular importance to the results in the (meanwhile worldwide) discussion of effects and benefits of heroin treatment. For the group of so-called most severely dependent patients, heroin treatment proves to be superior to the goals of methadone maintenance based on pharmacological maintenance treatment. This result should not be left without consequences. In accordance with the research results from other countries, it has to be investigated to what extent heroin-assisted treatment can be integrated into the regular treatment offers for severely ill i.v. opioid addicts."

Source: Naber, Dieter, and Haasen, Christian, Centre for Interdisciplinary Addiction Research of Hamburg University, "The German Model Project for Heroin Assisted Treatment of Opioid Dependent Patients — A Multi-Centre, Randomised, Controlled Treatment Study: Clinical Study Report of the First Study Phase," January 2006, p. 122.

9. "To conclude, it must be stated that heroin treatment involves a somewhat higher safety risk than methadone treatment. This is mainly due to the intravenous form of application. The rather frequently occurring respiratory depressions and cerebral convulsions are not unexpected and can easily be clinically controlled. Overall, the mortality rate was low during the first study phase, and no death occurred with a causal relationship with the study medication. Compared to much higher health risks related to the i.v. application of street heroin, the safety risk of medically controlled heroin prescription has to be considered as low."

Source: Naber, Dieter, and Haasen, Christian, Centre for Interdisciplinary Addiction Research of Hamburg University, "The German Model Project for Heroin Assisted Treatment of Opioid Dependent Patients — A Multi-Centre, Randomised, Controlled Treatment Study: Clinical Study Report of the First Study Phase," January 2006, p. 150.

Heroin-Assisted Therapy/Heroin Maintenance

10. "The UK is exceptional internationally because heroin is included in the range of legally sanctioned treatments for opiate dependence. In practice, this treatment option is rarely utilised: only about 448 heroin users receive heroin on prescription."

Source: Stimson, Gerry V., and Nicky Metrebian, Centre for Research on Drugs and Health Behavior, "Prescribing Heroin: What is the Evidence?" (London, England: Rowntree Foundation, 2003), p. 1.

11. "Many countries believe (erroneously) that the international drug conventions prohibit the use of heroin in medical treatment. Furthermore, the International Narcotics Control Board (INCB) has exerted great pressure on countries to cease prescribing heroin for any medical purpose. Nevertheless, a few countries, including the UK, Belgium, the Netherlands, Iceland, Malta, Canada and Switzerland, continue to use heroin (diamorphine) for general medical purposes, mostly in hospital settings (usually for severe pain relief). Until recently, however, Britain was the only country that allowed doctors to prescribe heroin for the treatment of drug dependence."

Source: Stimson, Gerry V., and Nicky Metrebian, Centre for Research on Drugs and Health Behavior, "Prescribing Heroin: What is the Evidence?" (London, England: Rowntree Foundation, 2003), p. 4.

HIV/AIDS & Injection Drug Use

1. "At the end of 2005, an estimated 421,873 persons in the 50 states and the District of Columbia were living with AIDS."

   Source: Centers for Disease Control (CDC), HIV/AIDS Surveillance Report 2005 (revised June 2007), Vol. 17, p. 8.

2. The estimated lifetime cost of treating an HIV positive person is at least $195,188.

   Source: Holtgrave, DR, Pinkerton, SD. "Updates of Cost of Illness and Quality of Life Estimates for Use in Economic Evaluations of HIV Prevention Programs." Journal of Acquired Immune Deficiency Syndromes and Human Retrovirology, Vol. 16, pp. 54-62 (1997).

3. "Of the estimated 341,524 male adults and adolescents living with HIV/AIDS, 61% had been exposed through male-to-male sexual\ contact, 18% had been exposed through injection drug use, 13% had been exposed through highrisk heterosexual contact, and 7% had been exposed through both male-to-male sexual contact and injection drug use. Of the estimated 126,964 female adults and adolescents living with HIV/AIDS, 72% had been exposed through high-risk heterosexual contact, and 26% had been exposed through injection drug use. Of the estimated 6,726 children living with HIV/AIDS, 90% had been exposed perinatally." (The CDC defines "high-risk heterosexual contact" as "Heterosexual contact with a person known to have, or to be at high risk for, HIV infection.")

   Source: Centers for Disease Control, HIV/AIDS Surveillance Report 2005 (revised June 2007), Vol. 17, p. 8.

4. Research published in the Journal of Urban Health estimated that in 1998, there were 1,364,874 injection drug users in the US.

   Source: Friedman, Samuel R., Barbara Tempalski, Hannah Cooper, Theresa Perlis, Marie Keem, Risa Friedman & Peter L. Flom, "Estimating Numbers of Injecting Drug Users in Metropolitan Areas for Structural Analyses of Community Vulnerability and for Assessing Relative Degrees of Service Provision for Injecting Drug Users," Journal of Urban Health (New York, NY: NY Academy of Medicine, 2004), Vol. 81, No. 3, p. 380.

5. According to the CDC, from the beginning of the AIDS epidemic through the end of 2005 there have been a total of 984,155 cases of AIDS reported in the US. Of these, 452,111 were reported to have been transmitted through male-to-male sexual contact, 241,364 were reported to have been transmitted through injection drug use, 65,881 were reportedly transmitted through male-to-male sexual contact and injection drug use, and 163,609 were reported to have been transmitted through "high-risk heterosexual contact."

   Source: Centers for Disease Control, HIV/AIDS Surveillance Report 2005 (revised June 2007), Vol. 17, Table 3, p. 12.

6. According to the CDC, from the beginning of the AIDS epidemic through the end of 2005 there have been a total of 9,101 cases of AIDS reported in the US among children under 13 years of age at the time of diagnosis.

   Source: Centers for Disease Control, HIV/AIDS Surveillance Report 2005 (revised 2007), Vol. 17, Table 3, p. 12.

7. The Centers for Disease Control reported that in 2003, HIV disease was the 22nd leading cause of death in the US for whites, the 9th leading cause of death for blacks, and the 13th leading cause of death for Hispanics.

HIV/AIDS & Injection Drug Use

Source: Heron, Melonie P., PhD, Smith, Betty L., BsED, Division of Vital Statistics, "Deaths: Leading Causes for 2003," National Vital Statistics Reports, Vol. 55, No. 10 (Hyattsville, MD: National Center for Health Statistics, CDC, March 15, 2007), p. 10, Table E, and p. 12, Table F.

8. The CDC estimates that of the 12,140 male adults or adolescent AIDS victims who died in 2005, 5,929 of the cases were reportedly transmitted through male-to-male sexual contact (MSM), 3,159 were reportedly transmitted through injection drug use, 1,364 were reportedly transmitted through male-to-male sexual contact and injection drug use, 1,584 were reportedly transmitted through high-risk heterosexual contact, and 104 were attributed to "other."

   Source: Centers for Disease Control, HIV/AIDS Surveillance Report 2005 (revised June 2007), Vol. 17, pp. 16-17, Table 7.

9. The CDC estimates that of the 4,128 female adults or adolescent AIDS victims who died in 2005, 1,651 of the cases were reportedly transmitted through injection drug use, 2,413 were reportedly transmitted through high-risk heterosexual contact, and 64 were attributed to "other."

   Source: Centers for Disease Control, HIV/AIDS Surveillance Report 2005 (revised June 2007), Vol. 17, pp. 16-17, Table 7.

10. "From 2001 through 2005, both among males and females, the estimated number of deaths of IDUs [with AIDS] decreased, but the number of deaths of persons exposed through high-risk heterosexual contact increased."

   Source: Centers for Disease Control, HIV/AIDS Surveillance Report 2005 (revised June 2007), Vol. 17, pp. 16-17, Table 7.

11. "Eastern Europe, the Commonwealth of Independent States, and significant parts of Asia are experiencing explosive growth in new HIV infections, driven largely by injecting drug use (UNAIDS, 2006). While the primary route of transmission in most of these areas is sharing of contaminated injecting equipment, sexual and perinatal transmission among IDUs and their partners also plays an important and growing role. In many highly affected countries, rapid growth in the number of IDUs infected with HIV has already created a public health crisis. Countries where the level of HIV infection is still relatively low have the chance — if they act now — to slow the spread of HIV."

   Source: Committee on the Prevention of HIV Infection among Injecting Drug Users in High-Risk Countries, "Preventing HIV Infection among Injecting Drug Users in High Risk Countries: An Assessment of the Evidence" (Washington, DC: National Academy Press, 2006), p. 141.

12. "On December 31, 2004, 1.9% of State prison inmates and 1.1% of Federal prison inmates were known to be infected with the human immunodeficiency virus (HIV). Correctional authorities reported that 21,366 State inmates and 1,680 Federal inmates were HIV positive. The number known to be HIV positive totaled 23,046, down from 23,663 at yearend 2003.
   "Of those known to be HIV positive in all U.S. prisons at yearend 2004, an estimated 6,027 were confirmed AIDS cases, up from 5,944 in 2003. Among State inmates, 0.5% had AIDS; among Federal inmates, 0.4%."

HIV/AIDS & Injection Drug Use

Source: Maruschak, Laura M. "HIV In Prisons, 2004," NCJ-213897 (Washington, DC: Department of Justice, Bureau of Justice Statistics, Nov. 2006), p. 1.

13. "In every year since 1991, the rate of confirmed AIDS has been higher among prison inmates than in the general population (figure 1). At yearend 2004 the rate of confirmed AIDS in State and Federal prisons was more than 3 times higher than in the total U.S. population. About 50 in every 10,000 prison inmates had confirmed AIDS, compared to 15 in 10,000 persons in the U.S. general population."

Source: Maruschak, Laura M. "HIV In Prisons, 2004," NCJ-213897 (Washington, DC: Department of Justice, Bureau of Justice Statistics, Nov. 2006), p. 5.

14. "Inmates held on a property offense in State and Federal prisons had the highest HIV-positive rate (both 2.6%) (table 11). Among State inmates, public-order offenders (0.9%) were least likely to report being HIV positive; among Federal prisoners, drug offenders (0.7%) were least likely to report being HIV positive."

Source: Maruschak, Laura M. "HIV In Prisons, 2004," NCJ-213897 (Washington, DC: Department of Justice, Bureau of Justice Statistics, Nov. 2006), p. 10.

15. "In personal interviews conducted in 2002, nearly two-thirds of local jail inmates reported ever being tested for HIV; of those, 1.3% disclosed that they were HIV positive."

Source: Maruschak, Laura M. "HIV In Prisons and Jails, 2002," NCJ-205333 (Washington, DC: Department of Justice, Bureau of Justice Statistics, Dec. 2004), p. 1.

16. "Those inmates held for a property offense in local jails reported the highest HIV positive rate (1.8%) (table 10). Drug offenders reported a slightly lower rate (1.6%). The percentage of public-order offenders who were HIV positive was 1.1%; the percentage of violent offenders, 0.7%."

Source: Maruschak, Laura M. "HIV In Prisons and Jails, 2002," NCJ-205333 (Washington, DC: Department of Justice, Bureau of Justice Statistics, Dec. 2004), p. 9.

17. "In 2004 for every 100,000 State inmates, 14 died from AIDS-related causes. The most AIDS-related deaths were reported in the South (84), followed by the Northeast (60). Together, these two regions accounted for more than three-quarters of AIDS-related deaths in State prisons."

Source: Maruschak, Laura M. "HIV In Prisons, 2004," NCJ-213897 (Washington, DC: Department of Justice, Bureau of Justice Statistics, Nov. 2006), p. 8.

18. "In 2002 the number of AIDS-related deaths in local jails was 42, down from 58 in 2000 (table 11). The rate of AIDS-related deaths was down from 9 per 100,000 inmates in 2000 to 6 per 100,000 in 2002. Of the 42 inmates who died from AIDS-related illnesses in 2002, 38 were male and 4 were female. Those who died from AIDS-related illnesses were most likely black (31 inmate deaths) and between the ages 35 and 44 (21 inmate deaths). Over the 3-year period beginning in 2000, a total of 155 local jail inmates died from AIDS-related causes."

Source: Maruschak, Laura M. "HIV In Prisons and Jails, 2002," NCJ-205333 (Washington, DC: Department of Justice, Bureau of Justice Statistics, Dec. 2004), p. 10.

Ibogaine

1. "Ibogaine, a natural alkaloid extracted from the root bark of the African shrub Tabernanthe Iboga, has attracted attention because of its reported ability to reverse human addiction to multiple drugs of abuse, including alcohol."

   Source: Dao-Yao He, Nancy N.H. McGough, Ajay Ravindranathan, Jerome Jeanblanc, Marian L. Logrip, Khanhky Phamluong, Patricia H. Janak, and Dorit Ron, "Glial Cell Line-Derived Neurotrophic Factor Mediates the Desirable Actions of the Anti-Addiction Drug Ibogaine against Alcohol Consumption," The Journal of Neuroscience, Jan. 19, 2005, Vol. 25, No. 3, p. 619.

2. "Studies also suggest that ibogaine attenuates drug- and ethanol-induced behaviors in rodents. For example, ibogaine reduces operant self-administration of heroin in rats, as well as naloxone-precipitated withdrawal in morphine-dependent rats (Glick et al., 1992; Dworkin et al., 1995). Administration of ibogaine decreases cocaine-induced locomotor activity and reduces cocaine self-administration in rats (Cappendijk and Dzoljic, 1993) and mice (Sershen et al., 1994)."

   Source: Dao-Yao He, Nancy N.H. McGough, Ajay Ravindranathan, Jerome Jeanblanc, Marian L. Logrip, Khanhky Phamluong, Patricia H. Janak, and Dorit Ron, "Glial Cell Line-Derived Neurotrophic Factor Mediates the Desirable Actions of the Anti-Addiction Drug Ibogaine against Alcohol Consumption," The Journal of Neuroscience, Jan. 19, 2005, Vol. 25, No. 3, p. 619.

3. "Despite its attractive properties, ibogaine is not approved as an addiction treatment because of the induction of side effects such as hallucinations. In addition, ibogaine at high doses causes degeneration of cerebellar Purkinje cells (O'Hearn and Molliver, 1993, 1997) and whole-body tremors and ataxia (Glick et al., 1992; O'Hearn and Molliver, 1993) in rats."

   Source: Dao-Yao He, Nancy N.H. McGough, Ajay Ravindranathan, Jerome Jeanblanc, Marian L. Logrip, Khanhky Phamluong, Patricia H. Janak, and Dorit Ron, "Glial Cell Line-Derived Neurotrophic Factor Mediates the Desirable Actions of the Anti-Addiction Drug Ibogaine against Alcohol Consumption," The Journal of Neuroscience, Vol. 25, No. 3, Jan. 19, 2005, p. 619.

4. "Based on anecdotal reports in humans, ibogaine has been claimed [1] to be effective in interrupting dependence on opioids, stimulants, alcohol and nicotine. Preclinical studies in rats have supported these claims: ibogaine has been reported to decrease the i.v. self-administration of morphine [2] and cocaine [3] and the oral intake of alcohol [4] and nicotine [5]. However, studies in rats have also raised concerns regarding potential adverse effects of ibogaine; most notably, high doses have been shown to be neurotoxic to the cerebellum [6,7]."

   Source: Glick, S.D., Maisonneuve, I.M., and Dickinson, H.A., "18-MC Reduces Methamphetamine and Nicotine Self-Administration in Rats," Neuropharmacology, Vol. 11, No. 9, June 26, 2000, p. 2013.

Ibogaine

5. "18-MC, a novel iboga alkaloid congener, reduces intravenous methamphetamine and nicotine self-administration in rats. These and previous results with morphine, cocaine and alcohol indicate that 18-MC warrants further development as a potential treatment for multiple forms of drug addiction."

   Source: Glick, S.D., Maisonneuve, I.M., and Dickinson, H.A., "18-MC Reduces Methamphetamine and Nicotine Self-Administration in Rats," Neuropharmacology, Vol. 11, No. 9, June 26, 2000, p. 2015.

6. "Although ibogaine has been reported to effectively reduce drug cravings and withdrawal symptoms in addicts (Sheppard, 1994), its tremorigenic, hallucinogenic, neurotoxic, and cardiovascular side effects (see Alper, 2001) have prevented its approval as a treatment for addiction. On the other hand, 18-methoxycoronaridine, although not yet tested in humans, has no apparent side effects in rats, presumably because it is more selective pharmacologically than ibogaine."

   Source: Pace, Christopher J., Glick, Stanley D., Maisonneuve, Isabelle M., He, Li-Wen, Jokiel, Patrick A., Kuehne, Martin E., and Fleck, Mark W., "Novel Iboga Alkaloid Congeners Block Nicotinic Receptors and Reduce Drug Self-Administration," European Journal of Pharmacology, Vol. 492, 2004, p. 159.

7. "In summary, repeated administration of drugs of abuse and alcohol induces a common pattern of changes in gene expression and protein levels selectively in the VTA. A subset of these changes is reversed by intra-VTA GDNF, as are some of the drug-induced behavioral effects. Endogenous GDNF systems appear to inhibit drug related behaviors, while repeated drug administration appears to inhibit GDIVF signaling itself. Based on these studies, we propose that GDNF is an endogenous anti-addiction agent. This possibility is directly supported by the finding that the activity of the anti-addiction drug, ibogaine, on alcohol consumption is mediated via increased expression of GDNF in the midbrain and the subsequent activation of the GDNF pathway."

   Source: Ron, Dorit, and Janak, Patricia H., Reviews in the Neurosciences, Vol. 16, No. 4, 2005, p. 281.

Interdiction

1. Interdiction efforts intercept 10-15% of the heroin and 30% of the cocaine. Drug traffickers earn gross profit margins of up to 300%. At least 75% of international drug shipments would need to be intercepted to substantially reduce the profitability of drug trafficking.

   Source: Associated Press, "U.N. Estimates Drug Business Equal to 8 Percent of World Trade," (1997, June 26).

2. "Global seizures of opiates reached 120 metric tons in 2004 (+ 9 per cent compared to 2003). Increases were particularly strong in South-East Europe (+109 per cent) reflecting the resumption of large-scale trafficking along the Balkan route. Highest seizures were reported by Iran, followed by Pakistan and China. The largest heroin seizures were reported from China (10.8 metric tons). The estimated global interception rate for opiates was 24 per cent of global production, a clear increase from the 10 percent recorded 10 years earlier."

   Source: United Nations Office on Drugs and Crime, "World Drug Report 2006, Volume 1: Analysis" (United Nations: Vienna, Austria, 2006), p. 14.

3. "In 2005, the estimated area under illicit opium poppy cultivation in the world decreased by 22 per cent (from 195,940 hectares to 151,500 hectares) due to lower cultivation in the three main source countries of illicit opium in the world: Afghanistan, Myanmar and Lao People's Democratic Republic (Lao PDR). Global opium production was estimated at 4,620 metric tons of which 4,100 metric tons (89 per cent) were produced in Afghanistan."

   Source: United Nations Office on Drugs and Crime, "World Drug Report 2006, Volume 1: Analysis" (United Nations: Vienna, Austria, 2006), p. 11.

4. "The potential production of cocaine reached 910 metric tons in 2005, about the same as a year earlier. Potential production in Colombia amounted to 640 metric tons, in Peru to 180 metric tons and in Bolivia to 90 metric tons. The level of overall production is practically unchanged from the levels of a decade ago."

   Source: United Nations Office on Drugs and Crime, "World Drug Report 2006, Volume 1: Analysis" (United Nations: Vienna, Austria, 2006), p. 82.

5. "For the third year in a row, Colombia seized most cocaine in the world (almost 188 metric tons), 32 per cent of the world total and an increase of 29 per cent compared to 2003. The second largest seizures were reported from the United States (166 metric tons, 28 per cent of the world total). In Ecuador, there has been a 9-fold increase in seizures (5 metric tons in 2004, 44 metric tons in 2005).
   "European cocaine seizures were close to 80 metric tons in 2004 and about 100 metric tons in 2005. Over the 1994-2004 period they increased by, on average, 10 per cent per year."

   Source: United Nations Office on Drugs and Crime, "World Drug Report 2006, Volume 1: Analysis" (United Nations: Vienna, Austria, 2006), p. 17.

Interdiction

6. "The rising importance of Africa, and notably of West Africa, as a transit point for cocaine shipments destined for European markets is becoming more evident. Seizures made in Africa increased more than three-fold in 2004 with seizures in West and Central Africa increasing more than six-fold. Most of this cocaine is destined for Spain and Portugal for onward shipment to other European countries. Largest seizures over the 2000-2004 period in Africa were made in Cape Verde, followed by South Africa, Kenya, Ghana and Nigeria. Despite this increase, African seizures still account for less than 1 per cent of global cocaine seizures but there are indications that only a very small proportion of cocaine transiting the African continent is actually seized."

   Source: United Nations Office on Drugs and Crime, "World Drug Report 2006, Volume 1: Analysis" (United Nations: Vienna, Austria, 2006), p. 17.

7. "The world's main cocaine trafficking routes continue to run from the Andean region, notably Colombia, to the United States. The trafficking patterns analysis of the Colombian authorities revealed that more than half of the country's seizures took place at the ports; with 60 per cent of the cocaine leaving the country via the Pacific coast and 40 per cent via the Atlantic coast in 2004. According to the United States Interagency Assessment of Cocaine Movement, half of the cocaine trafficked towards the United States in 2004 transited the Eastern Pacific, whereas 40 per cent were trafficked through the Western Caribbean."

   Source: United Nations Office on Drugs and Crime, "World Drug Report 2006, Volume 1: Analysis" (United Nations: Vienna, Austria, 2006), p. 87.

8. "The main intermediate target country of cocaine shipments from Colombia is Mexico. Mexico reports that, about 55 per cent of the cocaine is trafficked to Mexico by sea, another 30 per cent by land from Central America (Guatemala and Belize) and some 15 per cent comes by air. The direction of cocaine trafficking within Mexico is from the southern parts of the country to the northern border. In volume terms, most cocaine shipments are primarily by sea; in terms of trafficking operations, however, most cocaine deliveries are by land."

   Source: United Nations Office on Drugs and Crime, "World Drug Report 2006, Volume 1: Analysis" (United Nations: Vienna, Austria, 2006), p. 87.

9. "In the past, 30-50 per cent of the cocaine entered the USA directly via the Caribbean. For 2004, however, the United States Interagency Assessment of Cocaine Movement concluded that this proportion had fallen to below 10 per cent. The main smuggling vectors via the Caribbean in 2004 concerned Haiti and the Dominican Rep (2%), Jamaica (2%) and Puerto Rico (1%). The United States report that about 12 per cent of all cocaine entered the country by air in 2004. In contrast to the situation in the 1980s, direct shipments by air from Colombia are no longer very common."

   Source: United Nations Office on Drugs and Crime, "World Drug Report 2006, Volume 1: Analysis" (United Nations: Vienna, Austria, 2006), p. 88.

Interdiction

10. "As far as trafficking is concerned, a comparison with the interception rate of opiates in 1998 (17%), makes the interception rate of 46% reported for cocaine for the same year appear extremely high. Assuming a similar volume of seizures in 1999, the rate would be even higher (50%). For the reasons mentioned above, there are thus some doubts about the accuracy of the total potential cocaine production reported during the past few years (765 mt in 1999).
"Based on seizures and comsumption estimates, UNDCP considers that production might in fact be closer to 1,000 tons."
(In other words, governments make lowball estimates of cocaine production in order to look good.)

    Source: United Nations Office for Drug Control and Crime Prevention, Global Illicit Drug Trends 2000 (New York, NY: UNDCP, 2000), p. 32.

11. Thirteen truck loads of cocaine is enough to satisfy U.S. demand for one year. The United States has 19,924 kilometers of shoreline, 300 ports of entry and more than 7,500 miles of border with Mexico and Canada. Stopping drugs at the borders is like trying to find a needle in a haystack.

    Source: Frankel, G., "Federal Agencies Duplicate Efforts, Wage Costly Turf Battles," The Washington Post (June 8, 1997), p. A1; Central Intelligence Agency, World Factbook 1998, 1998.

12. One of the major problems with supply reduction efforts (source control, interdiction, and domestic enforcement) is that "suppliers simply produce for the market what they would have produced anyway, plus enough extra to cover anticipated government seizures."

    Source: Rydell, C.P. & Everingham, S.S., Controlling Cocaine, Prepared for the Office of National Drug Control Policy and the United States Army (Santa Monica, CA: Drug Policy Research Center, RAND, 1994), p. 6.

13. To achieve a one percent reduction in U.S. cocaine consumption, the United States could spend an additional $34 million on drug treatment programs, or 23 times as much — $783 million — on efforts to eradicate the supply at the source.

    Source: Rydell & Everingham, Controlling Cocaine (Santa Monica, CA: The RAND Corporation, 1994).

14. "Despite 2 years of extensive herbicide spraying [source country eradication], U.S. estimates show there has not been any net reduction in [Colombian] coca cultivation - net coca cultivation actually increased 50 percent."

    Source: US General Accounting Office, Drug Control: Narcotics Threat from Colombia Continues to Grow (Washington, DC: USGPO, 1999), p. 2.

15. In spite of US expenditures of $625 million in counter narcotics operations in Colombia between 1990 and 1998, Colombia was able to surpass Peru and Bolivia to become the world's largest coca producer. Additionally, "there has not been a net reduction in processing or exporting refined cocaine from Colombia or in cocaine availability within the United States."

Interdiction

Source: US General Accounting Office, Drug Control: Narcotics Threat from Colombia Continues to Grow (Washington, DC: USGPO, 1999), pp. 3, 4, 6.

16. "... While two major groups (the Medellin and Cali cartels) dominated drug-trafficking activities during the late 1980s and early 1990s, today there are hundreds of smaller and more decentralized organizations. These groups are now capable of producing 'black cocaine' that hinders detection and are improving their transportation capabilities by manufacturing boats capable of carrying up to 2 tons of cocaine at high speeds."

Source: US General Accounting Office, Drug Control: Narcotics Threat from Colombia Continues to Grow (Washington, DC: USGPO, 1999), pp. 4-5.

17. Black cocaine is created by a chemical process used by drug traffickers to evade detection by drug sniffing dogs and chemical tests. The traffickers add charcoal and other chemicals to cocaine, which transforms it into a black substance that has no smell and does not react when subjected to the usual chemical tests.

Source: US General Accounting Office, Drug Control: Narcotics Threat from Colombia Continues to Grow (Washington, DC: USGPO, 1999), p. 5.

Y

International Drug Facts

(Sections are divided as follows: A. Overview; B. Prevalence Estimates;
C. Problem Substance Use and Substance-Related Harm; D. Harm Reduction Efforts;
E. Treatment; F. Substance Use and the Justice System)

EUROPEAN UNION

A. Overview

1. "The EU drug strategy 2005–12, adopted by the European Council in December 2004, takes into account the results of the final evaluation of progress made during the previous period (2000–04). It aims to add value to the national strategies while respecting the principles of subsidiarity and proportionality set out in the treaties. It sets out two general goals for the EU with regard to drugs:
"-to achieve a high level of health protection, well-being and social cohesion by complementing the Member States' action in preventing and reducing drug use and dependence and drug-related harm to health and the fabric of society;
"-to ensure a high level of security for the general public by taking action against drug production and supply and cross-border trafficking, and intensifying preventive action against drug-related crime through effective cooperation between Member States."

   Source: "Annual Report 2005: The State of the Drugs Problem in Europe," European Monitoring Centre for Drugs and Drug Addiction (Luxembourg: Office for Official Publications of the European Communities, 2005), p. 18.

2. "Important policy differences between European Member States still exist, often reflecting differences in the national drug situations and in the configuration of responses. Nonetheless, the new drug strategy suggests that the European policy debate on drugs is increasingly characterised by agreement on a common framework for activities. For example, virtually all demand reduction strategies include prevention, treatment and harm reduction elements, although the emphasis on each varies between Member States."

   Source: "Annual Report 2006: The State of the Drugs Problem in Europe," European Monitoring Centre for Drugs and Drug Addiction (Luxembourg: Office for Official Publications of the European Communities, 2006), p. 11.

3. "A continuing trend, again evident in the new information reported this year, is for changes to national drug laws to emphasise more strongly a distinction between offences of drug possession for personal use and those involving trafficking and supply. Generally, there is a shift towards increased

International Drug Facts

EUROPEAN UNION

penalties for the latter and a reduced emphasis on custodial sentences for the former. This development is in line with a greater emphasis overall across Europe on widening the opportunities for drug treatment and on giving more attention to interventions that divert those with drug problems away from the criminal justice system towards treatment and rehabilitation options."

Source: "Annual Report 2006: The State of the Drugs Problem in Europe," European Monitoring Centre for Drugs and Drug Addiction (Luxembourg: Office for Official Publications of the European Communities, 2006), p. 11.

4. "For those countries that have made a legal distinction with respect to the possession of drugs for use rather than supply, the question arises whether there is an explicit need to legislate on what quantities of drugs constitute a threshold for personal use. Here no consensus currently prevails and different approaches have been adopted across Europe, ranging from the issuing of general operational guidelines through to specification of legal limits."

Source: "Annual Report 2006: The State of the Drugs Problem in Europe," European Monitoring Centre for Drugs and Drug Addiction (Luxembourg: Office for Official Publications of the European Communities, 2006), p. 11.

5. "Although expenditure is frequently measured over differing time periods, and there is no common definition of drugrelated public expenditure, available estimates suggest that drug spending has increased in several countries, including the Czech Republic, Denmark, Luxembourg, Austria and Poland.

"Countries reporting drug expenditure for the year 2004 included the Czech Republic (EUR 11.0 million), Spain (EUR 302 to 325 million), Cyprus (EUR 2.8 million), Poland (EUR 51 million) and Norway (EUR 46 million). Two countries reported more recent budgeted expenditure for tackling drugs: Luxembourg (EUR 6 million in 2005) and the United Kingdom (EUR 2 billion in 2004/05).

"In Slovakia, it is estimated that total public expenditure in the field of drugs in 2004 was EUR 14.5 million, of which law enforcement accounted for approximately EUR 8.4 million and social and healthcare for EUR 6.1 million.

"In Sweden, it is estimated that drug policy expenditure during 2002 was around EUR 0.9 billion (lower estimate EUR 0.5 billion, higher estimate EUR 1.2 billion). Comparing the 2002 estimates with figures for 1991 shows that public expenditure on drug policy has increased substantially.

"In Ireland, the mid-term review of the national drug strategy, published in June 2005, recognises that 'a measure of the expenditure is vital to gauge the cost effectiveness of the different elements of the strategy', and work will commence shortly to estimate police expenditure. In Portugal, the Institute for Drug and Drug Addiction (IDT) is funding research to develop and test a model to estimate the

International Drug Facts

EUROPEAN UNION

costs of drug abuse, and in Belgium a follow-up to a 2004 study on public expenditure was instituted at the end of 2005. Although sparse, these interesting data show that research on drug expenditure constitutes an increasingly important part of the policy agenda of some Member States."

Source: "Annual Report 2006: The State of the Drugs Problem in Europe," European Monitoring Centre for Drugs and Drug Addiction (Luxembourg: Office for Official Publications of the European Communities, 2006), pp. 18-19.

6. "Differences in the prevalence of drug use are influenced by a variety of factors in each country. As countries with more liberal drug policies (such as the Netherlands) and those with a more restricted approach (such as Sweden) have not very different prevalence rates, the impact of national drug policies (more liberal versus more restrictive approaches) on the prevalence of drug use and especially problem drug use remains unclear. However, comprehensive national drug policies are of high importance in reducing adverse consequences of problem drug use such as HIV infections, hepatitis B and C and overdose deaths."

Source: European Monitoring Center for Drugs and Drug Addiction, "2001 Annual Report on the State of the Drugs Problem in the European Union" (Brussells, Belgium: Office for Official Publications of the European Communities, 2001), p. 12.

7. "In Europe, the scope of drug policies is beginning to stretch beyond illicit drugs and to encompass other addictive substances or even types of behaviour. This is found in the drug policies of some Member States and in EU drug strategies. Increasingly, research is addressing the issue of addiction or addictive behaviours irrespective of the substances concerned."

Source: "Annual Report 2006: The State of the Drugs Problem in Europe," European Monitoring Centre for Drugs and Drug Addiction (Luxembourg: Office for Official Publications of the European Communities, 2006), p. 25.

8. "It can thus be concluded that consumption trends move in different directions in the European countries in question (Norway and the 15 countries which until recently made up the EU), the result being in fact a convergence of consumption patterns: 'wine countries' reduce their wine consumption and see beer and spirits account for ever-larger shares of total alcohol consumption, while trends are the direct opposite in typical 'spirits countries'. This convergence across countries of consumption levels also brings about a convergence of alcohol-related mortality. This is true in particular of liver-cirrhosis mortality, which has been falling in the 'wine countries' of the EU and rising in the 'beer countries' while Norway, Finland and Sweden, taken together, manifest a fairly stable level."

Source: Centralförbundet för alkohol- och narkotikaupplysning, "Drogutvecklingen i Sverige 2006" (Stockholm, Sweden: CAN, 2006), Report No. 98, p. 34.

International Drug Facts

EUROPEAN UNION

9. "When it comes to alcohol policy, it seems that the 15 'old' EU member states have converged to some extent. While alcohol policy has grown weaker in Finland and Sweden, several other countries — including Southern European ones — have reinforced their policies, for instance by lowering legal blood-alcohol levels for drivers and introducing stricter age limits for purchasing alcohol in both shops and restaurants."

Source: Centralförbundet för alkohol- och narkotikaupplysning, "Drogutvecklingen i Sverige 2006" (Stockholm, Sweden: CAN, 2006), Report No. 98, p. 34.

B. Prevalence Estimates

1. "Cannabis is the illegal substance most frequently used in Europe. Its use increased in almost all EU countries during the 1990s, in particular among young people, including school students.

"It is estimated that about 65 million European adults, that is about 20% of those aged 15–64, have tried the substance at least once, although it should be remembered that most of these will not be using the substance at the present time. National figures vary widely, ranging from 2% to 31%, with the lowest figures in Malta, Bulgaria and Romania, and the highest in Denmark (31%), Spain (29%), France (26%) and the United Kingdom (30%). Of the 25 countries for which information is available, 13 presented lifetime prevalence rates in the range 10–20%."

Source: "Annual Report 2006: The State of the Drugs Problem in Europe," European Monitoring Centre for Drugs and Drug Addiction (Luxembourg: Office for Official Publications of the European Communities, 2006), p. 38.

2. "Use of illegal drugs, including cannabis, is concentrated mainly among young people. In 2004, between 3% and 44% of Europeans aged 15–34 reported having tried cannabis, 3–20% had used it in the last year, and 1.5–13% had used it in the last month, with the highest figures again coming from the Czech Republic, Spain and the United Kingdom. The European averages for this age group are 32% for lifetime use, 14% for last year use (compared with 2% for 35- to 64-year-olds) and over 7% for last month use (compared with 1% for 35- to 64-year-olds).

"Cannabis use is even higher among 15- to 24-year-olds, with lifetime prevalence ranging between 3% and 44% (most countries report figures in the range 20–40%), last year use ranging from 4% to 28% (in most countries 10–25%) (Figure 2) and last month use ranging from 1% to 15% (in most countries 5–12%), with higher rates among males than females. In the new Member States levels of cannabis use among young adults aged 15–24 are typically in the same range as those in the EU-15 Member States, but among older age groups rates of use drop substantially."

International Drug Facts

EUROPEAN UNION

Source: "Annual Report 2006: The State of the Drugs Problem in Europe," European Monitoring Centre for Drugs and Drug Addiction (Luxembourg: Office for Official Publications of the European Communities, 2006), p. 39.

3. "By contrast, in the 2004 US national survey on drug use and health (60), 40.2% of adults (defined as aged 12 years and older) reported lifetime use [of cannabis], compared with the EU average of about 20%. This is higher even than in those European countries with the highest lifetime rates (Denmark 31.3% and the United Kingdom 29.7%) although differences in last year use estimates are less marked: this figure is 10.6% in the United States compared with a European average of 7%, and several European countries reported figures similar to those found in the United States."

Source: "Annual Report 2006: The State of the Drugs Problem in Europe," European Monitoring Centre for Drugs and Drug Addiction (Luxembourg: Office for Official Publications of the European Communities, 2006), p. 39-40.

4. "Although the predominant European trend since the mid-1990s has been upward, some countries exhibit a more stable pattern. For example, although rates of cannabis use in the United Kingdom since the 1990s have been particularly high, they have remained stable over this period. In addition, there has been little change in the levels of cannabis use in several low-prevalence countries, including Finland and Sweden in the north of Europe and Greece and Malta in the south. Most of the increases in cannabis use recorded in ESPAD since 1999 have occurred in the new EU Member States. Analysis of school data and general population survey evidence suggests that, on most measures, the Czech Republic, Spain and France have now joined the United Kingdom to form a group of high-prevalence countries."

Source: "Annual Report 2005: The State of the Drugs Problem in Europe," European Monitoring Centre for Drugs and Drug Addiction (Luxembourg: Office for Official Publications of the European Communities, 2005), p. 11.

5. "In many European countries the second most commonly used illegal substance is some form of synthetically produced drug. The use of these substances among the general population is typically low, but prevalence rates among younger age groups are significantly higher, and in some social settings or cultural groups the use of these drugs may be particularly high. Globally, amphetamines (amphetamine and methamphetamine) and ecstasy are among the most prevalent synthetic drugs."

Source: "Annual Report 2006: The State of the Drugs Problem in Europe," European Monitoring Centre for Drugs and Drug Addiction (Luxembourg: Office for Official Publications of the European Communities, 2006), p. 47.

6. "Globally, Europe remains the main centre of ecstasy production, although its relative importance appears to be declining as ecstasy manufacture has spread in recent years to other parts of the world, notably

International Drug Facts

EUROPEAN UNION

to North America (United States, Canada) and East and South-East Asia (China, Indonesia, Hong Kong) (CND, 2006; UNODC, 2006). Although the Netherlands remained in 2004 the main source of ecstasy for Europe and the world as a whole, ecstasy laboratories were also uncovered in Belgium, Estonia, Spain and Norway (Reitox national reports, 2005; UNODC, 2006). The ecstasy seized in the EU is reported to originate from the Netherlands and Belgium, and to a lesser extent Poland and the United Kingdom (Reitox national reports, 2005)."

Source: "Annual Report 2006: The State of the Drugs Problem in Europe," European Monitoring Centre for Drugs and Drug Addiction (Luxembourg: Office for Official Publications of the European Communities, 2006), p. 48.

7. "Traditionally, population surveys have shown that, next to cannabis, amphetamines and ecstasy are the illegal substances most commonly used, albeit the overall prevalence of their use is lower than that of cannabis. Use of ecstasy became popular during the 1990s, whereas amphetamines have been used for much longer."

Source: "Annual Report 2006: The State of the Drugs Problem in Europe," European Monitoring Centre for Drugs and Drug Addiction (Luxembourg: Office for Official Publications of the European Communities, 2006), p. 50.

8. "Among EU Member States, use of amphetamines and ecstasy appears to be relatively high in only a few countries, namely the Czech Republic, Estonia and the United Kingdom. Recent surveys among the adult population (15–64 years) report that lifetime prevalence of amphetamine use in Europe ranges from 0.1% to 5.9%, except in the United Kingdom (England and Wales), where it reaches 11.2%. On average about 3.1% of all European adults have used amphetamines at least once. After the United Kingdom, the countries with the next highest figures are Denmark (5.9%), Norway (3.6%) and Germany (3.4%). Last year use is much lower: 0.6% on average (range 0–1.4%). Based on general population surveys, it has been estimated that almost 10 million Europeans have tried this substance, and more than 2 million will have used amphetamine in the previous 12 months."

Source: "Annual Report 2006: The State of the Drugs Problem in Europe," European Monitoring Centre for Drugs and Drug Addiction (Luxembourg: Office for Official Publications of the European Communities, 2006), pp. 50-51.

9. "Among young adults (15–34 years) experience of amphetamine use is reported by 0.1–9.6%, with the United Kingdom (England and Wales) reporting a lifetime prevalence rate of 16.5% (which may reflect a historical phenomenon, see below). Half of the countries providing data have prevalence rates below 4%, with the highest rates after the United Kingdom reported by Denmark (9.6%), Norway (5.9%) and Germany (5.4%). An average of 4.8 % of young Europeans have tried amphetamine. Denmark (3.1%) and Estonia (2.9%) report the highest last year prevalence rates. It is estimated that, on average, 1.4% of young Europeans have used amphetamine in the last year (see also Figure 4)."

International Drug Facts

EUROPEAN UNION

Source: "Annual Report 2006: The State of the Drugs Problem in Europe," European Monitoring Centre for Drugs and Drug Addiction (Luxembourg: Office for Official Publications of the European Communities, 2006), p. 51.

10. "Ecstasy has been tried by 0.2–7.1 % of all adults [in EU member nations] (average 2.6%). Half of the countries report prevalence rates of 1.8% or lower, with highest prevalence rates being reported by the Czech Republic (7.1%) and the United Kingdom (6.7%). The prevalence of last year use of ecstasy ranges from 0.2% to 3.5%, but half of the countries report prevalence rates of 0.5% or below. It has been estimated that almost 8.5 million Europeans have tried ecstasy, and almost 3 million have used it in the last year."

Source: "Annual Report 2006: The State of the Drugs Problem in Europe," European Monitoring Centre for Drugs and Drug Addiction (Luxembourg: Office for Official Publications of the European Communities, 2006), p. 51.

11. "Among young adults across the European countries, the prevalence of lifetime use of ecstasy is 5.2%, ranging from 0.5% to 14.6%, although rates of less than 3.6% are reported by half of the countries. The Czech Republic (14.6%), the United Kingdom (12.7%) and Spain (8.3%) report the highest prevalence rates."

Source: "Annual Report 2006: The State of the Drugs Problem in Europe," European Monitoring Centre for Drugs and Drug Addiction (Luxembourg: Office for Official Publications of the European Communities, 2006), p. 51.

12. "For comparison, in the 2004 US national survey on drug use and health, 4.6% of adults (defined as 12 years and older) reported lifetime experience with ecstasy and 0.8% reported last year use (the corresponding figures for the EU are 2.6% and 0.9%). Among young adults aged 16–34 years, lifetime experience was 11.3%, and last year use 2.2% (5.2% and 1.9% respectively in Europe)."

Source: "Annual Report 2006: The State of the Drugs Problem in Europe," European Monitoring Centre for Drugs and Drug Addiction (Luxembourg: Office for Official Publications of the European Communities, 2006), p. 51.

13. "Lifetime experience of the use of LSD among adults ranges from 0.2% to 5.9%, with two thirds of countries reporting prevalence rates between 0.4% and 1.7%. Among young adults (15–34 years), lifetime prevalence of LSD use ranges from 0.3% to 9%, and among the 15–24 years age group it does not exceed 4.5%. The prevalence of last year use of this drug in the 15–24 years age group is over 1% only in the Czech Republic, Estonia, Latvia, Hungary, Poland and Bulgaria."

Source: "Annual Report 2006: The State of the Drugs Problem in Europe," European Monitoring Centre for Drugs and Drug Addiction (Luxembourg: Office for Official Publications of the European Communities, 2006), p. 51.

14. "Based on recent national population surveys, it is estimated that about 10 million Europeans have tried cocaine at least once (lifetime prevalence), representing over 3% of all adults. National figures on reported use range between 0.5% and 6%, with Italy (4.6%), Spain

International Drug Facts

EUROPEAN UNION

(5.9%) and the United Kingdom (6.1%) at the upper end of this range. It is estimated that about 3.5 million adults have used cocaine in the last year, representing 1% of all adults. National figures in most countries range between 0.3% and 1%, although prevalence levels are higher in Spain (2.7%) and the United Kingdom (2%)."

Source: "Annual Report 2006: The State of the Drugs Problem in Europe," European Monitoring Centre for Drugs and Drug Addiction (Luxembourg: Office for Official Publications of the European Communities, 2006), p. 59.

15. "As with other illegal drugs, cocaine use is concentrated among young adults. Lifetime experience is highest among young adults aged 15–34 years, although last year use is slightly higher among 15- to 24-year-olds. Cocaine seems to be predominantly a drug used by those in their 20s, but, compared with cannabis use, cocaine use is less concentrated among younger people. Lifetime experience among 15- to 34-year-olds ranges from 1% to 10%, with the highest levels again found in Spain (8.9%) and the United Kingdom (10.5%). Last year use ranges between 0.2% and 4.8%, with the figures for Denmark, Ireland, Italy and the Netherlands being around 2%, and for Spain and the United Kingdom over 4% (Figure 6). Data from school surveys show very low lifetime prevalence for the use of cocaine, ranging from 0% in Cyprus, Finland and Sweden to 6% in Spain, with even lower lifetime prevalence rates for use of crack cocaine, ranging from 0% to 3% (Hibell et al., 2004)."

Source: "Annual Report 2006: The State of the Drugs Problem in Europe," European Monitoring Centre for Drugs and Drug Addiction (Luxembourg: Office for Official Publications of the European Communities, 2006), p. 59.

16. "A rough estimate of current cocaine use in Europe would be about 1.5 million adults aged 15–64 years (80% in the age range 15–34 years). This can be considered as a minimum estimate, given probable under-reporting."

Source: "Annual Report 2006: The State of the Drugs Problem in Europe," European Monitoring Centre for Drugs and Drug Addiction (Luxembourg: Office for Official Publications of the European Communities, 2006), p. 61.

17. "For comparison, according to the 2004 United States national survey on drug use and health, 14.2% of adults (defined as 12 years or older) reported lifetime experience with cocaine, which contrasts with a European average of 3%. Last year use was 2.4%, compared with a European average of 1%, although in some EU countries, e.g. Spain (2.7%) and the United Kingdom (2%), reported figures are in the same range as in the United States. The comparatively higher lifetime figures in the United States may be in part related to earlier spread of cocaine use in that country."

Source: "Annual Report 2006: The State of the Drugs Problem in Europe," European Monitoring Centre for Drugs and Drug Addiction (Luxembourg: Office for Official Publications of the European Communities, 2006), p. 61.

International Drug Facts

EUROPEAN UNION

18. "The levels and patterns of illicit drug use in the selected English-speaking countries vary considerably (Table 4.3). Marijuana/cannabis use in the last 12 months was most prevalent in Canada (17%), and least prevalent in the Republic of Ireland and Northern Ireland (5%). Ecstasy and amphetamine use was most prevalent in Australia (4%). Cocaine use was most common in the USA (3%)."

   Source: Australian Institute of Health and Welfare, "Statistics on drug use in Australia 2006" (Canberra, Australia: Australian Institute of Health and Welfare, April 2007), Drug Statistics Series No. 18., Cat. no. PHE 80, p. 25.

19. "Among young adults (aged 16–34), US figures [for cocaine use] were 14.6% (lifetime), 5.1% (last year) and 1.7% (last month), whereas the EU average figures for 15- to 34-year-olds were, respectively, about 5% (lifetime), 2% (last year) and 1% (last month)."

   Source: "Annual Report 2006: The State of the Drugs Problem in Europe," European Monitoring Centre for Drugs and Drug Addiction (Luxembourg: Office for Official Publications of the European Communities, 2006), p. 61.

20. "Recent cocaine use (last year) increased markedly in the second half of the 1990s among young adults in the United Kingdom, until 2000, and in Spain, until 2001, with an apparent stabilisation in recent years. In Germany, a moderate increase was observed over the 1990s, but the figures have remained stable in recent years, at levels clearly lower than in Spain and the United Kingdom.
   "Moderate increases in last year use have been observed in Denmark (up to 2000), Italy, Hungary, the Netherlands (up to 2001) and Norway. This trend needs to be interpreted carefully as it is based on only two surveys in each country."

   Source: "Annual Report 2006: The State of the Drugs Problem in Europe," European Monitoring Centre for Drugs and Drug Addiction (Luxembourg: Office for Official Publications of the European Communities, 2006), p. 61.

21. "In Europe, two forms of imported heroin are found: the commonly available brown heroin (its chemical base form) and the less common and usually more expensive white heroin (a salt form), which typically originates from South-East Asia. In addition, some opioid drugs are produced within the EU, but manufacture is mainly confined to small-scale production of home-made poppy products (e.g. poppy straw, poppy concentrate from crushed poppy stalks or heads) in a number of eastern EU countries, for example Lithuania, where the market for poppy stalks and concentrate seems to have stabilised, and Poland, where production of 'Polish heroin' might be decreasing (CND, 2006)."

   Source: "Annual Report 2006: The State of the Drugs Problem in Europe," European Monitoring Centre for Drugs and Drug Addiction (Luxembourg: Office for Official Publications of the European Communities, 2006), p. 66.

International Drug Facts

EUROPEAN UNION

22. "Heroin consumed in Europe is predominantly manufactured in Afghanistan, which remains the world leader in illicit opium supply and in 2005 accounted for 89% of global illicit opium production, followed by Myanmar (7%)."

> Source: "Annual Report 2006: The State of the Drugs Problem in Europe," European Monitoring Centre for Drugs and Drug Addiction (Luxembourg: Office for Official Publications of the European Communities, 2006), p. 66.

23. "Worldwide, tobacco consumption seems to have been in decline since around 1996. Per capita demand for cigarettes in the industrialised countries started to decline in the early 1980s, and while per capita demand has not declined overall in countries outside the OECD, demand growth has slowed down since about 1995, and no longer compensates for declining demand in the industrialised countries (van Liemt 2002). World unmanufactured tobacco supply was projected to decline nearly 14% in 2002 in an effort to bring supplies more in line with consumption (USDA 2002)."

> Source: Australian Institute of Health and Welfare, "Statistics on drug use in Australia 2006" (Canberra, Australia: Australian Institute of Health and Welfare, April 2007), Drug Statistics Series No. 18., Cat. no. PHE 80, p. 11.

C. Problem Substance Use and Substance-Related Harm

1. "Estimates of the prevalence of problem opioid use at national level over the period 2000–04 range between one and eight cases per 1,000 population aged 15–64 (based on midpoints of estimates). Estimated prevalence rates of problem opioid use differ greatly between countries, although when different methods have been used within one country the results are largely consistent. Higher estimates of problem opioid use are reported by Ireland, Italy, Luxembourg, Malta and Austria (5–8 cases per 1,000 inhabitants aged 15–64 years), and lower rates are reported by the Czech Republic, Germany, Greece, Cyprus, Latvia and the Netherlands (fewer than four cases per 1,000 inhabitants aged 15–64 years) (Figure 8). Some of the lowest well-documented estimates now available are from the new countries of the EU, but in Malta a higher prevalence has been reported (5.4–6.2 cases per 1,000 aged 15–64). One can derive from the limited data a general EU prevalence of problem opioid use of between two and eight cases per 1 000 of the population aged 15–64. However, these estimates are still far from robust and will need to be refined as more data become available."

> Source: "Annual Report 2006: The State of the Drugs Problem in Europe," European Monitoring Centre for Drugs and Drug Addiction (Luxembourg: Office for Official Publications of the European Communities, 2006), pp. 68-69.

2. "Reports from some countries, supported by other indicator data, suggest that problem opioid use continued to increase during the latter half of the 1990s (Figure 9) but appears to have stabilised or declined somewhat in

International Drug Facts

EUROPEAN UNION

more recent years. Repeated estimates on problem opioid use for the period between 2000 and 2004 are available from seven countries (the Czech Republic, Germany, Greece, Spain, Ireland, Italy, Austria): four countries (the Czech Republic, Germany, Greece, Spain) have recorded a decrease in problem opioid use, while one reported an increase (Austria — although this is difficult to interpret as the data collection system changed during this period). Evidence from people entering treatment for the first time suggests that the incidence of problem opioid use may in general be slowly declining; therefore in the near future a decline in prevalence is to be expected."

Source: "Annual Report 2006: The State of the Drugs Problem in Europe," European Monitoring Centre for Drugs and Drug Addiction (Luxembourg: Office for Official Publications of the European Communities, 2006), p. 69.

3. "Getting homeless problem drug users into stable accommodation is the first step towards stabilisation and rehabilitation. Based on the estimated numbers of problem drug users and the proportion of homeless people among clients in treatment, there are approximately 75,600 to 123,300 homeless problem drug users in Europe. As facilities are currently available in most countries, and as some countries continue to implement new structures, the effect of these measures will depend on ensuring that homeless problem drug users can access these services."

Source: "Annual Report 2006: The State of the Drugs Problem in Europe," European Monitoring Centre for Drugs and Drug Addiction (Luxembourg: Office for Official Publications of the European Communities, 2006), pp. 34-35.

4. "In the Baltic states, the available seroprevalence data indicate that transmission among IDUs may still not be under control (Figure 10). In Estonia, a recent study suggests that prevalence in IDUs is increasing in one region (Tallinn: from 41% of a sample of 964 in 2001 to 54% of 350 in 2005) and exceptionally high in another (Kohtla-Järve: 90 % out of 100). In Latvia, two time series of seroprevalence data among IDUs show a continued increase until 2002/03 while a third series suggests a decrease since the peak in 2001. In Lithuania, data for 2003 suggest an increase in HIV among tested IDUs in drug treatment, needle exchanges schemes and hospitals, from between 1.0% and 1.7% during 1997–2002 to 2.4% (27/1,112) in 2003."

Source: "Annual Report 2006: The State of the Drugs Problem in Europe," European Monitoring Centre for Drugs and Drug Addiction (Luxembourg: Office for Official Publications of the European Communities, 2006), pp. 75-76.

5. "In the countries that have historically had high rates of HIV infection among IDUs (Spain, France, Italy, Poland and Portugal) there are new signs of continuing transmission at national level or in specific regions or among specific subgroups of IDUs. In these countries, it is important to note that the high background prevalence, resulting from the large-scale epidemics that occurred in the 1980s and 1990s, increases the likelihood that high-risk behaviour will lead to infection."

International Drug Facts

EUROPEAN UNION

Source: "Annual Report 2006: The State of the Drugs Problem in Europe," European Monitoring Centre for Drugs and Drug Addiction (Luxembourg: Office for Official Publications of the European Communities, 2006), p. 76.

6. "HIV prevalence among tested IDUs continues to vary widely between countries in the EU (Figure 10). In a number of countries HIV prevalence among IDUs has recently increased or has been high for many years. In contrast, in several countries, HIV prevalence among IDUs remained very low during 2003–04: HIV prevalence was less than or around 1% in the Czech Republic, Greece, Hungary, Malta, Slovenia (based on national samples), and in Slovakia, Bulgaria, Romania, Turkey and Norway (based on subnational samples). In some of these countries (e.g. Hungary), both HIV prevalence and hepatitis C virus (HCV) prevalence are among the lowest in Europe, suggesting low levels of injecting (see 'Hepatitis B and C'), although in some countries (e.g. Romania) there is evidence that the prevalence of hepatitis C is increasing."

Source: "Annual Report 2006: The State of the Drugs Problem in Europe," European Monitoring Centre for Drugs and Drug Addiction (Luxembourg: Office for Official Publications of the European Communities, 2006), p. 77.

7. "The prevalence of antibodies against hepatitis C virus (HCV) among IDUs is, in general, extremely high, although there is wide variation both within and between countries. Prevalence rates of over 60% among various IDU samples tested in 2003–04 are reported from Belgium, Denmark, Germany, Greece, Spain, Ireland, Italy, Poland, Portugal, the United Kingdom, Romania and Norway, while prevalence rates less than 40% have been found in samples from Belgium, the Czech Republic, Greece, Cyprus, Hungary, Malta, Austria, Slovenia, Finland and the United Kingdom."

Source: "Annual Report 2006: The State of the Drugs Problem in Europe," European Monitoring Centre for Drugs and Drug Addiction (Luxembourg: Office for Official Publications of the European Communities, 2006), p. 77.

8. "HCV antibody prevalence data among young IDUs (aged under 25) are available from 14 countries, although in some cases sample sizes are small. There is wide variation in results, with countries reporting both high and low figures from different samples. The highest prevalence rates among young IDUs in 2003–04 (over 40%) were found in samples from Belgium, Greece, Austria, Poland, Portugal, Slovakia and the United Kingdom, and the lowest prevalence (under 20%) in samples from Belgium, Greece, Cyprus, Hungary, Malta, Austria, Slovenia, Finland, the United Kingdom and Turkey. Considering only studies of young IDUs with national coverage, the highest prevalence rates (over 60%) are found in Portugal and the lowest (under 40%) in Cyprus, Hungary, Malta, Austria and Slovenia. Although the sampling procedures used may result in bias towards a more chronic group, the high prevalence of HCV antibodies found in a national sample in Portugal (67% among 108 IDUs under 25 years) is still worrying and may be indicative of continuing high-risk behaviour among young IDUs."

International Drug Facts

EUROPEAN UNION

Source: "Annual Report 2006: The State of the Drugs Problem in Europe," European Monitoring Centre for Drugs and Drug Addiction (Luxembourg: Office for Official Publications of the European Communities, 2006), pp. 77-78.

D. Harm Reduction Efforts

1. "Harm reduction strategies form an important part of the European response to drug use today, and improving access to services for the prevention and reduction of health-related harm is a main priority of the EU drug strategy 2005–12. The common strategic platform on the reduction of health related harm that the EU drug strategy provides is mirrored in many national policies across the EU and has supported a mainstreaming of evidence-based responses in this area."

   Source: "Annual Report 2006: The State of the Drugs Problem in Europe," European Monitoring Centre for Drugs and Drug Addiction (Luxembourg: Office for Official Publications of the European Communities, 2006), p. 33.

2. "Experiences in some Member States suggest that drug prevention interventions at the individual level may be more effective if also supported by regulatory policies on legal drugs that can limit the access of young people to these substances and reduce their social acceptability. As a result, environmental prevention strategies that address the normative and cultural framework of substance use are gaining ground in parts of Europe, supported by the first steps taken at EU level: the tobacco advertisement directive and the WHO framework convention on tobacco control."

   Source: "Annual Report 2006: The State of the Drugs Problem in Europe," European Monitoring Centre for Drugs and Drug Addiction (Luxembourg: Office for Official Publications of the European Communities, 2006), p. 27.

3. "While health promotion — as a framework condition for prevention — strives to encourage people to adopt healthy lifestyles and to create healthy living conditions for all, the new term 'public health prevention' is increasingly mentioned by some Member States (Italy, Netherlands, Slovakia) and Norway. Public health prevention entails a range of prevention measures aimed at improving the health of vulnerable sections of society, among which drug prevention is one element. These measures are particularly suited to the needs of young people, whose problem behaviours, including drug use, are strongly conditioned by vulnerability (social and personal) and by living conditions."

   Source: "Annual Report 2006: The State of the Drugs Problem in Europe," European Monitoring Centre for Drugs and Drug Addiction (Luxembourg: Office for Official Publications of the European Communities, 2006), p. 27.

4. "The reduction of drug-related deaths was defined for the first time as a European drug policy objective six years ago, and it is an objective of the current EU action plan. The number of countries which include a direct reference to the target of reducing drug-related deaths in their national policies

International Drug Facts

EUROPEAN UNION

has continued to increase in recent years, with eight countries adopting such strategies during 2004 and 2005 (bringing the total number to 15). Besides national policies, complementary approaches at city level are common: several capital cities (including Athens, Berlin, Brussels, Lisbon and Tallinn) but also wider semi-urban regions (e.g. the eastern region of Ireland, around Dublin) have their own strategies for reducing drug-related deaths. In the Czech Republic, Italy, the Netherlands and the United Kingdom, local or regional policies are reported to exist, and in Bulgaria strategies have been drawn up at local level in nine cities."

Source: "Annual Report 2006: The State of the Drugs Problem in Europe," European Monitoring Centre for Drugs and Drug Addiction (Luxembourg: Office for Official Publications of the European Communities, 2006), p. 31.

5. "In many EU countries, strategies aimed at reducing infectious disease are clearly geared towards HIV/AIDS, particularly Estonia, Spain, Cyprus, Latvia and Lithuania. However, in 10 countries (37%), infectious disease strategies explicitly mention the prevention of hepatitis C infection among drug users. Ireland launched a consultation process in 2004, preparing such a strategy, and in Germany recommendations on prevention and treatment were issued. Professional and public discussion in Austria was boosted by an international conference on the topic held in Vienna in 2005."

Source: "Annual Report 2006: The State of the Drugs Problem in Europe," European Monitoring Centre for Drugs and Drug Addiction (Luxembourg: Office for Official Publications of the European Communities, 2006), pp. 32-33.

6. "Although most European countries now distribute sterile injecting equipment, the nature and range of provision vary between countries. The most common model is to provide the service in a fixed location, usually a specialised drugs service, but often this type of provision is complemented by mobile services that attempt to reach out to drug users in community settings. Syringe exchange or vending machines complement the available NSP services in eight countries, although provision appears to be restricted to a handful of sites, with only Germany and France reporting substantial activities (around 200 and 250 machines respectively). Spain is the only EU country where needle and syringe exchange is regularly available in a prison setting, with provision available in 27 prisons in 2003. The only other EU country reporting activity in this area is Germany, where provision is limited to one prison."

Source: "Annual Report 2006: The State of the Drugs Problem in Europe," European Monitoring Centre for Drugs and Drug Addiction (Luxembourg: Office for Official Publications of the European Communities, 2006), p. 79.

7. "Pharmacy-based exchange schemes also help to extend the geographical coverage of the provision and, in addition, the sale of clean syringes in pharmacies may increase their availability. The sale of syringes without prescription is permitted in all EU countries except Sweden, although some pharmacists are unwilling to do so and some will even actively discourage drug users from patronising their premises."

International Drug Facts

EUROPEAN UNION

Source: "Annual Report 2006: The State of the Drugs Problem in Europe," European Monitoring Centre for Drugs and Drug Addiction (Luxembourg: Office for Official Publications of the European Communities, 2006), p. 79.

8. "Formally organised pharmacy syringe exchange or distribution networks exist in nine European countries (Belgium, Denmark, Germany, Spain, France, the Netherlands, Portugal, Slovenia and the United Kingdom), although participation in the schemes varies considerably, from nearly half of pharmacies (45%) in Portugal to less than 1% in Belgium. In Northern Ireland, needle and syringe exchange is currently organised exclusively through pharmacies."

Source: "Annual Report 2006: The State of the Drugs Problem in Europe," European Monitoring Centre for Drugs and Drug Addiction (Luxembourg: Office for Official Publications of the European Communities, 2006), p. 79.

9. "The purchase of syringes through pharmacies may be a major source of contact with the health service for some injectors, and the potential to exploit this contact point as a conduit to other services clearly exists. Work to motivate and support pharmacists to develop the services they offer to drug users could form an important part of extending the role of pharmacies, but to date only France, Portugal and the United Kingdom appear to be making significant investments in this direction."

Source: "Annual Report 2006: The State of the Drugs Problem in Europe," European Monitoring Centre for Drugs and Drug Addiction (Luxembourg: Office for Official Publications of the European Communities, 2006), p. 79.

10. "As a result of the serious health and social problems associated with crack cocaine use, there is more experience of developing services for this group, although activities are limited to those relatively few cities in Europe that have experienced a significant crack cocaine problem. In a number of cities crack cocaine users have been targeted by outreach schemes that attempt to engage with what is often viewed as a difficult group to work with. Although overall the evidence base remains relatively weak, some studies have suggested that benefits can accrue. For example, one study of an innovative outreach treatment programme in Rotterdam (Henskens, 2004, cited in the Dutch national report) identified factors that were observed to be important for treating this group of clients, who are often difficult to engage in conventional drug services."

Source: "Annual Report 2006: The State of the Drugs Problem in Europe," European Monitoring Centre for Drugs and Drug Addiction (Luxembourg: Office for Official Publications of the European Communities, 2006), p. 64.

11. "A more controversial approach has been adopted in some cities in Europe, where the concept of safe consumption rooms, usually targeting drug injection, has been extended to drug inhalation. Rooms for supervised inhalation have been opened in several Dutch, German and Swiss cities (EMCDDA, 2004c). Although the supervision of

International Drug Facts

EUROPEAN UNION

consumption hygiene is a main objective of such services, there is some evidence that they could also act as a conduit to other care options; for example, monitoring of one service in Frankfurt, Germany, reported that, during a six-month evaluation period in 2004, more than 1,400 consumptions were supervised, while 332 contact talks, 40 counselling sessions and 99 referrals to other drugs services were documented."

Source: "Annual Report 2006: The State of the Drugs Problem in Europe," European Monitoring Centre for Drugs and Drug Addiction (Luxembourg: Office for Official Publications of the European Communities, 2006), p. 64.

12. "Despite the overall expansion of treatment options, engaging with some groups of drug users, particularly those with long-term and chronic problems, remains a challenge for drug services. Outreach and low-threshold interventions are common approaches to attempting to make contact and engage with these hard-to-reach populations. A more controversial approach is the development in some countries of supervised drug consumption rooms mostly targeting drug injectors but now sometimes also extending provision to crack cocaine or heroin smoking (see EMCDDA, 2004c). Another controversial area of service development and experimentation is the use of heroin by a few countries as an agent for drug substitution treatment. Although, overall, activities in this area remain very limited compared with other treatment options, some studies have suggested that heroin prescribing may have potential benefits for clients where methadone maintenance treatment has failed. For example, a recent German randomised controlled trial of heroin-assisted treatment (Naber and Haasen, 2006) reported positive outcomes in terms of both health and reductions in use of illicit drugs. Nonetheless, no clear consensus currently exists across Europe on the cost and benefits of this approach and it remains an area where there is considerable political and scientific debate."

Source: "Annual Report 2006: The State of the Drugs Problem in Europe," European Monitoring Centre for Drugs and Drug Addiction (Luxembourg: Office for Official Publications of the European Communities, 2006), pp. 33-34.

13. "In the EU Member States, problem drug users can access social measures through facilities either exclusively dedicated to drug users or targeting socially deprived groups. Among these measures, housing is one of the key pillars. The service most commonly offered to homeless problem drug users is access to 'generic housing services' (in 21 countries), while 18 countries offer housing facilities solely for problem drug users and 13 countries combine the two systems. However, there are doubts about the effective access of homeless problem drug users to these facilities. Low availability, local resistance to providing drug users with new facilities, restricted criteria for access and difficulties for homeless problem drug users in sticking to the rules are among the problems reported."

International Drug Facts

EUROPEAN UNION

Source: "Annual Report 2006: The State of the Drugs Problem in Europe," European Monitoring Centre for Drugs and Drug Addiction (Luxembourg: Office for Official Publications of the European Communities, 2006), p. 34.

E. Treatment

1. "Substitution therapy for opioid dependence (mainly treatment with methadone or buprenorphine) is in place in all EU Member States as well as Bulgaria, Romania and Norway, and there is now a substantial European consensus that it is a beneficial approach to the treatment of problem opioid users, although in some countries it remains a sensitive topic (see Chapter 2). The role of substitution treatment is becoming less controversial internationally; the UN system came to a joint position on substitution maintenance therapy in 2004 (WHO/UNODC/UNAIDS, 2004), and in June 2006 WHO included both methadone and buprenorphine in its model list of essential medicines."

Source: "Annual Report 2006: The State of the Drugs Problem in Europe," European Monitoring Centre for Drugs and Drug Addiction (Luxembourg: Office for Official Publications of the European Communities, 2006), p. 72.

2. "While methadone continues to be the most commonly prescribed substitution treatment in Europe, treatment options are still expanding, and buprenorphine is now available in 19 EU countries, Bulgaria and Norway, although it is not clear whether it is officially approved for maintenance treatment in all countries where it is reported to be used. Considering that high-dosage buprenorphine treatment was introduced in Europe only 10 years ago, the drug's popularity as a therapeutic option has developed remarkably quickly (see Figure 1)."

Source: "Annual Report 2006: The State of the Drugs Problem in Europe," European Monitoring Centre for Drugs and Drug Addiction (Luxembourg: Office for Official Publications of the European Communities, 2006), p. 72.

3. "Some countries (Germany, Spain, the Netherlands and the United Kingdom) also have heroin prescription programmes, although the number of patients receiving this kind of treatment is very small compared with other forms of drug substitution (probably constituting less than 1% of the total). This form of treatment remains controversial and is generally provided on a scientific trial basis for long-term users in whom other therapeutic options have failed."

Source: "Annual Report 2006: The State of the Drugs Problem in Europe," European Monitoring Centre for Drugs and Drug Addiction (Luxembourg: Office for Official Publications of the European Communities, 2006), p. 72.

4. "It is estimated that in the EU more than half a million opioid users received substitution treatment in 2003, which represents one third of the currently estimated 1.5 million problem opioid users (EMCDDA, 2005a). The new Member States and candidate countries account for only a small fraction of the clients in substitution treatment in the European region, which can partly be explained by lower levels of opioid use in these countries. Although the overall provision of substitution treatment remains low in these countries, there are some indications of increases in Estonia, Lithuania and Bulgaria."

International Drug Facts

EUROPEAN UNION

Source: "Annual Report 2006: The State of the Drugs Problem in Europe," European Monitoring Centre for Drugs and Drug Addiction (Luxembourg: Office for Official Publications of the European Communities, 2006), p. 30.

5. "Over the last decade, but even more so in the last five years, many European countries have 'opened the doors' to treatment by expanding their provision of substitution treatment and reducing access limitations. Never before have such large numbers of drug users been reached by the system of care. Many but not all require assistance beyond the treatment of their dependency, and many seem to need low-threshold care as well as substantial support for their reintegration."

Source: "Annual Report 2006: The State of the Drugs Problem in Europe," European Monitoring Centre for Drugs and Drug Addiction (Luxembourg: Office for Official Publications of the European Communities, 2006), p. 31.

6. "A survey conducted among national focal points (NFPs) in 2005 assessed the general characteristics of treatment provision in Europe. National experts were asked whether the majority of opioid users were treated in drug-free or medically assisted programmes or whether both modalities were equally prevalent.

   "The results show a ratio largely in favour of medically assisted treatment, with the main substance used being methadone (except in the Czech Republic and France; for more details see Chapter 6). The results further show that drug-related treatment in most countries is predominantly provided in outpatient settings — only Latvia and Turkey provide most treatment in inpatient settings. Traditional psychotherapeutic treatment modalities (psychodynamic, cognitive-behavioural, systemic/family therapy or Gestalt therapy) are the most frequently used modalities in outpatient treatment in Ireland, Latvia, the United Kingdom, Bulgaria and Turkey. Nine countries report the provision of predominantly 'supportive' methods (which can include counselling, socio-educative and environmental therapy, motivational interviewing or relaxation techniques and acupuncture), and 10 countries combine the different methods in their outpatient work."

Source: "Annual Report 2006: The State of the Drugs Problem in Europe," European Monitoring Centre for Drugs and Drug Addiction (Luxembourg: Office for Official Publications of the European Communities, 2006), p. 31.

7. "Concerning inpatient care, the 12-step Minnesota model is frequently used in residential care in Ireland, Lithuania, Hungary and Turkey, while six countries predominantly apply psychotherapeutic treatment modalities, five countries 'supportive' methods and 10 countries a combination of such approaches."

Source: "Annual Report 2006: The State of the Drugs Problem in Europe," European Monitoring Centre for Drugs and Drug Addiction (Luxembourg: Office for Official Publications of the European Communities, 2006), p. 31.

International Drug Facts

EUROPEAN UNION

8. "Treatment units or programmes that exclusively service one specified target group are a common phenomenon across the EU. Children and young people under the age of 18 are treated in specialised agencies in 23 countries; the treatment of drug users with psychiatric co-morbidity takes place in specialised agencies in 18 countries; and women-specific services are reported to exist in all countries except Cyprus, Latvia, Lithuania, Bulgaria and Turkey. Services designed to meet the needs of immigrant drug users or of groups with specific language requirements or religious or cultural backgrounds are less common but have been reported from Belgium, Germany, Greece, Spain, Lithuania, the Netherlands, Finland, Sweden and the United Kingdom."

Source: "Annual Report 2006: The State of the Drugs Problem in Europe," European Monitoring Centre for Drugs and Drug Addiction (Luxembourg: Office for Official Publications of the European Communities, 2006), p. 33.

9. "The development of 'safer' substitution products (i.e. substances less likely to be diverted into the black market) makes it likely that drug dependency treatment will move even further towards the GP's surgery. This is also a process of normalisation, which allows drug dependency to be treated like a chronic disease such as diabetes."

Source: "Annual Report 2006: The State of the Drugs Problem in Europe," European Monitoring Centre for Drugs and Drug Addiction (Luxembourg: Office for Official Publications of the European Communities, 2006), p. 34.

10. "Some countries report that the large groups of heroin users in substitution treatment create a corresponding demand for social reintegration support, especially for paid work. Under the current economic circumstances, many countries may find it difficult to meet the vocational reintegration needs of older heroin users, even if they are stabilised in drug maintenance treatment. This situation is aggravated by the high levels of morbidity among this group."

Source: "Annual Report 2006: The State of the Drugs Problem in Europe," European Monitoring Centre for Drugs and Drug Addiction (Luxembourg: Office for Official Publications of the European Communities, 2006), p. 34.

F. Substance Use and the Justice System

1. "Over the five-year period 1999–2004, the number of 'reports' of drug law offences increased overall in most EU countries (in fact in all reporting countries except Italy and Portugal, with particularly marked increases — twofold or more — in Estonia, Lithuania, Hungary and Poland). In 2004, this increasing trend was confirmed in most reporting countries, although a few countries reported a fall over the previous year — the Czech Republic, Greece, Latvia, Luxembourg, Portugal, Slovenia (since 2001), Slovakia, Finland and Bulgaria."

Source: "Annual Report 2006: The State of the Drugs Problem in Europe," European Monitoring Centre for Drugs and Drug Addiction (Luxembourg: Office for Official Publications of the European Communities, 2006), pp. 23-24.

International Drug Facts

EUROPEAN UNION

2. "In most EU Member States the majority of reported drug law offences are related to drug use or possession for use, ranging in 2004 from 61% of all drug law offences in Poland to 90% in Austria. In the Czech Republic, Luxembourg, the Netherlands and Turkey, most reported drug law offences relate to dealing or trafficking, with the proportion varying from 48% of all drug offences in Luxembourg to 93% in the Czech Republic."

   Source: "Annual Report 2006: The State of the Drugs Problem in Europe," European Monitoring Centre for Drugs and Drug Addiction (Luxembourg: Office for Official Publications of the European Communities, 2006), p. 24.

3. "Over the same five-year period [1999-2004], the number of offences for use/possession for use increased overall in all reporting countries, except Italy, Portugal, Slovenia, Bulgaria and Turkey, which reported a declining trend. The share of all drug law offences accounted for by these offences also increased in most reporting countries over the period, although the rate of increase was generally low, except in Cyprus, Poland and Finland, where more marked upward trends were reported. However, in Luxembourg, Portugal, Bulgaria and Turkey, the proportion of drug offences related to use/possession for use fell overall."

   Source: "Annual Report 2006: The State of the Drugs Problem in Europe," European Monitoring Centre for Drugs and Drug Addiction (Luxembourg: Office for Official Publications of the European Communities, 2006), p. 24.

4. "In most of the Member States, cannabis is the illicit drug most often involved in reported drug law offences. In the countries where this is the case, cannabis-related offences in 2004 accounted for 34–87% of all drug law offences. In the Czech Republic and Lithuania, amphetamines-related offences predominated, accounting, respectively, for 50% and 31% of all drug law offences; while in Luxembourg cocaine is the most reported substance (in 43% of drug law offences)."

   Source: "Annual Report 2006: The State of the Drugs Problem in Europe," European Monitoring Centre for Drugs and Drug Addiction (Luxembourg: Office for Official Publications of the European Communities, 2006), p. 24.

5. "In 1999–2004, the number of 'reports' of drug law offences involving cannabis increased overall in the majority of reporting countries, while decreases were evident in Italy and Slovenia. Over the same period, the proportion of drug offences involving cannabis increased in Germany, Spain, France, Lithuania, Luxembourg, Portugal, the United Kingdom and Bulgaria, while it remained stable overall in Ireland and the Netherlands, and decreased in Belgium, Italy, Austria, Slovenia and Sweden. Although in all reporting countries (except in the Czech Republic and Bulgaria and for a few years in Belgium) cannabis is more predominant in offences for use/possession than in other drug law offences, the proportion of use-related offences involving cannabis has decreased since 1999 in several countries — namely Italy, Cyprus (2002–04), Austria, Slovenia and Turkey (2002–04) — and has fallen over the last year (2003–04) in most reporting countries, possibly indicating a reduced targeting of cannabis users by law enforcement agencies in these countries."

International Drug Facts

EUROPEAN UNION

Source: "Annual Report 2006: The State of the Drugs Problem in Europe," European Monitoring Centre for Drugs and Drug Addiction (Luxembourg: Office for Official Publications of the European Communities, 2006), p. 24.

6. "Over the same five-year period, the number of 'reports' and/or the proportion of drug law offences involving heroin decreased in the majority of reporting countries, except Belgium, Austria, Slovenia and Sweden, which reported upward trends in the number of 'reports' involving heroin and/or the proportion of drug offences that involved heroin.

"The opposite trend can be observed for cocaine-related offences: in terms of both number of 'reports' and the proportion of all drug offences, cocaine-related offences have increased since 1999 in most reporting countries. Bulgaria is the only country to report a downward trend in cocaine offences (both numbers and proportions of drug offences)."

Source: "Annual Report 2006: The State of the Drugs Problem in Europe," European Monitoring Centre for Drugs and Drug Addiction (Luxembourg: Office for Official Publications of the European Communities, 2006), p. 24.

7. "In 2004, an estimated 60,000 seizures of 74 tonnes of cocaine were made in the EU. Most seizures of cocaine are reported in western European countries, especially Spain, which accounts for about half the seizures and amounts recovered in the EU in the last five years. Over the period 1999–2004, the number of cocaine seizures increased overall at EU level, while quantities seized fluctuated within an upward trend. However, based on reporting countries, quantities appear to have declined in 2004 — perhaps in comparison with the exceptional amount recovered in Spain the year before."

Source: "Annual Report 2006: The State of the Drugs Problem in Europe," European Monitoring Centre for Drugs and Drug Addiction (Luxembourg: Office for Official Publications of the European Communities, 2006), p. 58.

8. "In 2004, the average retail price of cocaine varied widely across the EU, from EUR 41 per gram in Belgium to over EUR 100 per gram in Cyprus, Romania and Norway. The average prices of cocaine, corrected for inflation, showed an overall downward trend over the period 1999–2004 in all reporting countries except Luxembourg, where it declined until 2002 and then increased, and Norway, where prices rose sharply in 2001 and then stabilised."

Source: "Annual Report 2006: The State of the Drugs Problem in Europe," European Monitoring Centre for Drugs and Drug Addiction (Luxembourg: Office for Official Publications of the European Communities, 2006), pp. 58-59.

9. "Compared with heroin, the average purity of cocaine at user level [in the EU] is high, varying in 2004 from 24% in Denmark to 80% in Poland, with most countries reporting purities of 40–65%. Data available for 1999–2004 indicate an overall decrease in the average purity of cocaine in most reporting countries, although it increased in Estonia (since 2003), France and Lithuania, and remained stable in Luxembourg and Austria."

International Drug Facts

EUROPEAN UNION

Source: "Annual Report 2006: The State of the Drugs Problem in Europe," European Monitoring Centre for Drugs and Drug Addiction (Luxembourg: Office for Official Publications of the European Communities, 2006), p. 59.

10. "In 2004, the average retail price of brown heroin varied widely across Europe, from EUR 12 per gram in Turkey to EUR 141 per gram in Sweden, while that of white heroin varied between EUR 31 per gram in Belgium and EUR 202 per gram in Sweden, and the price of heroin of type undistinguished ranged from EUR 35 per gram in Slovenia to EUR 82 per gram in the United Kingdom. Data available for 1999–2004 show a decrease in the average price of heroin, corrected for inflation, in most reporting countries."

Source: "Annual Report 2006: The State of the Drugs Problem in Europe," European Monitoring Centre for Drugs and Drug Addiction (Luxembourg: Office for Official Publications of the European Communities, 2006), p. 67.

11. "The average purity of brown heroin at user level varied in 2004 from 10% in Bulgaria to 48% in Turkey, while that of white heroin varied between 20% in Germany and 63% in Denmark, and that of heroin of type undistinguished ranged from 16% in Hungary to 42–50% in the Netherlands. The average purity of heroin products has been fluctuating in most reporting countries since 1999, making it difficult to identify any overall trend."

Source: "Annual Report 2006: The State of the Drugs Problem in Europe," European Monitoring Centre for Drugs and Drug Addiction (Luxembourg: Office for Official Publications of the European Communities, 2006), p. 67.

12. "Data on drug use among the prison population in the last five years (1999–2004) were provided by most European countries (1). They show that, compared with the general population, drug users are overrepresented in prison. The proportion of detainees who report ever having used an illicit drug varies among prisons and detention centres, but average rates range from one third or less in Hungary and Bulgaria to two thirds or more in the Netherlands, the United Kingdom and Norway, with most countries reporting lifetime prevalence rates of around 50% (Belgium, Greece, Latvia, Portugal, Finland). Cannabis remains the most frequently used illicit drug, with lifetime prevalence rates among prisoners ranging between 4% and 86%, compared with lifetime prevalence rates of 3–57% for cocaine, 2–59% for amphetamines and 4–60% for heroin."

Source: "Annual Report 2006: The State of the Drugs Problem in Europe," European Monitoring Centre for Drugs and Drug Addiction (Luxembourg: Office for Official Publications of the European Communities, 2006), p. 69.

13. "Although the majority of drug users reduce or stop their drug use after incarceration, some detainees continue and others start using drugs (and/or injecting drugs) while in prison. According to available studies,

International Drug Facts

EUROPEAN UNION / AUSTRALIA

8–51% of inmates have used drugs within prison, 10–42% report regular drug use and 1–15% have injected drugs while in prison. This raises issues around the potential spread of infectious diseases, in particular in relation to access to sterile injection equipment and sharing practices among the prison population."

> Source: "Annual Report 2006: The State of the Drugs Problem in Europe," European Monitoring Centre for Drugs and Drug Addiction (Luxembourg: Office for Official Publications of the European Communities, 2006), p. 69.

14. On average per year from 1999 to 2001, the homicide rate in the European Union was 1.59 homicides per 100,000 population.

> Source: Barclay, Gordon & Cynthia Tavares, "International Comparisons of Criminal Justice Statistics 2001," Home Office Bulletin 12/03 (London, England, UK: Home Office Research, Development, and Statistics Directorate, October 24, 2003), p. 10, Table 1.1.

AUSTRALIA

A. Overview

1. "The National Drug Strategy 2004–2009 (NDS) provides a framework for a coordinated and integrated approach to drug issues in the Australian community. The MCDS has responsibility for the implementation of the NDS. The NDS is complemented, supported and integrated with a range of national, State and Territory government and non-government strategies, plans and initiatives.
"The mission of the NDS is 'to improve health, social and economic outcomes by preventing the uptake of harmful drug use and reducing the harmful effects of licit and illicit drugs in Australian society'.
"The challenge for all levels of government, the community and non-government organisations (NGOs) is to work together on these objectives to improve health, social and economic outcomes by preventing the uptake of harmful drug use and reducing the harmful effects of licit and illicit drugs in Australian society."

> Source: Intergovernmental Committee on Drugs, "National Drug Strategy 2004-2009: Annual Report July 2004-June 2005 to the Ministerial Council on Drug Strategy" (Canberra, Australia: Drug Strategy Branch, Australian Government Dept. of Health and Ageing, Dec. 2006), p. 5.

2. "The principle of harm minimisation has formed the basis of successive phases of Australia's National Drug Strategy since its inception in 1985.
"Harm minimisation does not condone drug use, rather it refers to policies and programs aimed at reducing drug-related harm. It aims to improve health, social and economic outcomes for both the community and the individual, and encompasses a wide range of approaches, including abstinence-oriented strategies.

International Drug Facts

AUSTRALIA

Source: Ministerial Council on Drug Strategy, "The National Drug Strategy: Australia's Integrated Framework 2004-2009" (Canberra, Australia: Drug Strategy Branch, Dept. of Health and Ageing, May 2004), p. 2.

3. "Australia's harm-minimisation strategy focuses on both licit and illicit drugs and includes preventing anticipated harm and reducing actual harm. Harm minimisation is consistent with a comprehensive approach to drug-related harm, involving a balance between demand reduction, supply reduction and harm reduction strategies. It encompasses:
"supply reduction strategies to disrupt the production and supply of illicit drugs, and the control and regulation of licit substances;
"demand reduction strategies to prevent the uptake of harmful drug use, including abstinence orientated strategies and treatment to reduce drug use; and
"harm reduction strategies to reduce drug-related harm to individuals and communities."

Source: Ministerial Council on Drug Strategy, "The National Drug Strategy: Australia's Integrated Framework 2004-2009" (Canberra, Australia: Drug Strategy Branch, Dept. of Health and Ageing, May 2004), p. 2.

4. "The success of Australia's drug policy is based on four features:
"the principle of harm minimisation, which recognises the need to use a wide range of approaches in dealing with drug related harm, including supply-reduction, demand-reduction (including abstinence oriented interventions) and harm-reduction strategies;
"the comprehensiveness of the approach, encompassing the harmful use of licit drugs (tobacco, alcohol and pharmaceutical drugs), illicit drugs and other substances (inhalants, kava);
"the promotion of partnerships between health, law enforcement and education agencies, affected communities, business and industry in tackling drug-related harm;
"a balanced approach — across all levels of government — between supply-reduction, demand-reduction and harm-reduction strategies, between preventing use and harms, and facilitating access to treatment."

Source: Ministerial Council on Drug Strategy, "The National Drug Strategy: Australia's Integrated Framework 2004-2009" (Canberra, Australia: Drug Strategy Branch, Dept. of Health and Ageing, May 2004), p. 11.

5. "According to the Australian Institute of Health and Welfare (AIHW) Australia's Health 2004 report, in 2000–01 expenditure on public health activities relating to the prevention of hazardous and harmful drug use in Australia was approximately $146.2 million."

Source: Intergovernmental Committee on Drugs, "National Drug Strategy 2004-2009: Annual Report July 2004-June 2005 to the Ministerial Council on Drug Strategy" (Canberra, Australia: Drug Strategy Branch, Australian Government Dept. of Health and Ageing, Dec. 2006), p. 7.

International Drug Facts

AUSTRALIA

B. Prevalence Estimates

1. "Based on responses to the 2004 NDSHS [National Drug Strategy Household Survey], 38% of Australians aged 14 years and over had used any illicit drug at least once in their lifetime, and 15% had used any illicit drug at least once in the last 12 months."

   Source: Australian Institute of Health and Welfare, "Statistics on drug use in Australia 2006" (Canberra, Australia: Australian Institute of Health and Welfare, April 2007), Drug Statistics Series No. 18., Cat. no. PHE 80, p. xi.

2. "The six most common illicit drugs used in the previous 12 months were marijuana/cannabis (11%), ecstasy, meth/amphetamine, and pain-killers/analgesics for non-medical purposes (all 3%), tranquillisers/sleeping pills and cocaine (1%)"

   Source: Australian Institute of Health and Welfare, "Statistics on drug use in Australia 2006" (Canberra, Australia: Australian Institute of Health and Welfare, April 2007), Drug Statistics Series No. 18., Cat. no. PHE 80, p. 21.

3. "Marijuana/cannabis was the most common illicit drug used, with one in three persons (34%) having used it at least once in their lifetime and 11% of the population having used it in the previous 12 months."

   Source: Australian Institute of Health and Welfare, "Statistics on drug use in Australia 2006" (Canberra, Australia: Australian Institute of Health and Welfare, April 2007), Drug Statistics Series No. 18., Cat. no. PHE 80, p. xi.

4. "Methamphetamine use was relatively uncommon in Australia in 2004: around 3% aged 14 years and over had used it in the last 12 months and 9% in their lifetime. Powder was the most common form of methamphetamine used (74%). The majority of users reported taking the drug in their own home or at a friend's house (66%)."

   Source: Australian Institute of Health and Welfare, "Statistics on drug use in Australia 2006" (Canberra, Australia: Australian Institute of Health and Welfare, April 2007), Drug Statistics Series No. 18., Cat. no. PHE 80, p. xi.

5. "The proportion of the population who had used any illicit drug in the last 12 months fluctuated between 1991 and 2004, reaching the same level in 2004 as the prevalence in 1991 (15%). While the proportion of people who had recently used marijuana/cannabis in 2004 (11%) was the lowest over this 13-year period, the proportion using ecstasy (3%) was the highest for that substance in the same period."

   Source: Australian Institute of Health and Welfare, "Statistics on drug use in Australia 2006" (Canberra, Australia: Australian Institute of Health and Welfare, April 2007), Drug Statistics Series No. 18., Cat. no. PHE 80, p. xi.

6. "The average age of first use of illicit drugs ranged from 18.6 years for inhalants, to 25.2 years for tranquillisers/sleeping pills and steroids for non-medical purposes. The average age of initiation was 18.7 years for marijuana/cannabis, 20.8 years for meth/amphetamine and 22.8 years for ecstasy."

International Drug Facts

AUSTRALIA

Source: Australian Institute of Health and Welfare, "Statistics on drug use in Australia 2006" (Canberra, Australia: Australian Institute of Health and Welfare, April 2007), Drug Statistics Series No. 18., Cat. no. PHE 80, p. 21.

7. "The overall prevalence of tobacco smoking in Australia is in decline, a trend which contributes to Australia being considered an international leader in tobacco control. Australians have decreased their daily tobacco use to 17.4 per cent in 2004 compared to 19.5 per cent in 2001 (NDSHS, AIHW 2004). This is among the lowest of any country in the world.

   "Even though these results are positive, tobacco remains the single largest preventable cause of disease and premature death in Australia and kills over 19,000 Australians each year. It is estimated to cost the Australian community approximately $21 billion in social costs per year."

   Source: Intergovernmental Committee on Drugs, "National Drug Strategy 2004-2009: Annual Report July 2004-June 2005 to the Ministerial Council on Drug Strategy" (Canberra, Australia: Drug Strategy Branch, Australian Government Dept. of Health and Ageing, Dec. 2006), p. 7.

8. "In 2004, around 84% of the population aged 14 years and over had consumed at least one full serve of alcohol in the last 12 months. People were most likely to drink either weekly (41%) or less than weekly (34%); 9% of Australians consumed alcohol on a daily basis. People aged 60 years and over recorded the highest prevalence of daily drinking (17%).

   "The pattern of alcohol consumption by the Australian population has remained relatively unchanged over the period 1991 to 2004."

   Source: Australian Institute of Health and Welfare, "Statistics on drug use in Australia 2006" (Canberra, Australia: Australian Institute of Health and Welfare, April 2007), Drug Statistics Series No. 18., Cat. no. PHE 80, p. x.

C. Problem Substance Use and Substance-Related Harm

1. "In 2003, it was estimated that 8% of the burden of disease in Australia was attributable to tobacco use and 2% to illicit drug use. Three per cent of the total burden of disease was attributable to alcohol consumption. However, alcohol was also estimated to prevent 1% of the burden of disease in 2003."

   Source: Australian Institute of Health and Welfare, "Statistics on drug use in Australia 2006" (Canberra, Australia: Australian Institute of Health and Welfare, April 2007), Drug Statistics Series No. 18., Cat. no. PHE 80, p. xi.

2. "Begg et al. (forthcoming) estimate that illicit drug use was responsible for 2% of the total burden of disease in Australia in 2003. There were 1,705 deaths and almost 51,500 DALYs [disability-adjusted life years] attributable to illicit drug use."

   Source: Australian Institute of Health and Welfare, "Statistics on drug use in Australia 2006" (Canberra, Australia: Australian Institute of Health and Welfare, April 2007), Drug Statistics Series No. 18., Cat. no. PHE 80, p. 36.

International Drug Facts

AUSTRALIA

3. "According to the annual Needle and Syringe Program (NSP) Survey, hepatitis C prevalence among people attending needle and syringe programs remained high over the period 1997 to 2005, at around 60%."

   Source: Australian Institute of Health and Welfare, "Statistics on drug use in Australia 2006" (Canberra, Australia: Australian Institute of Health and Welfare, April 2007), Drug Statistics Series No. 18., Cat. no. PHE 80, p. xi.

4. "Hepatitis C was the major condition for deaths attributable to illicit drug use in 2003 (759 deaths), followed by hepatitis B (329 deaths). Hepatitis C was also responsible for a significant proportion of DALYs attributable to illicit drugs (11,709 DALYs), while the main contributor was heroin/polydrug use (16,758 DALYs)."

   Source: Australian Institute of Health and Welfare, "Statistics on drug use in Australia 2006" (Canberra, Australia: Australian Institute of Health and Welfare, April 2007), Drug Statistics Series No. 18., Cat. no. PHE 80, p. xi.

5. "The number of new AIDS diagnoses in Australia among people who had a history of injecting drug use (including male homosexual contact and injecting drug use) varied over time from 31 diagnoses in 1997 down to 17 in 2001 and up to 29 diagnoses in 2004 (Table 6.7). In 2005 there was an increase of AIDS diagnoses among injecting drug users to 41."

   Source: Australian Institute of Health and Welfare, "Statistics on drug use in Australia 2006" (Canberra, Australia: Australian Institute of Health and Welfare, April 2007), Drug Statistics Series No. 18., Cat. no. PHE 80, p. 41.

6. "Between 1997 and 2004, the proportion of people who contracted AIDS and were injecting drug users remained relatively stable, ranging between 8% and 13% of new AIDS diagnoses. In 2005, there was an increase of new AIDS diagnoses among injecting drug users (16%), with 8% among injecting drug users with no male homosexual contact."

   Source: Australian Institute of Health and Welfare, "Statistics on drug use in Australia 2006" (Canberra, Australia: Australian Institute of Health and Welfare, April 2007), Drug Statistics Series No. 18., Cat. no. PHE 80, p. 41.

7. "The number of deaths from AIDS among injecting drug users decreased from 29 in 1997 to 17 in 2005 (Table 6.8). However, the proportion of AIDS deaths among people who had a history of injecting drug use increased by seven percentage points, from around 12% in 1997 to 19% in 2005."

   Source: Australian Institute of Health and Welfare, "Statistics on drug use in Australia 2006" (Canberra, Australia: Australian Institute of Health and Welfare, April 2007), Drug Statistics Series No. 18., Cat. no. PHE 80, p. 41.

8. "In 2005, 46% of injecting drug users surveyed for the IDRS had overdosed on heroin at some time in their lifetime (Table 6.11), and 9% of injecting drug users reported non-fatal heroin overdose on at least one occasion in the last 12 months. Nearly half (48%) of the injecting drug users responding to the survey reported that they were currently receiving treatment. Around 24% injected in a public space on the last occasion, ranging from 8% in the Northern Territory to 42% in Victoria."

International Drug Facts

AUSTRALIA

Source: Australian Institute of Health and Welfare, "Statistics on drug use in Australia 2006" (Canberra, Australia: Australian Institute of Health and Welfare, April 2007), Drug Statistics Series No. 18., Cat. no. PHE 80, p. 41.

9. "The death rate from accidental opioid overdose among people aged 15–54 years increased from 36.6 deaths per million persons in 1988 to peak at 101.9 deaths per million persons in 1999, before declining sharply to 34.6 deaths per million persons in 2001 (Figure 6.2). In the following 4 years, the death rate from accidental opioid overdose has declined slightly to 31.3 in 2004.

    "There were 357 accidental deaths due to opioid use among persons aged 15–54 years in Australia in both 2003 and 2004 (Table 6.12). The majority of accidental deaths due to opioid use in 2004 occurred in New South Wales (144 deaths) and Victoria (126 deaths)."

Source: Australian Institute of Health and Welfare, "Statistics on drug use in Australia 2006" (Canberra, Australia: Australian Institute of Health and Welfare, April 2007), Drug Statistics Series No. 18., Cat. no. PHE 80, pp. 45-46.

10. "Around one in five Australians (35%) aged 14 years and over consumed alcohol at risky or high-risk levels for short-term risk on at least one occasion in the last 12 months. One in ten Australians consumed alcohol at levels that are considered risky or high risk for alcohol-related harm in the long term."

Source: Australian Institute of Health and Welfare, "Statistics on drug use in Australia 2006" (Canberra, Australia: Australian Institute of Health and Welfare, April 2007), Drug Statistics Series No. 18., Cat. no. PHE 80, p. x.

11. "According to A Guide to Australian Alcohol Data 2004, alcohol is second only to tobacco as a preventable cause of death and hospitalisation in Australia. Alcohol is a significant contributor to public disorder and violence and crime. People seek treatment for alcohol abuse more frequently than for any other licit or illicit drug.

    "Reducing the level of alcohol abuse is a shared responsibility between the Australian and state and territory governments. The majority of Australians drink at low risk levels for most of the time (as defined by the Australian Alcohol Guidelines). However, risky or high risk drinking levels for both the short and long term is estimated to cause about 3,000 deaths per annum and is responsible for almost 5 per cent (gross harm) of the total disease burden in Australia. Alcohol abuse generates $7.6 billion in social cost to the community per annum."

Source: Intergovernmental Committee on Drugs, "National Drug Strategy 2004-2009: Annual Report July 2004-June 2005 to the Ministerial Council on Drug Strategy" (Canberra, Australia: Drug Strategy Branch, Australian Government Dept. of Health and Ageing, Dec. 2006), p. 8.

D. Harm Reduction Efforts

1. "A comprehensive harm-minimisation approach must take into account three interacting components: the individuals and the communities involved; their social, cultural, physical, legal and economic environment; and the drug itself. Harm minimisation approaches will vary according to the nature of the problem, the population group, the time and the locality. For example, strategies that aim to reduce harm for under-age drinkers will differ from strategies that target older smokers. Similarly, different strategies may be appropriate to accommodate the needs of injecting drug users living in rural Queensland and those living in metropolitan Sydney."

International Drug Facts

AUSTRALIA

Source: Ministerial Council on Drug Strategy, "The National Drug Strategy: Australia's Integrated Framework 2004-2009" (Canberra, Australia: Drug Strategy Branch, Dept. of Health and Ageing, May 2004), p. 11.

2. "The first National HIV/AIDS Strategy was launched in 1989. According to Professor Richard Feachem, from the World Bank, who oversaw the evaluation of the second National HIV/AIDS Strategy:

   "'The first National HIV/AIDS Strategy released by the Commonwealth Government in 1989 provided a framework for an integrated response to the HIV epidemic and a plan for action across a range of policy and program activities. Needle and Syringe Programs were a key component on the education and prevention strategy.'

   "Professor Feacham concluded: 'Needle and Syringe Exchange Programs must be a foundation of Australia's prevention efforts in a third Strategy and beyond'. The third National HIV/AIDS Strategy (Partnerships in Practice: National HIV/AIDS Strategy 1996-97 to 1998-99) continued to support Needle and Syringe Programs as an important part of its prevention program for people who inject drugs.

   "The fourth National HIV/AIDS Strategy and the first National Hepatitis C Strategy, continue to support Needle and Syringe Programs as effective harm reduction interventions."

   Source: Health Outcomes International, the National Centre for HIV Epidemiology and Clinical Research, and the Centre of Health Economics-York University, "Return on investment in needle and syringe programs in Australia" (Canberra, Australia: Australian Government Department of Health and Ageing, October 2002), p. 9.

3. "Between 1991 and 2000, an estimated $141 million ($150 million in 2000 prices) was expended on NSPs across Australia, comprised of $122 million (87%) by government, and $19 million (13%) in consumer expenditure."

   Source: Health Outcomes International, the National Centre for HIV Epidemiology and Clinical Research, and the Centre of Health Economics-York University, "Return on investment in needle and syringe programs in Australia" (Canberra, Australia: Australian Government Department of Health and Ageing, October 2002), p. 2.

4. "The first Australian Needle and Syringe Program began in Sydney in 1986 as a trial project. The testing of syringes returned to this Darlinghurst Program detected an increase in HIV prevalence, suggesting that HIV was spreading among clients. In the following year Needle and Syringe Programs became NSW Government policy. Other States and Territories followed soon after.

   "There are a number of different models of Needle and Syringe Programs operating in Australia that vary between different jurisdictions and sometimes by locality. Depending on the jurisdiction, the proportions of these that are government run and non-government run also vary. Furthermore, of the NSPs operating in the non-government sector, a number of these are 'peer-based' NSPs. Peer-based NSPs can be distinguished by the employment of past or current drug users in the development and provision of NSP services to networks of injecting drug users."

International Drug Facts

AUSTRALIA

Source: Health Outcomes International, the National Centre for HIV Epidemiology and Clinical Research, and the Centre of Health Economics-York University, "Return on investment in needle and syringe programs in Australia" (Canberra, Australia: Australian Government Department of Health and Ageing, October 2002), p. 9.

5. "Needle and Syringe Programs tend to be located in relatively public places because they need to be accessible. Various government-sponsored pharmacy schemes operate throughout Australia. Generally the schemes provide 1ml syringes, which can either be purchased, or, in NSW, exchanged free on return of a pack with used syringes. In addition to those participating in the government-sponsored schemes, other pharmacies sell needles and syringes and other equipment used for injecting on a commercial basis."

Source: Health Outcomes International, the National Centre for HIV Epidemiology and Clinical Research, and the Centre of Health Economics-York University, "Return on investment in needle and syringe programs in Australia" (Canberra, Australia: Australian Government Department of Health and Ageing, October 2002), p. 10.

6. "Australia's NSPs were estimated to have cost Commonwealth and State governments $122 million by 2000, but the return on this investment was the prevention of an estimated 25,000 HIV and 21,000 HCV infections. By 2010, our NSPs will have prevented an estimated 4500 deaths from AIDS and 90 deaths from HCV. The savings to governments for HIV and HCV were estimated to be at least $2.4 billion (allowing for conventional government 5% annual discounting of future costs) or as much as $7.7 billion (without discounting). By any reckoning, this represents an enormous saving in both lives and dollars. In light of these outcomes, opposition to NSPs amounts to public health vandalism and financial recklessness with taxpayers' dollars."

Source: Law, Matthew G. and Robert G. Batey, "Injecting Drug Use in Australia: Needle/Syringe Programs Prove Their Worth, but Hepatitis C Still on the Increase," Medical Journal of Australia, 2003; 178 (5):197-198, from the web at http://www.mja.com.au/public/issues/178_05_030303/law10754_fm.html, last accessed June 14, 2007.

7. "An extensive network of needle and syringe programs (NSPs) has been established in Australia; in the financial year 1994-95, around 700 NSPs distributed six million syringes nationally and an additional four million were distributed through pharmacies. Early and vigorous implementation of harm reduction measures, such as methadone maintenance, peer-based education and NSPs, has successfully maintained low seroprevalence of HIV infection among people who inject drugs in Australia."

Source: MacDonald, Margaret A., et al., "Hepatitis C Virus Antibody Prevalence Among Injecting Drug Users At Selected Needle and Syringe Programs In Australia, 1995-1997," Medical Journal of Australia, 2000;172:57-61, from the web athttp://www.mja.com.au/public/issues/172_02_170100/macdonald/macdonald.htmlla st accessed June 14, 2007.

International Drug Facts

AUSTRALIA

8. "The Sydney Medically Supervised Injecting Centre (MSIC) aims to reduce harm associated with illicit drug use by supervising injecting episodes that might otherwise occur in less safe circumstances such as public places or alone. Specifically, it is anticipated that supervising such injecting episodes will reduce the risk of morbidity and mortality associated with drug overdoses and transmission of blood-borne infections, while providing ready access to safe needle syringe disposal. It is also hoped that by extending the circumstances in which health professionals have contact with injecting drug users (IDUs) more, particularly those most 'at risk', will be engaged with the health and social welfare system sooner than otherwise.

"The Sydney MSIC is at 66 Darlinghurst Road Kings Cross, in the centre of the Kings Cross business district. Access is from Darlinghurst Road.

"No drugs are sold or kept on the premises. Registered clients receive clean needles and equipment, and advice about their health.

"The MSIC conducts tours of the premises for members of the public on a regular basis."

> Source: Website of the Sydney (Australia) Medically Supervised Injecting Centre at http://www.sydneymsic.com/index.htm, last accessed June 14, 2007.

9. "Based on the results presented in Chapter 2, it appears that there were no significant barriers to access and considerable demand for MSIC services, with the registration of almost 4,000 injecting drug users across 18-months and over 55,000 supervised injections. The MSIC engaged its target client group, individuals who inject on a regular basis with histories of public injecting and drug overdose. MSIC provided over 13,000 occasions of other onsite clinical service delivery such as vein care and injecting advice and counseling, and nearly 1,400 referrals for drug treatment, health care and social welfare assistance. During the trial period, MSIC staff effectively managed 409 drug overdoses without any fatalities."

> Source: MISC Evaluation Committee, "Final Report on the Evaluation of the Sydney Medically Supervised Injecting Centre" (Sydney, Australia: MISC Evaluation Committee, 2003), p. 202.

E. Treatment

1. "In the 2004–05 Alcohol and Other Drug Treatment Services National Minimum Data Set (AODTS-NMDS) collection, alcohol was the most common principal drug of concern in treatment episodes (37%), followed by marijuana/cannabis (23%), heroin (17%) and meth/amphetamine (11%). The proportion of treatment episodes where alcohol was the principal drug of concern increased with age, while the proportion of episodes where marijuana/cannabis was the principal drug of concern decreased with age."

> Source: Australian Institute of Health and Welfare, "Statistics on drug use in Australia 2006" (Canberra, Australia: Australian Institute of Health and Welfare, April 2007), Drug Statistics Series No. 18., Cat. no. PHE 80, p. xiii.

International Drug Facts

AUSTRALIA

2. "Almost 39,000 clients were receiving pharmacotherapy treatment at 30 June 2005, with the majority of these treatments received from a private prescriber (70%). Excluding clients where the type of drug used could not be identified, there were 25,369 (72%) methadone maintenance therapy clients and 9,947 (28%) buprenorphine maintenance therapy clients."

   Source: Australian Institute of Health and Welfare, "Statistics on drug use in Australia 2006" (Canberra, Australia: Australian Institute of Health and Welfare, April 2007), Drug Statistics Series No. 18., Cat. no. PHE 80, p. xiii.

F. Substance Use and the Justice System

1. "Marijuana/cannabis is the most common illicit drug for which people are arrested in Australia, accounting for almost three-quarters (71%) of arrests relating to illicit drugs in 2004–05 (Table 9.1). The proportion of arrests for amphetamine-type stimulants increased from 5% to 11% over the period of 1996–97 to 2000–01 and further increased to 13% in 2004–05. In absolute terms, the number of consumer and provider arrests for amphetaminetype stimulants increased from 3,907 in 1996–97 to 8,846 in 2000–01, increasing further to 10,068 in 2004–05."

   Source: Australian Institute of Health and Welfare, "Statistics on drug use in Australia 2006" (Canberra, Australia: Australian Institute of Health and Welfare, April 2007), Drug Statistics Series No. 18., Cat. no. PHE 80, p. 71.

2. "The overall number of consumer and provider arrests for illicit drugs fell from 85,046 in 1996–97 to 77,333 in 2004–05. Marijuana/cannabis arrests fell from 69,136 in 1996–97 to 54,936 in 2004–05."

   Source: Australian Institute of Health and Welfare, "Statistics on drug use in Australia 2006" (Canberra, Australia: Australian Institute of Health and Welfare, April 2007), Drug Statistics Series No. 18., Cat. no. PHE 80, p. 71.

3. "The majority of illicit drug arrests are related to the consumption rather than the provision or sale of substances (Table 9.1). For example, in 2004–05, over three-quarters of arrests for marijuana/cannabis (84%) and steroids (83%) were related to the consumption of those substances."

   Source: Australian Institute of Health and Welfare, "Statistics on drug use in Australia 2006" (Canberra, Australia: Australian Institute of Health and Welfare, April 2007), Drug Statistics Series No. 18., Cat. no. PHE 80, p. 71.

4. "Overall, total consumption-related illicit drug arrests in Australia declined from 73,800 in 1996–97 to 62,209 in 2004–05. Arrests relating to provision of illicit substances also decreased from 1996–97 to 2002–03, from 24,994 to 14,613 (ACC 2006)."

   Source: Australian Institute of Health and Welfare, "Statistics on drug use in Australia 2006" (Canberra, Australia: Australian Institute of Health and Welfare, April 2007), Drug Statistics Series No. 18., Cat. no. PHE 80, p. 71.

International Drug Facts

AUSTRALIA / CANADA

5. "Of the 2,021 persons in prison for drug-related offences at 30 June 2005, 1,607 (80%) were imprisoned for dealing/trafficking drugs, 257 (13%) for manufacturing/growing drugs and 157 (8%) for possessing/using drugs. "The proportion of people imprisoned with a drug-related most serious offence ranged between 9% and 11% over the period 1995 to 2005. In 2005, one in ten sentenced prisoners was imprisoned for drug-related offences."

   Source: Australian Institute of Health and Welfare, "Statistics on drug use in Australia 2006" (Canberra, Australia: Australian Institute of Health and Welfare, April 2007), Drug Statistics Series No. 18., Cat. no. PHE 80, p. 73.

6. "Almost 60% of prisoners reported a history of injecting drug use in 2004 (Table 7.9). The risk of carrying a bloodborne disease was greatly increased for those prisoners who injected drugs. Hepatitis C antibody was found in 35% of the prison population surveyed and in 56% of prisoners who injected drugs. This compares with an estimated prevalence of 1.3% in the general population (NCHECR 2005). One in five prisoners tested positive to the hepatitis B core antibody as did over one in four (27%) prisoners who reported injecting drugs. Less than 1% of prisoners tested positively to the HIV antibody; however, this was still higher than prevalence in the general population (0.07%) (NCHECR 2005)."

   Source: Australian Institute of Health and Welfare, "Statistics on drug use in Australia 2006" (Canberra, Australia: Australian Institute of Health and Welfare, April 2007), Drug Statistics Series No. 18., Cat. no. PHE 80, p. 60.

7. Australia's incarceration rate is 126 inmates per 100,000 of national population, with a total prison population of 25,353 out of an estimated national population of 20.2 million.

   Source: Walmsley, Roy, "World Prison Population List (Seventh Edition)" (London, England: International Centre for Prison Studies, 2007), p. 6, Table 5, citing the Australian Bureau of Statistics.

8. Australia's homicide rate is 1.87 per 100,000 national population (average per year 1999 to 2001).

   Source: Barclay, Gordon & Cynthia Tavares, "International Comparisons of Criminal Justice Statistics 2001," Home Office Bulletin 12/03 (London, England, UK: Home Office Research, Development, and Statistics Directorate, October 24, 2003), p. 10, Table 1.1.

CANADA

A. Overview

1. "The introduction of a new National Anti-Drug Strategy is an important commitment of Canada's New Government that is being supported in Budget 2007. This new strategy covers three priority areas, with common objectives, to combat illicit drug production, prevent illicit drug use and treat illicit drug dependency. This new approach will result in a more focused program for dealing with illicit drug use.

International Drug Facts

CANADA

"The investment of $63.8 million over two years will build on existing programs and initiatives ($385 million per year) that are being refocused to create a new National Anti-Drug Strategy. This new strategy places particular emphasis on additional actions to combat the illicit production and distribution of drugs, to address gaps in preventing illicit drug use, to create awareness of illicit drugs and their negative effects, particularly among youth, and to treat and rehabilitate those with drug dependencies."

Source: Canadian Dept. of Finance, The Budget Plan 2007, Tabled in the House of Commons by the Honourable James M. Flaherty, PC, MP, Minister of Finance, March 19, 2007, p. 257.

2. "Needle exchange and methadone programs are widely endorsed by United Nations agencies and supported by enormous bodies of published research as key HIV prevention measures. Numerous countries have operated supervised injection sites with great success for many years, and Canada's only such site, in Vancouver's Downtown Eastside, has been subject to rigorous evaluation that has produced a considerable body of peer-reviewed research showing its multiple benefits for both those who use the facility and the surrounding community.

"Yet the federal budget fails to mention harm reduction or to allocate any funds for harm reduction measures, representing a serious setback for HIV and hepatitis C programs in Canada. It is inevitable that cutting harm reduction out of the federal drug strategy undermines provincial and municipal efforts to sustain these essential and cost-effective programs. In the past, the federal government has supplemented provincial allocations for needle exchange programs and promoted awareness of and research on these programs. The allocations in Budget 2007 repudiate long experience and vast scientific evidence; the price will be paid for in increased risk of HIV and hepatitis transmission.

"In fact, what is contemplated appears to be a U.S.-style "war on drugs" - an approach that has been proven time and again to be counter-productive and a tragic waste of public funds, diverting resources from services that are desperately needed to address what is, at root, a health problem.

"While abandoning proven harm reduction measures, Budget 2007 includes significant resources for law enforcement initiatives dedicated to "combating illicit drug production and distribution." Previous analyses, including the 2001 report by the Auditor-General of Canada, have found that law enforcement has, for many years, represented by far the greatest portion of federal spending on drugs. Hundreds of millions of Canadians' tax dollars have been spent on law enforcement efforts to stem the supply of illicit drugs, with virtually no progress to show for this huge expenditure. In fact, as concluded in a recent study by the British Columbia Centre for Excellence in HIV/AIDS, many law enforcement measures that are heavily financed in Canada actually contribute to drug-related harms. To add to the waste, at least one third of the new funds allocated in the 2007 budget will go toward law enforcement."

International Drug Facts

CANADA

Source: Csete, Joanne, Executive Director, Canadian HIV/AIDS Legal Network, Letter to Members of Parliament and the Senate, March 30, 2007, from the web at http://www.aidslaw.ca/publications/interfaces/downloadFile.php?ref=1037, last accessed June 27, 2007.

3. "Although Canada's Drug Strategy was renewed in 2003 following criticisms regarding spending, activities, leadership and a lack of appropriate monitoring and evaluation, many of the problems of the past remain. Currently, through Canada's Drug Strategy, the federal government continues to invest heavily in policies and practices that have repeatedly been shown in the scientific literature to be ineffective or harmful. Specifically, while the stated goal of the Canada's Drug Strategy is to reduce harm, evidence obtained through this analysis indicates that the overwhelming emphasis continues to be on conventional enforcement-based approaches which are costly and often exacerbate, rather than reduce, drug-related harms. Further, Canada's Drug Strategy has not seized the opportunity to promote a national standard of care that reduces the most deadly harms associated with illicit drug use."

Source: DeBeck, Kora, Evan Wood, Julio Montaner and Thomas Kerr, "Canada's 2003 Renewed Drug Strategy — An Evidence-Based Review," HIV/AIDS Policy & Law Review (Toronto, Ontario, Canada: Canadian HIV/AIDS Legal Network, Dec. 2006), p. 10.

B. Prevalence Estimates

1. "Overall, 44.5% of Canadians report using cannabis at least once in their lifetime, and 14.1% report use during the 12 months before the survey. Males are more likely than females to have used cannabis in their lifetime (50.1% vs 39.2%) and during the past year (18.2% vs. 10.2%). Younger people are more likely to have ever used cannabis in their lifetime, with almost 70% of those between 18 and 24 having used it at least once. Younger people are also more likely to be past-year users. Almost 30% of 15-17 year olds and just over 47% of 18 and 19 year olds have used cannabis in the past year. Beyond age 45, less than 10% of the population has used cannabis in the past year."

Source: "Canadian Addiction Survey, A National Survey of Canadians Use of Alcohol and Other Drugs — Prevalence of Use and Related Harms: Highlights" (Canadian Centre on Substance Abuse, Nov. 2004), p. 6.

2. "Lifetime cannabis use increases with education, rising from 34.9% among those without high school completion to a peak of 52.4% among those with some postsecondary education and 44.2% among those with a university degree.

"Lifetime experiences with cannabis use increases with income adequacy (income relative to the number of people in a household), from 42.9% of those with a low income adequacy to 44.6% of those with a moderate income and 54.8% of those with a high income adequacy. The association between income adequacy and pastyear use is not significant."

International Drug Facts

CANADA

Source: "Canadian Addiction Survey, A National Survey of Canadians Use of Alcohol and Other Drugs — Prevalence of Use and Related Harms: Highlights" (Canadian Centre on Substance Abuse, Nov. 2004), p. 6.

3. "The use of illicit drugs is generally limited to cannabis only. About 28.7% of Canadians (63.4% of lifetime users) report using only cannabis during their lifetime, and 11.5% (79.1% of past-year users) used only cannabis during the past year.

   "Excluding cannabis, the illicit drug most commonly used during one's lifetime is reported to be hallucinogens, used by 11.4% of respondents, followed closely by cocaine (10.6%), speed (6.4%) and ecstasy (4.1%). The lifetime use of drugs such as inhalants, heroin, steroids and drugs taken intravenously is about 1% or less of the population. The percentage reporting the use of any five drugs other than cannabis (cocaine or crack; hallucinogens, PCP or LSD; speed or amphetamines; heroin; ecstasy [MDMA]), is 16.5%, and the percentage reporting the use of any of the eight drugs, including cannabis, is 45.2%."

Source: "Canadian Addiction Survey, A National Survey of Canadians Use of Alcohol and Other Drugs — Prevalence of Use and Related Harms: Highlights" (Canadian Centre on Substance Abuse, Nov. 2004), p. 7.

4. "Although about one in six Canadians has used an illicit drug other than cannabis in their lifetime, few have used these drugs during the past year. Rates of drug use in the past 12 months are generally 1% or less, with the exception of cocaine use (1.9%). About 3% of Canadians (4.3% of males and 1.8% of females) report using at least one of the five drugs other than cannabis, and 14.5% (18.7% of males and 10.6% of females) report using any of the eight drugs, including steroids and inhalants."

Source: "Canadian Addiction Survey, A National Survey of Canadians Use of Alcohol and Other Drugs — Prevalence of Use and Related Harms: Highlights" (Canadian Centre on Substance Abuse, Nov. 2004), p. 7.

5. "Self-reported rates of illicit drug use are increasing in Canada. The proportion of Canadians reporting any illicit drug use in their lifetime rose from 28.5% in 1994 to 45.0% in 2004, and in the past 12 months from 7.6% to 14.4%."

Source: "Canadian Addiction Survey, A National Survey of Canadians Use of Alcohol and Other Drugs — Prevalence of Use and Related Harms: Highlights" (Canadian Centre on Substance Abuse, Nov. 2004), p. 11.

6. "The past-year use of cannabis rose from 6.5% in 1989 to 7.4% in 1994, and to 14.1% in 2004. For cocaine and crack, rates declined from 1.4% in 1989 to 0.7% in 1994, and rose again to 1.9% in 2004. While past-year rates for the combined category of LSD/speed/heroin rose slightly from 0.4% in 1989, to 1.1% in 1994, and to 1.3% in 2004, these findings are not statistically significant."

Source: "Canadian Addiction Survey, A National Survey of Canadians Use of Alcohol and Other Drugs — Prevalence of Use and Related Harms: Highlights" (Canadian Centre on Substance Abuse, Nov. 2004), p. 11.

International Drug Facts

CANADA

7. "Most Canadians drink in moderation. In the 12 months before the survey, 79.3% of Canadians aged 15 or older report consuming alcohol, 14% are former drinkers and 7% lifetime abstainers. Of the past-year drinkers, 44% report drinking weekly. The rate of past-year drinking is significantly higher among males than females (82.0% vs. 76.8%, respectively). Past-year drinking rates peak among youth 18 to 24 years of age, with about 90% of people in that age range consuming alcohol during the course of the year."

Source: "Canadian Addiction Survey, A National Survey of Canadians Use of Alcohol and Other Drugs — Prevalence of Use and Related Harms: Highlights" (Canadian Centre on Substance Abuse, Nov. 2004), p. 4.

8. "According to this examination, the overall percentage of drinkers in Canada declined from 77.7% in 1989 to 72.3% in 1994 and has now risen again to 79.3% in 2004. Variations in drinking patterns across studies are consistent with the corresponding variations in rates of alcohol use. Furthermore, changes in rates of self-reported alcohol use are consistent with alcohol sales data."

Source: "Canadian Addiction Survey, A National Survey of Canadians Use of Alcohol and Other Drugs — Prevalence of Use and Related Harms: Highlights" (Canadian Centre on Substance Abuse, Nov. 2004), p. 10.

C. Problem Substance Use and Substance-Related Harm

1. "The most commonly reported drug-related harm involves physical health, reported by 30.3% of lifetime and 23.9% of past-year users of drugs other than cannabis, and 15.1% of lifetime and 10.1% of past-year users of any drug. Following physical health, a cluster of harms, represented somewhat equally, includes harms to one's friendship and social life (22.3% and 16.4% of users excluding cannabis, 10.7% and 6% of any drug users), home and marriage (18.9% and 14.1% excluding cannabis, 8.7% and 5.1% of any drug users), work (18.9% and 14.2% excluding cannabis, 9.2% and 5.1% of any drug users), and financial (19.6% and 18.9% excluding cannabis, 8.4% and 6.5% of any drug users).

Source: "Canadian Addiction Survey, A National Survey of Canadians Use of Alcohol and Other Drugs — Prevalence of Use and Related Harms: Highlights" (Canadian Centre on Substance Abuse, Nov. 2004), p. 7.

2. "The data indicate that the number of Canadians who report having used an injectable drug at some point in their life increased from 1.7 million in 1994 to a little over 4.1 million in 2004. Of those, 7.7% (132,000) reported having used a drug by injection in 1994 compared with 6.5% (269,000) in 2004."

Source: "Canadian Addiction Survey, A National Survey of Canadians Use of Alcohol and Other Drugs — Prevalence of Use and Related Harms: Highlights" (Canadian Centre on Substance Abuse, Nov. 2004), p. 11.

International Drug Facts

CANADA

3. "In Canada, as of 2004, 269,000 people reported using needles to inject drugs. In the first six months of 2005, over 20 percent of all newly recorded HIV infections in Canada were associated with injection drug use; among newly infected women, injection drug use accounted for 38 percent of recorded infections."

   Source: DeBeck, Kora, Evan Wood, Julio Montaner and Thomas Kerr, "Canada's 2003 Renewed Drug Strategy — An Evidence-Based Review," HIV/AIDS Policy & Law Review (Toronto, Ontario, Canada: Canadian HIV/AIDS Legal Network, Dec. 2006), pp. 1, 5.

4. "In 2004, the medical costs of HIV infection among injection drug users in the city of Vancouver was estimated to be in excess of $215 million. Nationally, direct health care costs attributable to illicit drug use were estimated to be over $1.13 billion for 2002. In that same year, illicit drug use is believed to have contributed to over 215,000 sick days resulting in income loss of over $21 million."

   Source: DeBeck, Kora, Evan Wood, Julio Montaner and Thomas Kerr, "Canada's 2003 Renewed Drug Strategy — An Evidence-Based Review," HIV/AIDS Policy & Law Review (Toronto, Ontario, Canada: Canadian HIV/AIDS Legal Network, Dec. 2006), p. 5.

D. Harm Reduction Efforts

1. "Vancouver Coastal Health (VCH) in partnership with the PHS Community Services Society opened North America's first legal supervised injection site (Insite) scientific research pilot project in September 2003.

   "Since opening its doors, Insite has been a safe, health-focused place where people can go to inject drugs and connect with health care professionals and addiction services. It is an integral part of Vancouver Coastal Health's continuum of care for people with addiction, mental illness and HIV/AIDS in the Vancouver community."

   Source: Vancouver Coastal Health Authority, "Insite - Supervised Injection Site - Health Services," from the web at http://www.vch.ca/sis/, last accessed June 27, 2007.

2. "On Friday, September 1, 2006, Federal Health Minister Tony Clement announced that the government had "deferred the decision" on Vancouver Coastal Health's application to extend the operating exemption for the SIS until December 31, 2007.

   "The Minister said that during that time, additional studies will be conducted into how supervised injection sites affect crime, prevention and treatment.

   "The SIS, Insite, will be allowed to continue operations during this review.

   "During the period until December 31, 2007, Health Canada will not entertain any applications for the establishment of additional injection sites in other parts of Canada until the NDS is in place, and the Vancouver review is completed."

   Source: Vancouver Coastal Health Authority, "Insite - Supervised Injection Site - Health Services," from the web at http://www.vch.ca/sis/, last accessed June 27, 2007.

International Drug Facts

CANADA

3. "About the study: The North American Opiate Medication Initiative is a clinical trial that will test whether heroin-assisted therapy benefits people suffering from chronic opiate addictions who have not benefited from other treatments.

   "Funded by the Canadian Institutes of Health Research, Canada's premier funding agency for health research, and approved by Health Canada, the study is enrolling participants in Vancouver and Montreal.

   "News: The NAOMI trial began enrolling in February 2005 in Vancouver and June 2005 in Montreal. These two cities have the largest heroin-addicted populations in Canada."

   Source: Website of the North American Opiate Medication Inititive, "NAOMI Study," from the web at http://www.naomistudy.ca/, last accessed June 27, 2007.

E. Treatment

1. "In 1998–99, there were 238 residential care facilities in Canada for people with alcohol and drug addiction problems, for which 6,019 beds were licensed or approved by provincial or municipal authorities. The 1998–99 Residential Care Facilities Survey reports on 183 of these 238 facilities, for a total of 4,752 licensed or approved beds. The survey found that of the 4,752 licensed or approved beds, 4,361 were available for use (391 were not). The occupancy rate for the available beds was 88.8%."

   Source: Canadian Community Epidemiology Network on Drug Use (CCENDU), "2002 National Report: Drug Trends and the CCENDU Network" (Ottawa, Ontario: Canadian Centre on Substance Abuse, 2003), p. 54.

2. "Interesting, however, is that in comparison with 1998–99, data from the 1993–94 Residential Care Facilities Survey revealed significantly more patients were on count on March 31, 1994 in reporting facilities (5,034). Further, there has also been a decline since 1993–94 in the total number of beds available (6,185) and the total number of facilities (262)."

   Source: Canadian Community Epidemiology Network on Drug Use (CCENDU), "2002 National Report: Drug Trends and the CCENDU Network" (Ottawa, Ontario: Canadian Centre on Substance Abuse, 2003), p. 54.

3. "The Canadian Centre on Substance Abuse maintains an on-line database of addiction treatment services in Canada to provide information to individuals seeking assistance for themselves or others and for health care professionals seeking to refer clients in or out of province. As of February, 2003, 1,012 addiction treatment programs were identified, which is estimated to be approximately 85% of all addiction treatment programs offered in Canada. The setting for which the largest number of treatment services was available was outpatient (618), and the least was medium-term residential (one to three months) (30) (see Figure 20). Data for type of addiction treated show that the greatest number of services were identified for alcohol (980) and the least for hallucinogens (543)."

   Source: Canadian Community Epidemiology Network on Drug Use (CCENDU), "2002 National Report: Drug Trends and the CCENDU Network" (Ottawa, Ontario: Canadian Centre on Substance Abuse, 2003), p. 55.

International Drug Facts

CANADA

4. "In Canada, as in many other countries, there is a national level regulatory framework for methadone prescription. The Office of Controlled Substances, Health Canada, works with provincial/territorial governments and medical licensing bodies, among others, to facilitate increased access to methadone maintenance treatment. To date in addition to the Health Canada guidelines on the use of opioids in the management of opioid dependence, several provinces have developed—or are in the process of developing— guidelines and training for practitioners interested in providing methadone maintenance treatment.

   "Although provinces have become increasingly involved in delineating the conditions under which they recommend to Health Canada physicians who should be allowed to prescribe methadone, only physicians who have received an exemption under Section 56 of the Controlled Drugs and Substances Act are allowed to prescribe methadone.

   "Methadone maintenance treatment may be delivered in a variety of different settings including:
   "* substance use treatment services/clinics (outpatient/inpatient);
   "* community-based health centres/clinics;
   "* private medical clinics;
   "* individual physicians' offices & community pharmacies;
   "* hospital-based health clinics;
   "* HIV/AIDS services/clinics;
   "* mental health agencies/clinics; and
   "* correctional facilities.

   "Practitioners from many different disciplines and backgrounds— including medicine, substance use treatment, social work and mental health, among others—are involved in delivering methadone maintenance treatment programs. Their roles vary, depending on factors such as qualifications, program setting, available resources and geographic location. There are also differences—across jurisdictions and among programs—in terms of program philosophy, range of services provided, client groups served, level of client involvement, program policies, and program settings."

   Source: Health Canada, Methadone Maintenance Treatment, from the web at http://www.hc-sc.gc.ca/hl-vs/pubs/adp-apd/methadone-treatment-traitement/methadone-canada_e.html last accessed July 2, 2007.

F. Substance Use and the Justice System

1. "In the area of law enforcement, it is noteworthy that 23 percent of all criminal charges processed through Canadian courts in 2002 were attributed to illicit drugs. This was associated with a cost of $330 million that year. Additionally, for 2002, policing costs and correctional service costs associated with illicit drugs were estimated to be $1.43 billion and $573 million respectively."

International Drug Facts

CANADA

Source: DeBeck, Kora, Evan Wood, Julio Montaner and Thomas Kerr, "Canada's 2003 Renewed Drug Strategy — An Evidence-Based Review," HIV/AIDS Policy & Law Review (Toronto, Ontario, Canada: Canadian HIV/AIDS Legal Network, Dec. 2006), p. 5.

2. "Data from the Uniform Crime Reporting Survey reveal an overall increase in the number of adults charged with a drug offence per 10,000 adult population from 1998 to 2001: 16.7 in 1998 and 19.7 in 2001 (see Figure 13). From 1998 to 2001, the majority of adults charged were male (average 86%). In 2001, cannabis charges represented the vast majority of drug offences adult males were charged with (71%), followed by cocaine (21%), other drugs (7%) and heroin (1%). In comparison, adult females received proportionally fewer charges for cannabis (62%), and more for cocaine (27%), other drugs (9%) and heroin (2%)."

Source: Canadian Community Epidemiology Network on Drug Use (CCENDU), "2002 National Report: Drug Trends and the CCENDU Network" (Ottawa, Ontario: Canadian Centre on Substance Abuse, 2003), p. 44.

3. "Within the federally incarcerated population, there was a continuous albeit nominal increase in the number of individuals incarcerated for a drug offence from 1994 to 2001 (1994: 5,117 and 2001: 5,761). They comprised nearly a quarter of the incarcerated population in both time periods, with the proportion steadily increasing from 1994 (23.1%) to 2001 (26.5%). The majority of incarcerated drug offenders in 2001 were male (94.1%). It is interesting to note, however, that even though the proportion of female involvement is limited (5.9% in 2001), it has increased over the seven-year period (from 3% in 1994 to 5.9% in 2001; that is, there were 163 federal female drug offenders in 1994 and 342 in 2001). The average age of males and females combined over the seven-year period is 35, ranging from 36 in 1996 to 33 in 2001."

Source: Canadian Community Epidemiology Network on Drug Use (CCENDU), "2002 National Report: Drug Trends and the CCENDU Network" (Ottawa, Ontario: Canadian Centre on Substance Abuse, 2003), p. 56.

4. "Recent studies have demonstrated that incarceration of injection drug users is independently associated with both syringe sharing and acquisition of HIV. In fact, estimates suggest that approximately 20 percent of HIV infections among injection drug users in Vancouver have been acquired in prison."

Source: DeBeck, Kora, Evan Wood, Julio Montaner and Thomas Kerr, "Canada's 2003 Renewed Drug Strategy — An Evidence-Based Review," HIV/AIDS Policy & Law Review (Toronto, Ontario, Canada: Canadian HIV/AIDS Legal Network, Dec. 2006), p. 5.

5. Canada's incarceration rate is 107 inmates per 100,000 of national population, with an average total prison population of 35,096 out of an estimated national population of 31.75 million.

International Drug Facts
CANADA / NETHERLANDS

Source: Walmsley, Roy, "World Prison Population List (Seventh Edition)" (London, England: International Centre for Prison Studies, 2007), p. 3, Table 2, citing Statistics Canada.

6. Canada's homicide rate is 1.77 per 100,000 national population (average per year 1999 to 2001).

Source: Barclay, Gordon & Cynthia Tavares, "International Comparisons of Criminal Justice Statistics 2001," Home Office Bulletin 12/03 (London, England, UK: Home Office Research, Development, and Statistics Directorate, October 24, 2003), p. 10, Table 1.1.

NETHERLANDS

A. Overview

1. "The national drug policy in the Netherlands has four major objectives: To prevent drug use and to treat and rehabilitate drug users. To reduce harm to users. To diminish public nuisance by drug users (the disturbance of public order and safety in the neighbourhood). To combat the production and trafficking of drugs.
   "The primary aim of Dutch drug policy is focused on health protection and health risk re-duction."

Source: Trimbos Institute, "Drug Situation 2006 The Netherlands by the Reitox National Focal Point: Report to the EMCDDA" (Utrecht, Netherlands: Trimbos-Instuut, 2007), p. 15.

2. "The sale of cannabis is illegal, yet coffee shops are tolerated in their sale of cannabis, if they adhere to certain criteria: no advertising, no sale of hard drugs, not selling to persons under the age of 18, not causing public nuisance and not selling more than 5 grams per transaction (AHOJ-G criteria). Three extra criteria are: no alcohol vendor, no more than 500 grams in stock and — in some cities — a minimum distance to a school or to the Dutch border. In recent years, government policy has aimed to reduce the number of coffee shops. However, the decision whether or not to tolerate a coffee shop lies with the local governments. At the end of 2005, the Netherlands had 729 officially tolerated cannabis outlets (coffee shops). This is a 1.0 percent overall decrease compared to the situation in 2004 (737 coffee shops, see paragraph 10.1). In 2005, the majority of the 467 municipalities in the Netherlands pursued a zero policy (72%) or a maximum policy (22%) with regard to the number of tolerated coffee shops."

Source: Trimbos Institute, "Drug Situation 2006 The Netherlands by the Reitox National Focal Point: Report to the EMCDDA" (Utrecht, Netherlands: Trimbos-Instuut, 2007), p. 18.

B. Prevalence Estimates

1. "In 2005, the prevalence of last year cannabis use was about 2.5 times higher among men than women (7.8% as against 3.1%). This male-female ratio was marginally smaller in previous years (almost 2). Apparently the gender gap is not narrowing."

Source: Trimbos Institute, "Drug Situation 2006 The Netherlands by the Reitox National Focal Point: Report to the EMCDDA" (Utrecht, Netherlands: Trimbos-Instuut, 2007), p. 26.

International Drug Facts

NETHERLANDS

2. Prevalence of drug use in the Dutch population 15-64 years of age:

	Lifetime Prevalence			Last Year Prevalence		
	1997	2001	2005	1997	2001	2005
Cannabis	19.1	19.5	22.6	5.5	5.5	5.4
Cocaine	2.6	2.1	3.4	0.7	0.7	0.6
Ecstasy	2.3	3.2	4.3	0.8	1.1	1.2
Amphetamine	2.2	2.0	2.1	0.4	0.4	0.3
LSD	1.5	1.2	1.4	-	0.0	0.1
Herion	0.3	0.2	0.6	0.0	0.0	0.0

Source: Trimbos Institute, "Drug Situation 2006 The Netherlands by the Reitox National Focal Point: Report to the EMCDDA" (Utrecht, Netherlands: Trimbos-Instuut, 2007), p. 26, Table 2.1.

3. "Among boys, the last month prevalence of cannabis use significantly decreased from 14% in 1996 to 10% in 2003 (figure 2.1). There was no significant change in cannabis use among girls (LMP 8% in 1996 and 7% in 2003).

"The proportion of lifetime cannabis users starting at an early age (13 or younger) increased from 21% in 1988 to 40% in 1996, and has remained fairly stable since then (37%) (Monshouwer et al., 2005).

"The percentage of pupils using other drugs, such as ecstasy, cocaine, amphetamine or heroin, also peaked in 1996 and stabilised or decreased since then (figure 2.2). In 2003, 4.5% of the pupils had ever tried one of these drugs and 1.5% was a current user."

Source: Trimbos Institute, "Drug Situation 2006 The Netherlands by the Reitox National Focal Point: Report to the EMCDDA" (Utrecht, Netherlands: Trimbos-Instuut, 2007), p. 27.

C. Problem Substance Use and Substance-Related Harm

1. "For the 2001 estimate, three methods were used, namely the multivariate social indicator method (MIM) (or regression imputation), the multiple imputation method (on the same data), and the treatment multiplier (TM). These methods yielded a central estimate of about 33,500 problem drug users, which implies 3.1 problem drug users per 1,000 inhabitants aged 15 to 64 years (range 2.2 – 4.3). Due to the large confidence intervals, the estimate for 2001 did not differ significantly from the previous estimate for the year 1999. For this previous year the number of problem drug users per 1,000 inhabitants aged 15 to 64 years was estimated at 2.7."

International Drug Facts

NETHERLANDS

Source: Trimbos Institute, "Drug Situation 2006 The Netherlands by the Reitox National Focal Point: Report to the EMCDDA" (Utrecht, Netherlands: Trimbos-Instuut, 2007), p. 37.

2. "The number of drug users who are currently injecting their drug can be estimated from treatment data given by the National Alcohol and Drugs Information System (LADIS, see also paragraph 4.2), in combination with the estimated number of problem hard drug users at national level. According to the LADIS, 10% of the opiate clients in 2005 in-jected their drug. There were 16,199 clients who had a primary or a secondary problem with opiates. This implies that there were about 1,620 currently injecting opiate users in treatment."

Source: Trimbos Institute, "Drug Situation 2006 The Netherlands by the Reitox National Focal Point: Report to the EMCDDA" (Utrecht, Netherlands: Trimbos-Instuut, 2007), p. 41.

3. "There were 11,652 clients in treatment that had a primary or a secondary problem with cocaine or crack, who were not yet counted among the clients with a primary or secondary problem with opiates. Of these cocaine/crack clients only 1% injected, whereas 59% smoked, and 40% sniffed the drug. The approximately 4,661 clients who snort their cocaine are less problematic and less marginalised and are not included in the estimated number of problem hard drug users at national level. Of the remaining 6,991 problematic cocaine/crack users who are in treatment, about 117 clients are estimated to be injecting drug users."

Source: Trimbos Institute, "Drug Situation 2006 The Netherlands by the Reitox National Focal Point: Report to the EMCDDA" (Utrecht, Netherlands: Trimbos-Instuut, 2007), p. 41.

4. "All in all, these figures from the opiate and cocaine/crack clients imply that, of the 18,643 problem hard drug clients in treatment, about 1,737 currently inject, which comes down to about 9.3%. Given the estimated number of 33,499 problem hard drug users at national level, it is then estimated that there are about 3,115 currently injecting problem hard drug users in the Netherlands, within a range of 2,211 to 4,321 injectors. Given the total of 11,008,282 inhabitants aged from 15 to 64 years in 2005, it is thus estimated that among the general population 0.03% are current injectors of hard drugs, within a range of 0.02% to 0.04% current injectors."

Source: Trimbos Institute, "Drug Situation 2006 The Netherlands by the Reitox National Focal Point: Report to the EMCDDA" (Utrecht, Netherlands: Trimbos-Instuut, 2007), pp. 41-42.

5. "The total number of recorded drug-related deaths increased between 1995 and 2001, decreased in 2002 and 2003, increased again in 2004 and stabilized in 2005. The increasing trend can be attributed to various factors, such as the change from ICD-9 to ICD-10 in 1996 (ICD-10 includes more cases), and the rise in acute cocaine deaths, which seems to parallel an increase in the problem use of this substance.

International Drug Facts

NETHERLANDS

"From the 122 cases in 2005, a total of 42 cases were coded to unspecified substances, compared to 54 in the 2004 registration year."

Source: Trimbos Institute, "Drug Situation 2006 The Netherlands by the Reitox National Focal Point: Report to the EMCDDA" (Utrecht, Netherlands: Trimbos-Instuut, 2007), p. 57.

6. "When generalising the figures from Amsterdam to the whole of the country, adjustments were therefore made for these differences in age and percentage of HIV infection. After these adjustments the total mortality among problem drug users for the whole of the Netherlands was estimated at 479 deaths, within a range between 340 and 664 deaths. From the estimated total mortality, 11% was considered to be a base-rate mortality which is not related to drugs, 23% was attributed directly to drugs, and 66% was attributed indirectly to drugs."

Source: Trimbos Institute, "Drug Situation 2006 The Netherlands by the Reitox National Focal Point: Report to the EMCDDA" (Utrecht, Netherlands: Trimbos-Instuut, 2007), p. 61.

7. "In 2005, 278 new AIDS diagnoses (of which 17 (6%) related to injecting drug use) were made, but this number is subject to change due to reporting delay (de Boer et al. 2006).
"In previous years, the number of cases related to injecting drug use peaked in 1995 (74), dropped to 9, 8, 13 and 6 cases in 2001, 2002, 2003, and 2004 respectively. Until 2005, 659 AIDS patients were registered as being infected through injecting drug use. The annual proportion of injecting drug users varied between 2% and 14% (De Boer et al. 2006)."

Source: Trimbos Institute, "Drug Situation 2006 The Netherlands by the Reitox National Focal Point: Report to the EMCDDA" (Utrecht, Netherlands: Trimbos-Instuut, 2007), p. 64.

D. Harm Reduction Efforts

1. "Despite fluctuations over the years, the total number of drug-related deaths in the Netherlands has remained relatively low. This might be explained by protective factors, such as the nationwide availability of methadone-maintenance treatment and the low rate of injecting drug use in the Netherlands."

Source: Trimbos Institute, "Drug Situation 2006 The Netherlands by the Reitox National Focal Point: Report to the EMCDDA" (Utrecht, Netherlands: Trimbos-Instuut, 2007), pp. 57-58.

2. "There are only limited data on needle exchange. Data from Amsterdam show that from 1990 to 1993 around one million needles were exchanged. After that this number gradually declined to some 500,000 in 1999, more than 300,000 in 2003 and only around 200,000 in 2004 and 2005 (M. Buster, personal communication). The total number of needle exchange programmes in the Netherlands is not known, nor are there national registration data on the number of exchanged syringes or needles. The website of Mainline (the grassroots organisation of drug users in Amsterdam) only presents some 120 exchange points in different cities (www.mainline.nl; updated in January 2005)."

International Drug Facts

NETHERLANDS

Source: Trimbos Institute, "Drug Situation 2006 The Netherlands by the Reitox National Focal Point: Report to the EMCDDA" (Utrecht, Netherlands: Trimbos-Instuut, 2007), pp. 74-75.

3. "Drug consumption rooms aim to reduce public nuisance, e.g. publicly using illegal drugs, leaving used needles around in the neighbourhood, or drug dealing. These rooms are also supposed to reduce the risk of transfer of infectious diseases and drug-related death, because drugs can be used in a safe, non-harassing and supervised environment with clean syringes and medical support on request. The number of drug consumption rooms in the Netherlands increased from some 20 to 32 in 2003. After that period some new rooms were initiated and others disappeared. The total number in 2006 was around 40."

Source: Trimbos Institute, "Drug Situation 2006 The Netherlands by the Reitox National Focal Point: Report to the EMCDDA" (Utrecht, Netherlands: Trimbos-Instuut, 2007), pp. 76-77.

4. "Medical heroin (co)prescription aims to improve the physical and psychosocial situation and to reduce drug-related crime within a selected group of opiate addicts. In the Netherlands it is also supposed to reduce drug-related nuisance and crime. An evaluation of the experiment with medical heroin prescription for treatment resistant opiate addicts showed that for more than 75% of the initial participants, the physical and psychosocial health situation improved substantially during the two years after the experiment. Criminal behaviour had become almost absent among this group. Moreover, thirteen percent voluntarily embarked on abstinence-based treatment or methadone maintenance treatment (Van den Brink et al. 2002). Therefore, medical heroin prescription will be continued and expanded for three years."

Source: Trimbos Institute, "Drug Situation 2006 The Netherlands by the Reitox National Focal Point: Report to the EMCDDA" (Utrecht, Netherlands: Trimbos-Instuut, 2007), pp. 77.

E. Treatment

1. "Due to mergers, the number of organisations of addiction care that are funded by public money, has decreased from 32 to 18 during the past six years (cf. (De Beer 2006)). The number of locations or units did not change much, i.e. somewhat more than two hundred."

Source: Trimbos Institute, "Drug Situation 2006 The Netherlands by the Reitox National Focal Point: Report to the EMCDDA" (Utrecht, Netherlands: Trimbos-Instuut, 2007), p. 51.

2. "In the Netherlands, methadone is mainly used in outpatient drug substitution treatment. A second substitution drug (buprenorphine) is not used on a regular basis (i.e. in only one organisation of addiction care). Methadone is dispensed in outpatient addiction units, methadone posts and in some cases special buses. In Amsterdam, the Municipal Health Service and a number of general practitioners are also involved in methadone distribu-tion. National registration data show that in 2005 methadone was dispensed 2.9 million times to 12,564 persons."

International Drug Facts

NETHERLANDS

Source: Trimbos Institute, "Drug Situation 2006 The Netherlands by the Reitox National Focal Point: Report to the EMCDDA" (Utrecht, Netherlands: Trimbos-Instuut, 2007), p. 55.

3. "In June 2004, the Dutch government decided that the treatment capacity for the medical prescription of heroin for chronic and treatment-resistant opiate addicts could be extended from 300 to 1,000 addicts (T.K.24077/137). This is a special treatment for a limited group in the setting of specialised addiction care. In December 2006, the Medicines Evaluation Board informed the Central Committee on the Treatment of Heroin Addicts (CCBH) that heroin was registered as a medicinal product for treatment-resistant heroin addicts (Central Committee on the Treatment of Heroin Addicts) (CCBH 2006). Most of the treatment costs for this special group of addicts have to be paid by the local munici-pal authorities. By the end of 2005 the Ministry of Health (VWS) adopted the plans of four out of the six municipalities already providing medical heroin co-prescription to in-crease their treatment capacity. Moreover, it approved the plans of eight other munici-palities to develop a treatment unit. In the autumn of 2006, a total of 815 treatment places in 18 municipalities were approved by the Minister. They are scheduled to be in operation by the end of 2007 (personal communication VWS)."

Source: Trimbos Institute, "Drug Situation 2006 The Netherlands by the Reitox National Focal Point: Report to the EMCDDA" (Utrecht, Netherlands: Trimbos-Instuut, 2007), p. 21.

F. Substance Use and the Justice System

1. "The criminal justice system in The Netherlands has to deal with several thousands of drug offences each year. These consist specifically of offences against the Opium Act in which possession, trafficking, production and cultivation — not drug use — are criminal acts."

Source: Trimbos Institute, "Drug Situation 2006 The Netherlands by the Reitox National Focal Point: Report to the EMCDDA" (Utrecht, Netherlands: Trimbos-Instuut, 2007), p. 83.

2. "In 2005, after four years of substantial and consecutive increase, the total number of Opium Act cases has decreased to 20,105: -8% in comparison to 2004. This drop con-cerns only hard drug cases, however, while soft drug cases still continued to increase to 9,298 cases in 2005: +2% compared to 2004. The number of soft drugs cases now is twice the number in 2000.
"Hard drug cases now account for less than half of total cases: 48% in 2005 (53% in 2004). Soft drug cases now make up 46% of all cases (41% in 2004). And 5% of the cases concern both hard and soft drugs.
"In 2005 Opium Act cases make up 7.5% of the total number of cases recorded by the Public Prosecution Service, slightly less than the year before (8.0% in 2004)."

Source: Trimbos Institute, "Drug Situation 2006 The Netherlands by the Reitox National Focal Point: Report to the EMCDDA" (Utrecht, Netherlands: Trimbos-Instuut, 2007), p. 83.

International Drug Facts

NETHERLANDS / RUSSIAN FEDERATION

3. "It was found that seven out of ten Opium Act cases (2004: 71%, and 2005: 69%) concern preparation, production and trafficking of drugs, the rest concerns possession only.

    "Moreover, two out of three cases of possession concern hard drugs (64% in 2004, and 66% in 2005)."

    Source: Trimbos Institute, "Drug Situation 2006 The Netherlands by the Reitox National Focal Point: Report to the EMCDDA" (Utrecht, Netherlands: Trimbos-Instuut, 2007), p. 84.

4. "The absolute number of possession cases remains unchanged in 2004 and 2005. But the number of cases of preparation, production and trafficking decreased by 10%. This drop involves hard drug cases only: cases of preparation, production and trafficking of hard drugs in 2005 are 25% below the level of 2004. In the meantime those for soft drugs increased — by 8%.

    "As a result of this development in 2005 more than half (53%) of the cases of preparation, production and trafficking concern soft drugs. The year before in 2004 hard drugs made up more than half (57%)."

    Source: Trimbos Institute, "Drug Situation 2006 The Netherlands by the Reitox National Focal Point: Report to the EMCDDA" (Utrecht, Netherlands: Trimbos-Instuut, 2007), p. 84.

5. "Opium Act offenders booked by the police have a relatively high chance of ending up in prison for a relatively long time. Opium Act offenders booked by the police account for 7% of the total number of offenders booked by the police. But their proportion in custodial sentences is higher (13%) and their proportion of detention years is even more substantial (21%)."

    Source: Trimbos Institute, "Drug Situation 2006 The Netherlands by the Reitox National Focal Point: Report to the EMCDDA" (Utrecht, Netherlands: Trimbos-Instuut, 2007), p. 89.

6. The incarceration rate in the Netherlands is 128 inmates per 100,000 of national population, with a total prison population 21,013 out of an estimated national population of 16.38 million.

    Source: Walmsley, Roy, "World Prison Population List (Seventh Edition)" (London, England: International Centre for Prison Studies, 2007), p. 5, Table 4, citing the national prison authority.

7. The homicide rate in the Netherlands is 1.51 per 100,000 national population (average per year 1999 to 2001).

    Source: Barclay, Gordon & Cynthia Tavares, "International Comparisons of Criminal Justice Statistics 2001," Home Office Bulletin 12/03 (London, England, UK: Home Office Research, Development, and Statistics Directorate, October 24, 2003), p. 10, Table 1.1.

RUSSIAN FEDERATION

A. Overview

1. "The drug enforcement agencies are supported in their functions by strong drug control laws and high-level Governmental attention. While recent years have seen some increase in the resources devoted to the prevention

148

International Drug Facts

RUSSIAN FEDERATION

of drug abuse and to the care for drug users, the major emphasis in the Government's policy is clearly targeted on addressing the problem of drug trafficking and production.

"Some outside observers believe that this heavy emphasis on law enforcement sometimes hampers efforts to address the problems of drug abuse, particularly among the youth. For one thing, there is some evidence that many drug users are sent to prison for drug trafficking, although they are arrested with small quantities of drugs in their possession. Since 1997, with the introduction of a new Criminal Code, the possession of a "small amount of narcotics" is not considered a criminal offence, but an administrative infraction. However, the definitions of what constitutes a "small amount" of the various drugs are established at extremely low levels. In the case of heroin, there is no quantity that can be considered a "small amount" and, thus, the possession of any quantity of that drug can be prosecuted as drug trafficking. This phenomenon, coupled with the fact that there are no juvenile courts in Russia, has resulted in the incarceration of many young drug users in adult prisons where there are few, if any, drug treatment programmes, and where they may be exposed to risks of violence, and of infection with tuberculosis and HIV/AIDS."

Source: United Nations Office on Drugs and Crime, "County Profile: Russian Federation" (Moscow, Russia: UNODC Regional Office, Russian Federation, 2003) p. 33.

2. "This was a couple of years after Russia had toughened its drug laws, lowering the minimum punishable dose to such a level that virtually any user could land behind bars. By 2004, the Justice Ministry estimated that 300,000 people were serving drug-related sentences in Russian prisons.

"That year the government — responding in part to pressure from the Justice Ministry, which was fighting prison overpopulation — raised the minimum punishable doses of illegal drugs, essentially ensuring that users who had no intent to sell would not be arrested. The police were incensed, arguing that some dealers took to carrying amounts just below the punishable level — but still sufficient to satisfy between one and nine users. In other words, the police complained, they were being prevented from arresting users and small-time dealers and forced to focus on real drug dealers, whom they didn't want to touch with a 10-foot pole.

"The more-liberal policy lasted less than two years. The minimum punishable dose has been lowered again — in most cases, by more than 50 percent. The dose is not quite as low as pre-2004 levels, but still low enough to put even casual users at risk."

Source: "Anti-Drug Laws for Drug Dealers," by Masha Gessen, Moscow Times, Feb. 16, 2006, from the web at http://www.mapinc.org/newscsdp/v06/n210/a10.html, last accessed Feb. 17, 2006.

International Drug Facts

RUSSIAN FEDERATION

B. Prevalence Estimates

1. "Since 2004 the overall number of drug abusers on register in the Russian Federation stayed almost unchanged with 342,719 in 2004 and 343,509 in 2005 (or 240.2 and 241.3 per 100,000 population accordingly). The number of newly registered cases of drug abuse has been gradually decreasing during the last 5 years but has for the first time shown a small increase (by 16.3%) in 2005 with 24,390 cases (or 17.1 per 100,000 population) compared to 21,027 (or 14,7 per 100,000) in 2004."

   Source: UNODC, "Illicit Drug Trends in the Russian Federation, 2005" (UNODC Regional Office for Russia and Belarus, Nov. 2006), p. 10.

2. "Estimates of the number of drug users range from 1.5 – 4.0 million drug users from the law enforcement services (and up to 6 million drug users from other sources). Regardless of the definitional differences at the basis of these estimates (i.e. drug addict vs. person who has tried drugs once in their life), there is a need to further gauge the extent of the drug problem."

   Source: UNODC, "Illicit Drug Trends in the Russian Federation, 2005" (UNODC Regional Office for Russia and Belarus, Nov. 2006), p. 12.

3. "By 2005, the Federal Drug Control Service reported that there were 1.5 million drug users in Russia, with 343,509 drug addicts officially registered in narcological centres. The Ministry of Health estimated that regular drug users may number up to 6 million Russians. Minister Nurgaliev stated that 4 million teenagers are drug users, with an estimated 1 million considered hardened addicts. Further, the epidemic has a young face, with the average age of users in some regions said to have dropped from 17 to 11 years in recent years and addiction rates in minors generally being cited as 2.5 times higher than that of the adult population."

   Source: UNODC, "Illicit Drug Trends in the Russian Federation, 2005" (UNODC Regional Office for Russia and Belarus, Nov. 2006), p. 14.

4. "There is some controversy over the number of narcotic drug users in Russia. Dr. Vadim Pokrovsky of the Federal AIDS Center said that estimates of the number of active drug users in Russia in February 2004 ranged from 1 to 4 million, and he believed the high end of that range reflected the reality. On February 20, 2004, Alexander Mikhailov, the deputy director of the State Drug Control Committee (SDCC), a federal body, was cited in Pravda as saying that Russia had over 4 million drug users, and that the "gloomy prediction" of his office was that Russia could have over 35 million drug users by 2014. In early January 2004, the executive secretary of the Commonwealth of Independent States, which includes twelve former Soviet states, predicted that in 2010 the twelve countries would have 25 million drug users of whom 10 million would be living with HIV/AIDS, the vast majority in Russia."

International Drug Facts

RUSSIAN FEDERATION

Source: Human Rights Watch, "Lessons Not Learned: Human Rights Abuses and HIV/AIDS in the Russian Federation," April 2004, Vol. 16, No. 5, pp. 14-15.

5. "There is no doubt that drug use and heroin use particularly have risen meteorically in Russia since 1990. Mikhailov said the total number of drug users had risen 900 percent in the decade ending in early 2004. A Max Planck Institute study of the drug trade in Russia concluded that drug-related crimes increased twelve-fold from 1990 to 1999. Many analysts have traced the dramatic rise in use of injected heroin since the fall of the Soviet Union to economic collapse and attendant rises in unemployment, poverty and desperation and to increased availability of cheap heroin trafficked through central Asia and across the former Soviet states. Some observers have suggested that the aftermath of the events of September 11, 2001 in Afghanistan and central Asia has done nothing to stem the flow of heroin through the region and may even exacerbate it in the long run. Mikhailov of the SDCC has told the press on numerous occasions that the United States military intervention in Afghanistan has contributed to heroin consumption in Russia because the Taliban had been able to suppress opium production before they were overthrown. In 2003, Victor Cherkesov, head of the SDCC, said the drug trade in Russia was valued at about U.S. $8 billion a year."

Source: Human Rights Watch, "Lessons Not Learned: Human Rights Abuses and HIV/AIDS in the Russian Federation," April 2004, Vol. 16, No. 5, p. 15.

C. Problem Substance Use and Substance-Related Harm

1. "From the point of view of drug-related health indicators two main problem regions can be pointed out in 2005 in scale of the whole country: south of Central / Eastern Siberia and west of Southern Federal District (regions near the Black Sea). In the majority of the problematic regions around 90% of registered users are intravenous drug users. Across the country the indicator of intravenous drug use among all stages of dependency is 74%. Still there are a few exceptions like the Tyva Republic where 83% of registered drug abusers have cannabis as the main drug."

Source: UNODC, "Illicit Drug Trends in the Russian Federation, 2005" (UNODC Regional Office for Russia and Belarus, Nov. 2006), p. 11.

2. "The epidemic disproportionately affects IDUs who comprise 87% of the cumulative number of registered HIV cases, however, with the epidemic becoming more mature, the infection tendency away from IDUs to heterosexual is also increasing with 68% of newly registered cases by the end of 2004 corresponding to IDU and 30% to heterosexuals (In the previous year heterosexual transmission accounted for 23.4% of new infections). The interpretation of the tendency towards less new infections diagnosed is not an indication of a slowing of the epidemic but rather reflective of the changes in HIV testing policy, the smaller number of tests performed in population groups with high-risk behaviors and also a shortage of test kits."

International Drug Facts

RUSSIAN FEDERATION

Source: UNODC, "Illicit Drug Trends in the Russian Federation, 2005" (UNODC Regional Office for Russia and Belarus, Nov. 2006), p. 14.

3. "The Russian Federation is facing a deadly epidemic of acquired immune deficiency syndrome (AIDS). It is driven in part by abuses of the human rights of those most at risk to get the disease and of the over 1 million Russians already living with the human immunodeficiency virus (HIV). The principal means of HIV transmission in Russia has been and remains injection drug use. But the Russian state has done little to support low-cost measures that would enable drug users to realize their right to be protected from this incurable disease. Instead, Russia has been a model of repression of drug users and stigmatization of HIV-positive people, putting the country squarely on the path of very high AIDS mortality and continued abuse of people affected by HIV/AIDS."

Source: Human Rights Watch, "Lessons Not Learned: Human Rights Abuses and HIV/AIDS in the Russian Federation," April 2004, Vol. 16, No. 5, p. 1.

4. "In 2002, an estimated 93 percent of persons registered by the government as HIVpositive since the beginning of the epidemic were injection drug users. In contrast, in 2002 an estimated 12 percent of new HIV transmission was sexual — that figure climbed to 17.5 percent in the first half of 2003 — indicating the foothold that the epidemic is gaining in the general population. The European Centre for the Epidemiological Monitoring of AIDS (EuroHIV), a center affiliated with the World Health Organization, noted that HIV prevalence may have 'reached saturation levels in at least some of the currently affected drug user populations' in eastern Europe, including in Russia, but cautioned against complacency 'as new outbreaks could still emerge among injection drug users…, particularly within the vast expanse of the Russian Federation.' Rhodes and colleagues in a February 2004 article echo this conclusion, noting evidence of recent examples of severe HIV outbreaks among drug users in Russia."

Source: Human Rights Watch, "Lessons Not Learned: Human Rights Abuses and HIV/AIDS in the Russian Federation," April 2004, Vol. 16, No. 5, p. 10.

D. Harm Reduction Efforts

1. "As indicated above, in recent years, the Government has announced the initiation of various programmes for expanding drug abuse preventive activities and treatment and rehabilitation of drug abusers. Largely due to the lack of resources, there have, in fact, been very few concrete actions in this field. There are almost no preventive education programmes aimed at informing the general public about the problems of illicit drugs. Targeted preventive programmes for high-risk groups, such as the unemployed and the youth, have been limited primarily to some small-scale, HIV/AIDS-related, activities undertaken by NGOs. The Ministry of Education has been attempting to develop some drug abuse preventive education programmes for the schools and has asked for some assistance from UNODC."

International Drug Facts

RUSSIAN FEDERATION

Source: United Nations Office on Drugs and Crime, "County Profile: Russian Federation" (Moscow, Russia: UNODC Regional Office, Russian Federation, 2003) p. 33.

2. "Researchers have found that police harassment is one of the most important factors that exacerbate risky behavior among drug users in Russia. In a 2002 study of drug use in five Russian cities, 44 percent of drug users said they had been stopped by the police in the month prior to being interviewed, and two third of these said that their injecting equipment had been confiscated by the police. Over 40 percent added that they rarely carried syringes for fear of encountering the police with them. In the Togliatti study, Rhodes and colleagues found that fear of being arrested or detained by the police was the most important factor behind the decision of drug users not to carry syringes, which in turn was an important determinant of sharing syringes during injection. This study concluded that drug users who had been arrested or detained by the police for drug-related offenses were over four times more likely than other users to have shared syringes in the previous four weeks. Drug users who feared the police in Togliatti tended to avoid not only syringe exchange services but also drug stores that sold syringes because police frequently targeted people buying syringes at such locations, a result also highlighted in a 2003 study of drug users in Moscow."

Source: Human Rights Watch, "Lessons Not Learned: Human Rights Abuses and HIV/AIDS in the Russian Federation," April 2004, Vol. 16, No. 5, p. 17.

3. "State action that impedes people from protecting themselves from a deadly epidemic is blatant interference with the right of Russians to the highest obtainable standard of health. There is no dispute as to the effectiveness of sterile syringes for preventing HIV, hepatitis C and other blood-borne infections. Public health experts are virtually unanimous in the view that providing access to sterile syringes neither encourages drug use nor dissuades drug users from entering drug treatment programs. In reality, the near absence of humane treatment programs for drug addiction in Russia and the very nature of drug use guarantee that there will always be people who either cannot or will not stop using drugs. Impeding this population from obtaining or using sterile syringes amounts to prescribing death as a punishment for illicit drug use."

Source: Human Rights Watch, "Lessons Not Learned: Human Rights Abuses and HIV/AIDS in the Russian Federation," April 2004, Vol. 16, No. 5, p. 3.

E. Treatment

1. "While provisions of the Federal Drug law guarantee state assistance to drug addicts, in fact, budgetary restraints have severely limited the capacity of state institutions to provide even a minimum level of support for drug users. Although the state drug-treatment centres are under the guidance of the Ministry of Health, they are, in fact, financed by the various administrative entities of the Federation. Since most of the oblasts

International Drug Facts

RUSSIAN FEDERATION

and republics have severe financial restraints, in most cases, the drug-treatment centres have not been able to cope with the sudden expansion in the number of drug users requiring assistance. They lack the financial, material and staff resources to carry out the tasks, which are assigned to them by law. There are a few private treatment centres in some of the major cities, but only the wealthy can make use of their facilities. This general lack of treatment and rehabilitation facilities and activities for drug users are some of the reasons why the country has been facing extreme difficulties in attempting to address the very serious problem of HIV/AIDS infection among injecting drug users."

Source: United Nations Office on Drugs and Crime, "County Profile: Russian Federation" (Moscow, Russia: UNODC Regional Office, Russian Federation, 2003) p. 34.

2. "Substitution (or replacement) therapy such as methadone maintenance therapy, which has been widely credited with controlling HIV transmission among injection drug users in many countries, is illegal in Russia, and the 2003 amendments to the drug law did not change this. Methadone is classified as 'illicit' by the terms of the three United Nations conventions on drug control, though most countries that are signatories to the conventions have methadone programs that are successful in substituting injected heroin with noninjected methadone. In this case, neither the SDCC nor the Ministry of Health seems necessarily disposed to review the status quo. Dr. Golyusov of the Ministry of Health said that he is concerned by first-hand accounts from drug users that methadone is more addictive or 'harder to get off' than heroin and that other countries' experiences have been 'contradictory.'"

Source: Human Rights Watch, "Lessons Not Learned: Human Rights Abuses and HIV/AIDS in the Russian Federation," April 2004, Vol. 16, No. 5, p. 22.

F. Substance Use and the Justice System

1. "In 2005, the number of drug related offences registered by all law enforcement agencies totaled 175,241 which is 17% higher compared to 2004."

Source: UNODC, "Illicit Drug Trends in the Russian Federation, 2005" (UNODC Regional Office for Russia and Belarus, Nov. 2006), p. 5.

2. "Drug distribution offences increased from 79,902 to 110,310 (+38%) and constituted 63% of all drug related crimes (53% in 2004). These changes were determined by the May 2004 amendment to the Criminal and Procedural Codes, which led to the retargeting the efforts of law enforcement agencies toward the most serious types of offences. The number of detected offences committed by organized groups in 2005 totaled 14,415."

Source: UNODC, "Illicit Drug Trends in the Russian Federation, 2005" (UNODC Regional Office for Russia and Belarus, Nov. 2006), p. 5.

International Drug Facts

RUSSIAN FEDERATION

3. "The most serious threat of illegal smuggling originates from Afghanistan (heroin and opium). Drugs are smuggled through Central Asia into Russia's domestic market and onwards into Europe. Since the withdrawal of Russian Border Guards from the Tajikistan / Afghanistan border in December 2004 heroin seizures have decreased significantly in all Central Asian States with seizures now the lowest on record since 2001."

   Source: UNODC, "Illicit Drug Trends in the Russian Federation, 2005" (UNODC Regional Office for Russia and Belarus, Nov. 2006), p. 8.

4. "The results of drug purity analysis are not readily available in part due to the fact that drug related sentencing is based on weight rather than other indicators. Nevertheless, some sources point to a continuing low heroin purity level reported in different parts of the country corroborating a trend first reported in 2001."

   Source: UNODC, "Illicit Drug Trends in the Russian Federation, 2005" (UNODC Regional Office for Russia and Belarus, Nov. 2006), p. 9.

5. "Because of drug laws that have historically criminalized the possession of very small amounts of narcotics, drug users in Russia face a high probability of spending time in prison or pretrial detention at some time in their lives. Injection drug use is widespread in prisons. But basic HIV prevention measures, including condoms and materials for sterilization of syringes, are largely lacking in Russian correctional facilities, making prisons across the country high-risk environments for AIDS. The vast numbers of prisoners released every year thus represent a public health challenge for the general population. Both in and outside of prison, the virtual absence of humane services to treat drug addiction and the illegality in Russia of methadone and other drugs used elsewhere to treat heroin addiction further compromise HIV prevention among drug users."

   Source: Human Rights Watch, "Lessons Not Learned: Human Rights Abuses and HIV/AIDS in the Russian Federation," April 2004, Vol. 16, No. 5, pp. 2-3.

6. "Being in prison or other state detention is an important risk factor for HIV in Russia. A very high percentage of drug users in the FSU find themselves in state custody at some time in their lives. Injection drug use is reportedly widespread in Russian prisons, and HIV prevention services such as provision of sterile syringes, disinfectant materials for syringes and condoms are virtually absent. Official statistics indicate that from 1996 to 2003, HIV prevalence in Russian prisons rose more than thirty-fold from less than one per 1,000 inmates to 42.1 per 1,000 inmates. According to a 2002 report, about 34,000 HIV-positive persons—over 15 percent of the persons officially counted as HIV-positive in the country—were in state custody, of which the large majority found out about their HIV status in prison. The Kresty pretrial detention facility in Saint Petersburg was reported in 2002 to have about 1,000 HIV-positive persons among its 7,800 inmates. Some 300,000 prisoners are released each year from penal institutions in Russia, representing an important public health challenge."

International Drug Facts

RUSSIAN FEDERATION / SWEDEN

Source: Human Rights Watch, "Lessons Not Learned: Human Rights Abuses and HIV/AIDS in the Russian Federation," April 2004, Vol. 16, No. 5, pp. 11-12.

7. "The system of penalties for juveniles facing criminal charges in Russia is based on suspended sentences or detention in educational correctional facilities, which house young offenders aged up to 21 years. The average sentence is four years. Only one quarter of adult recidivists considered a high-risk to society are said to have been admitted to a VK as juveniles."

Source: UNODC, "Illicit Drug Trends in the Russian Federation, 2005" (UNODC Regional Office for Russia and Belarus, Nov. 2006), p. 15.

8. The Russian Federation's incarceration rate is 611 inmates per 100,000 of national population, with a total prison population 869,814 out of an estimated national population of 142.3 million.

Source: Walmsley, Roy, "World Prison Population List (Seventh Edition)" (London, England: International Centre for Prison Studies, 2007), p. 5, Table 4, citing the national prison authority.

9. The Russian Federation's homicide rate is 22.05 per 100,000 national population (average per year 1999 to 2001).

Source: Barclay, Gordon & Cynthia Tavares, "International Comparisons of Criminal Justice Statistics 2001," Home Office Bulletin 12/03 (London, England, UK: Home Office Research, Development, and Statistics Directorate, October 24, 2003), p. 10, Table 1.1.

SWEDEN

A. Overview

1. "The goal and main message in the National Drug Strategy (Regeringens proposition 2002b) is the vision of a drug-free society. The efforts in that work can be summarised in the following way: more people are to become involved in work against drugs; more people are to say no to drugs; more people are to know about the medical and social consequences of drugs; fewer people should start using drugs; more abusers are to obtain help to a life free of drugs and criminality; and the availability of drugs is to be reduced. Particular priorities in the present strategy are directed to the prison and probation area and the treatment and care sector.

"The strategy is a downright drug strategy in terms of focusing on what is considered as illegal drugs. The only exception from that is a passage saying that leakage of narcotic pharmaceuticals into the illegal market should be narrowed. It is also a downright drug strategy in the meaning that substances are never mentioned. The aim is on political prioritising, demand and supply reduction, treatment and rehabilitation improvement and with no distinction between different illegal drugs."

Source: Statens Folkhalsoinstitut, "2005 National Report (2004 data) to the EMCDDA by the Reitox National Focal Point: Sweden — New Development, Trends and In-Depth Information on Selected Issues" (2006), p. 63.

International Drug Facts

SWEDEN

2. "Sweden has a restrictive policy on drugs (Proposition 2001/02:91. Nationell narkotikahandlingsplan); This was established already in 1968 when a drug policy bill was agreed upon in the Parliament, a year before a national Committee on the Treatment on Drug Abusers was ready to present its final report and recommendations on co-ordinating measures (SOU1969:52). A year before, 1967, an incident in a project with free prescriptions to drug abusers in Stockholm led to an intense debate in media and the closure of the project. This project was started in 1965. That was also the starting point for a project in the Central House of Detention in Stockholm, where Professor Nils Bejerot, by noting and counting fresh needle marks among new detainees wanted to demonstrate that the free prescription project would cause an increased prevalence of drug abuse in society. His views were much debated. Together with apprehensions of an escalating drug problem and in accordance with a restrictive alcohol policy the course was set."

Source: Swedish National Institute of Public Health & Swedish Council for Information on Alcohol and Other Drugs, "National Report: Sweden 2002" (Lisboa, Portugal: European Monitoring Centre for Drugs and Drug Addiction, 2003), p. 9.

3. "Between 1917 and 1955 Sweden had an alcohol rationing system, and even today embraces a comparatively restrictive alcohol policy. This tradition makes a restrictive drug policy a logical option."

Source: Boekhout van Solinge, Tim, "Dutch Drug Policy in a European Context" (Amsterdam, The Netherlands: Center for Drug Studies, University of Amsterdam, 1999), pre-publication version of an article appearing in Journal of Drug Issues 29(3), 511-528, 1999, from the web at http://www.cedro-uva.org/lib/boekhout.dutch.html last accessed July 2, 2007.

B. Prevalence Estimates

1. "The availability of cannabis, amphetamines, heroin and cocaine has increased strongly since the late 1980s, as illustrated by a doubling of seizures of these drugs over this period, in terms of both numbers and amounts seized. During the same time, prices of these drugs have roughly halved in real terms. The impression of increased drug availability in the 1990s is also confirmed by young people in various questionnaire surveys."

Source: Centralförbundet för alkohol- och narkotikaupplysning, "Drogutvecklingen i Sverige 2006" (Stockholm, Sweden: CAN, 2006), Report No. 98, p. 37.

2. "Since 1971, there are national data from surveys of school pupils and military conscripts. The share of ninth-year school pupils (aged 15–16) having tried illegal drugs was at its highest in the early 1970s, then fell to reach a low of 3–4 per cent in the second half of the 1980s. During the 1990s, this share more than doubled, and it was close to 10 per cent in 2001. From then on there has been a decrease; the share was 6 per cent in 2006."

Source: Centralförbundet för alkohol- och narkotikaupplysning, "Drogutvecklingen i Sverige 2006" (Stockholm, Sweden: CAN, 2006), Report No. 98, p. 38.

157

International Drug Facts

SWEDEN

3. "Surveys of 18-year-old men undergoing physical and psychological examination in connection with compulsory military conscription describe a similar trend as school surveys: falling levels in the 1980s and rises in the 1990s. Between 1992 and 2002, the share of conscripts who had tried illegal drugs at least once increased threefold, from 6 to 18 per cent. Since then, as among the two-years-younger school pupils, trying drugs has become less frequent: in 2005, 14 per cent of conscripts said they had used illegal drugs. A new series of annual surveys of second-year pupils at upper-secondary school (aged 17–18) has been started; between 2004 and 2006 some 15 per cent claimed to have tried illegal drugs."

    Source: Centralförbundet för alkohol- och narkotikaupplysning, "Drogutvecklingen i Sverige 2006" (Stockholm, Sweden: CAN, 2006), Report No. 98, p. 38.

4. "In school and conscription surveys, current use (30-day prevalence) has largely followed the same trends as lifetime prevalence. One exception is ninth-year pupils, where current use has not fallen in the 2000s but has been 3–4 per cent in the past two years. During the same period in the survey of upper-secondary pupils, 4 per cent claimed to have used illegal drugs in the past 30 days, with prevalence being higher for male pupils. These are relatively high levels. According to the survey of 16–24-year-olds, current use peaks at around the age of 21."

    Source: Centralförbundet för alkohol- och narkotikaupplysning, "Drogutvecklingen i Sverige 2006" (Stockholm, Sweden: CAN, 2006), Report No. 98, p. 38.

5. "The most recent survey of adults — a postal survey of 16–84-year-olds carried out in 2006 — shows that about 10 per cent have tried cannabis at least once, corresponding to over 700 000 people in the age range in question. Among 18–29-year-olds, about one-fourth of men and one-fifth of women claimed to have tried cannabis. In this age group, last-year prevalence of cannabis was 8 per cent for men and 4 per cent for women, as compared with 2 per cent for men and 1 per cent for women among all respondents."

    Source: Centralförbundet för alkohol- och narkotikaupplysning, "Drogutvecklingen i Sverige 2006" (Stockholm, Sweden: CAN, 2006), Report No. 98, p. 39.

6. "Total consumption in 2005 is estimated at 10.2 litres of pure alcohol per inhabitant aged 15 years or more. Much of the alcohol consumed nowadays comes from private imports, whose share was estimated at 22 per cent in 2005. In the same year, 2 per cent derived from legal home production, 11 per cent from smuggling and illicit home distilling (i.e. illegal sources), 15 per cent from restaurants and grocer's shops, and 48 per cent from the retailing monopoly. Between 1990 and 2005 the share of unrecorded alcohol has doubled from 18 to 36 per cent of total consumption. While part of this increase is due to a rising share for illegal alcohol, the main reason is growing volumes of privately imported alcohol, mainly as a consequence of the fact that since 1 January 2004, when the phasing-out of previously strict import regulations was completed, large volumes of alcohol may be imported from other EU countries."

International Drug Facts

SWEDEN

Source: Centralförbundet för alkohol- och narkotikaupplysning, "Drogutvecklingen i Sverige 2006" (Stockholm, Sweden: CAN, 2006), Report No. 98, p. 31.

7. "In the past four years, annual consumption has amounted to about 10 litres of pure alcohol, which is a historically very high level. Compared with the latter part of the 1990s, this represents an increase of around 2.5 litres or slightly more than 30 per cent, according to the estimates which include unrecorded alcohol."

Source: Centralförbundet för alkohol- och narkotikaupplysning, "Drogutvecklingen i Sverige 2006" (Stockholm, Sweden: CAN, 2006), Report No. 98, p. 32.

C. Problem Substance Use and Substance-Related Harm

1. "The calculation of the prevalence of abuse based on inpatient-care data has been updated, and in 2004 the number of people with heavy drug abuse was estimated at around 26,000 – that is, a return to the 1998 level."

Source: Centralförbundet för alkohol- och narkotikaupplysning, "Drogutvecklingen i Sverige 2006" (Stockholm, Sweden: CAN, 2006), Report No. 98, p. 40.

2. "The estimated number of problem drug users (PDUs) was close to 26,000 in 2003 giving a central rate/100,000 of 4.5 in the 15 - 64 interval. The figures are from a governmental report presented in October 2005 (SOU 2005:82). The estimated number of problem drug users in 2003 is about the same as in the latest case-finding study in 1998 (Lander, I. et al. 2002). According to the report, the number of PDUs has been rather constant over the years since 1998 with a peak in 2001 of close to 28,000-problem drug users."

Source: Statens Folkhalsoinstitut, "2005 National Report (2004 data) to the EMCDDA by the Reitox National Focal Point: Sweden — New Development, Trends and In-Depth Information on Selected Issues" (2006), p. 19.

3. "The vast majority of those whose abuse was classified as 'heavy' in these surveys had injected illegal drugs in the past 12 months. In 1979, 82 per cent had done this, as compared with 93 per cent in 1992 and 89 per cent in 1998. CNS stimulants (mainly amphetamines), opiates (mainly heroin) and cannabis have always been the predominant drugs. "Amphetamines were the main drug for about 48 per cent of heavy abusers both in 1979 and in 1992, but had become less important in 1998, when only 32 per cent had amphetamines as their main drug. Last-year prevalence of amphetamine use was found to be 77, 82 and 73 per cent, respectively.

"Heroin, on the other hand, has gained in importance since 1979. Last-year prevalence was 30, 34 and 47 per cent, respectively. Opiates were the main drug for 15 per cent of abusers in 1979, as compared with 26 per cent in 1992 and 28 per cent in 1998. The rise for heroin is also reflected, for instance, in seizures and prosecutions."

Source: Centralförbundet för alkohol- och narkotikaupplysning, "Drogutvecklingen i Sverige 2006" (Stockholm, Sweden: CAN, 2006), Report No. 98, p. 40.

International Drug Facts

SWEDEN

4. "Comparison between available indicators — mainly data on seizures and criminal-justice, health-care and cause-of-death statistics — and survey findings shows that they provide a relatively similar picture of trends in heavy drug abuse, with rises especially in the 1990s. The indicators point to a continued increase after 1998 as well.

   "For the most recent years, however, some sources indicate a stabilisation or even a decrease. Inpatient-care figures have been falling for a few years, even though this may be a result of the shift towards outpatient care. Drug deaths have stopped increasing and have indeed fallen by 4 per cent between 2001 and 2003, which may be due to the introduction of Subutex in substitution treatment for opiate addicts. Drug prices have also remained relatively unchanged in the 2000s, and even though seizure statistics are no longer fully comparable, at least there does not seem to have been any major rise in the number of seizures in the most recent years. At the same time, however, no fall is discernible in criminal-justice statistics."

   Source: Centralförbundet för alkohol- och narkotikaupplysning, "Drogutvecklingen i Sverige 2006" (Stockholm, Sweden: CAN, 2006), Report No. 98, p. 41.

5. "In 2002-2004, approximately 30 cases of HIV among intravenous drug users were notified annually, comprising approximately 6-12% of the total number of notified HIV cases (27 cases were notified in 2004, which was 6% of all notified cases). When interpreting time trends among HIV positive intravenous drug users, one should keep the low absolute number of cases in mind. The percentage of women varied between 11-36% in the years 1997-2004, with no clear time trend. There seems to be a slight increase in mean age at diagnosis among the intravenous drug users (mean age was 31 in 1991, compared to 40 years in 2004). The share of HIV cases among intravenous drug users, who were infected in Sweden, varied between 70% and 88% in the years 1997-2003. However, in 2004, the share was 56%."

   Source: Statens Folkhalsoinstitut, "2005 National Report (2004 data) to the EMCDDA by the Reitox National Focal Point: Sweden — New Development, Trends and In-Depth Information on Selected Issues" (2006), p. 29.

D. Harm Reduction Efforts

1. According to the Sweden's 2002 national drug report to the European Monitoring Centre for Drugs and Drug Addiction, "Harm reduction in its usual definition is not in practice. In conflict with the restrictive policy two needle exchange programmes exist. They are situated in Scania (Lund since 1986 and Malmö since 1987) on clinics for infectious diseases as a reaction on an expected HIV-epidemic at that time. The National Drug Coordinator will present a recommendation on the programmes future in February 2003. One alternative is to close them down."

   Source: Swedish National Institute of Public Health & Swedish Council for Information on Alcohol and Other Drugs, "National Report: Sweden 2002" (Lisboa, Portugal: European Monitoring Centre for Drugs and Drug Addiction, 2003), p. 47.

International Drug Facts

SWEDEN

E. Treatment

1. "Sweden has no registration that gives an overall view of clients in treatment."

    Source: Statens Folkhalsoinstitut, "2005 National Report (2004 data) to the EMCDDA by the Reitox National Focal Point: Sweden — New Development, Trends and In-Depth Information on Selected Issues" (2006), p. 21.

2. "The National Board of Health and Welfare (NBHW) has (2003) counted 611 specialized units for treatment of alcohol and drug problems (Socialstyrelsen 2004a) with a total of 23,500 clients (31 % women). Specialized units can be found in all systems; community social service, hospitals, therapeutic communities, and prisons. Outpatient treatment comprised 82% of all contacts, residential treatment 12% and 2% were undergoing inpatient treatment in hospitals. 4% participated in various programs in prison. 45% of all patients received treatment for alcohol misuse only, 22% for drugs and 33% for both alcohol and drug problems. 3,376 patients was identified as injecting drug users."

    Source: Statens Folkhalsoinstitut, "2005 National Report (2004 data) to the EMCDDA by the Reitox National Focal Point: Sweden — New Development, Trends and In-Depth Information on Selected Issues" (2006), p. 24.

3. "Sweden has five treatment units at hospitals in Uppsala (opened in 1966), Stockholm, Lund, Malmö and Helsingborg. Substitution treatment with methadone has always been surrounded with strict regulations. Even the number of patients that can be in the program has been regulated a few years ago. The 'roof' was set to 800 patients, but that has very recently been raised to 1,200. However, resources at the five units do not allow more than a few new patients per year to enter treatment. Methadone treatment demand much from patients as well as from staff and therefore it is also considered to be the most advanced and expensive form of treatment within the field.

    "Patients need a documented history of heroin addiction and several serious trials with other forms of treatment before they can have a referral from a specialist physician in a drug clinic. The patient then can be called to a methadone program for further investigation. If the patient is accepted, and a treatment plan has been set together with the responsible local social service, he enters a six months long day care treatment were he gets his very personal adjusted dose (the patient is not aware of the magnitude of the dose, but as a general rule doses are higher than in most programs around the world, which minimizes risk of relapse) of methadone and undergoes a training program during a full working day. Urine specimens are taken daily to secure he actually has taken his dose (which is taken in the premises) and that no illegal drugs have been used. After six months his contacts with the clinic is gradually reduced and he can collect his dose at a selected pharmacy, where he also delivers his urine specimen."

161

International Drug Facts

SWEDEN

Source: Statens Folkhalsoinstitut, "2005 National Report (2004 data) to the EMCDDA by the Reitox National Focal Point: Sweden — New Development, Trends and In-Depth Information on Selected Issues" (2006), p. 27.

4. "Buprenorphine (Subutex) has been under trials in specialized clinics during several years (Heilig and Kakko 2003). As the substance has not been regulated to the same degree as methadone there have appeared a few general practitioners in the arena who has prescribed Subutex. In one case a pensioner physician had more patients in substitution treatment than a methadone clinic usually has. His license as a physician is now suspended. As noted above buprenorphine treatment is now regulated in the same manner as methadone."

Source: Statens Folkhalsoinstitut, "2005 National Report (2004 data) to the EMCDDA by the Reitox National Focal Point: Sweden — New Development, Trends and In-Depth Information on Selected Issues" (2006), p. 27.

5. "Due foremost by financial shortcomings there has been a reduction in treatment programs and a transfer of patients from inpatient to outpatient treatment. Specially tailored treatment has decreased for several target groups in recent years and time spent in inpatient treatment has been seemingly shortened (Socialstyrelsen 2004a)."

Source: Statens Folkhalsoinstitut, "2005 National Report (2004 data) to the EMCDDA by the Reitox National Focal Point: Sweden — New Development, Trends and In-Depth Information on Selected Issues" (2006), p. 26.

F. Substance Use and the Justice System

1. "Since drug use is prohibited with a maximum of six months imprisonment, the police are allowed to conduct drug tests (blood or urine) if there is reasonable cause to believe that a person is under the influence of drugs, however not on persons younger than 15 years old. The conservatives have however suggested a change in the legislation so that also these persons could be tested."

Source: Report to the European Monitoring Center on Drugs and Drug Addiction by the Reitox National Focal Point of Sweden, Folkhalsoinstitutet (National Institute of Public Health), "Sweden Drug Situation 2000" (Stockholm, Sweden: NIPH and EMCDDA, December 2000), p. 13.

2. "In 2004 just over 45,000 crimes against the Narcotic punishment act were reported. This is little more than four per cent of all crimes reported in Sweden 2004 (BRC 2004a). The majority (48%) of the reports were on sole consumption.
"12,606 cases of illegal drug crimes arrived to the Prosecutors in 2004. This was an increase by 17 percent compared to 2003, 30 percent compared to 2002 and 49 percent compared to 2001. It was simultaneously reported that the Prosecutors closed 13 percent more cases of illegal drug related crimes in 2004 than in 2003. In total, the closure of all crimes counted increased by 4 percent (Cklagarmyndigheten 2005). Statistics from the National Council for Crime Prevention (NCCP) on arrests/reports for drug law offences (ST 11 to the 2005 NR) show that cannabis and amphetamine still are the dominating drugs."

International Drug Facts

SWEDEN / UNITED KINGDOM

Source: Statens Folkhalsoinstitut, "2005 National Report (2004 data) to the EMCDDA by the Reitox National Focal Point: Sweden — New Development, Trends and In-Depth Information on Selected Issues" (2006), p. 36.

3. "Street level prices have not followed the curve for seizures if the formula is that high prices mirror shortage of the substance caused by effective customs and police work. The number of seizures has grown from 294 (and 9 kilo) to 1,057 (13 kilo) between 1988 and 2003 (the reporting from 2004 is not fully compatible with earlier years, but were 900). Prices on the street dropped 60% during this period (CAN 2004b). Supply of heroin is seemingly good. In late 2004 one gram of heroin was prized 1,400 SEK [Swedish Krona] for white heroin (predominantly sold in Stockholm) and 1,200 SEK for brown heroin."

Source: Statens Folkhalsoinstitut, "2005 National Report (2004 data) to the EMCDDA by the Reitox National Focal Point: Sweden — New Development, Trends and In-Depth Information on Selected Issues" (2006), p. 21.

4. "The price at street level (adjusted to the 2004 monetary value) is about halved for hashish and cocaine since the end of the eighties. In 2004 one gram of hashish was reported to cost between 6.8 and 10.5 and one gram of cocaine between 63 and 105.3 . For amphetamine and brown heroin, prices are about 60 per cent lower today than 15 years ago. Prices in 2004 per gram of amphetamine had an interval of 15.8 – 52.6 , brown heroin 63 – 263.2 and white heroin 84.2 – 315.8."

Source: Statens Folkhalsoinstitut, "2005 National Report (2004 data) to the EMCDDA by the Reitox National Focal Point: Sweden — New Development, Trends and In-Depth Information on Selected Issues" (2006), p. 44.

5. Sweden's incarceration rate is 82 per 100,000 national population, with a total of prison population of 7,450 out of an estimated national population of 9.06 million.

Source: Walmsley, Roy, "World Prison Population List (Seventh Edition)" (London, England: International Centre for Prison Studies, 2007), p. 5, Table 4, citing a Swedish criminal justice expert.

6. Sweden's homicide rate is 1.11 per 100,000 national population (average per year 1998 to 2000).

Source: Barclay, Gordon & Cynthia Tavares, "International Comparisons of Criminal Justice Statistics 2001," Home Office Bulletin 12/03 (London, England, UK: Home Office Research, Development, and Statistics Directorate, October 24, 2003), p. 10, Table 1.1.

UNITED KINGDOM

A. Overview

1. "The Drug Strategy sets out a range of interventions that concentrate on the most dangerous drugs, the most damaged communities and individuals whose addiction and chaotic lifestyles are most harmful. "The Strategy complements action to restrict the supply of illegal drugs with action to diminish the demand for drugs.

International Drug Facts

UNITED KINGDOM

"Illegal drugs are controlled substances as defined by legislation; the Strategy does not cover alcohol misuse which is the responsibility of the Department of Health.

"The four strands of work within the Drug Strategy are:

"-reducing the supply of illegal drugs;

"-preventing young people from becoming drug misusers;

"-reducing drug-related crime; and

"-reducing the use of drugs through increased participation in treatment programmes."

Source: UK Home Office, Drug Strategy Overview, from the web at http://www. drugs.gov.uk/drug-strategy/overview/?version=1 last accessed June 19, 2007.

2. "The Government's Drug Strategy has the over-arching aim to 'reduce the harm caused by illegal drugs'. There are four key strands to the Drug Strategy: young people, treatment of problem drug users, supply of drugs and drug-related crime.

"Under the young people's target the Government has set the objective to: 'Reduce the use of Class A drugs and the frequent use of any illicit drug by all young people under the age of 25, especially by the most vulnerable groups' (Tackling Drugs, Changing Lives, Home Office 2004a, 20).

Source: Roe, Stephen and Louise Man, "Drug Misuse Declared: Findings from the 2005/06 British Crime Survey — England and Wales" (London, England: Research, Development and Statistics Directorate, Home Office Ministry, Oct. 2006), p. 5.

3. "A new Drug Strategy for Northern Ireland was published in May 2006, New Strategic Direction for Alcohol and Drugs 2006-2011 (DHSSPSNI 2006a), combining both drugs and alcohol in one strategic framework. The overall aim is to reduce the level of alcohol and drug related harm in Northern Ireland. Long term aims are to: provide accessible and effective treatment and support for people who are consuming alcohol and/or using drugs in a potentially hazardous, harmful or dependent way; reduce the level, breadth and depth of alcohol and drug-related harm to users, their families and/or their carers and the wider community; increase awareness on all aspects of alcohol and drug-related harm in all settings and for all age groups; integrate those policies which contribute to the reduction of alcohol and drugrelated harm into all Government Department strategies; develop a competent, skilled workforce across all sectors that can respond to the complexities of alcohol and drug use and misuse; promote opportunities for those under the age of 18 years to develop appropriate skills, attitudes and behaviours to enable them to resist societal pressures to drink alcohol and/or use illicit drugs, with particular emphasis on those identified as potentially vulnerable; and reduce the availability of illicit drugs in Northern Ireland.

"Five supporting pillars have been identified which are to provide the conceptual and practice base. These are: prevention and early intervention; treatment and support; law and criminal justice; harm reduction; monitoring, evaluation and research."

International Drug Facts

UNITED KINGDOM

Source: "United Kingdom Drug Situation: Annual Report to the European Monitoring Centre for Drugs and Drug Addiction (EMCDDA) 2006" (London, England: UK Focal Point in Drugs, Dept. of Health, Oct. 2006), p. 21.

4. "Our vision is of a Scotland whose people choose healthy lifestyles free from the harm of drug misuse. The strategy towards achieving that vision is set out in this document. It is underpinned by four key principles:

"Inclusion — Drug misuse occurs throughout society, but flourishes where individuals and communities feel marginalised from society and life choices are limited as a result of disadvantage. Deprivation is not the sole cause of drug misuse, but it is an important contributor. Tackling Scotland's drug problem has to be integrated with tackling social exclusion.

"Partnership — Co-ordinated and collective work on drug misuse achieves far more than independent and fragmented activity. The strategy recognises the benefits of partnership and encourages involvement at every level of implementation through suitable mechanisms and unifying action.

"Understanding — Scotland needs to base its anti-drugs work on well targeted and accurate research and information, which drives policies and programmes.

"Accountability — This strategy is clear about what results are required, and who should be charged with achieving them through a process of evaluation. The accountability structures are not ends but means to make a strong impact on Scotland's drug problem."

Source: "Tackling Drugs in Scotland: Action in Partnership," The Scottish Office, 1999, from the web at http://www.scotland.gov.uk/library/documents-w7/tdis-01.htm last accessed June 19, 2007.

B. Prevalence Estimates

1. "The 2005/06 BCS [British Crime Survey] estimates that 34.9% of 16 to 59 year olds have used one or more illicit drugs in their lifetime, 10.5% used one or more illicit drugs in the last year and 6.3% in the last month. "The survey also estimates that 13.9% of those aged 16 to 59 have used a Class A drug at least once in their lifetime, 3.4% used at least one Class A drug last year and 1.6% last month."

Source: Roe, Stephen and Louise Man, "Drug Misuse Declared: Findings from the 2005/06 British Crime Survey — England and Wales" (London, England: Research, Development and Statistics Directorate, Home Office Ministry, Oct. 2006), p. 1.

2. "Cannabis is the drug most likely to be used. The 2005/06 BCS indicates that 8.7% of 16 to 59 year olds reported using cannabis in the last year. Cocaine is the next most commonly used drug with 2.4% claiming to have used any form of it (either cocaine powder or crack cocaine) in the previous year. This is followed by ecstasy use at 1.6% and use of amphetamines at 1.3%. Amyl nitrite use in the last year is estimated at 1.2% and use of hallucinogens (LSD and magic mushrooms) at 1.1%. Other drugs are more rarely used."

International Drug Facts

UNITED KINGDOM

Source: Roe, Stephen and Louise Man, "Drug Misuse Declared: Findings from the 2005/06 British Crime Survey — England and Wales" (London, England: Research, Development and Statistics Directorate, Home Office Ministry, Oct. 2006), p. 1.

3. "It is estimated that over 11 million people aged 16 to 59 in England and Wales have used illicit drugs in their lifetime while less than three and a half million are estimated to have used illicit drugs in the last year and approximately two million in the last month.

   "It is also estimated that under four and a half million people aged 16 to 59 have used Class A drugs in their lifetime with over one million having used them in the past year and just over 500 thousand in the last month."

Source: Roe, Stephen and Louise Man, "Drug Misuse Declared: Findings from the 2005/06 British Crime Survey — England and Wales" (London, England: Research, Development and Statistics Directorate, Home Office Ministry, Oct. 2006), p. 2.

4. "Class A drug use in the past year among the 16 to 59 year olds increased between 1998 and 2005/06. This is mainly due to a comparatively large increase in cocaine powder use between 1998 and 2000. However between 2000 and 2005/06 the use of Class A drugs overall remained stable. Between 1998 and 2005/06 the use of LSD decreased.

   "Compared to 2004/05 the figures for 2005/06 show a stable pattern for most Class A drugs, except for an increase in the use of cocaine powder in the past year."

Source: Roe, Stephen and Louise Man, "Drug Misuse Declared: Findings from the 2005/06 British Crime Survey — England and Wales" (London, England: Research, Development and Statistics Directorate, Home Office Ministry, Oct. 2006), p. 2.

5. "The 2005/06 BCS estimates that 21.4% of 16 to 24 year olds used cannabis in the last year. Cocaine is the next most commonly used drug with 5.9% claiming to have used any form of it in the previous year. This is followed by ecstasy at 4.3%. Amyl nitrite use is estimated at 3.9%, use of hallucinogens at 3.4% and use of amphetamines at 3.3%. Other drugs are more rarely used."

Source: Roe, Stephen and Louise Man, "Drug Misuse Declared: Findings from the 2005/06 British Crime Survey — England and Wales" (London, England: Research, Development and Statistics Directorate, Home Office Ministry, Oct. 2006), p. 2.

6. "It is estimated that there are over two and three quarter million people aged 16 to 24 in England and Wales that have used illicit drugs at some point in their lives. Over one and a half million people are estimated to have used drugs in the previous year and under one million in the past month.

   "It is also estimated that over one million people aged 16 to 24 have used a Class A drug in their lifetime. Approximately 525 thousand young people are estimated to have used a Class A drug in the previous year and 250 thousand in the past month."

Source: Roe, Stephen and Louise Man, "Drug Misuse Declared: Findings from the 2005/06 British Crime Survey — England and Wales" (London, England: Research, Development and Statistics Directorate, Home Office Ministry, Oct. 2006), p. 2.

International Drug Facts

UNITED KINGDOM

7. "Prevalence of drug use varies between Government Office Regions. Amongst 16 to 59 year olds, those living in the South West reported higher levels of any illicit drug use compared to the total for England and Wales. Those living in London reported higher levels of Class A drug use than for England and Wales as a whole."

   Source: Roe, Stephen and Louise Man, "Drug Misuse Declared: Findings from the 2005/06 British Crime Survey — England and Wales" (London, England: Research, Development and Statistics Directorate, Home Office Ministry, Oct. 2006), p. 3.

C. Problem Substance Use and Substance-Related Harm

1. "Population-based surveys, because of the often hidden nature of problem drug use, are considered to be of limited use in estimating the full extent of problem drug use. More reliable estimates can be derived from alternative methods, with the multivariate indicator method being one such approach (Hickman et al. 2004). This combines local prevalence estimates with routinely available indicator data. Based on these, and reported in the UK Focal Point report for 2004, the estimate for problematic drug users was 9.35 per thousand (with a Confidence Interval or CI of 8.99 to 9.79 per thousand), with a total problem drug use population estimated at 360,811. For injecting drug use, the estimate was 3.2 per thousand (123,498 with a CI of 3.07 to 3.34 per thousand population aged 15 to 64 years). These rates varied across the UK (see Table 16)."

   Source: "United Kingdom Drug Situation: Annual Report to the European Monitoring Centre for Drugs and Drug Addiction (EMCDDA) 2006" (London, England: UK Focal Point in Drugs, Dept. of Health, Oct. 2006), p. 50.

2. "The 2006 Home Office report 'Measuring different aspects of problem drug use: methodological developments' describes how problem drug use can be estimated. This study provides a robust national estimate precise enough to allow monitoring over time. Four sources of data are used from which problem drug users (defined as those who use opiates and/or crack cocaine) can be identified. These sources of data are drug treatment, probation, police and prison data. Using these techniques it was estimated that there were 327,466 problem drug users in England, in 2004/05."

   Source: Information Centre, Lifestyle Statistics, "Statistics on Drug Misuse: England 2007" (London, England: National Health Service, 2007), p. 10.

3. "To obtain a national estimate of the prevalence of problem drug misuse in the year 2003, we have summed the local estimates for each of the 32 Council areas in Scotland. On this basis, we estimate that there are 51,582 individuals who are misusing opiates or benzodiazepines within Scotland. The 95% confidence interval attached to this estimate is 51,456 to 56,379. This corresponds to a prevalence rate of 1.84% of the Scottish population aged between 15 and 54 (95% CI 1.84-2.01%). As noted in the methods section the 95% confidence is skewed as it is derived from combining the distributions of the stratified estimates, which are themselves skewed."

International Drug Facts

UNITED KINGDOM

Source: Hay, Gordon, Maria Gannon, Neil McKenganey, Sharon Hutchinson and David Goldberg, "Estimating the National and Local Prevalence of Problem Drug Misuse in Scotland: Executive Report," Centre for Drug Misuse Research/University of Glasgow and Scottish Centre for Infection and Environmental Health, Nov. 2004, p. 15.

4. "Data collected from the Unlinked Anonymous Prevalence Monitoring Programme, includes information on current and former IDUs in contact with drug agencies in England, Wales and Northern Ireland. In 2005, HIV prevalence was higher among those IDUs contacting drug agencies in London than outside London (3.2% and 1.26% respectively). Prevalence of Hepatitis B and C among IDUs was much higher than HIV prevalence. In 2005, Hepatitis B prevalence among IDUs contacting drug agencies in London was 26%, and over half of IDUs (57%) contacting drug agencies in London were reported to have Hepatitis C. Outside London, prevalence of Hepatitis B among IDUs contacting drug agencies was 18% and Hepatitis C was 38% (no table)."

Source: Information Centre, Lifestyle Statistics, "Statistics on Drug Misuse: England 2007" (London, England: National Health Service, 2007), p. 70.

D. Harm Reduction Efforts

1. "In the 1980s, United Kingdom drug policy was led by a public health approach aimed at containing HIV transmission. The subsequent action, based on a harm reduction approach, is regarded as having been successful in containing HIV amongst injecting drug users (IDUs); providing free needles and syringes, promoting the safe disposal of used equipment, information campaigns on safer sex and safer injecting; and HIV/AIDS counselling, support and testing."

Source: "United Kingdom Drug Situation: Annual Report to the European Monitoring Centre for Drugs and Drug Addiction (EMCDDA) 2006" (London, England: UK Focal Point in Drugs, Dept. of Health, Oct. 2006), p. 85.

2. "In Scotland, Lanarkshire ADAT [Alcohol and Drug Action Team] is currently running a pilot project involving Naloxone the anti-overdose drug. This involves the training of ten front line addictions staff, ten clients and ten family/friends currently living with an injecting drug user. Each group is being trained by the Scottish Ambulance Service on Naloxone administration, basic life support and the unconscious patient. After successful completion of the course the participants are issued with a 400 mcg pre-filled Naloxone syringe, sharps bin and harm reduction/health promotion material. The pilot will be monitored after two months to assess both the effectiveness of the training and the impact of the Naloxone. A similar pilot project is also being run in Greater Glasgow (Scottish Executive - internal communication)."

Source: "United Kingdom Drug Situation: Annual Report to the European Monitoring Centre for Drugs and Drug Addiction (EMCDDA) 2006" (London, England: UK Focal Point in Drugs, Dept. of Health, Oct. 2006), p. 87.

International Drug Facts

UNITED KINGDOM

3. "The report for England found both pharmacy and agency based services provided syringe exchange in the overwhelming majority of (D(A)AT) [Drug and Alcohol Action Teams] areas though, overall, pharmacies constituted 80 per cent of facilities (Abdulrahim et al. 2006). On average, two agency based services and eight pharmacies provided facilities in each D(A)AT area.
"- The median number of visits by injectors to all needle exchange facilities in a D(A)AT area (pharmacies and specialist services), between April 2004 and March 2005, was 8,000;
"- the median number of clients who used needle exchange facilities in each D(A)AT area was 700, though this number has not been adjusted for double counting; and .
"- a median number of 150,000 syringes were distributed per D(A)AT area. There was, however, wide variation in activity between both services and D(A)AT areas."

   Source: "United Kingdom Drug Situation: Annual Report to the European Monitoring Centre for Drugs and Drug Addiction (EMCDDA) 2006" (London, England: UK Focal Point in Drugs, Dept. of Health, Oct. 2006), p. 89.

4. In Scotland, "Some form of needle exchange was available in every D(A)AT area. There were 188 exchanges; 136 pharmacy exchanges, 43 specialist exchanges, six police custody suite exchanges and three hospital A&E exchanges; nearly half of specialist service provision was through mobile/outreach facilities. The ratio of pharmacy to specialist exchanges was 3:1. In non-pharmacy services the median number of transactions per service was 1,054 (mean: 2,289):
"- the mean number of transactions per pharmacy was 1,458;
"- the median number of clients per service was 221 (mean: 491); and
"- the mean number of clients per pharmacy was 479.
"A roughly equal number of syringes were distributed by pharmacy and non-pharmacy services overall, though there was wide geographical variation. It is estimated that at least 1,563,312 syringes were returned to needle exchange services across Scotland, 849,113 to non-pharmacy services and 714,199 to pharmacy services; pharmacies having fewer returns than non-pharmacy exchanges."

   Source: "United Kingdom Drug Situation: Annual Report to the European Monitoring Centre for Drugs and Drug Addiction (EMCDDA) 2006" (London, England: UK Focal Point in Drugs, Dept. of Health, Oct. 2006), p. 90.

5. "Compared to England, services in Scotland were less likely to distribute filters, sterile water, stericups and Vitamin C to their clients, though more likely to distribute wipes or swabs. Services were less likely to provide on-site hepatitis B immunisation than in England. English services were much less likely to limit the number of syringes they gave out during any single needle exchange transaction; this is probably because of guidance in Scotland which limits the number given out.111 Scottish services were more likely than those in England to provide injecting equipment to young people aged 16 or 17. As in England, pharmacy schemes offered a smaller range of interventions."

169

International Drug Facts

UNITED KINGDOM

Source: "United Kingdom Drug Situation: Annual Report to the European Monitoring Centre for Drugs and Drug Addiction (EMCDDA) 2006" (London, England: UK Focal Point in Drugs, Dept. of Health, Oct. 2006), pp. 90-91.

6. "Northern Ireland is the only country within the United Kingdom with a national syringe exchange database. Nine pharmacies offer syringe exchange. In 2004/05:

"- 86,056 exchanges were made; there were 7,400 contacts, compared to 7,508 in the previous year;

"- the overall rate of transactions involving the return of used equipment fell in 2004/05 to 54 per cent compared to 59 per cent in the previous year;

"- just over half (54%) of all visits were made by clients aged 31 and over;

"- just under one in 20 visits (4%) were by clients reporting themselves to be new users of the needle and syringe exchange scheme;

"- twelve (0.2%) visits were by clients reporting to have shared needles (DHSSPSNI 2006b)."

Source: "United Kingdom Drug Situation: Annual Report to the European Monitoring Centre for Drugs and Drug Addiction (EMCDDA) 2006" (London, England: UK Focal Point in Drugs, Dept. of Health, Oct. 2006), p. 91.

E. Treatment

1. "Treatment providers are expected to offer advice and information, needle exchange, care planned counselling, structured day care programmes, community prescribing, inpatient drug treatment and residential rehabilitation. In addition, drug misusers are to be offered relapse prevention and aftercare programmes, hepatitis B vaccinations, and testing and counselling for hepatitis B and C, and HIV (DH 2002b). Oral methadone maintenance is the most common method used in treating heroin addiction; but buprenorphine and injectable methadone and heroin are also available."

Source: "United Kingdom Drug Situation: Annual Report to the European Monitoring Centre for Drugs and Drug Addiction (EMCDDA) 2006" (London, England: UK Focal Point in Drugs, Dept. of Health, Oct. 2006), p. 55.

2. "Based on the Treatment Demand Indicator a total of 117,783 individuals were reported as presenting for treatment during the period 2004/05, 36 per cent of whom were making their first ever treatment demand.

"There were 111,436 outpatient reports. This represents an overall increase of 22 per cent over the previous period, largely accounted for by an increase of 46 per cent in first treatment demands.

"There has been a 27 per cent increase in the number of self-referrals and a 71 per cent increase in those referred from the criminal justice system."

Source: "United Kingdom Drug Situation: Annual Report to the European Monitoring Centre for Drugs and Drug Addiction (EMCDDA) 2006" (London, England: UK Focal Point in Drugs, Dept. of Health, Oct. 2006), p. 56.

International Drug Facts

UNITED KINGDOM

3. "The number of individuals receiving structured treatment has increased by 13% from 160,450 in 2004/05 to 181,390 in 2005/06. This represents an increase of 113% on the 1998/99 baseline of 85,000 people receiving structured treatment. These figures demonstrate that the Government is succeeding in delivering treatment services and has actually exceeded the national treatment target of 170,000 people receiving structured treatment in 2007/08."

   Source: "Tackling Drugs. Changing Lives: Turning Strategy Into Reality" (London, England: UK Home Office Ministry, Jan. 2007).

4. "More than three quarters of clients entering treatment (78%) in 2005/06 remained in structured treatment for 12 weeks or more, when treatment is more likely to be effective."

   Source: "Tackling Drugs. Changing Lives: Turning Strategy Into Reality" (London, England. UK Home Office Ministry, Jan. 2007).

F. Substance Use and the Justice System

1. "In 2004/05 there were 186,783 incidents involving alleged drug offences recorded by the police in the United Kingdom, an increase of 0.5 per cent from the 185,924 offences reported in 2003/04."

   Source: "United Kingdom Drug Situation: Annual Report to the European Monitoring Centre for Drugs and Drug Addiction (EMCDDA) 2006" (London, England: UK Focal Point in Drugs, Dept. of Health, Oct. 2006), p. 100.

2. "The latest data on persons dealt with (persons found guilty, given a fiscal fine or dealt with by compounding) for drug offences is available for 2004 (Table 8.1). The total number of persons dealt with was 122,459. This is an increase of 4 per cent from the previous year (117,532). Eighty-eight per cent of persons were dealt with for drug possession offences. Trafficking and dealing offences (i.e. supplying or possession with intent to supply, and unlawful import or export), accounted for 12 per cent of all drug offences in 2004.
   "Sixty-eight per cent of offences (82,845) (not persons dealt with) related specifically to cannabis, eight per cent to cocaine and 10 per cent to heroin. The proportion of offences related to cannabis has decreased from the previous year."

   Source: "United Kingdom Drug Situation: Annual Report to the European Monitoring Centre for Drugs and Drug Addiction (EMCDDA) 2006" (London, England: UK Focal Point in Drugs, Dept. of Health, Oct. 2006), pp. 100-101.

3. "A survey of prisoners which gathers data on recent drug use reported that in October 2003 to September 2004, 39% of prisoners had used an illicit drug at some time in their current prison, 25% said they had used drugs in the past month and 16% in the past week. Almost a third (32%) had used cannabis and about a fifth (21%) had used opiates at least once in their current prison. About one in ten prisoners reported using each of these types of drug in the past week."

International Drug Facts

UNITED KINGDOM

Source: Information Centre, Lifestyle Statistics, "Statistics on Drug Misuse: England 2007" (London, England: National Health Service, 2007), p. 6.

4. The United Kingdom's incarceration rate is:
   England & Wales: 148 inmates per 100,000 of national population, with a total prison population 79,861 out of an estimated national population of 53.85 million.
   Northern Ireland: 84 inmates per 100,000 of national population, with a total prison population 1,466 out of an estimated national population of 1.74 million.
   Scotland: 139 inmates per 100,000 of national population, with a total prison population 7,131 out of an estimated national population of 5.12 million.

   Source: Walmsley, Roy, "World Prison Population List (Seventh Edition)" (London, England: International Centre for Prison Studies, 2007), p. 5, Table 4, citing the national prison authorities.

5. The United Kingdom's homicide rate is:
   England & Wales: 1.61 per 100,000 national population (average per year 1999 to 2001).
   Northern Ireland: 2.65 per 100,000 national population (average per year 1999 to 2001).
   Scotland: 2.16 per 100,000 national population (average per year 1999 to 2001).

   Source: Barclay, Gordon & Cynthia Tavares, "International Comparisons of Criminal Justice Statistics 2001," Home Office Bulletin 12/03 (London, England, UK: Home Office Research, Development, and Statistics Directorate, October 24, 2003), p. 10, Table 1.1.

6. "1.3 Since January 2004, police action in respect of cannabis possession has been subject to the Cannabis Enforcement Guidance issued by the Association of Chief Police Officers (ACPO). Under the Police and Criminal Evidence Code of Practice (G) for the Statutory Power of Arrest by Police Officers, which comes into force on 1 January 2006, arrest is subject to necessity criteria and will remain an operational decision at the discretion of the police officer, taking into account the particular circumstances.
   "1.4 In March 2002, the Council recommended that all cannabis products be reclassified from Class B to Class C. The Home Secretary accepted the Council's advice and the legislative changes came into force on 29 January 2004."

   Source: Advisory Council on the Misuse of Drugs, "Further consideration of the classification of cannabis under the Misuse of Drugs Act 1971" (London, England: Home Office Ministry, 2006), p. 4.

Mandatory Minimums

1. "Because it takes 100 times more powder cocaine than crack cocaine to trigger the same mandatory minimum penalty, this penalty structure is commonly referred to as the '100-to-1 drug quantity ratio.'"

   Source: US Sentencing Commission, "Report to Congress: Cocaine and Federal Sentencing Policy," May 2007, p. 3.

2. "Under current law, possession of five grams or more of crack cocaine triggers a mandatory minimum sentence of five years in prison; simple possession of any quantity of any other controlled substance (except flunitrazepan) by a first-time offender – including powder cocaine – is a misdemeanor offense punishable by a maximum of one year in prison."

   Source: US Sentencing Commission, "Report to Congress: Cocaine and Federal Sentencing Policy," May 2007, p. 4.

3. In fiscal year 2005, 53.1% of all federal powder cocaine defendants were low-level offenders such as mules or street-dealers. Only 12.8% were high-level dealers.

   Source: US Sentencing Commission, "Report to Congress: Cocaine and Federal Sentencing Policy," May 2007, p. 19, Figure 2-4.

4. In fiscal year 2005, 61.5% of all federal crack cocaine defendants were low-level offenders such as mules or street dealers. Only 8.4% were high-level dealers.

   Source: US Sentencing Commission, "Report to Congress: Cocaine and Federal Sentencing Policy," May 2007, p. 19, Figure 2-4.

5. "Current data and information continue to support the core findings contained in the 2002 Commission Report, among them: (1) The current quantity-based penalties overstate the relative harmfulness of crack cocaine compared to powder cocaine. (2) The current quantity-based penalties sweep too broadly and apply most often to lower level offenders. (3) The current quantity-based penalties overstate the seriousness of most crack cocaine offenses and fail to provide adequate proportionality. (4) The current severity of crack cocaine penalties mostly impacts minorities.
   "Based on these findings, the Commission maintains its consistently held position that the 100-to-1 drug quantity ratio significantly undermines the various congressional objectives set forth in the Sentencing Reform Act."

   Source: US Sentencing Commission, "Report to Congress: Cocaine and Federal Sentencing Policy," May 2007, pp. 7-8.

6. "Powder cocaine and crack cocaine offenses together historically have accounted for about half of the federally-sentenced drug trafficking offenders, approximately 11,000 in 2006. In 1992, powder cocaine offenses comprised 74 percent of the 8,972 cocaine offenses and crack cocaine offenses accounted for 26 percent of the cocaine offenses. By 1996, the total number of cocaine offenses decreased slightly to 8,705 and approximately half of cocaine offenses were powder cocaine and half were crack cocaine offenses. This even distribution of types of cocaine has remained consistent through 2006, with 5,744 powder cocaine offenses and 5,397 crack cocaine offenses sentenced in that Fiscal Year."

Mandatory Minimums

Source: US Sentencing Commission, "Report to Congress: Cocaine and Federal Sentencing Policy," May 2007, p. 12.

7. "Historically the majority of crack cocaine offenders are black, but the proportion steadily has declined since 1992: 91.4 percent in 1992, 84.7 percent in 2000, and 81.8 percent in 2006. Conversely, the proportion of white crack cocaine offenders has increased steadily from 3.2 percent in 1992 to 5.6 percent in 2002, to 8.8 percent in 2006. For powder cocaine, Hispanic offenders have comprised a growing proportion of cases. In 1992, Hispanics accounted for 39.8 percent of powder cocaine offenders. This proportion increased to over half (50.8%) by 2000 and continued increasing to 57.5 percent in 2006. There has been a corresponding decrease in the proportion of white offenders for powder cocaine, comprising 32.3 percent of offenders in 1992, decreasing by approximately half to 17.8 percent by 2000, and continuing to decrease to 14.3 percent by 2006."

Source: US Sentencing Commission, "Report to Congress: Cocaine and Federal Sentencing Policy," May 2007, p. 19.

8. Mandatory minimums have not actually reduced sentencing discretion. Control has merely been transferred from judges to prosecutors.

Source: Caulkins, J., et al., Mandatory Minimum Drug Sentences: Throwing Away the Key or the Taxpayers' Money? (Santa Monica, CA: RAND Corporation, 1997), p. 24.

9. "Justice Breyer delivered the opinion of the Court in part, concluding that 18 U. S. C. A. §3553(b)(1), which makes the Federal Sentencing Guidelines mandatory, is incompatible with today's Sixth Amendment 'jury trial' holding and therefore must be severed and excised from the Sentencing Reform Act of 1984 (Act). Section 3742(e), which depends upon the Guidelines' mandatory nature, also must be severed and excised. So modified, the Act makes the Guidelines effectively advisory, requiring a sentencing court to consider Guidelines ranges, see §3553(a)(4), but permitting it to tailor the sentence in light of other statutory concerns, see §3553(a)."

Source: Decision of the United States Supreme Court, United States v. Booker, Case No. 04-104, Argued Oct. 4, 2004, Decided Jan. 12, 2005.

10. "As previously noted, various drug offenses carry a mandatory minimum. For such offenses, the mandatory minimum precludes judges from sentencing at a lower guideline range minimum or from granting a downward departure that might otherwise be available, unless one of two statutory provisions applies. First, a judge may impose a sentence below the applicable mandatory minimum if the government (the federal prosecutor) files a motion with the court for such sentencing relief because of the defendant's 'substantial assistance' in the investigation or prosecution of another person. The discretion to make such a motion rests solely with the prosecutor. Second, in the absence of a substantial assistance motion, the 'safety

Mandatory Minimums

valve' provision affords relief from any otherwise applicable mandatory minimum sentence for drug offenders who have minimal criminal history (i.e., no more than 1 criminal history point); were not violent, armed, or high-level participants; and provided the government with truthful information regarding the offense. In these cases, the court is directed by statute to impose a sentence pursuant to the sentencing guidelines without regard to a mandatory minimum."

Source: General Accounting Office, "Federal Drug Offenses: Departures from Sentencing Guidelines and Mandatory Minimum Sentences, Fiscal Years 1999-2001," GAO-04-105, October 2003, pp. 9-10, from the web at www.gao.gov/cgi-bin/getrpt?GAO-04-105, last accessed Nov. 1, 2003.

11. "Similar to federal sentences overall, of the 69,279 drug sentences for which complete departure information was available, we found that most sentences were within guideline ranges (56 percent). Unlike federal sentences overall, from fiscal years 1999 to 2001, federal drug sentences departed downward more frequently due to substantial assistance (28 percent) than other reasons (16 percent), as shown in table 1. Other reasons that drug sentences departed downward included early disposition, that is, fast track, programs initiated by prosecutors; plea agreements; and judges' consideration of mitigating circumstances."

Source: General Accounting Office, "Federal Drug Offenses: Departures from Sentencing Guidelines and Mandatory Minimum Sentences, Fiscal Years 1999-2001," GAO-04-105, October 2003, p. 11, from the web at www.gao.gov/cgi-bin/getrpt?GAO-04-105, last accessed Nov. 1, 2003.

12. "After eleven years, it should be obvious that the system has failed and that it cannot be fixed — even by the Supreme Court — because the criminal justice system has been distorted: the enhanced power of the prosecutor in sentencing has diminished the traditional role of the judge. The result has been even less fairness, and a huge rise in the prison population."

Source: Smith, Alexander, and Polack, Harriet, "Curtailing the Sentencing Power of Trial Judges: The Unintended Consequences", Court Review (Williamsburg, VA: American Judges Association, Summer 1999), p. 6-7.

13. "Most of the judges we interviewed were quite bitter about the operation of the sentencing guidelines. As one of them remarked: 'The people who drew up these guidelines never sat in a court andhad to look a defendant in the eye while imposing some of these sentences.'"

Source: Smith, Alexander, and Polack, Harriet, "Curtailing the Sentencing Power of Trial Judges: The Unintended Consequences", Court Review (Williamsburg, VA: American Judges Association, Summer 1999), p. 6.

14. "Though it is still too early to make a final judgment, RAND found that three strikes and truth-in-sentencing laws have had little significant impact on crime and arrest rates. According to the Uniform Crime Reports, states with neither a three strikes nor a truth-in-sentencing law had the lowest rates of index crimes, whereas index crime rates were highest in states with both types of get-tough laws."

Mandatory Minimums

Source: Turner, Susan, RAND Corporation Criminal Justice Program, Justice Research & Statistics Association, "Impact of Truth-in-Sentencing and Three Strikes Legislation on Crime" Crime and Justice Atlas 2000 (Washington, DC: US Dept. of Justice, June 2000), p. 10.

15. The ONDCP in its 2000 annual report detailed administration requests for major increases in funding to the Federal Bureau of Prisons for drug-related prison construction. These include an extra $420 Million in fiscal year 2001, and advanced appropriations of $467 Million in 2002, and an additional $316 Million in 2003 — all drug-related.

Sources: Office of National Drug Control Policy, Executive Office of the White House, National Drug Control Strategy: Annual Report 2000 (Washington, DC: US Government Printing Office, 2000), p. 96.

aa

Marijuana

1. In 2005, 42.6 percent of the 1,846,351 total arrests for drug abuse violations in the US were for marijuana — a total of 786,545. Of those, 696,074 people were arrested for possession alone. By contrast in 2000, a total of 734,497 Americans were arrested for marijuana offenses, of which 646,042 were for possession alone.

   Sources: Crime in America: FBI Uniform Crime Reports 2005 (Washington, DC: US Dept. of Justice, 2006), Table 29, from the web at http://www.fbi.gov/ucr/05cius/data/table_29.html and Arrest Table: Arrests for Drug Abuse Violations, from the web http://www.fbi.gov/ucr/05cius/arrests/index.htm last accessed Sept. 20, 2006; Federal Bureau of Investigation, Uniform Crime Reports for the United States 2000 (Washington DC: US Government Printing Office, 2001), pp. 215-216, Tables 4.1 and 29.

2. "Cannabis remains by far the most commonly used drug in the world. An estimated 162 million people used cannabis in 2004, equivalent to some 4 per cent of the global population age 15-64. In relative terms, cannabis use is most prevalent in Oceania, followed by North America and Africa. While Asia has the lowest prevalence expressed as part of the population, in absolute terms it is the region that is home to some 52 million cannabis users, more than a third of the estimated total. The next largest markets, in absolute terms, are Africa and North America."

   Source: United Nations Office on Drugs and Crime, "World Drug Report 2006, Volume 1: Analysis" (United Nations: Vienna, Austria, 2006), p. 23.

3. Marijuana was first federally prohibited in 1937. Today, more than 97 million Americans admit to having tried it.

   Sources: Marihuana Tax Act of 1937; Substance Abuse and Mental Health Services Administration, US Department of Health and Human Services, Results from the 2005 National Survey on Drug Use and Health: National Findings (Rockville, MD: Office of Applied Studies, Sept. 2006), p. 224, Table G.1.

4. "Tetrahydrocannabinol is a very safe drug. Laboratory animals (rats, mice, dogs, monkeys) can tolerate doses of up to 1,000 mg/kg (milligrams per kilogram). This would be equivalent to a 70 kg person swallowing 70 grams of the drug — about 5,000 times more than is required to produce a high. Despite the widespread illicit use of cannabis there are very few if any instances of people dying from an overdose. In Britain, official government statistics listed five deaths from cannabis in the period 1993-1995 but on closer examination these proved to have been deaths due to inhalation of vomit that could not be directly attributed to cannabis (House of Lords Report, 1998). By comparison with other commonly used recreational drugs these statistics are impressive."

   Source: Iversen, Leslie L., PhD, FRS, "The Science of Marijuana" (London, England: Oxford University Press, 2000), p. 178, citing House of Lords, Select Committee on Science and Technology, "Cannabis — The Scientific and Medical Evidence" (London, England: The Stationery Office, Parliament, 1998).

5. "A review of the literature suggests that the majority of cannabis users, who use the drug occasionally rather than on a daily basis, will not suffer any lasting physical or mental harm. Conversely, as with other

Marijuana

'recreational' drugs, there will be some who suffer adverse consequences from their use of cannabis. Some individuals who have psychotic thought tendencies might risk precipitating psychotic illness. Those who consume large doses of the drug on a regular basis are likely to have lower educational achievement and lower income, and may suffer physical damage to the airways. They also run a significant risk of becoming dependent upon continuing use of the drug. There is little evidence, however, that these adverse effects persist after drug use stops or that any direct cause and effect relationships are involved."

Source: Iversen, Leslie L., PhD, FRS, "Long-Term Effects of Exposure to Cannabis," Current Opinion in Pharmacology, Feb. 2005, Vol. 5, No. 1, p. 71.

6. According to research published in the journal Addiction, "First, the use of cannabis and rates of psychotic symptoms were related to each other, independently of observed/non-observed fixed covariates and observed time dynamic factors (Table 2). Secondly, the results of structural equation modelling suggest that the direction of causation is that the use of cannabis leads to increases in levels of psychotic symptoms rather than psychotic symptoms increasing the use of cannabis. Indeed, there is a suggestion from the model results that increases in psychotic symptoms may inhibit the use of cannabis."

Source: Fergusson, David M., John Horwood & Elizabeth M. Ridder, "Tests of Causal Linkages Between Cannabis Use and Psychotic Symptoms," Addiction, Vol. 100, No. 3, March 2005, p. 363.

7. The Christchurch Press reported on March 22, 2005, that "The lead researcher in the Christchurch study, Professor David Fergusson, said the role of cannabis in psychosis was not sufficient on its own to guide legislation. 'The result suggests heavy use can result in adverse side-effects,' he said. 'That can occur with (heavy use of) any substance. It can occur with milk.' Fergusson's research, released this month, concluded that heavy cannabis smokers were 1.5 times more likely to suffer symptoms of psychosis that non-users. The study was the latest in several reports based on a cohort of about 1000 people born in Christchurch over a four-month period in 1977. An effective way to deal with cannabis use would be to incrementally reduce penalties and carefully evaluate its impact, Fergusson said. 'Reduce the penalty, like a parking fine. You could then monitor (the impact) after five or six years. If it did not change, you might want to take another step."

Source: Bleakley, Louise, "NZ Study Used in UK Drug Review," The Press (Christchurch, New Zealand: March 22, 2005), from the web at http://www.mapinc.org/ newscsdp/v05/n490/a08.html, last accessed March 28, 2005.

8. "The results of our meta-analytic study failed to reveal a substantial, systematic effect of long-term, regular cannabis consumption on the neurocognitive functioning of users who were not acutely intoxicated. For six of the eight neurocognitive ability areas that were surveyed. the confidence intervals for the average effect sizes across studies overlapped zero in each instance, indicating that the effect size could not be distinguished from zero. The two exceptions were in the domains of learning and forgetting."

Source: Grant, Igor, et al., "Non-Acute (Residual) Neurocognitive Effects Of Cannabis Use: A Meta-Analytic Study," Journal of the International Neuropsychological Society (Cambridge University Press: July 2003), 9, p. 685.

Marijuana

9. "These results can be interpreted in several ways. A statistically reliable negative effect was observed in the domain of learning and forgetting, suggesting that chronic long-term cannabis use results in a selective memory defect. While the results are compatible with this conclusion, the effect size for both domains was of a very small magnitude. The 'real life' impact of such a small and selective effect is questionable. In addition, it is important to note that most users across studies had histories of heavy longterm cannabis consumption. Therefore, these findings are not likely to generalize to more limited administration of cannabis compounds, as would be seen in a medical setting."

Source: Grant, Igor, et al., "Non-Acute (Residual) Neurocognitive Effects Of Cannabis Use: A Meta-Analytic Study," Journal of the International Neuropsychological Society (Cambridge University Press: July 2003), 9, p. 686.

10. "In conclusion, our meta-analysis of studies that have attempted to address the question of longer term neurocognitive disturbance in moderate and heavy cannabis users has failed to demonstrate a substantial, systematic, and detrimental effect of cannabis use on neuropsychological performance. It was surprising to find such few and small effects given that most of the potential biases inherent in our analyses actually increased the likelihood of finding a cannabis effect."

Source: Grant, Igor, et al., "Non-Acute (Residual) Neurocognitive Effects Of Cannabis Use: A Meta-Analytic Study," Journal of the International Neuropsychological Society (Cambridge University Press: July 2003), 9, p. 687.

11. "Nevertheless, when considering all 15 studies (i.e., those that met both strict and more relaxed criteria) we only noted that regular cannabis users performed worse on memory tests, but that the magnitude of the effect was very small. The small magnitude of effect sizes from observations of chronic users of cannabis suggests that cannabis compounds, if found to have therapeutic value, should have a good margin of safety from a neurocognitive standpoint under the more limited conditions of exposure that would likely obtain in a medical setting."

Source: Grant, Igor, et al., "Non-Acute (Residual) Neurocognitive Effects Of Cannabis Use: A Meta-Analytic Study," Journal of the International Neuropsychological Society (Cambridge University Press: July 2003), 9, pp. 687-8.

12. A Johns Hopkins study published in May 1999, examined marijuana's effects on cognition on 1,318 participants over a 15 year period. Researchers reported "no significant differences in cognitive decline between heavy users, light users, and nonusers of cannabis." They also found "no male-female differences in cognitive decline in relation to cannabis use." "These results ... seem to provide strong evidence of the absence of a long-term residual effect of cannabis use on cognition," they concluded.

Source: Constantine G. Lyketsos, Elizabeth Garrett, Kung-Yee Liang, and James C. Anthony. (1999). "Cannabis Use and Cognitive Decline in Persons under 65 Years of Age," American Journal of Epidemiology, Vol. 149, No. 9.

Marijuana

13. "Current marijuana use had a negative effect on global IQ score only in subjects who smoked 5 or more joints per week. A negative effect was not observed among subjects who had previously been heavy users but were no longer using the substance. We conclude that marijuana does not have a long-term negative impact on global intelligence. Whether the absence of a residual marijuana effect would also be evident in more specific cognitive domains such as memory and attention remains to be ascertained."

   Source: Fried, Peter, Barbara Watkinson, Deborah James, and Robert Gray, "Current and former marijuana use: preliminary findings of a longitudinal study of effects on IQ in young adults," Canadian Medical Association Journal, April 2, 2002, 166(7), p. 887.

14. "Although the heavy current users experienced a decrease in IQ score, their scores were still above average at the young adult assessment (mean 105.1). If we had not assessed preteen IQ, these subjects would have appeared to be functioning normally. Only with knowledge of the change in IQ score does the negative impact of current heavy use become apparent."

   Source: Fried, Peter, Barbara Watkinson, Deborah James, and Robert Gray, "Current and former marijuana use: preliminary findings of a longitudinal study of effects on IQ in young adults," Canadian Medical Association Journal, April 2, 2002, 166(7), p. 890.

15. A 1999 federal report conducted by the Institute of Medicine found that, "For most people, the primary adverse effect of acute marijuana use is diminished psychomotor performance. It is, therefore, inadvisable to operate any vehicle or potentially dangerous equipment while under the influence of marijuana, THC, or any cannabinoid drug with comparable effects."

   Source: Janet E. Joy, Stanley J. Watson, Jr., and John A Benson, Jr., Marijuana and Medicine: Assessing the Science Base, Division of Neuroscience and Behavioral Research, Institute of Medicine (Washington, DC: National Academy Press, 1999).

bb 16. The DEA's Administrative Law Judge, Francis Young concluded: "In strict medical terms marijuana is far safer than many foods we commonly consume. For example, eating 10 raw potatoes can result in a toxic response. By comparison, it is physically impossible to eat enough marijuana to induce death. Marijuana in its natural form is one of the safest therapeutically active substances known to man. By any measure of rational analysis marijuana can be safely used within the supervised routine of medical care."

   Source: US Department of Justice, Drug Enforcement Agency, "In the Matter of Marijuana Rescheduling Petition," [Docket #86-22], (September 6, 1988), p. 57.

17. Commissioned by President Nixon in 1972, the National Commission on Marihuana and Drug Abuse concluded that "Marihuana's relative potential for harm to the vast majority of individual users and its actual impact on society does not justify a social policy designed to seek out and firmly punish those who use it. This judgment is based on prevalent use patterns, on behavior exhibited by the vast majority of users and on our interpretations of existing medical and scientific data. This position also is consistent with the estimate by law enforcement personnel that the elimination of use is unattainable."

   Source: Shafer, Raymond P., et al, Marihuana: A Signal of Misunderstanding, Ch. V, (Washington DC: National Commission on Marihuana and Drug Abuse, 1972).

Marijuana

18. When examining the relationship between marijuana use and violent crime, the National Commission on Marihuana and Drug Abuse concluded, "Rather than inducing violent or aggressive behavior through its purported effects of lowering inhibitions, weakening impulse control and heightening aggressive tendencies, marihuana was usually found to inhibit the expression of aggressive impulses by pacifying the user, interfering with muscular coordination, reducing psychomotor activities and generally producing states of drowsiness lethargy, timidity and passivity."

Source: Shafer, Raymond P., et al, Marihuana: A Signal of Misunderstanding, Ch. III, (Washington DC: National Commission on Marihuana and Drug Abuse, 1972).

19. When examining the medical affects of marijuana use, the National Commission on Marihuana and Drug Abuse concluded, "A careful search of the literature and testimony of the nation's health officials has not revealed a single human fatality in the United States proven to have resulted solely from ingestion of marihuana. Experiments with the drug in monkeys demonstrated that the dose required for overdose death was enormous and for all practical purposes unachievable by humans smoking marihuana. This is in marked contrast to other substances in common use, most notably alcohol and barbiturate sleeping pills." The WHO reached the same conclusion in 1995.

Source: Shafer, Raymond P., et al, Marihuana: A Signal of Misunderstanding, Ch. III, (Washington DC: National Commission on Marihuana and Drug Abuse, 1972); Hall, W., Room, R. & Bondy, S., WHO Project on Health Implications of Cannabis Use: A Comparative Appraisal of the Health and Psychological Consequences of Alcohol, Cannabis, Nicotine and Opiate Use, August 28, 1995, (Geneva, Switzerland: World Health Organization, March 1998).

20. The World Health Organization released a study in March 1998 that states: "there are good reasons for saying that [the risks from cannabis] would be unlikely to seriously [compare to] the public health risks of alcohol and tobacco even if as many people used cannabis as now drink alcohol or smoke tobacco."

Source: Hall, W., Room, R. & Bondy, S., WHO Project on Health Implications of Cannabis Use: A Comparative Appraisal of the Health and Psychological Consequences of Alcohol, Cannabis, Nicotine and Opiate Use, August 28, 1995, (contained in original version, but deleted from official version) (Geneva, Switzerland: World Health Organization, March 1998).

21. The authors of a 1998 World Health Organization report comparing marijuana, alcohol, nicotine and opiates quote the Institute of Medicine's 1982 report stating that there is no evidence that smoking marijuana "exerts a permanently deleterious effect on the normal cardiovascular system."

Source: Hall, W., Room, R. & Bondy, S., WHO Project on Health Implications of Cannabis Use: A Comparative Appraisal of the Health and Psychological Consequences of Alcohol, Cannabis, Nicotine and Opiate Use, August 28, 1995 (Geneva, Switzerland: World Health Organization, March 1998).

Marijuana

22. Some claim that cannabis use leads to "adult amotivation." The World Health Organization report addresses the issue and states, "it is doubtful that cannabis use produces a well defined amotivational syndrome." The report also notes that the value of studies which support the "adult amotivation" theory are "limited by their small sample sizes" and lack of representative social/cultural groups.

    Source: Hall, W., Room, R. & Bondy, S., WHO Project on Health Implications of Cannabis Use: A Comparative Appraisal of the Health and Psychological Consequences of Alcohol, Cannabis, Nicotine and Opiate Use, August 28, 1995 (Geneva, Switzerland: World Health Organization, March 1998).

23. Australian researchers found that regions giving on-the-spot fines to marijuana users rather than harsher criminal penalties did not cause marijuana use to increase.

    Source: Ali, Robert, et al., The Social Impacts of the Cannabis Expiation Notice Scheme in South Australia: Summary Report (Canberra, Australia: Department of Health and Aged Care, 1999), p. 44.

24. "Cannabis is only considered a risk factor for traffic accidents if drivers operate vehicles after consuming the drug. Robbe (1994) found that 30% to 90% of his participants were willing to drive after consuming a typical dose of cannabis. This is consistent with a recent Australian survey in which more than 50% of users drove after consuming cannabis (Lenne, Fry, Dietze, & Rumbold, 2000). A self administered questionnaire given to 508 students in grades 10 to 13 in Ontario, Canada, found that 19.7% reported driving within an hour after using cannabis (Adlaf, Mann, & Paglia, 2003)."

    Source: Laberge, Jason C., Nicholas J. Ward, "Research Note: Cannabis and Driving — Research Needs and Issues for Transportation Policy," Journal of Drug Issues, Dec. 2004, pp. 974-5.

25. "Several studies have examined cannabis use in driving simulator and on-road situations. The most comprehensive review was done by Smiley in 1986 and then again in 1999. Several trends are evident and can be described by three general performance characteristics:
    "1. Cannabis increased variability of speed and headway as well as lane position (Attwood, Williams, McBurney, & Frecker, 1981; Ramaekers, Robbe, & O'Hanlon, 2000; Robbe, 1998; Sexton et al., 2000; Smiley, Moskowitz, & Zeidman, 1981; Smiley, Noy, & Tostowaryk, 1987). This was more pronounced under high workload and unexpected conditions, such as curves and wind gusts.
    "2. Cannabis increased the time needed to overtake another vehicle (Dott, 1972 [as cited in Smiley, 1986]) and delayed responses to both secondary and tracking tasks (Casswell, 1977; Moskowitz, Hulbert, & McGlothlin, 1976; Sexton et al., 2000; Smiley et al., 1981).
    "3. Cannabis resulted in fewer attempts to overtake another vehicle (Dott, 1972) and larger distances required to pass (Ellingstad et al., 1973 [as cited in Smiley, 1986]). Evidence of increased caution also included slower speeds (Casswell, 1977; Hansteen, Miller, Lonero, Reid, & Jones, 1976; Krueger & Vollrath, 2000; Peck, Biasotti, Boland, Mallory, & Reeve, 1986; Sexton et al., 2000; Smiley et al., 1981; Stein, Allen, Cook, & Karl, 1983) and larger headways (Robbe, 1998; Smiley et al., 1987)."

Marijuana

Source: Laberge, Jason C., Nicholas J. Ward, "Research Note: Cannabis and Driving — Research Needs and Issues for Transportation Policy," Journal of Drug Issues, Dec. 2004, pp. 977-8.

26. "Both simulator and road studies showed that relative to alcohol use alone, participants who used cannabis alone or in combination with alcohol were more aware of their intoxication. Robbe (1998) found that participants who consumed 100 g/kg of cannabis rated their performance worse and the amount of effort required greater compared to those who consumed alcohol (0.05 BAC). Ramaekers et al. (2000) showed that cannabis use alone and in combination with alcohol consumption increased self-ratings of intoxication and decreased self-ratings of performance. Lamers and Ramaekers (2001) found that cannabis use alone (100 g/kg) and in combination with alcohol consumption resulted in lower ratings of alertness, greater perceptions of effort, and worse ratings of performance."

Source: Laberge, Jason C., Nicholas J. Ward, "Research Note: Cannabis and Driving — Research Needs and Issues for Transportation Policy," Journal of Drug Issues, Dec. 2004, pp. 978.

27. "Both Australian studies suggest cannabis may actually reduce the responsibility rate and lower crash risk. Put another way, cannabis consumption either increases driving ability or, more likely, drivers who use cannabis make adjustments in driving style to compensate for any loss of skill (Drummer, 1995). This is consistent with simulator and road studies that show drivers who consumed cannabis slowed down and drove more cautiously (see Ward & Dye, 1999; Smiley, 1999. This compensation could help reduce the probability of being at fault in a motor vehicle accident since drivers have more time to respond and avoid a collision. However, it must be noted that any behavioral compensation may not be sufficient to cope with the reduced safety margin resulting from the impairment of driver functioning and capacity."

Source: Laberge, Jason C., Nicholas J. Ward, "Research Note: Cannabis and Driving — Research Needs and Issues for Transportation Policy," Journal of Drug Issues, Dec. 2004, pp. 980.

28. A literature review of the effects of cannabis on driving found, "Another paradigm used to assess crash risk is to use cross-sectional surveys of reported nonfatal accidents that can be related to the presence of risk factors, such as alcohol and cannabis consumption. Such a methodology was employed in a provocative dissertation by Laixuthai (1994). This study used data from two large surveys that were nationally representative of high school students in the United States during 1982 and 1989. Results showed that cannabis use was negatively correlated with nonfatal accidents, but these results can be attributed to changes in the amount of alcohol consumed. More specifically, the decriminalization of cannabis and the subsequent reduction

Marijuana

in penalty cost, as well as a reduced purchase price of cannabis, made cannabis more appealing and affordable for young consumers. This resulted in more cannabis use, which substituted for alcohol consumption, leading to less frequent and less heavy drinking. The reduction in the amount of alcohol consumed resulted in fewer nonfatal accidents."

Source: Laberge, Jason C., Nicholas J. Ward, "Research Note: Cannabis and Driving — Research Needs and Issues for Transportation Policy," Journal of Drug Issues, Dec. 2004, pp. 980-1.

29. Since 1969, government-appointed commissions in the United States, Canada, England, Australia, and the Netherlands have concluded, after reviewing the scientific evidence, that marijuana's dangers had previously been greatly exaggerated, and urged lawmakers to drastically reduce or eliminate penalties for marijuana possession.

Source: Advisory Committee on Drug Dependence, Cannabis (London, England: Her Majesty's Stationery Office, 1969); Canadian Government Commission of Inquiry, The Non-Medical Use of Drugs (Ottawa, Canada: Information Canada, 1970); The National Commission on Marihuana and Drug Abuse, Marihuana: A Signal of Misunderstanding, (Nixon-Shafer Report) (Washington, DC: USGPO, 1972); Werkgroep Verdovende Middelen, Background and Risks of Drug Use (The Hague, The Netherlands: Staatsuigeverij, 1972); Senate Standing Committee on Social Welfare, Drug Problems in Australia-An Intoxicated Society (Canberra, Australia: Australian Government Publishing Service, 1977); Advisory Council on the Misuse of Drugs, "The classification of cannabis under the Misuse of Drugs Act 1971" (London, England, UK: Home Office, March 2002), available on the web from http://www.drugs.gov.uk/Reportsand Publications/Communities/1034155489/Classific_Cannabis_MisuseDrugsAct1971.pdf ; House of Commons Home Affairs Committee Third Report, "The Government's Drugs Policy: Is It Working?" (London, England, UK: Parliament, May 9, 2002), from the web at http://www.publications.parliament.uk/pa/cm200102/cmselect/cmhaff/318/31802.hmand "Cannabis: Our Position for a Canadian Public Policy," report of the Canadian Senate Special Committee on Illegal Drugs (Ottawa, Canada: Senate of Canada, September 2002).

bb

30. The Canadian Senate's Special Committee on Illegal Drugs recommended in its 2002 final report on cannabis policy that "the Government of Canada amend the Controlled Drugs and Substances Act to create a criminal exemption scheme. This legislation should stipulate the conditions for obtaining licenses as well as for producing and selling cannabis; criminal penalties for illegal trafficking and export; and the preservation of criminal penalties for all activities falling outside the scope of the exemption scheme."

Source: "Cannabis: Our Position for a Canadian Public Policy," report of the Canadian Senate Special Committee on Illegal Drugs (Ottawa, Canada: Senate of Canada, September 2002), p. 46.

31. The United Kingdom officially downgraded the classification of cannabis from Class B to Class C effective Jan. 29, 2004. The London Guardian reported that "Under the switch, cannabis will be ranked alongside bodybuilding steroids and some anti-depressants. Possession of cannabis will no longer be an arrestable offence in most cases, although police will retain the power to arrest users in certain

Marijuana

aggravated situations - such as when the drug is smoked outside schools. The home secretary, David Blunkett, has said the change in the law is necessary to enable police to spend more time tackling class A drugs such as heroin and crack cocaine which cause the most harm and trigger far more crime."

Source: Tempest, Matthew, "MPs Vote To Downgrade Cannabis," The Guardian (London, England), Oct. 29, 2003.

32. In May of 1998, the Canadian Centre on Substance Abuse, National Working Group on Addictions Policy released policy a discussion document which recommended, "The severity of punishment for a cannabis possession charge should be reduced. Specifically, cannabis possession should be converted to a civil violation under the Contraventions Act." The paper further noted that, "The available evidence indicates that removal of jail as a sentencing option would lead to considerable cost savings without leading to increases in rates of cannabis use."

Source: Single, Eric, Cannabis Control in Canada: Options Regarding Possession (Ottawa, Canada: Canadian Centre on Substance Abuse, May 1998).

33. "Our conclusion is that the present law on cannabis produces more harm than it prevents. It is very expensive of the time and resources of the criminal justice system and especially of the police. It inevitably bears more heavily on young people in the streets of inner cities, who are also more likely to be from minority ethnic communities, and as such is inimical to police-community relations. It criminalizes large numbers of otherwise law-abiding, mainly young, people to the detriment of their futures. It has become a proxy for the control of public order; and it inhibits accurate education about the relative risks of different drugs including the risks of cannabis itself."

Source: Police Foundation of the United Kingdom, "Drugs and the Law: Report of the Independent Inquiry into the Misuse of Drugs Act of 1971", April 4, 2000. The Police Foundation, based in London, England, is a nonprofit organization presided over by Charles, Crown Prince of Wales, which promotes research, debate and publication to improve the efficiency and effectiveness of policing in the UK.

34. "Statements in the popular media that the potency of cannabis has increased by ten times or more in recent decades are not support by the data from either the USA or Europe. As discussed in the body of this report, systematic data are not available in Europe on long-term trends and analytical and methodological issues complicate the interpretation of the information that is available. Data are stronger for medium and short-term trends where no major differences are apparent in Europe, although some modest increases are found in some countries. The greatest long-term changes in potency appear to have occurred in the USA. It should be noted here that before 1980 herbal cannabis potency in the USA was, according to the available data, very low by European standards."

Marijuana

Source: European Monitoring Centre for Drugs and Drug Addiction, "EMCDDA Insights - An Overview of Cannabis Potency in Europe" (Luxembourg: Office for Official Publications of the European Communities, 2004), p. 59.

35. "Although marijuana grown in the United States was once considered inferior because of a low concentration of THC, advancements in plant selection and cultivation have resulted in higher THC-containing domestic marijuana. In 1974, the average THC content of illicit marijuana was less than one percent. Today most commercial grade marijuana from Mexico/Columbia and domestic outdoor cultivated marijuana has an average THC content of about 4 to 6 percent. Between 1998 and 2002, NIDA-sponsored Marijuana Potency Monitoring System (MPMP) analyzed 4,603 domestic samples. Of those samples, 379 tested over 15 percent THC, 69 samples tested between 20 and 25 percent THC and four samples tested over 25 percent THC."

Source: US Drug Enforcement Administration, "Drugs of Abuse" (Washington, DC: US Dept. of Justice, 2005), from the web athttp://www.dea.gov/pubs/abuse/7-pot.htm last accessed Jan. 27, 2005.

bb

Medical Marijuana

1. Since 1996, twelve states have legalized medical marijuana use: AK, CA, CO, HI, ME, MT, NV, NM, OR, RI, VT, and WA. Eight of the twelve did so through the initiative process. Hawaii's law was enacted by the legislature and signed by the governor in 2000, Vermont's was enacted by the legislature and passed into law without the governor's signature in May 2004, Rhode Island's was passed into law over the governor's veto in January 2006, and New Mexico's legislation was signed into law by Governor Bill Richardson on April 2, 2007.

   Source: National Organization for the Reform of Marijuana Laws (NORML), from the web at http://www.norml.org/index.cfm?Group_ID=3391 last accessed May 24, 2007, and Marijuana Policy Project (MPP), from the web at http://www.mpp.org/ RI_number_11.html last accessed Jan. 4, 2006.

2. The Institute of Medicine's 1999 report on medical marijuana stated, "The accumulated data indicate a potential therapeutic value for cannabinoid drugs, particularly for symptoms such as pain relief, control of nausea and vomiting, and appetite stimulation."

   Source: Janet E. Joy, Stanley J. Watson, Jr., and John A Benson, Jr., Marijuana and Medicine: Assessing the Science Base. Division of Neuroscience and Behavioral Research, Institute of Medicine (Washington, DC: National Academy Press, 1999).

3. The Institute of Medicine's 1999 report on medical marijuana examined the question whether the medical use of marijuana would lead to an increase of marijuana use in the general population and concluded that, "At this point there are no convincing data to support this concern. The existing data are consistent with the idea that this would not be a problem if the medical use of marijuana were as closely regulated as other medications with abuse potential." The report also noted that, "this question is beyond the issues normally considered for medical uses of drugs, and should not be a factor in evaluating the therapeutic potential of marijuana or cannabinoids."

   Source: Janet E. Joy, Stanley J. Watson, Jr., and John A Benson, Jr., Marijuana and Medicine: Assessing the Science Base. Division of Neuroscience and Behavioral Research, Institute of Medicine (Washington, DC: National Academy Press, 1999).

4. In the Institute of Medicine's report on medical marijuana, the researchers examined the physiological risks of using marijuana and cautioned, "Marijuana is not a completely benign substance. It is a powerful drug with a variety of effects. However, except for the harms associated with smoking, the adverse effects of marijuana use are within the range of effects tolerated for other medications."

   Source: Janet E. Joy, Stanley J. Watson, Jr., and John A Benson, Jr., Marijuana and Medicine: Assessing the Science Base. Division of Neuroscience and Behavioral Research, Institute of Medicine (Washington, DC: National Academy Press, 1999).

5. The Institute of Medicine's 1999 report on medical marijuana examined the question of whether marijuana could diminish patients' immune system - an important question when considering its use by AIDS and cancer patients. The report concluded, "the short-term immunosuppressive effects are not well established but, if they exist, are not likely great enough to preclude a legitimate medical use."

Medical Marijuana

Source: Janet E. Joy, Stanley J. Watson, Jr., and John A Benson, Jr., Marijuana and Medicine: Assessing the Science Base. Division of Neuroscience and Behavioral Research, Institute of Medicine (Washington, DC: National Academy Press, 1999).

6. "Conclusions: Smoked and oral cannabinoids did not seem to be unsafe in people with HIV infection with respect to HIV RNA levels, CD4+ and CD8+ cell counts, or protease inhibitor levels over a 21-day treatment."

   Source: Abrams, Donald I., MD, et al., "Short-Term Effects of Cannabinoids in Patients with HIV-1 Infection - A Randomized, Placebo-Controlled Clinical Trial," Annals of Internal Medicine, Aug. 19, 2003, Vol. 139, No. 4 (American College of Physicians), p. 258.

7. "This study provides evidence that short-term use of cannabinoids, either oral or smoked, does not substantially elevate viral load in individuals with HIV infection who are receiving stable antiretroviral regimens containing nelfinavir or indinavir. Upper confidence bounds for all estimated effects of cannabinoids on HIV RNA level from all analyses were no greater than an increase of 0.23 log10 copies/mL compared with placebo. Because this study was randomized and analyses were controlled for all known potential confounders, it is very unlikely that chance imbalance on any known or unknown covariate masked a harmful effect of cannabinoids. Study participants in all groups may have been expected to benefit from the equivalent of directly observed antiretroviral therapy, as well as decreased stress and, for some, improved nutrition over the 25-day inpatient stay."

   Source: Abrams, Donald I., MD, et al., "Short-Term Effects of Cannabinoids in Patients with HIV-1 Infection - A Randomized, Placebo-Controlled Clinical Trial," Annals of Internal Medicine, Aug. 19, 2003, Vol. 139, No. 4 (American College of Physicians), p. 264.

8. "Over a 5-day inpatient intervention period, smoking cannabis cigarettes three times a day reduced HIV-SN [Sensory Neuropathy] pain by 34%, significantly more than the 17% reduction with placebo cigarettes. A >30% reduction in pain has been validated as a clinically significant level of improvement. In the current study, half (52%) of those randomized to cannabis experienced at least a 30% reduction in pain, while a quarter (24%) of those randomized to placebo experienced a similar reduction in pain."

   Source: Abrams, Donald I., MD, Jay, A., Shade, S.B., Vizoso, H., Reda, H., Press, S., Kelly, M.E., Rowbotham, M.C., and Petersen, K.L., "Cannabis in Painful HIV-Associated Sensory Neuropathy: A Randomized Placebo-Controlled Trial," Neurology, Vol. 68, Feb. 13, 2007, p. 519.

9. "Nevertheless, when considering all 15 studies (i.e., those that met both strict and more relaxed criteria) we only noted that regular cannabis users performed worse on memory tests, but that the magnitude of the effect was very small. The small magnitude of effect sizes from observations of chronic users of cannabis suggests that cannabis compounds, if found to have therapeutic value, should have a good margin of safety from a neurocognitive standpoint under the more limited conditions of exposure that would likely obtain in a medical setting."

Medical Marijuana

Source: Grant, Igor, et al., "Non-Acute (Residual) Neurocognitive Effects Of Cannabis Use: A Meta-Analytic Study," Journal of the International Neuropsychological Society (Cambridge University Press: July 2003), 9, pp. 687-8.

10. In spite of the established medical value of marijuana, doctors are presently permitted to prescribe cocaine and morphine — but not marijuana.

    Source: The Controlled Substances Act of 1970, 21 U.S.C. §§ 801 et seq.

11. According to a review by the General Accounting Office (GAO) of medical cannabis programs in four states, "Most medical marijuana recommendations in states where data are collected have been made for applicants with severe pain or muscle spasticity as their medical condition. Conditions allowed by the states' medical marijuana laws ranged from illnesses such as cancer and AIDS, to symptoms, such as severe pain. Information is not collected on the conditions for which marijuana has been recommended in Alaska or California. However, data from Hawaii's registry showed that the majority of recommendations have been made for the condition of severe pain or the condition of muscle spasticity. Likewise, data from Oregon's registry showed that, 84 percent of recommendations were for the condition of severe pain or for muscle spasticity."

    Source: General Accounting Office, "Marijuana: Early Experiences with Four States' Laws That Allow Use for Medical Purposes" (Washington, DC: Government Printing Office, Nov. 2002), GAO-03-189, p. 24.

12. Though doctors in the US are not permitted to prescribe marijuana, they are allowed to discuss it with their patients and to recommend marijuana to those patients for whom it would be useful. This was clarified by the federal courts in the case of Conant v. McCaffrey in Sept. 2000: "The government is permanently ENJOINED from (i) revoking a class-member physician's DEA registration merely because the doctor recommends medical marijuana to a patient based on a sincere medical judgment and (ii) from initiating any investigation solely on that ground. This injunction applies whether or not the physician anticipates that the recommendation will, in turn, be used by the patient to obtain marijuana in violation of federal law. The Court finds that all other issues tendered are not justiciable." A federal appeal of the case was rejected by the US Supreme Court in Oct. 14, 2003 (Case No. 03-40, Walters v. Conant).

    Source: Conant v. McCaffrey, Case No. C 97-00139 WHA, US District Court for the Northern District of California (9th Circuit), "Order Granting in Part and Denying in Part Cross-Motions for Summary Judgment; Dissolving Preliminary Injunction; Entering Permanent Injunction," Sept. 2000, pp. 22-23; Associated Press, "Supreme Court Rejects Anti-Marijuana Case," Oct. 14, 2003.

13. Organizations that have endorsed medical access to marijuana include: the Institute of Medicine, the American Academy of Family Physicians; American Bar Association; American Public Health Association; American Society of Addiction Medicine; AIDS Action

Medical Marijuana

Council; British Medical Association; California Academy of Family Physicians; California Legislative Council for Older Americans; California Medical Association; California Nurses Association; California Pharmacists Association; California Society of Addiction Medicine; California-Pacific Annual Conference of the United Methodist Church; Colorado Nurses Association; Consumer Reports Magazine; Kaiser Permanente; Lymphoma Foundation of America; Multiple Sclerosis California Action Network; National Association of Attorneys General; National Association of People with AIDS; National Nurses Society on Addictions; New Mexico Nurses Association; New York State Nurses Association; New England Journal of Medicine; and Virginia Nurses Association.

14. A few of the editorial boards that have endorsed medical access to marijuana include: Boston Globe; Chicago Tribune; Miami Herald; New York Times; Orange County Register; and USA Today.

15. Many organizations have favorable positions (e.g., unimpeded research) on medical marijuana. These groups include: The Institute of Medicine, The American Cancer Society; American Medical Association; Australian Commonwealth Department of Human Services and Health; California Medical Association; Federation of American Scientists; Florida Medical Association; and the National Academy of Sciences.

16. The Controlled Substances Act of 1970 established five categories, or "schedules," into which all illicit and prescription drugs were placed. Marijuana was placed in Schedule I, which defines the substance as having a high potential for abuse, no currently accepted medical use in the United States, and a lack of accepted safety for use under medical supervision. To contrast, over 90 published reports and studies have shown marijuana has medical efficacy.

   Sources: The Controlled Substances Act of 1970, 21 U.S.C. §§ 801 et seq.; Common Sense for Drug Policy, Compendium of Reports, Research and Articles Demonstrating the Effectiveness of Medical Marijuana, Vol. I & Vol. II (Falls Church, VA: Common Sense for Drug Policy, March 1997).

17. The U.S. Penal Code states that any person can be imprisoned for up to one year for possession of one marijuana cigarette and imprisoned for up to five years for growing a single marijuana plant.

   Source: The Controlled Substances Act of 1970, 21 U.S.C. §§ 801 et seq.

18. On September 6, 1988, the Drug Enforcement Administration's Chief Administrative Law Judge, Francis L. Young, ruled: "Marijuana, in its natural form, is one of the safest therapeutically active substances known. ...[T]he provisions of the [Controlled Substances] Act permit and require the transfer of marijuana from Schedule I to Schedule II. It would be unreasonable, arbitrary and capricious for the DEA to continue to stand between those sufferers and the benefits of this substance."

   Source: US Department of Justice, Drug Enforcement Agency, "In the Matter of Marijuana Rescheduling Petition," [Docket #86-22] (September 6, 1988), p. 57.

Medical Marijuana

19. The DEA's Administrative Law Judge, Francis Young concluded: "In strict medical terms marijuana is far safer than many foods we commonly consume. For example, eating 10 raw potatoes can result in a toxic response. By comparison, it is physically impossible to eat enough marijuana to induce death. Marijuana in its natural form is one of the safest therapeutically active substances known to man. By any measure of rational analysis marijuana can be safely used within the supervised routine of medical care."

    Source: US Department of Justice, Drug Enforcement Agency, "In the Matter of Marijuana Rescheduling Petition," [Docket #86-22], (September 6, 1988), p. 57.

20. Between 1978 and 1997, 35 states and the District of Columbia passed legislation recognizing marijuana's medicinal value. States include: AL, AZ, AR, CA, CO, CT, FL, GA, IL, IA, LA, MA, ME, MI, MN, MO, MT, NV, NH, NJ, NM, NY, NC, OH, OK, OR, RI, SC, TN, TX, VT, VA, WA, WV, and WI.

CC

Methadone & Buprenorphine Treatment

1. According to the National Institutes of Health (NIH), "Methadone maintenance treatment is effective in reducing illicit opiate drug use, in reducing crime, in enhancing social productivity, and in reducing the spread of viral diseases such as AIDS and hepatitis."

    Source: Effective Medical Treatment of Opiate Addiction. NIH Consensus Statement 1997 Nov. 17-19; 15(6): 4.

2. According to the NIH, "All opiate-dependent persons under legal supervision should have access to methadone maintenance therapy..."

    Source: Effective Medical Treatment of Opiate Addiction. NIH Consensus Statement 1997 Nov. 17-19; 15(6): 2.

3. "The safety and efficacy of narcotic agonist (methadone) maintenance treatment has been unequivocally established."

    Source: Effective Medical Treatment of Opiate Addiction. NIH Consensus Statement 1997 Nov. 17-19; 15(6): 4.

4. "In summary, data from studies conducted in Australia, Europe, Asia and the United States have, with few exceptions, found strong associations between participation in methadone treatment and reductions in the frequency of opioid use, fewer injections and injection-related HIV risk behaviors, and lower rates of HIV prevalence and incidence. Few randomized controlled trials have been conducted due to ethical concerns regarding the random assignment of individuals to no treatment or other potentially less effective treatment modalities. Despite this fact, the consistency of findings from the observational and case–controlled studies cited here provide a preponderance of evidence suggesting that sustained treatment of opioid-dependent injection drug users with methadone is associated strongly with protection from HIV infection."

    Source: Sullivan, Lynn David S. Metzger, Paul J. Fudala & David A. Fiellin, "Decreasing International HIV Transmission: The Role of Expanding Access to Opioid Agonist Therapies for Injection Drug Users," Addiction, February 2005, Vol. 100, No. 2, p. 152.

5. "The wide international variation in the availability of opioid agonist treatment for opioid-dependent injection drug users, despite documented scientific evidence in support of its efficacy, highlights the impact of political and philosophical forces that determine the availability of this treatment. Few proven therapies for medical conditions are restricted in this fashion. Therefore, efforts to address the political and philosophical opposition to opioid agonist treatment are needed to meet the global needs to prevent HIV transmission."

    Source: Sullivan, Lynn, David S. Metzger, Paul J. Fudala & David A. Fiellin, "Decreasing International HIV Transmission: The Role of Expanding Access to Opioid Agonist Therapies for Injection Drug Users," Addiction, February 2005, Vol. 100, No. 2, p. 153.

6. "The unnecessary regulations of methadone maintenance therapy and other long-acting opiate agonist treatment programs should be reduced, and coverage for these programs should be a required benefit in public and private insurance programs."

Methadone & Buprenorphine Treatment

Source: *Effective Medical Treatment of Opiate Addiction. NIH Consensus Statement 1997 Nov. 17-19; 15(6): 2.*

7. "The unparalleled international epidemic of injection drug use as a major cause of global HIV transmission, coupled with the research evidence supporting the efficacy of methadone treatment in decreasing drug injection and HIV transmission, and the unique pharmacological properties and potential acceptance of buprenorphine and the buprenorphine/naloxone combination, mean that the world is poised for implementation and evaluation of these treatments as a method to stem the spread of HIV."

Source: Sullivan, Lynn, David S. Metzger, Paul J. Fudala & David A. Fiellin, "Decreasing International HIV Transmission: The Role of Expanding Access to Opioid Agonist Therapies for Injection Drug Users," Addiction, February 2005, Vol. 100, No. 2, p. 153.

8. "The current narcotic treatment system is able to provide the most effective medical treatment for opioid dependence, opioid agonist maintenance, to only 170,000 of the estimated 810,000 opioid-dependent individuals in the United States."

Source: Fiellin, David A., MD, Patrick G. O'Connor, MD, MPH, Marek Chawarski, PhD, Juliana P. Pakes, MEd, Michael V. Pantalon, PhD, and Richard S. Schottenfeld, MD, "Methadone Maintenance in Primary Care: A Randomized Controlled Trial," Journal of the American Medical Association (Chicago, IL: American Medical Association, Oct. 10, 2001), Vol. 286, No. 14, p. 1724.

9. "NTPs (Narcotics Treatment Programs) are the most highly regulated form of medicine practiced in the US, as they are subject to Federal, State, and local regulation. Under this regulatory burden, expansion of this system has been static for many years. This has resulted in a 'treatment gap', which is defined as the difference between the number of opiate dependent persons and those in treatment. The gap currently is over 600,000 persons and represents 75-80% of all addicts."

Source: "Buprenorphine Update: Questions and Answers," National Institute on Drug Abuse (Rockville, MD: National Institutes of Health), from the web at http://www.nida.nih.gov/Bupupdate.html last accessed Dec. 12, 2006.

10. "The financial costs of untreated opiate dependence to the individual, the family, and society are estimated to be approximately $20 billion per year."

Source: Effective Medical Treatment of Opiate Addiction. NIH Consensus Statement 1997 Nov. 17-19; 15(6): 11.

11. "Although a drug-free state represents an optimal treatment goal, research has demonstrated that this goal cannot be achieved or sustained by the majority of opiate-dependent people."

Source: Effective Medical Treatment of Opiate Addiction. NIH Consensus Statement 1997 Nov. 17-19; 15(6): 5.

12. "Of the various treatments available, Methadone Maintenance Treatment, combined with attention to medical, psychiatric and socioeconomic issues, as well as drug counseling, has the highest probability of being effective."

Methadone & Buprenorphine Treatment

Source: Effective Medical Treatment of Opiate Addiction. NIH Consensus Statement 1997 Nov. 17-19; 15(6): 7.

13. "Over the past two decades, clear and convincing evidence has been collected from multiple studies showing that effective treatment of opiate dependence markedly reduces the rates of criminal activity."

Source: Effective Medical Treatment of Opiate Addiction. NIH Consensus Statement 1997 Nov. 17-19; 15(6): 12.

14. "Our results support the hypothesis that harm-reduction-based methadone maintenance treatment decreases the risk of natural-cause and overdose mortality. Furthermore, our data suggest that in harm-reduction-based methadone programs, being in methadone treatment is important in itself, independent of the pharmacologic effect of methadone dosage. To decrease mortality among drug users, prevention measures should be expanded for those who dropout of treatment."

Source: Langendam, Miranda W., PhD, Giel H.A.van Brussel, MD, Roel A. Coutinho, MD, PhD, and Erik J.C. van Ameijden, PhD, "The Impact of Harm-Reduction-Based Methadone Treatment on Mortality Among Heroin Users," American Journal of Public Health (Washington, DC: American Public Health Association, May 2001), Vol. 95, No. 5, p. 779.

15. "Methadone's half-life is approximately 24 hours and leads to a long duration of action and once-a-day dosing. This feature, coupled with its slow onset of action, blunts its euphoric effect, making it unattractive as a principal drug of abuse."

Source: Effective Medical Treatment of Opiate Addiction. NIH Consensus Statement 1997 Nov. 17-19; 15(6): 14.

16. "Prolonged oral treatment with this medicine [methadone] diminishes and often eliminates opiate use, reduces transmission of many infections, including HIV and hepatitis B and C, and reduces criminal activity."

Source: Effective Medical Treatment of Opiate Addiction. NIH Consensus Statement 1997 Nov. 17-19; 15(6): 16.

17. "Methadone maintenance treatment (MMT) has been shown to improve life functioning and decrease heroin use; criminal behavior; drug use practices, such as needle sharing, that increase human immunodeficiency virus (HIV) risk; and HIV infection."

Source: Sees, Karen, DO, et al., "Methadone Maintenance vs. 180-Day Psychosocially Enriched Detoxification for Treatment of Opiod Dependence: A Randomized Controlled Trial", Journal of the American Medical Association, 2000, 283:1303.

18. A study reported in the March 8, 2000 edition of the Journal of the American Medical Association shows that traditional methadone maintenance therapy is superior to both short-term and long-term detoxification treatment as a method to treat heroin dependence.

Source: Sees, Karen, DO, et al., "Methadone Maintenance vs. 180-Day Psychosocially Enriched Detoxification for Treatment of Opiod Dependence: A Randomized Controlled Trial", Journal of the American Medical Association, 2000, 283:1303-1310.

Methadone & Buprenorphine Treatment

19. "In summary, levomethadyl acetate, buprenorphine, and high-dose methadone were more effective than low-dose methadone in reducing the use of illicit opioids. As compared with low-dose methadone, levomethadyl acetate produced the longest duration of continuous abstinence; buprenorphine administered three times weekly was similar to levomethadyl acetate in terms of study retention and was similar to high-dose methadone in terms of abstinence."

Source: Johnson, Rolley E., Pharm. D., Mary Ann Chutuape, PhD, Eric C. Strain, MD, Sharon L. Walsh, PhD, Maxine L. Stitzer, PhD, and George E. Bigelow, PhD, "A Comparison of Levomethadyl Acetate, Buprenorphine, and Methadone for Opioid Dependence," New England Journal of Medicine (Boston, MA: Massachusetts Medical Society, Nov. 2, 2000), Vol. 343, No. 18, p. 1296.

20. "Office-based methadone maintenance administered by appropriately trained primary care and specialist physicians has the potential to provide an alternative for selected patients to the current narcotic treatment system that would allow for greater physician involvement and perhaps increased quality of care. Potential benefits from this type of care include increased attention to comorbid medical and psychiatric conditions, decreased stigma associated with the diagnosis and treatment, decreased contact with active heroin users, and increased access to treatment. These benefits may increase patient satisfaction and enhance clinical outcomes."

Source: Fiellin, David A., MD, Patrick G. O'Connor, MD, MPH, Marek Chawarski, PhD, Juliana P. Pakes, MEd, Michael V. Pantalon, PhD, and Richard S. Schottenfeld, MD, "Methadone Maintenance in Primary Care: A Randomized Controlled Trial," Journal of the American Medical Association (Chicago, IL: American Medical Association, Oct. 10, 2001), Vol. 286, No. 14, p. 1725.

21. "Our results demonstrate that methadone maintenance using weekly physician office-based dispensing is feasible, that treatment retention and patient and clinician satisfaction are high, and that illicit drug use does not differ significantly compared with continued treatment in an NTP. Stable patients demonstrated high functional status and low levels of health and social service use on transfer from an NTP to office-based care. The high level of patient and clinician satisfaction with office-based care and the outcomes observed with office-based treatment run counter to concerns regarding the potential quality of this type of care and the ability to identify a group of physicians interested in providing treatment for opioid-dependent patients."

Source: Fiellin, David A., MD, Patrick G. O'Connor, MD, MPH, Marek Chawarski, PhD, Juliana P. Pakes, MEd, Michael V. Pantalon, PhD, and Richard S. Schottenfeld, MD, "Methadone Maintenance in Primary Care: A Randomized Controlled Trial," Journal of the American Medical Association (Chicago, IL: American Medical Association, Oct. 10, 2001), Vol. 286, No. 14, p. 1729.

22. "This study has implications for future treatment of opioid dependence. First, the results support the feasibility of transferring stable patients from NTPs to the offices of trained primary care physicians and extends prior research in this field. These findings, along with recent trials demonstrating the effectiveness of buprenorphine for untreated opioid-dependent patients in primary care settings, offer encouragement regarding the use of primary care offices to help expand access to treatment for opioid dependence."

Methadone & Buprenorphine Treatment

Source: Fiellin, David A., MD, Patrick G. O'Connor, MD, MPH, Marek Chawarski, PhD, Juliana P. Pakes, MEd, Michael V. Pantalon, PhD, and Richard S. Schottenfeld, MD, "Methadone Maintenance in Primary Care: A Randomized Controlled Trial," Journal of the American Medical Association (Chicago, IL: American Medical Association, Oct. 10, 2001), Vol. 286, No. 14, p. 1730.

23. "Prescription of methadone by primary care physicians can safely increase the availability of an important treatment modality, and at the same time improve health care for this difficult-to-reach population."

    Source: Weinrich, Michael, MD, and Stuart, Mary, ScD, "Provision of Methadone Treatment in Primary Care Medical Practices: Review of the Scottish Experience and Implications for US Policy", Journal of the American Medical Association, 2000, 283:1343-1348, p. 1347.

24. The Journal of the American Medical Association notes in an editorial in its March 8, 2000 edition that following the Scottish example, and allowing primary care physicians to dispense methadone, could provide a three- to five-fold increase in access, as well as reducing the cost per patient.

    Source: Rounsaville, Bruce J., MD, and Kosten, Thomas R., MD, "Treatment for Opioid Dependence: Quality and Access", Journal of the American Medical Association, 2000, 283:1337:1339.

25. "Taken together, the data confirm a correlation between increased methadone distribution through pharmacy channels and the rise in methadone-associated mortality. The data, thus, support the hypothesis that the growing use of oral methadone, prescribed and dispensed for the outpatient management of pain, explains the dramatic increases in methadone consumption and the growing availability of the drug for diversion to illicit use. Although the data remain incomplete, National Assessment meeting participants concurred that methadone tablets and/or diskettes distributed through channels other than OTPs most likely are the central factor in methadone-associated mortality."

    Source: Center for Substance Abuse Treatment, Methadone-Associated Mortality: Report of a National Assessment, May 8-9, 2003, CSAT Publication No. 28-03 (Rockville, MD: Center for Substance Abuse Treatment, Substance Abuse and Mental Health Services Administration, 2004), p. 25.

26. The Treatment Outcome Prospective Study (TOPS)-a long-term, large-scale longitudinal study of drug treatment-found that patients drastically reduced heroin use while in treatment, with 10% using heroin or other narcotics weekly or daily after just three months in treatment.

    Sources: Hubbard, R.L., et al., "Treatment Outcome Prospective Study (TOPS): Client Characteristics and Behaviors before, during, and after Treatment," in Tims, F.M. & Ludford, J.P. (eds.), Drug Abuse Treatment Evaluation: Strategies, Progress and Prospects (Rockville, MD: National Institute on Drug Abuse, 1984), p. 60.

27. Methadone treatment greatly reduces criminal behavior. The decline in predatory crimes is likely in part because methadone maintenance treatment patients no longer need to finance a costly heroin addiction, and because treatment allows many patients to stabilize their lives and return to legitimate employment.

Methadone & Buprenorphine Treatment

Sources: Hubbard, R.L., et al., "Treatment Outcome Prospective Study (TOPS): Client Characteristics and Behaviors before, during, and after Treatment," in Tims, F.M. & Ludford, J.P. (eds.), Drug Abuse Treatment Evaluation: Strategies, Progress and Prospects (Rockville, MD: National Institute on Drug Abuse, 1984), p. 60; Ball, J.C. & Ross, A., The Effectiveness of Methadone Maintenance Treatment, (New York, NY: Springer-Verlag, 1991), pp. 195-211; Newman, R.G. & Peyser, N., "Methadone Treatment: Experiment and Experience," Journal of Psychoactive Drugs, 23: 115-21 (1991).

28. In support of methadone as an effective treatment for heroin addiction, then-Drug Czar Barry McCaffrey issued the following statement: "Methadone is one of the longest-established, most thoroughly evaluated forms of drug treatment. The science is overwhelming in its findings about methadone treatment's effectiveness. The National Institute on Drug Abuse (NIDA) Drug Abuse Treatment Outcome Study found, for example, that methadone treatment reduced participants' heroin use by 70%, their criminal activity by 57%, and increased their full-time employment by 24%."

Source: McCaffrey, Barry, Statement of ONDCP Director Barry McCaffrey on Mayor Giuliani's Recent Comments on Methadone Therapy, (Press Release) (Washington, DC: ONDCP), July 24, 1998.

29. Methadone is cost effective. Methadone costs about $4,000 per year, while incarceration costs about $20,200 to $23,500 per year.

Sources: Institute of Medicine, Treating Drug Problems (Washington DC: National Academy Press, 1990), Vol. 1, pp. 151-52; Rosenbaum, M., Washburn, A., Knight, K., Kelley, M., & Irwin, J., "Treatment as Harm Reduction, Defunding as Harm Maximization: The Case of Methadone Maintenance," Journal of Psychoactive Drugs, 28: 241-249 (1996); Criminal Justice Institute, Inc., The Corrections Yearbook 1997 (South Salem, NY: Criminal Justice Institute, Inc., 1997) [estimating cost of a day in jail on average to be $55.41 a day, or $20,237 a year, and the cost of prison to be on average to be about $64.49 a day, or $23,554 a year].

30. Methadone does not make patients "high" or interfere with normal functioning.

Source: Lowinson, J.H., et al., (1997), "Methadone Maintenance," Substance Abuse: A Comprehensive Textbook, (3rd Ed.) (Baltimore, MD: Williams & Wilkins, 1997), pp. 405-15.

31. Methadone maintenance treatment helps clients to reduce high risk behaviors like needle sharing and unsafe sex.

Source: Rosenbaum, et al., "Treatment as Harm Reduction, Defunding as Harm Maximization: The Case of Methadone Maintenance," Journal of Psychoactive Drugs, 28: 241-249 (1996).

32. "Prior to the enactment of DATA 2000 [Drug Addiction Treatment Act of 2000], the use of opioid medications to treat opioid addiction was permissible only in federally approved Opioid Treatment Programs (OTPs) (i.e., methadone clinics), and only with the Schedule II opioid medications methadone and levo-alpha-acetyl-methadol (LAAM), which could only be dispensed, not prescribed. Now, under the provisions of DATA 2000, qualifying physicians in the medical office and other appropriate settings outside the OTP system may prescribe and/or dispense Schedule III, IV, and V opioid medications for the treatment of opioid addiction if such medications have been specifically approved by the Food and Drug Administration (FDA) for that indication. (The text of DATA 2000 can be viewed at http://www.buprenorphine.samhsa.gov/fulllaw.html.)

Methadone & Buprenorphine Treatment

"In October 2002, FDA approved two sublingual formulations of the Schedule III opioid partial agonist medication buprenorphine for the treatment of opioid addiction. These medications, Subutex® (buprenorphine) and Suboxone® (buprenorphine/naloxone), are the first and, as of this writing, the only Schedule III, IV, or V medications to have received such FDA approval and, thus, to be eligible for use under DATA 2000."

Source: Center for Substance Abuse Treatment, Clinical Guidelines for the Use of Buprenorphine in the Treatment of Opioid Addiction, Treatment Improvement Protocol (TIP) Series 40, DHHS Publication No. (SMA) 04-3939 (Rockville, MD: Substance Abuse and Mental Health Services Administration, 2004), p. xv. For more information or to get a copy of the Buprenorphine TIP go to http://buprenorphine.samhsa.gov/.

33. "Buprenorphine can be used for either longterm maintenance or for medically supervised withdrawal (detoxification) from opioids. The preponderance of research evidence and clinical experience, however, indicates that opioid maintenance treatments have a much higher likelihood of long-term success than do any forms of withdrawal treatment. In any event, the immediate goals in starting buprenorphine should be stabilization of the patient and abstinence from illicit opioids, rather than any arbitrary or predetermined schedule of withdrawal from the prescribed medication."

Source: Center for Substance Abuse Treatment, Clinical Guidelines for the Use of Buprenorphine in the Treatment of Opioid Addiction, Treatment Improvement Protocol (TIP) Series 40, DHHS Publication No. (SMA) 04-3939 (Rockville, MD: Substance Abuse and Mental Health Services Administration, 2004), p. 20.

34. "A number of clinical trials have established the effectiveness of buprenorphine for the maintenance treatment of opioid addiction. These have included studies that compared buprenorphine to placebo (Johnson et al. 1995; Ling et al. 1998; Fudala et al. 2003), as well as comparisons to methadone (e.g., Johnson et al. 1992; Ling et al. 1996; Pani et al. 2000; Petitjean et al. 2001; Schottenfeld et al. 1997; Strain et al. 1994a, 1994b) and to methadone and levo-alpha-acetyl-methadol (LAAM) (Johnson et al. 2000). Results from these studies suggest that buprenorphine in a dose range of 8–16 mg a day sublingually is as clinically effective as approximately 60 mg a day of oral methadone, although it is unlikely to be as effective as full therapeutic doses of methadone (e.g., 120 mg per day) in patients requiring higher levels of full agonist activity for effective treatment.

"A meta-analysis comparing buprenorphine to methadone (Barnett et al. 2001) concluded that buprenorphine was more effective than 20–35 mg of methadone but did not have as robust an effect as 50–80 mg methadone — much the same effects as the individual studies have concluded."

Source: Center for Substance Abuse Treatment, Clinical Guidelines for the Use of Buprenorphine in the Treatment of Opioid Addiction, Treatment Improvement Protocol (TIP) Series 40, DHHS Publication No. (SMA) 04-3939 (Rockville, MD: Substance Abuse and Mental Health Services Administration, 2004), pp. 20-21.

Methadone & Buprenorphine Treatment

35. "Buprenorphine and naloxone in combination and buprenorphine alone are safe and reduce the use of opiates and the craving for opiates among opiate-addicted persons who receive these medications in an office-based setting."

   Source: Fudula, Paul J., PhD, T. Peter Bridge, MD, Susan Herbert, MA, William O. Williford, PhD, C. Nora Chiang, PhD, Karen Jones, MS, Joseph Collins, ScD, Dennis Raisch, PhD, Paul Casadonte, MD, R. Jeffrey Goldsmith, MD, Walter Ling, MD, Usha Malkerneker, MD, Laura McNicholas, MD, PhD, John Renner, MD, Susan Stine, MD, PhD, & Donald Tusel, MD for the Buprenorphine/Naloxone Collaborative Study Group, "Office-Based Treatment of Opiate Addiction with a Sublingual-Tablet Formulation of Buprenorphine and Naloxone," New England Journal of Medicine, Sept. 4, 2003, Vol. 349, No. 10, p. 949.

36. Researchers from Yale University "investigated the use of counseling and different frequencies of medication dispensing in primary care treatment with buprenorphine-naloxone. Neither the primary outcomes (the frequency of illicit opioid use, the percentage of opioid-negative urine specimens, and the maximum number of consecutive weeks of abstinence from illicit opioids) nor the proportion of patients who completed the study differed significantly among the three groups. Specifically, outcomes among patients receiving brief counseling combined with once-weekly medication dispensing did not differ significantly from outcomes among patients receiving either extended counseling or thrice-weekly medication dispensing. Patient satisfaction was significantly higher with once-weekly than with thrice-weekly medication dispensing, although because of the large number of statistical tests conducted, this may represent a chance finding."

   Source: Fiellin, David A., MD, Michael V. Pantalon, PhD, Marek C. Chawarski, PhD, Brent A. Moore, PhD, Lynn E. Sullivan, MD, Patrick G. O'Connor, MD, MPH, and Richard S. Schottenfeld, MD, "Counseling plus Buprenorphine-Naloxone Maintenance Therapy for Opioid Dependence," New England Journal of Medicine Vol. 355, No. 4, July 27, 2006, pp. 370-371.

37. According to research published in the New England Journal of Medicine, "Consistent with the findings of previous research with buprenorphine, the frequency of illicit opioid use decreased significantly from baseline to induction and was lowest during maintenance for all three groups. The mean percentages of patients who completed the 24-week study, which ranged between 39 and 48 percent, were similar to those found in previous studies, including one conducted in an office-based setting. Therefore, the majority of patients who entered this study either left treatment or were considered appropriate for transfer to a more structured treatment setting with methadone. Nonetheless, although we did not demonstrate the superiority of extended counseling or thrice-weekly medication dispensing over the relatively limited nurse-administered counseling and once-weekly dispensing, our findings support the feasibility of buprenorphine–naloxone maintenance in primary care."

Methadone & Buprenorphine Treatment

Source: Fiellin, David A., MD, Michael V. Pantalon, PhD, Marek C. Chawarski, PhD, Brent A. Moore, PhD, Lynn E. Sullivan, MD, Patrick G. O'Connor, MD, MPH, and Richard S. Schottenfeld, MD, "Counseling plus Buprenorphine-Naloxone Maintenance Therapy for Opioid Dependence," New England Journal of Medicine Vol. 355, No. 4, July 27, 2006, p. 371.

38. "Because buprenorphine is a partial opioid agonist, it is thought to have some advantages over methadone and levomethadyl acetate, including fewer withdrawal symptoms and a lower risk of overdose. Buprenorphine is as effective as methadone if a sufficient dose is used. Like levomethadyl acetate, buprenorphine has the advantage of being long-acting; it can also be effectively administered three times per week."

    Source: O'Connor, Patrick G., MD, MPH, "Treating Opioid Dependence — New Data and New Opportunities," New England Journal of Medicine, Nov. 2, 2000 (Boston, MA: Massachusetts Medical Society, 2000), Vol. 343, No. 18, from the web at http://www.nejm.org/content/2000/0343/0018/1332.asp last accessed Feb. 12, 2001, citing Schottenfeld RS, Pakes JR, Oliveto A, Ziedonis D, Kosten TR, "Buprenorphine vs methadone maintenance treatment for concurrent opioid dependence and cocaine abuse," Arch Gen Psychiatry 1997;54:713-20; and Schottenfeld RS, Pakes J, O'Connor P, Chawarski M, Oliveto A, Kosten TR, "Thrice-weekly versus daily buprenorphine maintenance," Biol Psychiatry 2000;47:1072-9.

39. The New England Journal of Medicine in Nov. of 2000 published a study comparing methadone with LAAM and buprenorphine. According to the report, "Most of the development and evaluation research on buprenorphine has been based on daily doses. Our study used thrice-weekly doses and found that outcomes were approximately equivalent to those with either daily methadone or thrice-weekly levomethadyl acetate. Thus, thrice-weekly buprenorphine may also offer greater convenience to patients and clinic staff."

    Source: Johnson, Rolley E., Pharm. D., Mary Ann Chutuape, PhD, Eric C. Strain, MD, Sharon L. Walsh, PhD, Maxine L. Stitzer, PhD, and George E. Bigelow, PhD, "A Comparison of Levomethadyl Acetate, Buprenorphine, and Methadone for Opioid Dependence," New England Journal of Medicine (Boston, MA: Massachusetts Medical Society, Nov. 2, 2000), Vol. 343, No. 18, p. 1296.

dd

Methamphetamine

1. "Methamphetamine, sometimes used medically (for attention-deficit hyperactivity disorder, obesity, and narcolepsy), is easily manufactured illicitly, and its use has become widespread in Holland, Great Britain, and North America. Illicit use of methamphetamine is the chief type of amphetamine abuse in North America."

   Source: "Amphetamine," The Merck Manual, Section 15. Psychiatric Disorders, Chapter 198. Drug Use and Dependence, Merck & Co. Inc., from the web at http://www.merck.com/ mmpe/sec15/ch198/ch198c.html last accessed May 31, 2007.

2. Just 4.5% of those aged 12 and over in the US have ever tried methamphetamine, and approximately 0.2% of the population has used methamphetamine in the past month. In comparison, 40.1% were reported to have tried marijuana in their lifetimes and 6.0% of the population were estimated to have tried marijuana in the past month; 13.8% of the population were reported to have ever tried cocaine and 1.0% were past month users; 1.5% of the US population have ever tried heroin and 0.1% were estimated to be past month users; and 4.7% of the US population have ever tried Ecstasy (MDMA) while 0.2% were estimated to be past month users.

   Source: Substance Abuse and Mental Health Services Administration. (2006). Results from the 2005 National Survey on Drug Use and Health: National Findings (Office of Applied Studies, NSDUH Series H-30, DHHS Publication No. SMA 06-4194). Rockville, MD, p. 225, Table G.2, p. 229, Table G.6, and p. 238, Table G.15.

3. "The rates for past month and past year methamphetamine use did not change between 2004 and 2005, but the lifetime rate declined from 4.9 to 4.3 percent. From 2002 to 2005, decreases were seen in lifetime (5.3 to 4.3 percent) and past year (0.7 to 0.5 percent) use, but not past month use (0.3 percent in 2002 vs. 0.2 percent in 2005). Although the number of past month users has remained steady since 2002, the number of methamphetamine users who were dependent on or abused some illicit drug did rise significantly during this period, from 164,000 in 2002 to 257,000 in 2005 (Figure 2.3)."

   Source: Substance Abuse and Mental Health Services Administration. (2006). Results from the 2005 National Survey on Drug Use and Health: National Findings (Office of Applied Studies, NSDUH Series H-30, DHHS Publication No. SMA 06-4194). Rockville, MD, p. 16.

4. "The number of new users of stimulants generally increased during the 1990s, but there has been little change since 2000. Incidence of methamphetamine use generally rose between 1992 and 1998. Since then, there have been no statistically significant changes."

   Source: Substance Abuse and Mental Health Services Administration. (2004). Results from the 2003 National Survey on Drug Use and Health: National Findings (Office of Applied Studies, NSDUH Series H-25, DHHS Publication No. SMA 04-3964). Rockville, MD, p. 46. Also available on the web at http://www.oas.samhsa.gov/nhsda/2k3nsduh/ 2k3Results.htm#ch5, last accessed Aug. 31, 2005.

5. "The number of recent new users of methamphetamine taken nonmedically among persons aged 12 or older was 192,000 in 2005 (Figure 5.4). Between 2002 and 2004, the number of methamphetamine initiates remained steady at around 300,000 per year, but there was a decline from 2004 (318,000 initiates) to 2005. The average age of new methamphetamine users aged 12 to 49 was 18.9 years in 2002, 20.4 years in 2003, 20.6 years in 2004, and 18.6 years in 2005."

Methamphetamine

Source: Substance Abuse and Mental Health Services Administration. (2006). Results from the 2005 National Survey on Drug Use and Health: National Findings (Office of Applied Studies, NSDUH Series H-30, DHHS Publication No. SMA 06-4194). Rockville, MD, p. 50.

6. "Methamphetamine is an addictive stimulant drug that strongly activates certain systems in the brain. Methamphetamine is chemically related to amphetamine, but the central nervous system effects of methamphetamine are greater. Both drugs have some limited therapeutic uses, primarily in the treatment of obesity.

   "Methamphetamine is made in illegal laboratories and has a high potential for abuse and addiction. Street methamphetamine is referred to by many names, such as 'speed,' 'meth,' and 'chalk.' Methamphetamine hydrochloride, clear chunky crystals resembling ice, which can be inhaled by smoking, is referred to as 'ice,' 'crystal,' 'glass,' and 'tina.'"

Source: National Institute on Drug Abuse, InfoFacts: Methamphetamine (Rockville, MD: US Department of Health and Human Services), from the web at http://www.nida.nih.gov/ infofacts/methamphetamine.html last accessed January 9, 2006.

7. "80 percent of all methamphetamine in the United States comes from super labs in Mexico and California. However, the purity of that methamphetamine ranges from 15 percent to 20 percent. Individuals who manufacture meth, often dubbed 'cookers' usually only make about an ounce for personal use, but the product is about 85 percent to 95 percent pure."

Source: Testimony of Commissioner Michael Campion, Minnesota Department of Public Safety, US House of Representatives Committee on Government Reform Subcommittee on Criminal Justice, Drug Policy & Human Resources, June 27, 2005, available at http://www.csdp.org/research/Campion_Testimony.pdf .

8. "Law enforcement pressure and strong precursor chemical sales restrictions have achieved marked success in decreasing domestic methamphetamine production. Mexican DTOs, however, have exploited the vacuum created by rapidly expanding their control over methamphetamine distribution — even to eastern states — as users and distributors who previously produced the drug have sought new, consistent sources. These Mexican methamphetamine distribution groups (supported by increased methamphetamine production in Mexico) are often more difficult for local law enforcement agencies to identify, investigate, and dismantle because they typically are much more organized and experienced than local independent producers and distributors. Moreover, these Mexican criminal groups typically produce and distribute ice methamphetamine that usually is smoked, potentially resulting in a more rapid onset of addiction to the drug."

Source: National Drug Intelligence Center, "National Methamphetamine Threat Assessment" (Johnstown, PA: US Dept. of Justice, Nov. 2006), p. 1.

9. "Methamphetamine releases high levels of the neurotransmitter dopamine, which stimulates brain cells, enhancing mood and body movement. It also appears to have a neurotoxic effect, damaging brain cells that contain dopamine as well as serotonin, another neurotransmitter. Over time, methamphetamine appears to cause reduced levels of dopamine, which can result in symptoms like those of Parkinson's disease, a severe movement disorder."

Methamphetamine

Source: National Institute on Drug Abuse, InfoFacts: Methamphetamine (Rockville, MD: US Department of Health and Human Services), from the web at http://www.nida.nih.gov/ infofacts/methamphetamine.html last accessed January 9, 2006.

10. "The psychologic effects of using amphetamines are similar to those produced by cocaine and include alertness, euphoria, and feelings of competence and power. Amphetamines typically cause erectile dysfunction in men but enhance sexual desire. Use is associated with unsafe sex practices, and users are at higher risk of sexually transmitted infections, including HIV infection."

Source: "Amphetamine," The Merck Manual, Section 15. Psychiatric Disorders, Chapter 198. Drug Use and Dependence, Merck & Co. Inc., from the web at http://www.merck.com/mmpe/sec15/ch198/ch198c.html last accessed May 31, 2007.

11. "Repeated use of amphetamines has been shown to cause death of large numbers of brain cells. Repeated use also induces dependence. Tolerance develops slowly, but amounts several hundred-fold greater than the amount originally used may eventually be ingested or injected. Tolerance to various effects develops unequally, so that tachycardia and enhanced alertness diminish, but hallucinations and delusions may occur. However, even massive doses are rarely fatal. Long-term users have reportedly injected as much as 15,000 mg of amphetamine in 24 h without observable acute illness."

Source: "Amphetamine," The Merck Manual, Section 15. Psychiatric Disorders, Chapter 198. Drug Use and Dependence, Merck & Co. Inc., from the web at http://www.merck.com/ mmpe/sec15/ch198/ch198c.html last accessed May 31, 2007.

12. "Although research on the medical and developmental effects of prenatal methamphetamine exposure is still in its early stages, our experience with almost 20 years of research on the chemically related drug, cocaine, has not identified a recognizable condition, syndrome or disorder that should be termed 'crack baby' nor found the degree of harm reported in the media and then used to justify numerous punitive legislative proposals.
"The term 'meth addicted baby' is no less defensible. Addiction is a technical term that refers to compulsive behavior that continues in spite of adverse consequences. By definition, babies cannot be 'addicted' to methamphetamines or anything else. The news media continues to ignore this fact.
"In utero physiologic dependence on opiates (not addiction), known as Neonatal Narcotic Abstinence Syndrome, is readily diagnosable and treatable, but no such symptoms have been found to occur following prenatal cocaine or methamphetamine exposure."

Source: Open letter to the press and the public signed by 93 medical and psychological researchers, from the web at http://www.csdp.org/news/news/Meth_Letter.pdf, last accessed Jan. 9, 2006.

13. "During Vietnam both the Air Force and Navy made amphetamines available to aviators. Intermittently since Vietnam up through Desert Storm the Air Force has used both amphetamines and sedatives in selected aircraft for specific missions."

Methamphetamine

Source: "Performance Maintenance During Continuous Flight Operations: A Guide For Flight Surgeons," NAVMED P-6410, Naval Strike and Air Warfare Center, Jan. 1, 2000, p. 8, available online through the Virtual Naval Hospital of the University of Iowa, at http://www.vnh.org/PerformMaint/

14. "Following Desert Storm an anonymous survey of deployed fighter pilots was completed. 464 surveys were returned (43%). For Desert Storm: 57% used stimulants at some time (17% routinely, 58% occasionally, 25% only once). Within individual units, usage varied from 3% to 96%, with higher usage in units tasked for sustained combat patrol (CAP) missions. Sixty one percent of those who used stimulants reported them essential to mission accomplishment."

Source: "Performance Maintenance During Continuous Flight Operations: A Guide For Flight Surgeons," NAVMED P-6410, Naval Strike and Air Warfare Center, Jan. 1, 2000, p. 11, available online through the Virtual Naval Hospital of the University of Iowa, at http://www.vnh.org/PerformMaint/

15. "Amphetamine abusers are prone to accidents, because the drug produces excitation and grandiosity followed by excess fatigue and sleeplessness. Taken IV, amphetamine may lead to serious antisocial behavior and can precipitate a schizophrenic episode."

Source: "Amphetamine," The Merck Manual, Section 15. Psychiatric Disorders, Chapter 198. Drug Use and Dependence, Merck & Co. Inc., from the web at http://www.merck.com/mmpe/sec15/ch198/ch198.html last accessed May 31, 2007.

16. "Methamphetamine causes increased heart rate and blood pressure and can cause irreversible damage to blood vessels in the brain, producing strokes. Other effects of methamphetamine include respiratory problems, irregular heartbeat, and extreme anorexia. Its use can result in cardiovascular collapse and death."

Source: National Institute on Drug Abuse, InfoFacts: Methamphetamine (Rockville, MD: US Department of Health and Human Services), from the web at http://www.nida.nih.gov/ infofacts/methamphetamine.html last accessed January 9, 2006.

17. "An exhaustion syndrome occurs with repeated use of methamphetamine, involving intense fatigue and need for sleep after the stimulation phase. Methamphetamine can also produce a psychosis in which the person misinterprets others' actions, hallucinates, and becomes unrealistically suspicious. Some users experience a prolonged depression, during which suicide is possible. Methamphetamine use has also led to deaths attributed to severe dehydration, disseminated intravascular coagulation, and renal failure. Users have a high rate of severe tooth decay affecting multiple teeth; causes involve decreased salivation, acidic combustion products, and poor oral hygiene."

Source: "Amphetamine," The Merck Manual, Section 15. Psychiatric Disorders, Chapter 198. Drug Use and Dependence, Merck & Co. Inc., from the web at http://www.merck.com/mmpe/sec15/ch198/ch198c.html last accessed May 31, 2007.

Methamphetamine

18. "People who use high IV doses usually accept that they will eventually experience paranoia and often do not act on it. Nevertheless, with very intense drug use or near the end of weeks of use, awareness may fail and the user may respond to the delusions. Recovery from even prolonged amphetamine psychosis is usual. Thoroughly disorganized and paranoid users recover slowly but completely. The more florid symptoms fade within a few days or weeks, but some confusion, memory loss, and delusional ideas commonly persist for months."

    Source: "Amphetamine," The Merck Manual, Section 15. Psychiatric Disorders, Chapter 198. Drug Use and Dependence, Merck & Co. Inc., from the web at http://www.merck.com/mmpe/sec15/ch198/ch198c.html last accessed May 31, 2007.

19. "Further contributing to the threat posed by the trafficking and abuse of methamphetamine, some chemicals used to produce methamphetamine are flammable, and improper storage, use, or disposal of such chemicals often leads to clandestine laboratory fires and explosions. National Clandestine Laboratory Seizure System (NCLSS) 2003 data show that there were 529 reported methamphetamine laboratory fires or explosions nationwide, a slight decrease from 654 reported fires or explosions in 2002."

    Source: National Drug Threat Assessment 2004 (Johnstown, PA: National Drug Intelligence Center, April 2004), pp. 17-18.

20. "Toxic chemicals used to produce methamphetamine often are discarded in rivers, fields, and forests, causing environmental damage that results in high cleanup costs. For example, DEA's annual cost for cleanup of clandestine laboratories (almost entirely methamphetamine laboratories) in the United States has increased steadily from FY1995 ($2 million), to FY1999 ($12.2 million), to FY 2002 ($23.8 million). Moreover, the Los Angeles County Regional Criminal Information Clearinghouse, a component of the Los Angeles HIDTA, reports that in 2002 methamphetamine laboratory cleanup costs in the combined Central Valley and Los Angeles HIDTA areas alone reached $3,909,809. Statewide, California spent $4,974,517 to remediate methamphetamine laboratories and dumpsites in 2002."

    Source: National Drug Threat Assessment 2004 (Johnstown, PA: National Drug Intelligence Center, April 2004), p. 18.

21. "In fact, according to National Drug Threat Survey (NDTS) 2006 data, 38.8 percent of state and local law enforcement officials nationwide report methamphetamine as the greatest drug threat to their areas, a higher percentage than that for any other drug."

    Source: National Drug Intelligence Center, "National Methamphetamine Threat Assessment" (Johnstown, PA: US Dept. of Justice, Nov. 2006), p. 1.

Militarization of the Drug War

Brief Chronology of Domestic Military Involvement

1878-The Posse Comitatus Act makes it illegal for the military to act as police on U.S. territory or waters.

1981-Posse Comitatus Act is amended to allow limited military involvement in policing.

1989-Joint Task Force 6 (JTF-6, renamed Joint Task Force North (JTF-North) on Sept. 28, 2004) is established. According to the US Northern Command's website at http://www.jtfn.northcom.mil/subpages/mission.html, JTF-6/JTF-North is "a joint service command comprised of active duty and reserve component Soldiers, Sailors, Airmen, Marines, and Department of Defense civilian employees and contracted support personnel. JTF North, formerly known as Joint Task Force Six, is the Department of Defense organization tasked to support our nation's federal law enforcement agencies in the interdiction of suspected transnational threats within and along the approaches to the continental United States," including narcotics trafficking.

1991-Posse Comitatus Act is amended to allow counter-drug training of civilian police by the military.

1995-JTF-6 is expanded to the entire continental United States. It has 700 troops, including 125 combat-ready troops on the U.S.-Mexican border. (Houston Chronicle, 1997, June 22).

May 1997-Esequiel Hernandez becomes the first U.S. citizen shot and killed by JTF-6 troops.

2000-US Coast Guard begins deploying helicopters equipped with machine guns and 50 caliber sniper rifles to help interdiction efforts.

July 2000-US Congress approves $1.3 Billion in military aid to Colombia to fight their drug war as part of "Plan Colombia". An additional 60 combat helicopters are approved for use in Colombia, and the cap on US military personnel assisting in the Colombian conflict is doubled to 500.

April 2001-Peruvian Air Force working with American anti-drug forces in Air Bridge Denial program shoots down legitimate civilian aircraft, killing two US citizens (a missionary and her child). ABD program temporarily halted.

August 2003-ABD program restarts in Colombia.

2004-Office of Congressman Mark Souder (R-IN) reports that Colombia ABD program forced down, immobilized and/or destroyed 21 suspected narcotics trafficking aircraft.

2005-US Congress approves Administration request to increase "Byrd Caps" on personnel in Colombia to 800 military personnel and 600 "civilian contractor" personnel.

1. "The US Congress approved in July 2000 an emergency supplemental assistance request for fiscal years 2000-2001 of $1.32 billion, of which $862.3 million was allocated to Colombia and the balance to neighboring countries (primarily Peru, Bolivia, and Ecuador) and to US agencies' Andean region antidrug operations. Of the $862.3 million allocated to Colombia, $521.2 million is new assistance to the Colombian armed

Militarization of the Drug War

forces and $123.1 is assistance to the police, with the rest ($218 million) going to alternative economic development, aid to displaced persons, judicial reform, law enforcement, and promotion of human rights.

"The bulk of the military assistance will support the Colombian armed forces' three counter-narcotics battalions, which are to receive 16 UH-60 Black Hawk and 30 UH-1H Huey transport helicopters."

Source: Rabasa, Angel & Peter Chalk, "Colombian Labyrinth: The Synergy of Drugs and Insurgency and Its Implications for Regional Instability" (Santa Monica, CA: RAND Corporation, 2001), pp. 62-3, from the web at http://www.rand.org/publications/ MR/MR1339/ last accessed August 11, 2002.

2. "Although US assistance is provided for counter-narcotics purposes only, there is a clear linkage between the Colombian government's counter-narcotics and counter-insurgency strategies. the Colombian government believes that, by striking at the drug trade, it also strikes at the economic center of gravity of the guerrillas. That is, by destroying the coca and poppy fields, drug-production facilities, and transportation networks, the government can also degrade the guerrillas' ability to carry on the war. "Whether this is an accurate assessment remains to be seen."

    Source: Rabasa, Angel & Peter Chalk, "Colombian Labyrinth: The Synergy of Drugs and Insurgency and Its Implications for Regional Instability" (Santa Monica, CA: RAND Corporation, 2001), p. 65, from the web at http://www.rand.org/publications/ MR/MR1339/ last accessed August 11, 2002.

3. "The FARC clearly believes that US counter-narcotics assistance is directed against it, that it is, in effect, disguised counter-insurgency assistance, and that if they, the guerrillas, were to gain the upper hand, the United States would intervene on the side of the Bogota government. Therefore, in its public posture, the FARC has stressed the threat that US military assistance to Colombia poses to the peace process, a theme that plays well with some domestic and international audiences. The FARC professes to be opposed in principle to the narcotics trade, while criticizing the methods employed by the Colombian government — aerial spraying in particular. It has also sought to forestall direct US intervention by drawing parallels between Colombia and Vietnam."

    Source: Rabasa, Angel & Peter Chalk, "Colombian Labyrinth: The Synergy of Drugs and Insurgency and Its Implications for Regional Instability" (Santa Monica, CA: RAND Corporation, 2001), p. 68, from the web at http://www.rand.org/publications/ MR/MR1339/ last accessed August 11, 2002.

4. "Since fiscal year 2000, the availability of U.S. and allied assets spent on interdiction operations in the transit zone — as measured in on-station ship days and flight hours — has varied. U.S. and allied on-station ship days decreased from approximately 3,600 days in fiscal year 2000 to about 3,300 in fiscal year 2005, and U.S. and allied on-station flight hours increased from approximately 10,500 hours in fiscal year 2000 to almost 12,900 in fiscal year 2005. However, on-station ship days peaked in fiscal year 2001 and flight hours peaked

Militarization of the Drug War

in fiscal year 2002, but both have generally declined since then, primarily because Defense has provided fewer assets. Declines in Defense assets were largely offset by the Coast Guard, CBP US Bureau for Customs and Border Protection), and several allied European nations — France, the Netherlands, and the United Kingdom. Nevertheless, with the assets available in recent years, JIATF-South (Joint Interagency Task Force-South) reports that it detected (made visual contact with) less than one-third of the known maritime drug movements."

Source: "Drug Control: Agencies Need to Plan for Likely Decline in Drug Interdiction Assets, and Develop Better Performance Measures for Transit Zone Operations," Government Accountability Office (Washington, DC: USGAO, Nov. 2005), GAO-06-200, p. 4.

5. Eighty-nine percent (89%) of police departments have paramilitary units, and 46% have been trained by active duty armed forces. The most common use of paramilitary units is serving drug-related search warrants (usually no-knock entries into private homes). Twenty percent (20%) of police departments use paramilitary units to patrol urban areas.

Source: Kraska, P. & Kappeler, V., "Militarizing American Police: The Rise and Normalization of Paramilitary Units," Social Problems, Vol. 44, No. 1 (February 1997).

6. In 1996 "Drug Czar" Retired General Barry McCaffrey said of the Drug War, "It makes us all very uncomfortable to see uniformed military units getting heavily involved."

Source: McGee, J., "Military Seeks Balance in Delicate Mission: The Drug War," Washington Post, (November 29, 1996).

7. On February 15, 2000, before the House Subcommittee on Criminal Justice, Drug Policy, and Human Resources, Gen. McCaffrey testified about sending military aid to Colombia to fight their drug war: "Military support will be required to provide a sufficient level of security for the CNP (Colombian National Police) to perform their law enforcement mission. The proposed assistance package would enable the Colombian Army to operate jointly with the CNP as they move into the dangerous drug production sanctuaries in southern Colombian by providing funds to stand up two additional Army Counternarcotics Battalions. The first Army Counternarcotics Battalion, which was trained and equipped by the US, was brought on line in late 1999."

Source: Testimony of ONDCP Director McCaffrey, February 15, 2000, before the House Subcommittee on Criminal Justice, Drug Policy, and Human Resources, from the ONDCP website at www.whitehousedrugpolicy.gov/news/testimony/021500/index.html

Overdose

HEROIN:

1. "Acute intoxication (overdose) is characterized by euphoria, flushing, itching (particularly with morphine), miosis, drowsiness, decreased respiratory rate and depth, hypotension, bradycardia, and decreased body temperature."

   Source: "Opioids," The Merck Manual, Section 15. Psychiatric Disorders, Chapter 198. Drug Use and Dependence, Merck & Co. Inc., from the web at http://www.merck.com/ mmpe/sec15/ch198/ch198l.html last accessed May 29, 2007.

2. "A first priority for prevention must be to reduce the frequency of drug overdoses. We should inform heroin users about the risks of combining heroin with alcohol and other depressant drugs. Not all users will act on such information, but if there are similar behavioral changes to those that occurred with needle-sharing overdose deaths could be substantially reduced. Heroin users should also be discouraged from injecting alone and thereby denying themselves assistance in the event of an overdose."

   Source: Dr. W.D. Hall, "How can we reduce heroin 'overdose' deaths?" The Medical Journal of Australia (MJA 1996; 164:197), from the web at http://www.mja.com.au/ public/issues/feb19/hall/hall.html last accessed on November 17, 2000.

3. Fear of official involvement may contribute to the problem of overdose deaths. According to research in Australia, "Our findings that an ambulance was called while the subject was still alive in only 10% of cases, and that a substantial minority of heroin users died alone, strongly suggest that education campaigns should also emphasise that it is safer to inject heroin in the company of others, and important to call for an ambulance early in the event of an overdose. Consideration should also be given to trialling the distribution of the opioid antagonist naloxone to users to reduce mortality from heroin use."

   Source: Zador, Deborah, Sunjic, Sandra, and Darke, Shane, "Heroin-related deaths in New South Wales, 1992: toxicological findings and circumstances," The Medical Journal of Australia, (MJA 1996; 164:204) published on the web at http://www.mja. com.au/public/issues/ feb19/zador/zador.html last accessed on November 17, 2000.

4. "This pilot trial is the first in North America to prospectively evaluate a program of naloxone distribution to IDUs to prevent heroin overdose death. After an 8-hour training, our study participants' knowledge of heroin overdose prevention and management increased, and they reported successful resuscitations during 20 heroin overdose events. All victims were reported to have been unresponsive, cyanotic, or not breathing, but all survived. These findings suggest that IDUs can be trained to respond to heroin overdose by using CPR and naloxone, as others have reported. Moreover, we found no evidence of increases in drug use or heroin overdose in study participants. These data corroborate the findings of several feasibility studies recommending the prescription and distribution of naloxone to drug users to prevent fatal heroin overdose."

Overdose

Source: Seal, Karen H., Robert Thawley, Lauren Gee, Joshua Bamberger, Alex H. Kral, Dan Ciccarone, Moher Downing, and Brian R. Edlin, "Naloxone Distribution and Cardiopulmonary Resuscitation Training for Injection Drug Users to Prevent Heroin Overdose Death: A Pilot Intervention Study," Journal of Urban Medicine (New York, NY: New York Academy of Medicine, 2005), Vol. 82, No. 2, p. 308.

5. "The disadvantage of continuing to describe heroin-related fatalities as 'overdoses' is that it attributes the cause of death solely to heroin and detracts attention from the contribution of other drugs to the cause of death. Heroin users need to be educated about the potentially dangerous practice of concurrent polydrug and heroin use."

    Source: Zador, Deborah, Sunjic, Sandra, and Darke, Shane, "Heroin-related deaths in New South Wales, 1992: toxicological findings and circumstances," The Medical Journal of Australia, (MJA 1996; 164:204) published on the web at http://www.mja. com.au/public/issues/ feb19/zador/zador.html last accessed on November 17, 2000.

6. "In addition to the effects of the drug itself, street heroin may have additives that do not readily dissolve and result in clogging the blood vessels that lead to the lungs, liver, kidneys, or brain. This can cause infection or even death of small patches of cells in vital organs."

    Source: National Institute on Drug Abuse, Infofax on Heroin No. 13548 (Rockville, MD: US Department of Health and Human Services), from the web at http://www.nida.nih.gov/ Infofax/heroin.html last accessed November 16, 2000.

7. "A striking finding from the toxicological data was the relatively small number of subjects in whom morphine only was detected. Most died with more drugs than heroin alone 'on board', with alcohol detected in 45% of subjects and benzodiazepines in just over a quarter. Both of these drugs act as central nervous system depressants and can enhance and prolong the depressant effects of heroin."

    Source: Zador, Deborah, Sunjic, Sandra, and Darke, Shane, "Heroin-related deaths in New South Wales, 1992: toxicological findings and circumstances," The Medical Journal of Australia, (MJA 1996; 164:204) published on the web at http://www.mja. com.au/public/issues/ feb19/zador/zador.html last accessed on November 17, 2000.

COCAINE:

1. "An overdose [of cocaine] may produce tremors, seizures, and delirium. Death may result from MI, arrhythmias, and heart failure. Patients with extreme clinical toxicity may, on a genetic basis, have decreased (atypical) serum cholinesterase, an enzyme needed for clearance of cocaine. The concurrent use of cocaine and alcohol produces a condensation product, cocaethylene, which has stimulant properties and may contribute to toxicity."

    Source: "Cocaine," The Merck Manual, Section 15. Psychiatric Disorders, Chapter 198. Drug Use and Dependence, Merck & Co. Inc., from the web at http://www.merck.com/ mmpe/sec15/ch198/ch198f.html last accessed May 29, 2007.

Overdose

METHAMPHETAMINE:

1. "Repeated use of amphetamines has been shown to cause death of large numbers of brain cells. Repeated use also induces dependence. Tolerance develops slowly, but amounts several hundred-fold greater than the amount originally used may eventually be ingested or injected. Tolerance to various effects develops unequally, so that tachycardia and enhanced alertness diminish, but hallucinations and delusions may occur. However, even massive doses are rarely fatal. Long-term users have reportedly injected as much as 15,000 mg of amphetamine in 24 h without observable acute illness."

   Source: "Amphetamines," The Merck Manual, Section 15. Psychiatric Disorders, Chapter 198. Drug Use and Dependence, Merck & Co. Inc., from the web at http://www.merck.com/ mmpe/sec15/ch198/ch198c.html last accessed May 29, 2007.

2. "People in the acute agitated psychotic state, with paranoid delusions and auditory and visual hallucinations, respond well to phenothiazines; chlorpromazine 25 to 50 mg IM rapidly reverses this state but may produce severe postural hypotension. Haloperidol 2.5 to 5 mg IM is effective; it rarely produces hypotension but may produce an alarming acute extrapyramidal motor reaction. Usually, reassurance and a quiet, nonthreatening environment are conducive to recovery and are often all that is needed. Ammonium chloride 1 g po q 2 to 4 h to acidify the urine hastens amphetamine excretion."

   Source: "Amphetamines," The Merck Manual, Section 15. Psychiatric Disorders, Chapter 198. Drug Use and Dependence, Merck & Co. Inc., from the web at http://www.merck.com/ mmpe/sec15/ch198/ch198c.html last accessed May 29, 2007.

3. "A paranoid psychosis may result from long-term use of high IV or oral doses. Rarely, the psychosis is precipitated by a single high dose or by repeated moderate doses. Typical features include delusions of persecution, ideas of reference, and feelings of omnipotence. People who use high IV doses usually accept that they will eventually experience paranoia and often do not act on it. Nevertheless, with very intense drug use or near the end of weeks of use, awareness may fail and the user may respond to the delusions. Recovery from even prolonged amphetamine psychosis is usual. Thoroughly disorganized and paranoid users recover slowly but completely. The more florid symptoms fade within a few days or weeks, but some confusion, memory loss, and delusional ideas commonly persist for months."

   Source: "Amphetamines," The Merck Manual, Section 15. Psychiatric Disorders, Chapter 198. Drug Use and Dependence, Merck & Co. Inc., from the web at http://www.merck.com/ mmpe/sec15/ch198/ch198c.html last accessed May 29, 2007.

METHADONE:

1. "Still, methadone is a potent drug; fatal overdoses have been reported over the years (Baden, 1970; Gardner, 1970; Clark, et al., 1995; Drummer, et al., 1992). As with most other opioids, the primary toxic effect of excessive methadone is respiratory depression and hypoxia, sometimes accompanied by pulmonary edema and/or aspiration pneumonia (White and Irvine, 1999; Harding-Pink, 1993). Among patients in addiction treatment, the largest proportion of methadone-

Overdose

associated deaths have occurred during the drug's induction phase, usually when (1) treatment personnel overestimate a patient's degree of tolerance to opioids, or (2) a patient uses opioids or other central nervous system (CNS) depressant drugs in addition to the prescribed methadone (Karch and Stephens, 2000; Caplehorn, 1998; Harding-Pink, 1991; Davoli, et al., 1993). In fact, when deaths occur during later stages of treatment, other drugs usually are detected at postmortem examination (Appel, et al., 2000). In particular, researchers have called attention to the 'poison cocktail' resulting from the intake of multiple psychotropic drugs (Borron, et al., 2001; Haberman, et al., 1995) such as alcohol, benzodiazepines, and other opioids. When used alone, many of these substances are relatively moderate respiratory depressants; however, when combined with methadone, their additive or synergistic effects can be lethal (Kramer, 2003; Payte and Zweben, 1998).

"It is important to note that postmortem blood concentrations of methadone do not appear to reliably distinguish between individuals who have died from methadone toxicity and those in whom the presence of methadone is purely coincidental (Drummer, 1997; Caplan, et al., 1983)."

Source: Center for Substance Abuse Treatment, Methadone-Associated Mortality: Report of a National Assessment, May 8-9, 2003, CSAT Publication No. 28-03 (Rockville, MD: Center for Substance Abuse Treatment, Substance Abuse and Mental Health Services Administration, 2004), p. 11, available at http://www.csdp.org/research/ methadone.samhsa204.pdf.

2. "Three primary scenarios characterize current reports of methadone-associated mortality:

"1. In the context of legitimate patient care, methadone accumulates to harmful serum levels during the first few days of treatment for addiction or pain (that is, the induction period before methadone steady state is achieved or tolerance develops).

"2. Illicitly obtained methadone is used by some individuals who have diminished or no tolerance to opioids and who may use excessive and/or repetitive doses in an attempt to achieve euphoric effects.

"3. Methadone – either licitly administered or illicitly obtained – is used in combination with other CNS depressant agents (such as benzodiazepines, alcohol, or other opioids)."

Source: Center for Substance Abuse Treatment, Methadone-Associated Mortality: Report of a National Assessment, May 8-9, 2003, CSAT Publication No. 28-03 (Rockville, MD: Center for Substance Abuse Treatment, Substance Abuse and Mental Health Services Administration, 2004), p. 24, available at http://www.csdp.org/research/ methadone.samhsa204.pdf.

ALCOHOL:

1. According to the US National Library of Medicine's MEDLINEplus Medical Encyclopedia, Ethanol Overdose is defined as "Poisoning from an overdose of ethanol secondary to excessive consumption of alcoholic beverages." Symptoms of overdose include slowed respirations, vomiting, abdominal pain, intestinal bleeding, stupor, and

Overdose

coma. They advise that "If able to rouse an adult who has overconsumed alcohol, move the person to a comfortable place to sleep off the effects. Make sure the person won't fall, get hurt, and is not lying in vomit. If the patient is semi-conscious or unconscious, emergency assistance may be needed. WHEN IN DOUBT, CALL for medical help. DO NOT INDUCE VOMITING UNLESS INSTRUCTED TO DO SO BY Poison Control, because an individual can accidentally inhale vomit into the lungs." [Emphasis in original.] TheNLMnotes that "In cases of acute toxic alcohol consumption, survival over 24 hours usually indicates recovery will follow."

> *Source: "Ethanol Overdose," MEDLINEplus Medical Encyclopedia, US National Library of Medicine (Bethesda, MD: American Accreditation HealthCare Commission, Dec. 1, 2001), from the web at http://www. nlm.nih.gov/medlineplus/ency/article/ 002644.htm last accessed Sept. 20, 2002.*

2. "In 2003, a total of 20,687 persons died of alcohol-induced causes in the United States (Tables 23 and 24). The category 'alcohol-induced causes' includes not only deaths from dependent and nondependent use of alcohol, but also accidental poisoning by alcohol. It excludes unintentional injuries, homicides, and other causes indirectly related to alcohol use as well as deaths due to fetal alcohol syndrome."

> *Source: Hoyert, Donna L., PhD, Heron, Melonie P., PhD, Murphy, Sherry L., BS, Kung, Hsiang-Ching, PhD; Division of Vital Statistics, "Deaths: Final Data for 2003," National Vital Statistics Reports, Vol. 54, No. 13 (Hyattsville, MD: National Center for Health Statistics, April 19, 2006), p. 10.*

MARIJUANA:

1. "Tetrahydrocannabinol is a very safe drug. Laboratory animals (rats, mice, dogs, monkeys) can tolerate doses of up to 1,000 mg/kg (milligrams per kilogram). This would be equivalent to a 70 kg person swallowing 70 grams of the drug—about 5,000 times more than is required to produce a high. Despite the widespread illicit use of cannabis there are very few if any instances of people dying from an overdose. In Britain, official government statistics listed five deaths from cannabis in the period 1993-1995 but on closer examination these proved to have been deaths due to inhalation of vomit that could not be directly attributed to cannabis (House of Lords Report, 1998). By comparison with other commonly used recreational drugs these statistics are impressive."

> *Source: Iversen, Leslie L., PhD, FRS, "The Science of Marijuana" (London, England: Oxford University Press, 2000), p. 178, citing House of Lords, Select Committee on Science and Technology, "Cannabis — The Scientific and Medical Evidence" (London, England: The Stationery Office, Parliament, 1998).*

2. An exhaustive search of the literature finds no deaths induced by marijuana. The US Drug Abuse Warning Network (DAWN) records instances of drug mentions in medical examiners' reports, and though marijuana is mentioned, it is usually in combination with alcohol or other drugs. Marijuana alone has not been shown to cause an overdose death.

Overdose

Source: Drug Abuse Warning Network (DAWN), available on the web at http://www.samhsa.gov/ ; also see Janet E. Joy, Stanley J. Watson, Jr., and John A. Benson, Jr., "Marijuana and Medicine: Assessing the Science Base," Division of Neuroscience and Behavioral Research, Institute of Medicine (Washington, DC: National Academy Press, 1999), available on the web at http://www.nap.edu/html/marimed/; and US Department of Justice, Drug Enforcement Administration, "In the Matter of Marijuana Rescheduling Petition" (Docket #86-22), September 6, 1988, p. 57.

THE BOTTOM LINE:

1. "In 2003, a total of 28,723 persons died of drug-induced causes in the United States (Tables 21 and 22). The category 'drug-induced causes' includes not only deaths from dependent and nondependent use of drugs (legal and illegal use), but also poisoning from medically prescribed and other drugs. It excludes unintentional injuries, homicides, and other causes indirectly related to drug use. Also excluded are newborn deaths due to mother's drug use."

    Source: Hoyert, Donna L., PhD, Heron, Melonie P., PhD, Murphy, Sherry L., BS, Kung, Hsiang-Ching, PhD; Division of Vital Statistics, "Deaths: Final Data for 2003," National Vital Statistics Reports, Vol. 54, No. 13 (Hyattsville, MD: National Center for Health Statistics, April 19, 2006), p. 10.

2. According to the federal Drug Abuse Warning Network, most drug-induced deaths involve multiple drugs. "DAWN accepts reports of illicit drugs, alcohol, prescription and over-the-counter pharmaceuticals, dietary supplements, and non-pharmaceutical inhalants. Multiple substances (as many as 6) can be reported for a single case. In 2003, the typical DAWN case involved between 2 and 3 drugs. Multiple drugs were as common in drug misuse deaths as in drug-related suicide cases; each averaged 2.7 drugs per case.

    "When multiple drugs are involved in a single case, the cause of death often cannot be attributed to any one substance. Instead, the cause may be attributed to 'combined effects' of multiple drugs. To illustrate this important concept, the area profiles in this publication differentiate the number of deaths that involved only one drug (termed 'single-drug' deaths) from all deaths. On average, participating metropolitan areas reported only 24% of drug misuse deaths (range 2% to 50%) and 19% of drug-related suicides (range 0% to 50%) with a single drug. Similarly, in the 6 States 24% of misuse deaths (range 7% to 35%) and 27% of drug-related suicides (range 10% to 57%) involved a single drug.

    "Across the metropolitan areas, the most common single-drug deaths involved opiates/opioids alone, followed by cocaine and stimulants. The most frequent multiple-drug deaths involved various combinations of opiates/opioids, cocaine, and alcohol. In new DAWN, alcohol is reported in combination with other drugs and, for individuals under age 21, alcohol is reported even when no other drugs are present. Across the 32 metropolitan areas, the most common unique combinations were: Cocaine with opiates/opioids, Alcohol with opiates/opioids, Alcohol with cocaine and opiates/opioids, and Alcohol with cocaine."

    Source: Substance Abuse and Mental Health Services Administration, Office of Applied Studies "Drug Abuse Warning Network, 2003: Area Profiles of Drug-Related Mortality," DAWN Series D-27, DHHS Publication No. (SMA) 05-4023. Rockville, MD, 2005, p. 17.

Pain Management

Many doctors are afraid to prescribe adequate pain medication for fear of prosecution.

1. "Unbalanced and misleading media coverage on the abuse of opioid analgesics not only perpetuates misconceptions about pain management; it compromises the access to adequate pain relief sought by over 50 million Americans living with pain.

   "In the past several years, there has been growing recognition on the part of health care providers, government regulators, and the public that the undertreatment of pain is a major societal problem.

   "Pain of all types is undertreated in our society. The pediatric and geriatric populations are especially at risk for undertreatment. Physicians' fears of using opioid therapy, and the fears of other health professionals, contribute to the barriers to effective pain management."

   Source: American Medical Association, "About the AMA Position on Pain Management Using Opioid Analgesics," 2004, from the web at http://www.ama-assn.org/ama/pub/category/11541.html, last accessed March 1, 2004.

2. "The AMA supports the position that (1) physicians who appropriately prescribe and/or administer controlled substances to relieve intractable pain should not be subject to the burdens of excessive regulatory scrutiny, inappropriate disciplinary action, or criminal prosecution. It is the policy of the AMA that state medical societies and boards of medicine develop or adopt mutually acceptable guidelines protecting physicians who appropriately prescribe and/or administer controlled substances to relieve intractable pain before seeking the implementation of legislation to provide that protection; (2) education of medical students and physicians to recognize addictive disorders in patients, minimize diversion of opioid preparations, and appropriately treat or refer patients with such disorders; and (3) the prevention and treatment of pain disorders through aggressive and appropriate means, including the continued education of physicians in the use of opioid preparations."

   Source: American Medical Association, "About the AMA Position on Pain Management Using Opioid Analgesics," 2004, from the web at http://www.ama-assn.org/ama/pub/category/11541.html, last accessed March 1, 2004.

3. The Gallup polling organization performed a survey on pain for the Arthritis Foundation. They found that:

   "* Nine in 10 Americans aged 18 and older (89%) suffer from pain at least once a month.

   "* Forty-three percent of adults - a projected 83 million - report that pain frequently affects their participation in some activities.

   "* Fewer than half (43%) of respondents report they have a "great deal of control" over their pain.

   "* More than half (54%) of adults report that they prefer to be alone when in pain and 50 percent say they are in a bad mood when in pain.

   "* One in four Americans (23%) experience joint pain daily or every few days and 18% report suffering pain from arthritis, a disease that affects areas in or around the joints.

215

Pain Management

"* More than 26 million Americans (15%) who suffer pain monthly have severe pain.

"* More than half (55%) of Americans aged 65 and older have pain daily.

"* Older pain sufferers are considerably less likely than younger pain sufferers to talk to family and friends about pain (38% of those aged 65 and older and 46% of those aged 50 to 64 are likely to discuss their pain vs. 58% of those aged 18 to 34).

"* Older Americans (age 65 and older) are most likely to cite getting older (88%) and arthritis (69%) as causes of their pain. Younger Americans (aged 18 to 34), on the other hand, are more likely to say tension or stress (73%), overwork or overexertion (64%) or their lifestyle (51%) cause their pain.

"* Eighty percent of Americans believe their aches and pains are "just part of getting older" and 28 percent believe there is no solution to their pain.

"* Pain experienced by older Americans tends to be more frequent (55% of those aged 65 and older compared to 32% of those aged 18 to 34 suffer daily pain) and lasts longer (110 weeks for those aged 65 and older vs. 49 weeks for those aged 18 to 34 with severe or moderate pain).

"* Forty-six percent of women report experiencing daily pain compared to only 37 percent of men.

"* Women feel they have significantly less control over their pain than men - only 39 percent of women with severe or moderate pain claim to have a 'great deal of control over their pain' compared to 48 percent of men.

"* While tension and stress are significant causes of pain for both men and women, they are the leading causes of pain among women (72% of women vs. 56% of men).

"* Women more often become upset when their pain prevents them from doing things they enjoy (60% of women vs. 50% of men).

"* Women are more likely to want to be alone when in pain (61% of women vs. 46% of men).

"* Men are more likely than women to see a doctor only when they are urged by others to do so. Thirty-eight percent of men say they will wait to see a doctor until someone encourages them to go compared with 27% of women.

"* One in three women (35%) cite the trials of balancing work and family life as the most significant cause of their pain compared to only 24 percent of men.

"* Women are more likely than men to experience frequent pain, particularly headache (17% vs. 8%), backache (24% vs. 19%), arthritis (20% vs. 15%) and sore feet (25% vs. 17%).

"* Sixty-four percent of pain sufferers will see a doctor only when they cannot stand the pain any longer.

"* Less than half (42%) of people who visit their doctor for pain believe that their doctor completely understands how their pain makes them feel."

216

Pain Management

*Source: The Arthritis Foundation, "Pain In America: Highlights from a Gallup Survey,"
2000, from the web at http://www.arthritis.org/conditions/speakingofpain/factsheet.asp,
last accessed March 1, 2004.*

4. "It is estimated that 9% of the U.S. adult population suffer from moderate to severe non-cancer related chronic pain."

   Source: Roper Starch Worldwide, Inc., "Chronic Pain In America: Roadblocks To Relief," research conducted for the American Pain Society, the American Academy of Pain Medicine and Janssen Pharmaceutica, Jan. 1999, from the web at http://www.ampainsoc.org/whatsnew/conclude_road.htm, last accessed March 2, 2004.

5. "Conventional wisdom suggests that the abuse potential of opioid analgesics is such that increases in medical use of these drugs will lead inevitably to increases in their abuse. The data from this study with respect to the opioids in the class of morphine provide no support for this hypothesis. The present trend of increasing medical use of opioid analgesics to treat pain does not appear to be contributing to increases in the health consequences of opioid analgesic abuse."

   Source: Joranson, David E., MSSW, Karen M. Ryan, MA, Aaron M. Gilson, PhD, June L. Dahl, PhD, "Trends in Medical Use and Abuse of Opioid Analgesics," Journal of the American Medical Association, Vol. 283, No. 13, April 5, 2000, p. 1713.

6. "Opioid analgesics are useful in managing severe acute or chronic pain. They are often underused, resulting in needless pain and suffering because clinicians often underestimate the required dosage, overestimate the duration of action and risk of adverse effects, and have unreasonable concerns about addiction (see Drug Use and Dependence: Opioids). Physical dependence (development of withdrawal symptoms when a drug is stopped) should be assumed to exist in all patients treated with opioids for more than a few days. However, addiction (loss of control, compulsive use, craving and use despite harm) is very rare in patients with no history of substance abuse. Before opioid therapy is initiated, clinicians should ask about risk factors for abuse and addiction. These risk factors include prior alcohol or drug abuse, a family history of alcohol or drug abuse, and a prior major psychiatric disorder. If risk factors are present, treatment may still be appropriate; however, the clinician should use more controls to prevent abuse (eg, small prescriptions, frequent visits, no refills for 'lost' prescriptions) or should refer the patient to a pain specialist or an addiction medicine specialist experienced in pain management."

   Source: "Pain," The Merck Manual, Section 16. Neurologic Disorders, Chapter 209. Pain, Merck & Co. Inc., from the web at http://www.merck.com/mmpe/sec16/ch209/ch209a.html last accessed May 31, 2007.

7. "Therapeutic doses taken regularly over 2 to 3 days can lead to some tolerance and dependence, and when the drug is stopped, the user may have mild withdrawal symptoms which are scarcely noticed or are flu-like.
   "Patients with chronic pain requiring long-term use should not be labeled addicts, although they may have some problems with tolerance

Pain Management

and physical dependence. Opioids induce cross-tolerance so that abusers can substitute one for another. People who have developed tolerance may show few signs of drug use and may function normally in their usual activities, but obtaining the drug is an ever-present problem. Tolerance to the various effects of these drugs frequently develops unevenly. Heroin users, for example, may become largely tolerant to the drug's euphoric and lethal effects but continue to have constricted pupils and constipation."

Source: "Opioids," The Merck Manual, Section 15: Psychiatric Disorders, Chapter 198: Drug Use and Dependence, Merck & Co. Inc., from the web at http://www.merck.com/ mmpe/sec15/ch198/ch198l.html last accessed May 24, 2007.

8. "The undertreatment of pain is a significant concern in populations with chemical dependency. In painful disorders for which there is a broad consensus about the role of opioid therapy, specifically cancer and AIDS-related pain, studies have documented that this treatment commonly diverges from accepted guidelines. Undertreatment is far more challenging to assess when a broad consensus concerning optimal treatment approaches does not exist. It would be difficult, therefore, to determine the extent to which the pain and functional impairments experienced by patients in this study relate to inadequate pain management. However, given the number of barriers identified as potential reasons for inadequate pain management, it is appropriate to raise concerns about undertreatment and to investigate it further."

Source: Rosenblum, Andrew, PhD, Herman Joseph, PhD, Chunki Fong, MS, Steven Kipnis, MD, Charles Cleland, PhD, Russell K. Portenoy, MD, "Prevalence and Characteristics of Chronic Pain Among Chemically Dependent Patients in Methadone Maintenance and Residential Treatment Facilities," Journal of the American Medical Association (Chicago, IL: American Medical Association, May 14, 2003), Vol. 289, No. 18, p. 2377.

9. "In our study, there was greater evidence for an association between substance use and chronic pain among inpatients than among MMTP [Methadone Maintenance Treatment Program] patients. Among inpatients, there were significant bivariate relationships between chronic pain and pain as a reason for first using drugs, multiple drug use, and drug craving. In the multivariate analysis, only drug craving remained significantly associated with chronic pain. Not surprisingly, inpatients with pain were significantly more likely than those without pain to attribute the use of alcohol and other illicit drugs, such as cocaine and marijuana, to a need for pain control. These results suggest that chronic pain contributes to illicit drug use behavior among persons who were recently using alcohol and/or cocaine. Inpatients with chronic pain visited physicians and received legitimate pain medications no more frequently than those without pain, raising the possibility that undertreatment or inability to access appropriate medical care may be a factor in the decision to use illicit drugs for pain."

Source: Rosenblum, Andrew, PhD, Herman Joseph, PhD, Chunki Fong, MS, Steven Kipnis, MD, Charles Cleland, PhD, Russell K. Portenoy, MD, "Prevalence and Characteristics of Chronic Pain Among Chemically Dependent Patients in Methadone Maintenance and Residential Treatment Facilities," Journal of the American Medical Association (Chicago, IL: American Medical Association, May 14, 2003), Vol. 289, No. 18, pp. 2376-2377.

Pain Management

10. "There were 6.4 million (2.6 percent) persons aged 12 or older who used prescription-type psychotherapeutic drugs nonmedically in the past month. Of these, 4.7 million used pain relievers, 1.8 million used tranquilizers, 1.1 million used stimulants (including 512,000 using methamphetamine), and 272,000 used sedatives. Each of these estimates is similar to the corresponding estimate for 2004."

    Source: Substance Abuse and Mental Health Services Administration, US Department of Health and Human Services, Results from the 2005 National Survey on Drug Use and Health: National Findings (Rockville, MD: Office of Applied Studies, Sept. 2006), p. 1.

11. "Among persons aged 12 or older who used pain relievers nonmedically in the past 12 months, 59.8 percent reported that the source of the drug the most recent time they used was from a friend or relative for free. Another 16.8 percent reported they got the drug from one doctor. Only 4.3 percent got the pain relievers from a drug dealer or other stranger, and only 0.8 percent reported buying the drug on the Internet."

    Source: Substance Abuse and Mental Health Services Administration, US Department of Health and Human Services, Results from the 2005 National Survey on Drug Use and Health: National Findings (Rockville, MD: Office of Applied Studies, Sept. 2006), p. 26.

12. According to a review by the General Accounting Office (GAO) of medical cannabis programs in four states, "Most medical marijuana recommendations in states where data are collected have been made for applicants with severe pain or muscle spasticity as their medical condition. Conditions allowed by the states' medical marijuana laws ranged from illnesses such as cancer and AIDS, to symptoms, such as severe pain. Information is not collected on the conditions for which marijuana has been recommended in Alaska or California. However, data from Hawaii's registry showed that the majority of recommendations have been made for the condition of severe pain or the condition of muscle spasticity. Likewise, data from Oregon's registry showed that, 84 percent of recommendations were for the condition of severe pain or for muscle spasticity."

    Source: General Accounting Office, "Marijuana: Early Experiences with Four States' Laws That Allow Use for Medical Purposes" (Washington, DC: Government Printing Office, Nov. 2002), GAO-03-189, p. 24.

13. According to a survey conducted by Roper Starch Worldwide for the American Pain Society, "Chronic pain as defined by this study is a severe and ever present problem. It can be as much of a problem to middle age adults as seniors and is one women are more likely to face than men. The majority of chronic pain sufferers have been living with their pain for over 5 years. Although the more common type is pain that flares up frequently versus being constant, it is still present on average almost 6 days in a typical week.
    "About one third of all chronic sufferers describe their pain as being almost the worst pain one can possibly imagine. Their pain is more likely to be constant than flaring up frequently and two-thirds of them have been living with it for over 5 years."

219

Pain Management

Source: Roper Starch Worldwide, Inc., "Chronic Pain In America: Roadblocks To Relief," research conducted for the American Pain Society, the American Academy of Pain Medicine and Janssen Pharmaceutica, Jan. 1999, from the web at http://www.ampainsoc.org/whatsnew/conclude_road.htm, last accessed March 2, 2004.

14. "Just over one-half of chronic pain sufferers say their pain is pretty much under control. But, this can be attributed primarily to those with moderate pain. The majority of those with the most severe pain do not have it under control and among those who do, it took almost half of them over a year to reach that point. In contrast, 7 of every 10 with moderate pain say they have it under control and it took the majority less than a year to reach that point. Pain can become more severe even when it is under control. Among those with very severe pain, 4 of every 10 said their pain was moderate or severe before getting their pain under control."

Source: Roper Starch Worldwide, Inc., "Chronic Pain In America: Roadblocks To Relief," research conducted for the American Pain Society, the American Academy of Pain Medicine and Janssen Pharmaceutica, Jan. 1999, from the web at http://www.ampainsoc.org/whatsnew/conclude_road.htm, last accessed March 2, 2004.

15. "Almost all chronic pain sufferers have gone to a doctor for relief of their pain at one time or another. Almost 4 of every 10 are not currently doing so, since they think either there is nothing more a doctor can do or in one way or another their pain is under control or they can deal with it themselves.

"This is not the case with those having very severe pain; over 7 of every 10 are currently going to a doctor for pain relief. In addition, significant numbers of those with very severe pain are significantly more likely to require emergency room visits, hospitalization and even psychological counseling or therapy to treat their pain.

"A significant proportion (over one-fourth) of all chronic pain sufferers wait for at least 6 months before going to a doctor for relief of their pain because they underestimate the seriousness of it and think they can tough it out."

Source: Roper Starch Worldwide, Inc., "Chronic Pain In America: Roadblocks To Relief," research conducted for the American Pain Society, the American Academy of Pain Medicine and Janssen Pharmaceutica, Jan. 1999, from the web at http://www.ampainsoc.org/whatsnew/conclude_road.htm, last accessed March 2, 2004.

hh

16. "Chronic pain sufferers are having difficulty in finding doctors who can effectively treat their pain, since almost one half have changed doctors since their pain began; almost a fourth have made at least 3 changes. The primary reasons for a change are the doctor not taking their pain seriously enough, the doctor's unwillingness to treat it aggressively, the doctor's lack of knowledge about pain and the fact they still had too much pain. This level of frustration is significantly higher among those with very severe pain where the majority have changed doctors at least once and almost of every 3 have done it 3 or more times. Their primary reason for changing was still having too much pain after treatment."

Pain Management

Source: Roper Starch Worldwide, Inc., "Chronic Pain In America: Roadblocks To Relief," research conducted for the American Pain Society, the American Academy of Pain Medicine and Janssen Pharmaceutica, Jan. 1999, from the web at http://www.ampainsoc.org/ whatsnew/conclude_road.htm, last accessed March 2, 2004.

17. "Almost all chronic pain sufferers have used OTC [Over The Counter medications] to relieve their pain and over one half have used Rx NSAIDs [Prescription Non-Steroidal Anti-Inflammatory Drugs]. Narcotic pain relievers have been tried by just over 4 of every 10 sufferers; their use, along with Rx NSAIDs, anti-depressants and anti-seizure drugs, varies directly with the severity of pain."

Source: Roper Starch Worldwide, Inc., "Chronic Pain In America: Roadblocks To Relief," research conducted for the American Pain Society, the American Academy of Pain Medicine and Janssen Pharmaceutica, Jan. 1999, from the web at http://www.ampainsoc.org/ whatsnew/summary3_road.htm, last accessed March 2, 2004.

18. "Medical therapies are not providing sufficient relief, since the majority of chronic pain sufferers, especially those with severe pain, have also turned to non-medicinal therapies. The primary one is a hot/cold pack. Surprisingly, almost all of the major non-medicinal therapies currently used are perceived as providing more relief by their users than OTCs, the most widely used medicines; the one exception are herbs/dietary supplements/vitamins which are perceived as offering the least amount of relief than any medicines or other major non-medicinal therapies.
"The overall favorable perceptions of non-medicinal therapies are driven by those with moderate pain. Although those with very severe pain are more likely to use them, they have a significantly lower opinion of their efficacy versus medicinal therapies."

Source: Roper Starch Worldwide, Inc., "Chronic Pain In America: Roadblocks To Relief," research conducted for the American Pain Society, the American Academy of Pain Medicine and Janssen Pharmaceutica, Jan. 1999, from the web at http://www.ampainsoc.org/ whatsnew/conclude_road.htm, last accessed March 2, 2004.

19. "A small, but significant, percent of chronic pain sufferers have at one time or another turned to alcohol for relief; this occurred more often among middle age adults and men."

Source: Roper Starch Worldwide, Inc., "Chronic Pain In America: Roadblocks To Relief," research conducted for the American Pain Society, the American Academy of Pain Medicine and Janssen Pharmaceutica, Jan. 1999, from the web at http://www.ampainsoc.org/ whatsnew/conclude_road.htm, last accessed March 2, 2004.

20. "Chronic pain sufferers currently taking narcotic pain relievers differ from other chronic pain sufferers as to the severity of their pain, being less likely to have it under control, changing doctors more often, requiring more intensive treatment at hospitals, taking more pills per day, more likely following their doctors prescribed regimen and lastly, to being referred to a specialized program/clinic for their pain."

Source: Roper Starch Worldwide, Inc., "Chronic Pain In America: Roadblocks To Relief," research conducted for the American Pain Society, the American Academy of Pain Medicine and Janssen Pharmaceutica, Jan. 1999, from the web at http://www.ampainsoc.org/ whatsnew/summary4_road.htm, last accessed March 2, 2004.

Pain Management

21. "The quality of life has improved significantly among those who have their pain under control."

    Source: Roper Starch Worldwide, Inc., "Chronic Pain In America: Roadblocks To Relief," research conducted for the American Pain Society, the American Academy of Pain Medicine and Janssen Pharmaceutica, Jan. 1999, from the web at http://www.ampainsoc.org/ whatsnew/summary4_road.htm, last accessed March 2, 2004.

22. "Overall, the estimated $61.2 billion per year in pain-related lost productive time in our study accounts for 27% of the total estimated work-related cost of pain conditions in the US workforce."

    Source: Stewart, Walter F., PhD, MPH, Judith A. Ricci, ScD, MS, Elsbeth Chee, ScD, David Morganstein, MS, Richard Lipton, MD, "Lost Productive Time and Cost Due to Common Pain Conditions in the US Workforce," Journal of the American Medical Association (Chicago, IL: American Medical Association, Nov. 12, 2003), Vol. 290, No. 18, p. 2449.

23. "Our estimate of $61.2 billion per year in pain-related lost productive time does not include costs from other causes. First, we did not include lost productive time costs associated with dental pain, cancer pain, gastrointestinal pain, neuropathy, or pain associated with menstruation. Second, we do not account for pain-induced disability that leads to continuous absence of 1 week or more. Third, we did not consider secondary costs from other factors such as the hiring and training of replacement workers or the institutional effect among coworkers. Taking these other factors into consideration could increase, decrease, or have no net effect on health-related lost productive time cost estimates. Fourth, we may be prone to underestimating current lost productive time among those with persistent pain problems (eg, chronic daily headache). To the extent that these workers remain employed,they may adjust both their performance and perception of their performance over time. The latter, a form of perceptual accommodation, makes it difficult to accurately ascertain the impact of a chronic pain condition on work in the recent past through self-report."

    Source: Stewart, Walter F., PhD, MPH, Judith A. Ricci, ScD, MS, Elsbeth Chee, ScD, David Morganstein, MS, Richard Lipton, MD, "Lost Productive Time and Cost Due to Common Pain Conditions in the US Workforce," Journal of the American Medical Association (Chicago, IL: American Medical Association, Nov. 12, 2003), Vol. 290, No. 18, p. 2452.

24. "Lost productive time varied to some degree in the workforce. First, little or no variation was observed by age. In large part, the lack of differences by age was due to the counterbalancing effects of different pain conditions. Headache, common at younger ages (ie, 18-34 years), rapidly declines in prevalence thereafter. In contrast, the other 3 pain conditions are either more common with increasing age (eg, arthritis) or peak at a later age than headache (eg, back pain)."

    Source: Stewart, Walter F., PhD, MPH, Judith A. Ricci, ScD, MS, Elsbeth Chee, ScD, David Morganstein, MS, Richard Lipton, MD, "Lost Productive Time and Cost Due to Common Pain Conditions in the US Workforce," Journal of the American Medical Association (Chicago, IL: American Medical Association, Nov. 12, 2003), Vol. 290, No. 18, p. 2449.

Pain Management

25. "A total of 52.7% of the workforce reported having headache, back pain, arthritis, or other musculoskeletal pain in the past 2 weeks. Overall, 12.7% of the workforce lost productive time in a 2-week period due to a common pain condition; 7.2% lost 2 h/wk or more of work. Headache was the most common pain condition resulting in lost productive time, affecting 5.4% (2.7% with >= 2/wk) of the workforce (Table 1), which was followed by back pain (3.2%), arthritis (2.0%), and other musculoskeletal pain (2.0%)."

Source: Stewart, Walter F., PhD, MPH, Judith A. Ricci, ScD, MS, Elsbeth Chee, ScD, David Morganstein, MS, Richard Lipton, MD, "Lost Productive Time and Cost Due to Common Pain Conditions in the US Workforce," Journal of the American Medical Association (Chicago, IL: American Medical Association, Nov. 12, 2003), Vol. 290, No. 18, p. 2446.

26. "Among those who lost productive time due to a pain condition, an average of 4.6 h/wk was lost (Table 1). The mean lost productive time was for headache (3.5 h/wk) and highest for other musculoskeletal pain (5.5 h/wk). Absence days were uncommon. A total of 1.1% of the workforce was absent from work 1 or more days per week from 1 of the 4 pain conditions; 0.12% were absent 2 d/wk or more. Headache and back pain were dominant causes of missed days of work. Overall, lost productive time due to health-related reduced performance on days at work accounted for 4 times more lost time than absenteeism. The ratio of lost productive time due to health-related performance on days at work compared with absenteeism varied among categories of pain disorders: headache, 4.5 h/wk; arthritis, 6.5 h/wk; back pain, 2.9 h/wk; and other musculoskeletal pain, 3.6 h/wk."

Source: Stewart, Walter F., PhD, MPH, Judith A. Ricci, ScD, MS, Elsbeth Chee, ScD, David Morganstein, MS, Richard Lipton, MD, "Lost Productive Time and Cost Due to Common Pain Conditions in the US Workforce," Journal of the American Medical Association (Chicago, IL: American Medical Association, Nov. 12, 2003), Vol. 290, No. 18, p. 2446.

27. "National survey data that provide detailed data on use of treatments are limited. Of the common pain conditions, sufficient details have only been reported on migraine headaches. Recent data indicate that only 41% of individuals who have migraine headaches in the US population ever receive any prescription drug for migraine. Only 29% report that satisfaction with treatment is moderate, especially among those who are often disabled by their episodes. Randomized trials demonstrate that optimal therapy for migraine dramatically reduces headache-related disability time in comparison with usual care."

Source: Stewart, Walter F., PhD, MPH, Judith A. Ricci, ScD, MS, Elsbeth Chee, ScD, David Morganstein, MS, Richard Lipton, MD, "Lost Productive Time and Cost Due to Common Pain Conditions in the US Workforce," Journal of the American Medical Association (Chicago, IL: American Medical Association, Nov. 12, 2003), Vol. 290, No. 18, p. 2453.

28. "Pain was very prevalent in representative samples of 2 distinct populations with chemical dependency, and chronic severe pain was experienced by a substantial minority of both groups. Methadone patients differed from patients recently admitted to a residential

Pain Management

treatment center in numerous ways and had a significantly higher prevalence of chronic pain (37% vs. 24%). Although comparisons with other studies of pain epidemiology are difficult to make because of methodological differences, the prevalence of chronic pain in these samples is in the upper range reported in surveys of the general population. The prevalence of chronic pain in these chemically dependent patients also compares with that in surveys of cancer patients undergoing active therapy, approximately a third of whom have pain severe enough to warrant opioid therapy."

Source: Rosenblum, Andrew, PhD, Herman Joseph, PhD, Chunki Fong, MS, Steven Kipnis, MD, Charles Cleland, PhD, Russell K. Portenoy, MD, "Prevalence and Characteristics of Chronic Pain Among Chemically Dependent Patients in Methadone Maintenance and Residential Treatment Facilities," Journal of the American Medical Association (Chicago, IL: American Medical Association, May 14, 2003), Vol. 289, No. 18, p. 2376.

29. "Although MMTP [Methadone Maintenance Treatment Program] patients were significantly more likely than inpatients to report chronic pain, and almost a quarter reported that pain was one of the reasons for first using drugs, there was relatively little evidence that pain was associated with current levels of substance abuse. In the multivariate analysis, the associations between chronic pain and the substance abuse behaviors observed in the bivariate analysis (pain as a reason for first using drugs and drug craving) were not sustained. Moreover, the bivariate associations that were found in the inpatient group between chronic pain and multiple drug use, and between pain and the use of illicit drugs to treat pain complaints, were not identified among MMTP patients."

Source: Rosenblum, Andrew, PhD, Herman Joseph, PhD, Chunki Fong, MS, Steven Kipnis, MD, Charles Cleland, PhD, Russell K. Portenoy, MD, "Prevalence and Characteristics of Chronic Pain Among Chemically Dependent Patients in Methadone Maintenance and Residential Treatment Facilities," Journal of the American Medical Association (Chicago, IL: American Medical Association, May 14, 2003), Vol. 289, No. 18, p. 2377.

30. "Physicians are concerned that their prescribing decisions and patterns may be questioned and that they could be investigated without sufficient cause. Some physicians contend that patients may suffer because physicians will be reluctant to prescribe appropriate controlled substances to manage a patient's pain or treat their condition. Patients are concerned that their personal information may be used inappropriately by those with authorized access or shared with unauthorized entities. Pharmacists have also expressed concerns."

Source: General Accounting Office, "Prescription Drugs: State Monitoring Programs Provide Useful Tool to Reduce Diversion" (Washington, DC: Government Printing Office, May 2002), GAO-PO-634, p. 18.

Let the state medical boards, not the Justice Department, regulate and discipline doctors.

Prisons, Jails and Probation — An Overview

1. "Overall, the United States incarcerated 2,320,359 persons at yearend 2005." This total represents persons held in —

Federal and State Prisons	1,446,269 (which excludes State and Federal prisoners in local jails)
Territorial Prisons	15.735
Local Jails	747,529
Facilities Operated by or Exclusively for the Bureau of Immigration and Customs Enforcement	10,104
Military Facilities	2,322
Jails in Indian Country	1,745 (as of midyear 2004)
Juvenile Facilities	96,655 (as of 2003)

Source: Harrison, Paige M. & Beck, Allen J., Ph.D., US Department of Justice, Bureau of Justice Statistics, Prisoners in 2005 (Washington DC: US Department of Justice, Nov. 2006), p. 1.

2. "The rate of incarceration in prison and jail was 737 inmates per 100,000 U.S. residents in 2005, up from 601 in 1995. At yearend 2005, 1 in every 136 U.S. residents was incarcerated in a State or Federal prison or a local jail."

Source: Harrison, Paige M. & Beck, Allen J., Ph.D., US Department of Justice, Bureau of Justice Statistics, Prisoners in 2005 (Washington DC: US Department of Justice, Nov. 2006), p. 2.

3. According to the American Corrections Association, the average daily cost per state prison inmate per day in the US in 2005 was $67.55.

Sources: American Correctional Association, 2006 Directory of Adult and Juvenile Correctional Departments, Institutions, Agencies and Probation and Parole Authorities, 67th Edition (Alexandria, VA: ACA, 2006), p. 16.

4. "On December 31, 2005, a total of 1,446,269 inmates were in the custody of State and Federal prison authorities, and 747,529 were in the custody of local jail authorities (table 1). The total incarcerated population increased by 58,463, or 2.7% from yearend 2004. This is less than the average annual increase of 3.3% since 1995."

Source: Harrison, Paige M. & Beck, Allen J., Ph.D., US Department of Justice, Bureau of Justice Statistics, Prisoners in 2005 (Washington DC: US Department of Justice, Nov. 2006), p. 2.

5. "The rate of growth of the State prison population slowed between 1995 and 2001 and then began to rise. During this time the percentage change in the first 6 months of each year steadily decreased, reaching a low of 0.6% in 2001, and then rose to 1.0% in 2005 (table 2). The percentage change in the second 6 months of each year showed a similar trend, resulting in an actual decrease in State prison populations for the second half of 2000 and 2001.

Prisons, Jails and Probation —
An Overview

"Since 1995 the Federal system has grown at a much higher rate than the States, peaking at 6.0% growth in the first 6 months of 1999. In the first 6 months of 2005, the number of Federal inmates increased 2.3%, more than twice the rate of State growth."

> *Source: Harrison, Paige M. & Allen J. Beck, Allen J., PhD, US Department of Justice, Bureau of Justice Statistics, Prison and Jail Inmates at Midyear 2005 (Washington DC: US Department of Justice, May 2006), p. 2.*

6. "While the number of offenders in each major offense category increased [from 1995 to 2003], the number incarcerated for a drug offense accounted for the largest percentage of the total growth (49%), followed by public-order offenders (38%)."

> *Source: Harrison, Paige M. & Allen J. Beck, Allen J., PhD, US Department of Justice, Bureau of Justice Statistics, Prisoners in 2005 (Washington DC: US Department of Justice, Nov. 2006), p. 10.*

7. "The United States has the highest prison population rate in the world, some 738 per 100,000 of the national population, followed by Russia (611), St Kitts & Nevis (547), U.S. Virgin Is. (521), Turkmenistan (c.489), Belize (487), Cuba (c.487), Palau (478), British Virgin Is. (464), Bermuda (463), Bahamas (462), Cayman Is. (453), American Samoa (446), Belarus (426) and Dominica (419).
"However, more than three fifths of countries (61%) have rates below 150 per 100,000. (The rate in England and Wales - 148 per 100,000 of the national population - is above the mid-point in the World List.)"

> *Source: Walmsley, Roy, "World Prison Population List (Seventh Edition)" (London, England: International Centre for Prison Studies, 2007), p. 1.*

8. "More than 9.25 million people are held in penal institutions throughout the world, mostly as pre-trial detainees (remand prisoners) or as sentenced prisoners. Almost half of these are in the United States (2.19m), China (1.55m plus pretrial detainees and prisoners in 'administrative detention') or Russia (0.87m)." According to the US Census Bureau, the population of the US represents 4.6% of the world's total population (291,450,886 out of a total 6,303,683,217).

> *Source: Walmsley, Roy, "World Prison Population List (Seventh Edition)" (London, England: International Centre for Prison Studies, 2007), p. 1; US Census Bureau, Population Division, from the web at http://www.census.gov/main/www/popclock.html accessed July 8, 2003.*

9. The U.S. nonviolent prisoner population is larger than the combined populations of Wyoming and Alaska.

> *Source: John Irwin, Ph. D., Vincent Schiraldi, and Jason Ziedenberg, America's One Million Nonviolent Prisoners (Washington, DC: Justice Policy Institute, 1999), pg. 4.*

10. According to a report on prison growth by the Urban Institute's Justice Policy Center, "Over the last 25 years, the number of state facilities increased from just fewer than 600 to over 1,000 in the year 2000, an increase of about 70 percent. In other words, more than 40 percent of state prisons in operation today opened in the last 25 years."

ii

Prisons, Jails and Probation — An Overview

Source: Lawrence, Sarah and Jeremy Travis, "The New Landscape of Imprisonment: Mapping America's Prison Expansion" (Washington, DC: Urban Institute, April 2004), p. 2.

11. "During 2005 the total Federal, State, and local adult correctional population - incarcerated or in the community - grew by 60,700 to over 7 million. The growth of 0.9% during the year was less than half of the average annual increase of 2.5% since 1995. About 3.2% of the U.S. adult population, or 1 in every 32 adults, were incarcerated or on probation or parole at yearend 2005." According to the Department of Justice in 2005, there were 7,056,000 persons in the correctional population, of whom 4,162,536 were on probation, 784,408 were on parole, 747,529 were in jails, and 1,446,269 were in state and federal prisons. In 1995, there were 5,342,900 people in the correctional population of whom 3,077,861 were on probation, 679,421 were on parole, 507,044 were in jails, and 1,078,542 were in state and federal prisons. In 2000, there were 6,445,100 people in the correctional population of whom 3,826,209 were on probation, 723,898 were on parole, 621,149 were in jails, and 1,316,333 were in state and federal prisons.

Source: Glaze, Lauren E. and Thomas P. Bonczar, US Department of Justice, Bureau of Justice Statistics, Probation and Parole in the United States, 2005 (Washington DC: US Department of Justice, November 2006), p. 1.

12. "Department of corrections data show that about a fourth of those initially imprisoned for nonviolent crimes are sentenced for a second time for committing a violent offense. Whatever else it reflects, this pattern highlights the possibility that prison serves to transmit violent habits and values rather than to reduce them."

Source: Craig Haney, Ph.D., and Philip Zimbardo, Ph.D., "The Past and Future of U.S. Prison Policy: Twenty-five Years After the Stanford Prison Experiment," American Psychologist, Vol. 53, No. 7 (July 1998), p. 721.

13. "Over the past twenty-five years, the United States has built the largest prison system in the world. But despite a recent downturn in the crime rate, we remain far and away the most violent advanced industrial society on earth."

Source: Currie, E., Crime and Punishment in America (New York, NY: Metropolitan Books, Henry Holt and Company, Inc., 1998), p. 3.

14. According to the Department of Justice, studies of recidivism reveal that "the amount of time inmates serve in prison does not increase or decrease the likelihood of recidivism, whether recidivism is measured as parole revocation, re-arrest, reconviction, or return to prison."

Source: An Analysis of Non-Violent Drug Offenders with Minimal Criminal Histories, Washington D.C.: U.S. Department of Justice (1994, February), p. 41.

15. According to a report on prison growth by the Urban Institute's Justice Policy Center, "Another issue related to prison expansion of the 1980s and 1990s is the disparity between where prisoners come from ('home counties') and where prisoners serve their sentences ('prison counties'). Many believe that the prison construction boom of the last 20 years happened in areas that were located far away from prisoners' homes.

Prisons, Jails and Probation —
An Overview

This has been an area of concern because greater distances between a prisoner's home and where he or she is incarcerated can negatively impact a prisoner and his or her family members. Being incarcerated far away from home makes it more challenging to maintain familial relationships and parent/child relationships in particular. In addition, challenges related to reintegrating into the community increase when a prisoner is housed far away from home. For example, steps that may facilitate prisoner reentry, such as finding a job and a place to live, are more difficult when a prisoner is imprisoned a long distance from the place to which he or she will return after release."

Source: Lawrence, Sarah and Jeremy Travis, "The New Landscape of Imprisonment: Mapping America's Prison Expansion" (Washington, DC: Urban Institute, April 2004), p. 33.

16. States spent $42.89 billion on Corrections in 2005 alone. To compare, states only spent $24.69 billion on public assistance.

Source: National Association of State Budget Officers (NASBO), 2005 State Expenditure Report (Washington, DC: NASBO, June 2005), p. 35, Table 18, and p. 58, Table 32.

17. "At yearend 2005, 26 States reported that they were operating below 100% of their highest capacity, and 23 States and the Federal prison system reported operating at 100% or more of their highest capacity. Nevada, operating at 56% of its highest capacity, reported the lowest percent of capacity occupied. Alabama and California, both 93% over their lowest reported capacity, had the highest percent of capacity occupied. "At yearend 2005 the Federal prison system was operating at 34% over capacity. Overall, State prisons were operating between 99% of their highest capacity and 114% of their lowest capacity (table 9)."

Source: Harrison, Paige M. & Allen J. Beck, PhD, US Department of Justice, Bureau of Justice Statistics, Prisoners in 2005 (Washington DC: US Department of Justice, Nov. 2006), pp. 7-8.

18. From 1984 to 1996, California built 21 new prisons, and only one new university.

Source: Ambrosio, T. & Schiraldi, V., "Trends in State Spending, 1987-1995," Executive Summary-February 1997 (Washington DC: The Justice Policy Institute, 1997).

19. California state government expenditures on prisons increased 30% from 1987 to 1995, while spending on higher education decreased by 18%.

Source: National Association of State Budget Officers, 1995 State Expenditures Report (Washington DC: National Association of State Budget Officers, 1996).

20. According to a report on prison growth by the Urban Institute's Justice Policy Center, "Every dollar transferred to a 'prison community' is a dollar that is not given to the home community of a prisoner, which is often among the country's most disadvantaged urban areas. According to one account, Cook County Illinois will lose nearly $88 million in federal benefits over the next decade because residents were counted in the 2000 Census in their county of incarceration rather than their county of origin (Duggan 2000). Losing funds from the 'relocation' of prisoners is also an issue for New York City, as two-thirds of state prisoners are from the city, while 91 percent of prisoners are incarcerated in upstate counties (Wagner 2002a)."

Prisons, Jails and Probation — An Overview

Source: Lawrence, Sarah and Jeremy Travis, "The New Landscape of Imprisonment: Mapping America's Prison Expansion" (Washington, DC: Urban Institute, April 2004), p. 3.

21. According to a report on prison growth by the Urban Institute's Justice Policy Center, "The effect of prisoner location on population counts may also influence the allocation of political representation and, therefore, political influence (Haberman 2000). In Wisconsin, the number of state prisoners who were housed in other states (known as interstate transfers) caused concern because these prisoners would be counted in the decennial census in the states where they were incarcerated. In 1999, U.S. Representative Mark Green introduced a bill (unsuccessfully) that proposed changes to the census policy so Wisconsin prisoners held in other states would be counted as Wisconsin residents."

Source: Lawrence, Sarah and Jeremy Travis, "The New Landscape of Imprisonment: Mapping America's Prison Expansion" (Washington, DC: Urban Institute, April 2004), p. 3.

22. "In December 2000, the Prison Journal published a study based on a survey of inmates in seven men's prison facilities in four states. The results showed that 21 percent of the inmates had experienced at least one episode of pressured or forced sexual contact since being incarcerated, and at least 7 percent had been raped in their facility. A 1996 study of the Nebraska prison system produced similar findings, with 22 percent of male inmates reporting that they had been pressured or forced to have sexual contact against their will while incarcerated. Of these, over 50 percent had submitted to forced anal sex at least once. Extrapolating these findings to the national level gives a total of at least 140,000 inmates who have been raped."

Source: Human Rights Watch, "No Escape: Male Rape in US Prisons - Summary and Recommendations," 2001, from the web at http://www.hrw.org/reports/2001/prison/report.html last accessed May 18, 2004.

ii

Prisons and Drug Offenders

1. The Department of Justice reported that at year-end 2003, federal prisons held a total of 158,426 inmates, of whom 86,972 (55%) were drug offenders. By comparison in 2000 federal prisons held 131,739 total inmates of whom 74,276 (56%) were drug offenders, and in 1995 federal prisons held a total of 88,658 inmates of whom 52,782 (60%) were drug offenders.

   Source: Harrison, Paige M. & Allen J. Beck, PhD, US Department of Justice, Bureau of Justice Statistics, Prisoners in 2005 (Washington, DC: US Department of Justice, November 2006), p. 10, Table 14.

2. In 2003, drug law violators comprised 20.0% of all adults serving time in State prisons - 250,900 out of 1,256,400 State prison inmates.

   Source: Harrison, Paige M. & Allen J. Beck, PhD, US Department of Justice, Bureau of Justice Statistics, Prisoners in 2005 (Washington, DC: US Department of Justice, November 2006), p. 9.

3. According to the US Justice Department, 27.9% of drug offenders in state prisons are serving time for possession; 69.4% are serving time for trafficking offenses; and 2.7% are in for "other."

   Source: Mumola, Christopher J., and Karberg, Jennifer C., "Drug Use and Dependence, State and Federal Prisoners, 2004," (Washington, DC: US Dept. of Justice, Oct. 2006) (NCJ213530), p. 4.

4. According to the Justice Department, 5.3% of drug offenders in federal prisons are serving time for possession; 91.4% are serving time for trafficking offenses; and 3.3% are in for "other."

   Source: Mumola, Christopher J., and Karberg, Jennifer C., "Drug Use and Dependence, State and Federal Prisoners, 2004," (Washington, DC: US Dept. of Justice, Oct. 2006) (NCJ213530), p. 4.

5. "Between 1984 and 1999, the number of defendants charged with a drug offense in U.S. district courts increased about 3% annually, on average, from 11,854 to 29,306."

   Source: Scalia, John, US Department of Justice, Bureau of Justice Statistics, Federal Drug Offenders, 1999 with Trends 1984-99 (Washington, DC: US Dept. of Justice, August 2001), p. 7.

6. "As a result of increased prosecutions and longer time served in prison, the number of drug offenders in Federal prisons increased more than 12% annually, on average, from 14,976 during 1986 to 68,360 during 1999."

   Source: Scalia, John, US Department of Justice, Bureau of Justice Statistics, Federal Drug Offenders, 1999 with Trends 1984-99 (Washington, DC: US Dept. of Justice, August 2001), p. 7.

7. "In 1995, 23% of state prisoners were incarcerated for drug offenses in contrast to 9% of drug offenders in state prisons in 1986. In fact, the proportion of drug offenders in the state prison population nearly tripled by 1990, when it reached 21%, and has remained at close to that level since then. The proportion of federal prisoners held for drug violations doubled during the past 10 years. In 1985, 34% of federal prisoners were incarcerated for drug violations. By 1995, the proportion had risen to 60%."

Prisons and Drug Offenders

Source: Craig Haney, Ph.D., and Philip Zimbardo, Ph.D., "The Past and Future of U.S. Prison Policy: Twenty-five Years After the Stanford Prison Experiment," American Psychologist, Vol. 53, No. 7 (July 1998), p. 715.

8. According to ONDCP, federal spending to incarcerate drug offenders totals nearly $3 Billion a year — $2.525 Billion by the Bureau of Prisons, and $429.4 Million by Federal Prisoner Detention.

   Source: Office of National Drug Control Policy, "National Drug Control Strategy: FY 2003 Budget Summary" (Washington, DC: Office of the President, February 2002), Table 3, pp. 7-9.

9. According to the American Corrections Association, the average daily cost per state prison inmate per day in the US in 2005 was $67.55. That means it costs states approximately $16,948,295 per day to incarcerate drug offenders in state prison, or $6,186,127,675 per year.

   Sources: American Correctional Association, 2006 Directory of Adult and Juvenile Correctional Departments, Institutions, Agencies and Probation and Parole Authorities, 67th Edition (Alexandria, VA: ACA, 2006), p. 16; Harrison, Paige M. & Allen J. Beck, PhD, US Department of Justice, Bureau of Justice Statistics, Prisoners in 2005 (Washington, DC: US Department of Justice, November 2006), p. 9.

10. "17% of State and 18% of Federal prisoners committed their crime to obtain money for drugs."

    Source: Mumola, Christopher J., and Karberg, Jennifer C., "Drug Use and Dependence, State and Federal Prisoners, 2004," (Washington, DC: US Dept. of Justice, Oct. 2006) (NCJ213530), p. 1.

11. "Violent offenders in State prison (50%) were less likely than drug (72%) and property (64%) offenders to have used drugs in the month prior to their offense."

    Source: Mumola, Christopher J., and Karberg, Jennifer C., "Drug Use and Dependence, State and Federal Prisoners, 2004," (Washington, DC: US Dept. of Justice, Oct. 2006) (NCJ213530), p. 1.

12. "Violent offenders (47%) were the only offender group in State prisons with less than half meeting the DSM-IV criteria for drug dependence or abuse. Property and drug offenders (63% of each) were the most likely to be drug dependent or abusing.

    "Drug offenders (52%) were the only group of Federal inmates with at least half meeting the drug dependence or abuse criteria. Property offenders (27%) reported the lowest percentage of drug dependence or abuse."

    Source: Mumola, Christopher J., and Karberg, Jennifer C., "Drug Use and Dependence, State and Federal Prisoners, 2004," (Washington, DC: US Dept. of Justice, Oct. 2006) (NCJ213530), p. 7.

13. According to a federal survey of jail inmates, of the total 440,670 jail inmates in the US in 2002, 112,447 were drug offenders: 48,823 for possession, 56,574 for trafficking.

    Source: Karberg, Jennifer C. and Doris J. James, US Dept. of Justice, Bureau of Justice Statistics, "Substance Dependence, Abuse, and Treatment of Jail Inmates, 2002" (Washington, DC: US Dept. of Justice, July 2005), Table 7, p. 6.

Prisons and Drug Offenders

14. According to a federal survey of jail inmates, in 2002, of the 96,359 violent offenders in jail, 37.6% used alcohol at the time of their offense, 21.8% used drugs, and 47.2% used alcohol or drugs; of the 112,895 property offenders in jail that year, 28.5% used alcohol at the time of their offense, 32.5% used drugs, and 46.8% used alcohol or drugs; of the 112,447 drug offenders in jail that year, 22.4% used alcohol at the time of their offense, 43.2% used drugs, and 51.7% used drugs or alcohol at the time of their offense.

    Source: Karberg, Jennifer C. and Doris J. James, US Dept. of Justice, Bureau of Justice Statistics, "Substance Dependence, Abuse, and Treatment of Jail Inmates, 2002" (Washington, DC: US Dept. of Justice, July 2005), Table 7, p. 6.

15. According to the US Justice Department, in federal prisons, "While the number of offenders in each major offense category increased [from 1995 to 2003], the number incarcerated for a drug offense accounted for the largest percentage of the total growth (49%), followed by public-order offenders (38%)."

    Source: Harrison, Paige M. & Allen J. Beck, Allen J., PhD, US Department of Justice, Bureau of Justice Statistics, Prisoners in 2005 (Washington DC: US Department of Justice, Nov. 2006), p. 10.

16. According to the US Justice Department, between 1990 and 2000 "Overall, the percentage of violent Federal inmates declined from 17% to 10%. While the number of offenders in each major offense category increased, the number incarcerated for a drug offense accounted for the largest percentage of the total growth (59%), followed by public-order offenders (32%)."

    Source: Harrison, Paige M. & Allen J. Beck, Allen J., PhD, US Department of Justice, Bureau of Justice Statistics, Prisoners in 2001 (Washington DC: US Department of Justice, July 2002), p. 14.

17. "Department of corrections data show that about a fourth of those initially imprisoned for nonviolent crimes are sentenced for a second time for committing a violent offense. Whatever else it reflects, this pattern highlights the possibility that prison serves to transmit violent habits and values rather than to reduce them."

    Source: Craig Haney, Ph.D., and Philip Zimbardo, Ph.D., "The Past and Future of U.S. Prison Policy: Twenty-five Years After the Stanford Prison Experiment," American Psychologist, Vol. 53, No. 7 (July 1998), p. 721.

18. "We must have law enforcement authorities address the issue because if we do not, prevention, education, and treatment messages will not work very well. But having said that, I also believe that we have created an American gulag."

    Source: Source: Gen. Barry R. McCaffrey (USA, Ret.), Director, ONDCP, Keynote Address, Opening Plenary Session, National Conference on Drug Abuse Prevention Research, National Institute on Drug Abuse, September 19, 1996, Washington, DC, on the web at http://www.nida.gov/MeetSum/CODA/Keynote2.html last accessed May 25, 2007.

Prisons and Drug Offenders

19. The table below shows the average time (mean and median) imposed on Federal convicts for various offenses in 2000.

Average Federal Sentence

Offense	Mean	Median
All Offenses	56.8 months	33.0 months
All Felonies	58.0 months	36.0 months
Violent Felonies	86.6 months	63.0 months
Drug Felonies	75.6 months	55.0 months
Property Felony - Fraud	22.5 months	14.0 months
Property Felony - Other	33.4 months	18.0 months
Public Order Felony - Regulatory	28.0 months	15.0 months
Public Order Felony - Other	46.5 months	30.0 months
Misdemeanors	10.3 months	6.0 months

Source: US Department of Justice, Bureau of Justice Statistics, Federal Criminal Case Processing 2000, With Trends 1982-2000 (Washington, DC: US Department of Justice, November 2001), p. 12, Table 6.

Prison, Race, and the Drug Laws

1. Of the 250,900 state prison inmates serving time for drug offenses in 2004, 133,100 (53.05%) were black, 50,100 (19.97%) were Hispanic, and 64,800 (25.83%) were white.

   Source: Harrison, Paige M. & Allen J. Beck, PhD, US Dept. of Justice, Bureau of Justice Statistics, Prisoners in 2005 (Washington, DC: US Dept. of Justice, Nov. 2006) (NCJ215092), Table 12, p. 9.

2. "The racially disproportionate nature of the war on drugs is not just devastating to black Americans. It contradicts faith in the principles of justice and equal protection of the laws that should be the bedrock of any constitutional democracy; it exposes and deepens the racial fault lines that continue to weaken the country and belies its promise as a land of equal opportunity; and it undermines faith among all races in the fairness and efficacy of the criminal justice system. Urgent action is needed, at both the state and federal level, to address this crisis for the American nation."

   Source: Key Recommendations from Punishment and Prejudice: Racial Disparities in the War on Drugs (Washington, DC: Human Rights Watch, June 2000), from the web at http://www.hrw.org/campaigns/drugs/war/key-reco.htm

3. "Our criminal laws, while facially neutral, are enforced in a manner that is massively and pervasively biased. The injustices of the criminal justice system threaten to render irrelevant fifty years of hard-fought civil rights progress."

   Source: Welch, Ronald H. and Angulo, Carlos T., Justice On Trial: Racial Disparities in the American Criminal Justice System (Washington, DC: Leadership Conference on Civil Rights/Leadership Conference Education Fund, May 2000), p. v.

4. "When incarceration rates by State (excluding Federal inmates) are estimated separately by gender, race, and Hispanic origin, male rates are found to be 10 times higher than female rates; black rates 5-1/2 times higher than white rates; and Hispanic rates nearly 2 times higher than white rates (table 14)."

   Source: Harrison, Paige M., & Beck, Allen J., PhD, Bureau of Justice Statistics, Prison and Jail Inmates at Midyear 2005 (Washington, DC: US Dept. of Justice, May 2006) (NCJ213133), p. 10.

5. The incarceration rate in state or federal prison and jail for men was 1,371 per 100,000 residents, for women 129 per 100,000 residents. The rate for white men was 709 per 100,000, for black men 4,682 per 100,000, for Hispanic men 1,856 per 100,000. The rate for white women was 88 per 100,000, for black women 347 per 100,000, and for Hispanic women 144 per 100,000.

   Source: Harrison, Paige M., & Beck, Allen J., PhD, Bureau of Justice Statistics, Prison and Jail Inmates at Midyear 2005 (Washington, DC: US Dept. of Justice, May 2006) (NCJ213133), p. 10, Table 13.

6. According to the US Census Bureau, the US population in 2000 was 281,421,906. Of that, 194,552,774 (69.1%) were white; 33,947,837 (12.1%) were black; and 35,305,818 (12.5%) were of Hispanic origin. Additionally, 2,068,883 (0.7%) were Native American, and 10,123,169 (3.8%) were Asian.

Prison, Race, and the Drug Laws

Source: US Census Bureau, Department of Commerce, Census 2000 Redistricting Data (P.L. 94-171) Summary File for states, Population by Race and Hispanic or Latino Origin for the United States: 2000 (PHC-T-1) Table 1, from the web at http://www.census.gov/population/cen2000/ phc-t1/tab01.txt, last accessed September 8, 2001.

7. Regarding State prison population growth from 1990 through 2000, the US Dept. of Justice reports, "Overall, the increasing number of drug offenses accounted for 27% of the total growth among black inmates, 7% of the total growth among Hispanic inmates, and 15% of the growth among white inmates (table 19)."

   Source: Harrison, Paige M. & Allen J. Beck, PhD, US Dept. of Justice, Bureau of Justice Statistics, Prisoners in 2001 (Washington, DC: US Dept. of Justice, July 2002), p. 13.

8. According to the federal Household Survey, "most current illicit drug users are white. There were an estimated 9.9 million whites (72 percent of all users), 2.0 million blacks (15 percent), and 1.4 million Hispanics (10 percent) who were current illicit drug users in 1998." And yet, blacks constitute 36.8% of those arrested for drug violations and over 42% of those in federal prisons for drug violations. African-Americans comprise almost 57% of those in state prisons for drug felonies; Hispanics account for 17.2%.

   Sources: Substance Abuse and Mental Health Services Administration, National Household Survey on Drug Abuse: Summary Report 1998 (Rockville, MD: Substance Abuse and Mental Health Services Administration, 1999), p. 13; Bureau of Justice Statistics, Sourcebook of Criminal Justice Statistics 1998 (Washington DC: US Department of Justice, August 1999), p. 343, Table 4.10, p. 435, Table 5.48, and p. 505, Table 6.52; Beck, Allen J., Ph.D. and Mumola, Christopher J., US Department of Justice, Bureau of Justice Statistics, Prisoners in 1998 (Washington DC: US Department of Justice, August 1999), p. 10, Table 16; Harrison, Paige M. & Allen J. Beck, PhD, Bureau of Justice Statistics, Prisoners in 2001 (Washington, DC: US Dept. of Justice, July 2002), p. 13, Table 17.

9. Among persons convicted of drug felonies in state courts, whites were less likely than African-Americans to be sent to prison. Thirty-three percent (33%) of convicted white defendants received a prison sentence, while 51% of African-American defendants received prison sentences. It should also be noted that Hispanic felons are included in both demographic groups rather than being tracked separately so no separate statistic is available.

   Source: Durose, Matthew R., and Langan, Patrick A., Bureau of Justice Statistics, State Court Sentencing of Convicted Felons, 1998 Statistical Tables (Washington DC: US Department of Justice, December 2001), Table 25, available on the web at http://www.ojp.usdoj.gov/ bjs/abstract/scsc98st.htm, last accessed December 21, 2001.

10. At the start of the 1990s, the U.S. had more Black men (between the ages of 20 and 29) under the control of the nation's criminal justice system than the total number in college. This and other factors led some scholars to conclude that, "crime control policies are a major contributor to the disruption of the family, the prevalence of single parent families, and children raised without a father in the ghetto, and the 'inability of people to get the jobs still available.'"

Prison, Race, and the Drug Laws

Source: Craig Haney, Ph.D., and Philip Zimbardo, Ph.D., "The Past and Future of U.S. Prison Policy: Twenty-five Years After the Stanford Prison Experiment," American Psychologist, Vol. 53, No. 7 (July 1998), p. 716.

11. "Since 1997, 16 states have implemented reforms to their felony disenfranchisement policies
    "These reforms have resulted in the restoration of voting rights to an estimated 621,400 persons
    "By 2004, the total number of people disenfranchised due to a felony conviction had risen to 5.3 million
    "Among those disenfranchised, 74% are currently living in the community
    "In 2004, 1 in 12 African Americans was disenfranchised because of a felony conviction, a rate nearly five times that of non-African Americans
    "Voting is linked with reduced recidivism; one study shows that 27 percent of non-voters were rearrested, compared with 12 percent of voters"

    Source: King, Ryan S., "A Decade of Reform: Felony Disenfranchisement Policy in the United States" (Washington, DC: Sentencing Project, 2006), p. 2.

12. "Thirteen percent of all adult black men — 1.4 million — are disenfranchised, representing one-third of the total disenfranchised population and reflecting a rate of disenfranchisement that is seven times the national average. Election voting statistics offer an approximation of the political importance of black disenfranchisement: 1.4 million black men are disenfranchised compared to 4.6 million black men who voted in 1996."

    Source: Jamie Fellner and Mark Mauer, Losing the Vote: The Impact of Felony Disenfranchisement Laws in the United States (Washington, DC: Human Rights Watch & The Sentencing Project, 1998), p. 8. Election data cited comes from the US Census Bureau, Voting and Registration in the Election of November 1996 (P20-504) (Washington, DC: US Census Bureau, July 1998).

13. "In 2001, the chances of going to prison were highest among black males (32.2%) and Hispanic males (17.2%) and lowest among white males (5.9%). The lifetime chances of going to prison among black females (5.6%) were nearly as high as for white males. Hispanic females (2.2%) and white females (0.9%) had much lower chances of going to prison."

    Source: Bonczar, Thomas P., US Department of Justice, Bureau of Justice Statistics, "Prevalence of Imprisonment in the US Population, 1974-2001," NCJ197976 (Washington DC: US Department of Justice, August 2003), p. 8.

14. Due to harsh new sentencing guidelines, such as 'three-strikes, you're out,' "a disproportionate number of young Black and Hispanic men are likely to be imprisoned for life under scenarios in which they are guilty of little more than a history of untreated addiction and several prior drug-related offenses... States will absorb the staggering cost of not only constructing additional prisons to accommodate increasing numbers of prisoners who will never be released but also warehousing them into old age."

    Source: Craig Haney, Ph.D., and Philip Zimbardo, Ph.D., "The Past and Future of U.S. Prison Policy: Twenty-five Years After the Stanford Prison Experiment," American Psychologist, Vol. 53, No. 7 (July 1998), p. 718.

kk

Race, HIV/AIDS and the Drug War

1. According to the US Centers for Disease Control (CDC), in 2005, of the 433,760 persons in the US living with AIDS, an estimated 149,658 were Non-Hispanic Whites; 185,988 were Non-Hispanic Blacks; and 78,054 were Hispanic.

   Source: Centers for Disease Control, HIV/AIDS Surveillance Report 2005 (revised June 2007), Vol. 17, p. 21, Table 10.

2. "From 2001 through 2005, the estimated number of AIDS cases increased among all racial and ethnic groups (Table 3). In 2005, rates of AIDS cases were 54.1 per 100,000 in the black population, 18.0 per 100,000 in the Hispanic population, 7.4 per 100,000 in the American Indian/Alaska Native population, 5.9 per 100,000 in the white population, and 3.6 per 100,000 in the Asian/Pacific Islander population (Table 5a)."

   Source: Centers for Disease Control, HIV/AIDS Surveillance Report 2005 (revised June 2007), Vol. 17, p. 6.

3. According to the US Centers for Disease Control, in 2005, of the 123,803 Non-Hispanic Black Male adults or adolescents living with AIDS, 44% of cases were transmitted through male-to-male sexual contact, 28% of cases were transmitted by injection drug use, 8% were transmitted by male-to-male sexual contact and injection drug use, and 19% were transmitted by high-risk sexual contact.

   Of the 56,689 Non-Hispanic Black Female adults or adolescents living with AIDS in 2005, 32% of cases were transmitted by injection drug use and 66% were transmitted by high-risk heterosexual contact.

   Of the 130,464 Non-Hispanic White Male adults or adolescents living with AIDS in 2005, 75% of cases were transmitted through male-to-male sexual contact, 10% of cases were transmitted by injection drug use, 9% were transmitted by male-to-male sexual contact and injection drug use, and 4% were transmitted by high-risk sexual contact.

   Of the 18,641 Non-Hispanic White Female adults or adolescents living with AIDS in 2005, 39% of cases were transmitted by injection drug use and 58% were transmitted by high-risk sexual contact.

   Of the 61,416 Hispanic Males adults or adolescents living with AIDS in 2005, 56% of cases were transmitted through male-to-male sexual contact, 25% of cases were transmitted by injection drug use, 7% were transmitted by male-to-male sexual contact and injection drug use, and 12% were transmitted by high-risk heterosexual contact.

   Of the 15,953 Hispanic Female adults or adolescents living with AIDS in 2005, 32% of cases were transmitted by injection drug use and 66% were transmitted by high-risk heterosexual contact.

   Source: Centers for Disease Control, HIV/AIDS Surveillance Report 2005 (revised June 2007), Vol. 17, p. 22, Table 11.

4. The Centers for Disease Control reported that in 2003, HIV disease was the 22nd leading cause of death in the US for whites, the 9th leading cause of death for blacks, and the 13th leading cause of death for Hispanics.

   Source: Heron, Melonie P., PhD, Smith, Betty L., BsED, Division of Vital Statistics, "Deaths: Leading Causes for 2003," National Vital Statistics Reports, Vol. 55, No. 10 (Hyattsville, MD: National Center for Health Statistics, CDC, March 15, 2007), p. 10, Table E, and p. 12, Table F.

Race, HIV/AIDS and the Drug War

5. According to the US Centers for Disease Control, among non-Hispanic Blacks in the US in 2003 HIV/AIDS was the eighth leading cause of death for those 5-9 years of age, the eighth leading cause of death in the US for those aged 10-14, the ninth among those aged 15-19, the sixth leading cause for those aged 20-24, the fourth leading cause of death for those aged 25-34, the third leading cause of death for those aged 35-44, the third leading cause of death for those aged 45-54, and the ninth leading cause of death for those aged 55-64.

    Source: Heron, Melonie P., PhD, and Betty L. Smith, BSEd, Centers for Disease Control, Division of Vital Statistics, "Deaths: Leading Causes for 2003," National Vital Statistics Reports (Hyattsville, MD: National Center for Health Statistics, March 15, 2007), Vol. 55, No. 10, pp. 68-69, Table 2.

6. "More than 165,000 African Americans were living with injection-related AIDS or had already died from it by the end of 2001. Many thousands more were infected with the HIV virus.

    "The HIV/AIDS epidemic has fallen much more harshly upon African Americans than on whites who inject drugs. Among those who inject drugs, African Americans are five times as likely as whites to get AIDS.

    "In 2000, with all the advances in AIDS treatment, AIDS was still among the top three leading causes of death for African Americans aged 25-54 years. More than half of those deaths were caused by contaminated needles."

    Source: Dawn Day, Ph.D., Health Emergency 2003: The Spread of Drug-Related AIDS and Hepatitis C Among African Americans and Latinos (The Dogwood Center: Princeton, NJ, 2002), p. i.

7. According to the US Centers for Disease Control, among Hispanics in the US in 2003 HIV/AIDS was the eighth leading cause of death for those aged 20-24, the sixth leading cause of death among those aged 25-34, the fourth leading cause for those aged 35-44, the fifth leading cause of death for those aged 45-54, and the tenth leading cause of death for those aged 55-64.

    Source: Heron, Melonie P., PhD, and Betty L. Smith, BSEd, Centers for Disease Control, Division of Vital Statistics, "Deaths: Leading Causes for 2003," National Vital Statistics Reports (Hyattsville, MD: National Center for Health Statistics, March 15, 2007), Vol. 55, No. 10, pp. 53-54, Table 2.

8. "More than 76,000 Latinos living in the United States and Puerto Rico had injection-related AIDS or had already died from it by the end of 2001. Thousands more were infected with the HIV virus.

    "The HIV/AIDS epidemic has fallen more harshly upon Latinos than on whites who inject drugs. Among those who inject drugs, Latinos are at least one and a half times as likely as whites to get AIDS.

    "In 2000, with all the advances in AIDS treatment, AIDS was still among the top five leading causes of death for Latinos aged 25-54. More than half of those deaths were caused by contaminated needles."

    Source: Dawn Day, Ph.D., Health Emergency 2003: The Spread of Drug-Related AIDS and Hepatitis C Among African Americans and Latinos (The Dogwood Center: Princeton, NJ, 2002), p. i.

Race, HIV/AIDS and the Drug War

9. According to the US Centers for Disease Control, among non-Hispanic Whites in the US in 2003 HIV/AIDS was the sixth leading cause of death among those aged 25-34, and the sixth leading cause of death for those aged 35-44.

    Source: Heron, Melonie P., PhD, and Betty L. Smith, BSEd, Centers for Disease Control, Division of Vital Statistics, "Deaths: Leading Causes for 2003," National Vital Statistics Reports (Hyattsville, MD: National Center for Health Statistics, March 15, 2007), Vol. 55, No. 10, p. 61, Table 2.

Substance Abuse Prevention & Education

1. A report by the U.S. Center on Substance Abuse Prevention stated that "alternatives programming appears to be most effective among those youth at greatest risk for substance abuse and related problems." According to the report, alternatives are defined as, "those that provide targeted populations with activities that are free of alcohol, tobacco, and illicit drugs."

   Source: Maria Carmona and Kathryn Stewart, "A Review of Alternative Activities and Alternatives Programs in Youth-Oriented Prevention," National Center for the Advancement of Prevention, under contract for the US Dept. of Health and Human Services, Substance Abuse and Mental Health Services Administration (SAMHSA), Center for Substance Abuse Prevention, CSAP Technical Report 13, 1996, pp. 3, 20.

2. "Universal prevention efforts face a more challenging task in a society in which, for instance, binge drinking and smoking in public spaces are widely accepted and have positive value associations such as extroversion and fun (in the former case) and civil liberty (in the latter case). This weakens the credibility of prevention measures, because it appears to adolescents that disapproval of illicit drug use, and attempts to prevent it, stem only from legal concerns and not from a real social commitment to avoid harmful substance use."

   Source: "Selected Issues: Annual Report 2006: The State of the Drugs Problem in Europe," European Monitoring Centre for Drugs and Drug Addiction (Luxembourg: Office for Official Publications of the European Communities, 2006), p. 17.

3. "Does drug testing prevent or inhibit student drug use? Members of the Supreme Court appear to believe it does. However, among the eighth-, 10th-, and 12th-grade students surveyed in this study, school drug testing was not associated with either the prevalence or the frequency of student marijuana use, or of other illicit drug use. Nor was drug testing of athletes associated with lower-than-average marijuana and other illicit drug use by high school male athletes. Even among those who identified themselves as fairly experienced marijuana users, drug testing also was not associated with either the prevalence or the frequency of marijuana or other illicit drug use."

   Source: Yamaguchi, Ryoko, Lloyd D. Johnston & Patrick M. O'Malley, Relationship Between Student Illicit Drug Use and School Drug-Testing Policies," Journal of School Health, April 2003, Vol. 73, No. 4, p. 164.

4. "Drug testing of students is more prevalent in schools where drugs are used, kept or sold than in schools that are drug free. While only 23 percent of drug-free schools drug test students, 38 percent of non-drug-free schools conduct some type of drug testing.
   "Drug testing is not associated with either significantly lower risk scores or lower estimates of student body drug use. The average risk score of teens attending a school that is not drug free but has drug testing is 1.69; the average risk score of students at non-drug-free schools without drug testing is 1.50. The estimate of students using illegal drugs averages 40 percent for non-drug-free schools with testing and 34 percent at non-drug-free schools without testing."

Substance Abuse Prevention & Education

Source: QEV Analytics, "National Survey of American Attitudes on Substance Abuse VIII: Teens and Parents" (New York, NY: National Center on Addiction and Substance Abuse at Columbia University, August 2003), pp. 20-21.

5. "In 2004, 60.3 percent of youths aged 12 to 17 reported that they had talked at least once in the past year with at least one of their parents about the dangers of drug, tobacco, or alcohol use; this rate represents an increase from the 2003 rate of 58.9 percent and the 2002 rate of 58.1 percent. Among youths who reported having had such conversations with their parents, rates of current alcohol and cigarette use and past year and lifetime use of alcohol, cigarettes, and illicit drugs were lower than among youths who did not report such conversations. For example, past month binge drinking was reported by 10.5 percent of youths who had talked with their parents about drug, tobacco, or alcohol use compared with 12.0 percent of those who had not. Past month use of illicit drugs other than marijuana was reported by 4.6 percent of youths who had such conversations with their parents compared with 6.3 percent of those who had not."

Source: Substance Abuse and Mental Health Services Administration, "Results from the 2004 National Survey on Drug Use and Health: National Findings," Office of Applied Studies, NSDUH Series H-28, DHHS Publication No. SMA 05-4062) (Rockville, MD: NIDA, Sept. 2005), p. 65.

6. "The profiles of young cannabis users, at least in the early stages of consumption, do not differ from those of young alcohol or tobacco users. This supports the idea that universal prevention for young people should not focus on cannabis alone, but should be aimed at preventing use of alcohol and tobacco too."

Source: "Annual Report 2006: The State of the Drugs Problem in Europe," European Monitoring Centre for Drugs and Drug Addiction (Luxembourg: Office for Official Publications of the European Communities, 2006), pp. 43-44.

7. "GAO's review of Westat's evaluation reports and associated documentation leads to the conclusion that the evaluation provides credible evidence that the campaign was not effective in reducing youth drug use, either during the entire period of the campaign or during the period from 2002 to 2004 when the campaign was redirected and focused on marijuana use."

Source: Government Accountability Office, "ONDCP Media Campaign: Contractor's National Evaluation Did Not Find That the Youth Anti-Drug Media Campaign Was Effective in Reducing Youth Drug Use" (Washington, DC: US Government Printing Office, August 2006), GAO-06-818.

8. "The NSPY [National Survey of Parents and Youth] did not find significant reductions in marijuana use either leading up to or after the Marijuana campaign for youth 12 to 18 years old between 2002 and 2003. Indeed there was evidence for an increase in past month and past year use among the target audience of 14- to 16-year-olds, although it appears that the increase was already in place in the last half of 2002,

Substance Abuse Prevention & Education

before the launch of the Marijuana Initiative. It will be worthwhile to track whether the nonsignificant decline from the second half of 2002 through the first half of 2003 is the beginning of a true trend. There was a significant decrease in lifetime marijuana use among youth 16 to 18 years of age from 2002 to 2003; however, since this significant decrease was not replicated in either the directly relevant past year or past month time periods, it is difficult to ascribe the change to the campaign."

Source: Hornik, Robert, David Maklan, Diane Cadell, Carlin Henry Barmada, Lela Jacobsohn, Vani R. Henderson, Anca Romantan, Jeffrey Niederdeppe, Robert Orwin, Sanjeev Sridharan, Adam Chu, Carol Morin, Kristie Taylor, Diane Steele, "Evaluation of the National Youth Anti-Drug Media Campaign: 2003 Report of Findings," Delivered to National Institute on Drug Abuse, National Institutes of Health, Department of Health and Human Services By Westat & the Annenberg School for Communication, Contract No. N01DA-8-5063, December 22, 2003, p. 4-15.

9. "In sum, the analysis of the NSPY data does not support a claim that use among the target audience of 14- to 16-year-olds has declined with the initiation of the Marijuana Initiative. Contrarily, it appears to have increased in the past year compared to prior measurement, although the increase appears to have occurred before the start of the Marijuana Initiative and was only maintained during the first half of 2003. The MTF [Monitoring the Future] data does show declines, particularly for 8th and 10th graders. However, these declines cannot be confidently attributed to the operation of the Campaign."

Source: Hornik, Robert, David Maklan, Diane Cadell, Carlin Henry Barmada, Lela Jacobsohn, Vani R. Henderson, Anca Romantan, Jeffrey Niederdeppe, Robert Orwin, Sanjeev Sridharan, Adam Chu, Carol Morin, Kristie Taylor, Diane Steele, "Evaluation of the National Youth Anti-Drug Media Campaign: 2003 Report of Findings," Delivered to National Institute on Drug Abuse, National Institutes of Health, Department of Health and Human Services By Westat & the Annenberg School for Communication, Contract No. N01DA-8-5063, December 22, 2003, p. 4-15.

10. In their evaluation of ONDCP's Antidrug Media Campaign, researchers from Westat and the Annenberg School of Communication concluded: "In the previous reports, based on both favorable trends over time and cross-sectional associations, there was evidence supportive of Campaign effects on talking with children; on beliefs and attitudes regarding monitoring of children; and, in the case of the cross-sectional associations, on doing fun activities with them. These results still hold when Wave 7 parent reports are added, although youth reports of monitoring and talking behaviors are not consistent with parent reports and thus call into question the favorable changes in behavior that may be associated with the Campaign."

Source: Hornik, Robert, David Maklan, Diane Cadell, Carlin Henry Barmada, Lela Jacobsohn, Vani R. Henderson, Anca Romantan, Jeffrey Niederdeppe, Robert Orwin, Sanjeev Sridharan, Adam Chu, Carol Morin, Kristie Taylor, Diane Steele, "Evaluation of the National Youth Anti-Drug Media Campaign: 2003 Report of Findings," Delivered to National Institute on Drug Abuse, National Institutes of Health, Department of Health and Human Services By Westat & the Annenberg School for Communication, Contract No. N01DA-8-5063, December 22, 2003, p. 6-1.

Substance Abuse Prevention & Education

11. The Government Accountability Office reported that "Westat's analysis of the relationship between exposure to campaign advertisements and youth self-reported drug use in the NSPY data for the entire period covered by its evaluation — assessments that used statistical methods to adjust for individual differences and control for other factors that could explain changes in self-reported drug use — showed no significant effects of exposure to the campaign on initiation of marijuana by prior nonusing youth. Westat's analysis found significant unfavorable effects — that is, a relationship between campaign exposure and higher rates of initiation — during one round of NSPY data and for the whole period of the campaign among certain subgroups of the sample (e.g., 12-1/2- to 13-year-olds and girls). Westat found no effects of campaign exposure on rates of quitting or use by prior users of marijuana."

Source: Government Accountability Office, "ONDCP Media Campaign: Contractor's National Evaluation Did Not Find That the Youth Anti-Drug Media Campaign Was Effective in Reducing Youth Drug Use" (Washington, DC: US Government Printing Office, August 2006), GAO-06-818, pp. 6-7.

12. "Out-of-school exposure to drug or alcohol prevention messages in the past year was reported by 83.0 percent of youths aged 12 to 17 in 2004, a percentage similar to that in 2002 and 2003. Most indicators of current alcohol and drug use were similar for youths exposed to such out-of-school messages and those reporting no such exposure. However, past month use of illicit drugs was lower among those who were exposed than among those not exposed (10.3 vs. 11.8 percent)."

Source: Substance Abuse and Mental Health Services Administration, "Results from the 2004 National Survey on Drug Use and Health: National Findings," Office of Applied Studies, NSDUH Series H-28, DHHS Publication No. SMA 05-4062) (Rockville, MD: NIDA, Sept. 2005), p. 65.

13. "Our results are consistent in documenting the absence of beneficial effects associated with the DARE program. This was true whether the outcome consisted of actual drug use or merely attitudes toward drug use. In addition, we examined processes that are the focus of intervention and purportedly mediate the impact of DARE (e.g., self- esteem and peer resistance), and these also failed to differentiate DARE participants from nonparticipants. Thus, consistent with the earlier Clayton et al. (1996) study, there appear to be no reliable short-term, long-term, early adolescent, or young adult positive outcomes associated with receiving the DARE intervention."

Source: Lynam, Donald R., Milich, Richard, et al., "Project DARE: No Effects at 10-Year Follow-Up," Journal of Consulting and Clinical Psychology (Washington, DC: American Psychological Association, August 1999), Vol. 67, No. 4, 590-593.

14. A federally funded Research Triangle Institute study of Drug Abuse Resistance Education (DARE) found that "DARE's core curriculum effect on drug use relative to whatever drug education (if any) was offered in the control schools is slight and, except for tobacco use, is not statistically significant."

Substance Abuse Prevention & Education

Source: Ennett, S.T., et al., "How Effective Is Drug Abuse Resistance Education? A Meta-Analysis of Project DARE Outcome Evaluations," American Journal of Public Health, 84: 1394-1401 (1994).

15. Dr. Dennis Rosenbaum, a professor at the University of Illinois at Chicago, completed a six-year study of 1,798 students and found that "DARE had no long-term effects on a wide range of drug use measures"; DARE does not "prevent drug use at the stage in adolescent development when drugs become available and are widely used, namely during the high school years"; and that DARE may actually be counter productive. According to the study, "there is some evidence of a boomerang effect among suburban kids. That is, suburban students who were DARE graduates scored higher than suburban students in the Control group on all four major drug use measures."

Source: Rosenbaum, Dennis, "Assessing the Effects of School-based Drug Education: A Six Year Multilevel Analysis of Project DARE," Abstract of article published in Journal of Research in Crime and Delinquency, Vol. 35, No. 4 (November, 1998).

16. A federal report by the U.S. Center on Substance Abuse Prevention noted that "adolescence is a period in which youth reject conventionality and traditional authority figures in an effort to establish their own independence. For a significant number of adolescents, this rejection consists of engaging in a number of 'risky' behaviors, including drug and alcohol use. Within the past few years, researchers and practitioners have begun to focus on this tendency, suggesting that drug use may be a 'default' activity engaged in when youth have few or no opportunities to assert their independence in a constructive manner."

Source: Maria Carmona and Kathryn Stewart, A Review of Alternative Activities and Alternatives Programs in Youth-Oriented Prevention (National Center for the Advancement of Prevention, under contract for the Substance Abuse Mental Health Services Administration(SAMHSA), Center for Substance Abuse Prevention, 1996), p. 5.

17. The World Health Organization noted that, while some studies indicate that adolescents who use marijuana might be more likely to drop out of high school and experience job instability in young adulthood, "the apparent strength of these cross-sectional studies . . . has been exaggerated because those adolescents who are most likely to use cannabis have lower academic aspirations and poorer high school performance prior to using cannabis, than their peers who do not."

Source: Hall, W., Room, R., & Bondy, S., WHO Project on Health Implications of Cannabis Use: A Comparative Appraisal of the Health and Psychological Consequences of Alcohol, Cannabis, Nicotine and Opiate Use, August 28, 1995 (Geneva, Switzerland: World Health Organization, 1998).

Substance Use and Pregnancy

1. Criminalizing substance abuse during pregnancy discourages substance-using or abusing women from seeking prenatal care, drug treatment, and other social services, and sometimes leads to unnecessary abortions.

   Sources: Cole, H.M., "Legal Interventions During Pregnancy: Court-Ordered Medical Treatment and Legal Penalties for Potentially Harmful Behavior by Pregnant Women," Journal of the American Medical Association, 264: 2663-2670 (1990); Polan, M.L., Dombrowski, M.P., Ager, J.W., & Sokol, R.J., "Punishing Pregnant Drug Users: Enhancing the Flight from Care," Drug and Alcohol Dependence, 31: 199-203 (1993); Koren, G., Gladstone, D. Robeson, C. & Robieux, I., "The Perception of Teratogenic Risk of Cocaine," Teratology, 46: 567-571 (1992).

2. "Our study found significant cognitive deficits with cocaine-exposed children twice as likely to have significant delay throughout the first 2 years of life. The 13.7% rate of mental retardation is 4.89 times higher than that expected in the population at large, and the percentage of children with mild or greater delays requiring intenvetion was 38%, almost double the rate of the high-risk noncocaine- but polydrug-exposed comparison group. Because 2-year Mental Development Index scores are predictive of later cognitive outcomes, it is possible that these children will continue to have learning difficulties at school age.

   "Cognitive delays could not be attributed to exposure to other drugs or to a large number of potentially confounding variables. Further, poorer cognitive outcomes were related to higher amounts of cocaine metabolites in infant meconium as well as to maternal self-reported measures of amount and frequency of cocaine use during pregnancy, providing further support for a teratologic model."

   "Some limitations to this study should be considered. Although examiners were masked to infant drug status, it may have been possible to identify drug exposure through maternal or caregiver characteristics, since all children were assessed with the caregiver present. The sample was also recruited according to hospital screening measures and reflects outcomes only of more heavily exposed infants. Also, the drug assessments were made retrospectively, making reliability of maternal report problematic."

   Source: Singer, Lynn T., PhD, Robert Arendt, PhD, Sonia Minnes, PhD, Kathleen Farkas, PhD, Ann Salvator, MS, H. Lester Kirchner, PhD, Robert Kliegman, MD, "Cognitive and Motor Outcomes of Cocaine-Exposed Infants," Journal of the American Medical Association, April 17, 2002, Vol. 287, No. 15, pp. 1957-1959.

3. Research funded by the National Institute on Drug Abuse (NIDA) and the Albert Einstein Medical Center in Philadelphia states, "Although numerous animal experiments and some human data show potent effects of cocaine on the central nervous system, we were unable to detect any difference in Performance, Verbal or Full Scale IQ scores between cocaine-exposed and control children at age 4 years."

   Source: Hallam Hurt, MD; Elsa Malmud, PhD; Laura Betancourt; Leonard E. Braitman, PhD; Nancy L. Brodsky, Phd; Joan Giannetta, "Children with In Utero Cocaine Exposure Do Not Differ from Control Subjects on Intelligence Testing," Archives of Pediatrics & Adolescent Medicine, Vol. 151: 1237-1241 (American Medical Association, 1997).

Substance Use and Pregnancy

4. Well-controlled studies find minimal or no increased risk of Sudden Infant Death Syndrome (SIDS) among cocaine-exposed infants.

   Sources: Bauchner, H., Zuckerman, B., McClain, M., Frank, D., Fried, L.E., & Kayne, H., "Risk of Sudden Infant Death Syndrome among Infants with In Utero Exposure to Cocaine," Journal of Pediatrics, 113: 831-834 (1988). (Note: Early studies reporting increased risk of SIDS did not control for socioeconomic characteristics and other unhealthy behaviors. See, e.g., Chasnoff, I.J., Hunt, C., & Kletter, R., et al., "Increased Risk of SIDS and Respiratory Pattern Abnormalities in Cocaine-Exposed Infants," Pediatric Research, 20: 425A (1986); Riley, J.G., Brodsky, N.L. & Porat, R., "Risk for SIDS in Infants with In Utero Cocaine Exposure: a Prospective Study," Pediatric Research, 23: 454A (1988)).

5. Among the general population there has been no detectable increase in birth defects which may be associated with cocaine use during pregnancy.

   Source: Martin, M.L., Khoury, M.J., Cordero, J.F. & Waters, G.D., "Trends in Rates of Multiple Vascular Disruption Defects, Atlanta, 1968-1989: Is There Evidence of a Cocaine Teratogenic Epidemic?" Teratology, 45: 647-653 (1992).

6. The lack of quality prenatal care is associated with undesirable effects often attributed to cocaine exposure: prematurity, low birth weight, and fetal or infant death.

   Sources: Klein, L., & Goldenberg, R.L., "Prenatal Care and its Effect on Pre-Term Birth and Low Birth Weight," in Merkatz, I.R. & Thompson, J.E. (eds.), New Perspectives on Prenatal Care (New York, NY: Elsevier, 1990), pp. 511-513; MacGregor, S.N., Keith, L.G., Bachicha, J.A. & Chasnoff, I.J., "Cocaine Abuse during Pregnancy: Correlation between Prenatal Care and Perinatal Outcome," Obstetrics and Gynecology, 74: 882-885 (1989).

7. Provision of quality prenatal care to heavy cocaine users (with or without drug treatment) has been shown to significantly improve fetal health and development.

   Source: Chazotte, C., Youchah, J., & Freda, M.C., "Cocaine Use during Pregnancy and Low Birth Weight: The Impact of Prenatal Care and Drug Treatment," Seminars in Perinatology, 19: 293-300 (1995).

8. Presented with children randomly labeled "prenatally cocaine-exposed" and "normal," childcare professionals ranked the performance of the "prenatally cocaine-exposed" children below that of "normal," despite actual performance.

   Source: Thurman, S.K., Brobeil, R.A., Duccette, J.P., & Hurt, H., "Prenatally Exposed to Cocaine: Does the Label Matter?" Journal of Early Intervention, 18: 119-130 (1994).

9. According to a study published by the Journal of the American Medical Association in 2002, "Consistent with previous studies, we found that maternal cigarette smoking was associated with reduced birth weight and an increased risk of LBW, shortened gestation and an increased risk of preterm birth, and intrauterine growth restriction. Our data indicate that maternal cigarette smoking likely affects infant birth weight via both reduced fetal growth and shortened gestation."

   Source: Wang, Xiaobin, MD, MPH, ScD, Barry Zuckerman, MD, et al., "Maternal Cigarette Smoking, Metabolic Gene Polymorphism, and Infant Birth Weight," Journal of the American Medical Association (Chicago, IL: American Medical Association, January 9, 2002), Vol. 287, No. 2, p. 200.

Substance Use and Pregnancy

10. According to a study published by the Journal of the American Medical Association in 2002, "For the ever smokers, the mean birth weight was 280 g lower (95% confidence interval [CI], -413 to -147) and the odds ratio (OR) for LBW was higher (OR, 1.8; 95% CI, 1.3-2.7) compared with the never smokers. The mean gestational age for ever smokers was 0.8 weeks shorter (95% CI, -1.3 to -0.2) and the OR of preterm birth was higher (OR, 1.8; 95% CI, 1.3-2.7)."

    Source: Wang, Xiaobin, MD, MPH, ScD, Barry Zuckerman, MD, et al., "Maternal Cigarette Smoking, Metabolic Gene Polymorphism, and Infant Birth Weight," Journal of the American Medical Association (Chicago, IL: American Medical Association, January 9, 2002), Vol. 287, No. 2, p. 198.

11. According to a study published by the British Medical Journal in 2002, "In utero exposures due to smoking during pregnancy may increase the risk of both diabetes and obesity through programming, resulting in lifelong metabolic dysregulation, possibly due to fetal malnutrition or toxicity. The odds ratios for obesity without type 2 diabetes are more modest than those for diabetes and the scope for confounding may be greater. Smoking during pregnancy may represent another important determinant of metabolic dysregulation and type 2 diabetes in offspring. Smoking during pregnancy should always be strongly discouraged."

    Source: Montgomery, Scott M., and Anders Ekborn, "Smoking During Pregnancy and Diabetes Mellitus In a British Longitudinal Birth Cohort," British Medical Journal (London, England: British Medical Association, January 5, 2002), Vol. 321, p. 27.

Supervised Consumption Facilities (SCFs) & Safe Injection Facilities (SIFs)

1. "Governmentally sanctioned 'safer injection facilities' (SIFs) are a health service that several countries around the world have been adding to the array of public health programs they offer. These countries include:

   "Canada where the federal government, in collaboration with the Federal, Territorial and Provincial Advisory Committee on Population Health, has created a task force to examine the feasibility of a national research-based trial of SIFs (Kerr & Palepu, 2001); Vancouver, BC where SIFs are included in the Mayor's 'Four Pillar Drug Strategy,' and a formal proposal to implement 2 SIFs has been put forward (Kerr, 2000; MacPherson, 2001)

   "Germany with 13 SIFs operating in 4 cities

   "The Netherlands with 16 SIFs operating in 9 cities

   "Switzerland with 17 SIFs operating in 12 cities

   "Spain with 1 SIF operating in Madrid

   "Australia where an SIF began operations in May, 2001 in Sydney, and legislation has been approved to operate an SIF in Canberra and is pending in Melbourne (New York Times, 2001; Dolan, 2000)."

   Source: Broadhead, Robert S., Thomas Kerr, Jean-Paul C. Grund, and Frederick L. Altice, "Safer Injection Facilities in North America: Their Place in Public Policy and Health Initiatives," Journal of Drug Issues (Tallahassee, FL: Florida State University, Winter 2002), Vol. 32, No. 1, p. 331.

2. "Our review suggests that SIFs target several public health problems that municipalities in North America may wish to consider, problems largely unaddressed by needle exchange, street-outreach, education campaigns, HIV counseling, and other conventional services. SIFs target injectors' use of public spaces to inject drugs in order to reduce the many risks associated with the practice. Compared to conventional services, SIFs provide greater opportunities for health workers to connect with injectors, and to move them into primary care, drug treatment, and other rehabilitation services. Finally, SIFs target the 'nuisance factor' of drug scenes — the hazardous litter and intimidating presence of injectors congregating in city parks, public playgrounds and on street corners — by offering them an alternative, supervised 'public' space. Our review also suggests that, for municipalities considering SIFs in order to address these problems, their implementation would not necessarily require any significant or fundamental changes in public policy or law: SIFs require the same working agreements with social service providers and the police that needle exchange, street-outreach, drug treatment and similar health programs for injectors already receive."

   Source: Broadhead, Robert S., Thomas Kerr, Jean-Paul C. Grund, and Frederick L. Altice, "Safer Injection Facilities in North America: Their Place in Public Policy and Health Initiatives," Journal of Drug Issues (Tallahassee, FL: Florida State University, Winter 2002), Vol. 32, No. 1, p. 347-8.

Supervised Consumption Facilities (SCFs) & Safe Injection Facilities (SIFs)

3. "The present study demonstrates that the opening of the Vancouver SIF was associated with a greater than 30% increase in the rate of detoxification service use among SIF users in comparison to the year prior to the SIF's opening. Subsequent analyses demonstrated that detoxification service use was associated with increased use of methadone and other forms of addiction treatment, as well as reduced injecting at the SIF."

    Source: Wood, Evan, Tyndall, Mark W., Zhang, Ruth, Montaner, Julio S.G., and Kerr, Thomas, "Rate of Detoxification Service Use and its Impact among a Cohort of Supervised Injecting Facility Users," Addiction, 2007, Vol. 102, p. 918.

4. "In summary, the present study demonstrates that the SIF was associated with increased use of detoxification service use and that residential detoxification was associated with increased rates of methadone use and other forms of addiction treatment. Given the known role of methadone and other forms of addiction treatment in reducing levels of injection drug use, and given that detoxification programme use was associated with reduced injecting at the SIF, our findings imply that the SIF has probably helped to reduce rates of injection drug use among users of the facility."

    Source: Wood, Evan, Tyndall, Mark W., Zhang, Ruth, Montaner, Julio S.G., and Kerr, Thomas, "Rate of Detoxification Service Use and its Impact among a Cohort of Supervised Injecting Facility Users," Addiction, 2007, Vol. 102, p. 918.

5. In an evaluation of the Vancouver supervised injection facility, researchers concluded that: "Our study indicates that the opening of North America's first supervised injection facility was not associated with measurable negative changes in the use of injected drugs. Indeed, we found a substantial reduction in the starting of binge drug use after the opening of the facility, suggesting that it had not prompted 'risk compensation' among local injecting drug users, whereby the benefits of a safer environment are overcome by more risky behaviours such as higher intensity drug use."

    Source: Kerr, Thomas, Jo-Anne Stoltz, Mark Tyndall, Kathy Li, Ruth Zhang, Julio Montaner, Evan Wood, "Impact of a medically supervised safer injection facility on community drug use patterns: a before and after study," British Medical Journal, Vol. 332, Jan. 28, 2006, pp. 221-222.

6. In an evaluation of the Vancouver supervised injection facility, researchers concluded that: "Although there was a substantial increase in the number of participants who started smoking crack cocaine, it is unlikely that the facility, which does not allow smoking in the facility, prompted this change. These findings are relevant to a recent review of supervised injection facilities by the European Monitoring Centre on Drugs and Drug Addiction, which highlighted concerns that these facilities could potentially 'encourage increased levels of drug use' and 'make drug use more acceptable and comfortable, thus delaying initiation into treatment.'"

Supervised Consumption Facilities (SCFs) & Safe Injection Facilities (SIFs)

Source: Kerr, Thomas, Jo-Anne Stoltz, Mark Tyndall, Kathy Li, Ruth Zhang, Julio Montaner, Evan Wood, "Impact of a medically supervised safer injection facility on community drug use patterns: a before and after study," British Medical Journal, Vol. 332, Jan. 28, 2006, p. 222.

7. "Evaluation of the Vancouver facility has shown that its opening has been associated with reductions in public drug use and publicly discarded syringes and reductions in syringe sharing among local injecting drug users. Our study suggests that these benefits have not been offset by negative changes in community drug use."

Source: Kerr, Thomas, Jo-Anne Stoltz, Mark Tyndall, Kathy Li, Ruth Zhang, Julio Montaner, Evan Wood, "Impact of a medically supervised safer injection facility on community drug use patterns: a before and after study," British Medical Journal, Vol. 332, Jan. 28, 2006, p. 222.

8. "In summary, there have been many overdose events within Vancouver's SIF, although the rate of overdoses is similar to rates observed in SIF in other settings. The majority of these overdoses involved the injection of opiates, and most events were successfully managed within the SIF through the provision of oxygen. It is noteworthy that none of the overdose events occurring at the SIF resulted in a fatality. These findings suggest that SIF can play a role in managing overdoses among IDU and indicate the potential of SIF to reduce morbidity and mortality associated with illicit drug-related overdoses."

Source: Thomas Kerr, Mark W. Tyndall, Calvin Lai, Julio S.G. Montaner, Evan Wood, "Drug-related overdoses within a medically supervised safer injection facility," International Journal of Drug Policy, 2006.

9. "Little evaluative work has been conducted into supervised injection facilities in other countries. In Hanover, however, 98% of users of the medically supervised injecting centre did not encounter any negative experience with local residents and 94% reported no negative police encounters. Research from Frankfurt showed that a drug user who overdoses on the street is 10 times more likely to stay in hospital for one night than a drug user who overdoses in a medically supervised injecting centre. In addition, no one has died from heroin overdose in any medically supervised injecting centre. Therefore, establishing such centres in the United Kingdom is likely to reduce the number of drug related deaths."

Source: Wright, Nat M.J., Charlotte N.E. Tompkins, "Supervised Injecting Centres," British Medical Journal, Vol. 328, Jan. 10, 2004, p. 101.

10. Researchers for the EU's drugs monitoring agency looking into safer injection facilities and drug consumption rooms found that "Consumption rooms reach a population of often older, long-term users some of whom have had no previous treatment contact. Services appear particularly successful in attracting groups that are difficult to reach. No evidence was found to suggest that naive users are initiated into injecting as a result of the presence of consumption rooms."

Supervised Consumption Facilities (SCFs) & Safe Injection Facilities (SIFs)

Source: Hedrich, Dagmar, "European Report on Drug Consumption Rooms" (Lisbon, Portugal: European Monitoring Centre on Drugs and Drug Addiction, Feb. 2004), p. 42.

11. Researchers for the EU's drugs monitoring agency looking into safer injection facilities and drug consumption rooms found that "Service users' sociodemographic data and drug use profile are similar across countries. Data show that the rooms reach the intended target groups of long-term addicts, street injectors, homeless drug users and drug-using sex workers and are thus facilitating contact with the most problematic and marginalised drug users. Demographic information also shows that these services can be successful in reaching long-term drug users with no previous contact with treatment services."

Source: Hedrich, Dagmar, "European Report on Drug Consumption Rooms" (Lisbon, Portugal: European Monitoring Centre on Drugs and Drug Addiction, Feb. 2004), p. 42.

12. "Consumption rooms achieve the immediate objective of providing a safe place for lower risk, more hygienic drug consumption without increasing the levels of drug use or risky patterns of consumption. Direct benefits of supervised injecting appear to be a reduction in some of the risk behaviours related to injecting, in particular improvements in injecting practice, use of sterile equipment and lack of opportunity for sharing drugs. Other benefits are that, if medical emergencies should occur, immediate medical intervention is possible, and the consumption equipment used in the rooms is correctly disposed of. Client surveys consistently show that service users appreciate the hygienic conditions, safety and peace that the rooms provide."

Source: Hedrich, Dagmar, "European Report on Drug Consumption Rooms" (Lisbon, Portugal: European Monitoring Centre on Drugs and Drug Addiction, Feb. 2004), p. 48.

13. "There is no evidence that consumption rooms encourage increased drug use or initiate new users. There is little evidence that by providing better conditions for drug consumption they perpetuate drug use in clients who would otherwise discontinue consuming drugs such as heroin or cocaine, nor that they undermine treatment goals.
"When managed in consultation with local authorities and police, they do not increase public order problems by increasing local drug scenes or attracting drug users and dealers from other areas. If consultation and cooperation between key actors does not take place, then there can be a risk of a 'pull effect' and consumption rooms run the risk of being blamed for aggravating local problems of public order including drug dealing."

Source: Hedrich, Dagmar, "European Report on Drug Consumption Rooms" (Lisbon, Portugal: European Monitoring Centre on Drugs and Drug Addiction, Feb. 2004), p. 84.

Supervised Consumption Facilities (SCFs) & Safe Injection Facilities (SIFs)

14. "According to the few studies that have examined the effects of consumption rooms on acquisitive crime, there is no evidence from police data of a negative effect on local levels of theft, robbery and burglary."

    Source: Hedrich, Dagmar, "European Report on Drug Consumption Rooms" (Lisbon, Portugal: European Monitoring Centre on Drugs and Drug Addiction, Feb. 2004), pp. 83-4.

15. "There is no evidence that the operation of consumption rooms leads to more acquisitive crime. There is small-scale drug dealing in the vicinity of many services, which is not surprising given their location."

    Source: Hedrich, Dagmar, "European Report on Drug Consumption Rooms" (Lisbon, Portugal: European Monitoring Centre on Drugs and Drug Addiction, Feb. 2004), p. 83.

16. "Neighbourhood attitudes and perceptions. Surveys of local residents and businesses, as well as registers of complaints made to the police, generally show positive changes following the establishment of consumption rooms, including perceptions of decreased nuisance and increases in acceptance of the rooms. Police, too, often acknowledge that consumptions contribute to minimising or preventing open drug scenes.

    "Open drug scenes and police policy. There are instances where consumption rooms have been blamed for increasing public nuisance, including open drug scenes and dealing. These arose where police actions in other areas had the effect of relocating drug markets and open scenes.

    "Pull effect. Available evidence is not sufficient to draw conclusions on whether consumption rooms exert a 'pull-effect' by attracting drug users from other areas, thus adding to the situation already created by established drug markets. Attempts to decentralise drug scenes by dispersing consumption rooms have not led to increased nuisance around the rooms. However, they have not attracted large numbers of clients either."

    Source: Hedrich, Dagmar, "European Report on Drug Consumption Rooms" (Lisbon, Portugal: European Monitoring Centre on Drugs and Drug Addiction, Feb. 2004), p. 82.

17. "There is no evidence that consumption rooms increase levels of drug use or encourage riskier patterns of use, nor that they increase morbidity and mortality.

    "Few clients use the facilities only for drug consumption. Most at some point use other services, especially medical and in some cases drug treatment.

    "There is little evidence that consumption rooms undermine treatment by making drug use more 'comfortable'. Whether clients in oral methadone treatment are allowed to use the rooms for injection, is dealt with in different ways."

    Source: Hedrich, Dagmar, "European Report on Drug Consumption Rooms" (Lisbon, Portugal: European Monitoring Centre on Drugs and Drug Addiction, Feb. 2004), pp. 80-81.

Supervised Consumption Facilities (SCFs) & Safe Injection Facilities (SIFs)

18. "Consumption rooms achieve the immediate objective of providing a safe place for lower risk, more hygienic drug consumption without increasing the levels of drug use or risky patterns of consumption."

    Source: Hedrich, Dagmar, "European Report on Drug Consumption Rooms" (Lisbon, Portugal: European Monitoring Centre on Drugs and Drug Addiction, Feb. 2004), p. 77.

19. "We found significant reductions in public injection drug use, publicly discarded syringes and injection-related litter after the opening of the medically supervised safer injecting facility in Vancouver. These reductions were independent of law enforcement activities and changes in rainfall patterns.

    "Our findings are consistent with anecdotal reports of improved public order following the establishment of safer injecting facilities and are not surprising given that a commonly reported reason for public drug use is the lack of an alternative place to inject and that IDUs who go to safer injecting facilities are often homeless or marginally housed. Our findings are also highly plausible since more than 500 IDUs visited the facility daily after it opened, and several feasibility studies have suggested that IDUs who inject in public would be the most likely to use safer injecting facilities. Our observations suggest that the establishment of the safer injecting facility has resulted in measurable improvements in public order, which in turn may improve the liveability of communities and benefit tourism while reducing community concerns stemming from public drug use and discarded syringes. It is also noteworthy that we did not observe an increase in the number of drug dealers in the vicinity of the facility, which indicates that the facility's opening did not have a negative impact on drug dealing in the area. Although further study of these issues is necessary, the safer injecting facility may also offer public health benefits, since public injection drug use has been associated with an array of health-related harms."

    Source: Wood, Evan, Thomas Kerr, Will Small, Kathy Li, David C. Marsh, Julio S.G. Montaner & Mark W. Tyndall, "Changes in Public Order After the Opening of a Medically Supervised Safer Injecting Facility for Illicit Injection Drug Users," Canadian Medical Association Journal, Vol. 171, No. 7, Sept. 28, 2004, p. 733.

20. "In summary, we documented significant reductions in the number of IDUs injecting in public, publicly discarded syringes and injection-related litter after the opening of the medically supervised safer injecting facility. These reductions appeared to be independent of several potential confounders, and our findings were supported by external data sources. Although the overall health impacts of the facility will take several years to evaluate, the findings from this study should be valuable to other cities that are contemplating similar evaluations and should have substantial relevance to many urban areas where public injection drug use has been associated with substantial public health risks and adverse community impacts."

Supervised Consumption Facilities (SCFs) & Safe Injection Facilities (SIFs)

Source: Wood, Evan, Thomas Kerr, Will Small, Kathy Li, David C. Marsh, Julio S.G. Montaner & Mark W. Tyndall, "Changes in Public Order After the Opening of a Medically Supervised Safer Injecting Facility for Illicit Injection Drug Users," Canadian Medical Association Journal, Vol. 171, No. 7, Sept. 28, 2004, p. 734.

21. According to the final report of the evaluation of the Sydney, Australia, Medically Supervised Injecting Centre (MSIC) by the MSIC Evaluation Committee (established by the New South Wales Dept. of Health): "In summary, the evidence available from this Evaluation indicates that:

"- operation of the MSIC in the King Cross area is feasible;

"- the MSIC made service contact with its target population, including many who had no prior treatment for drug dependence;

"- there was no detectable change in heroin overdoses at the community level;

"- a small number of opioid overdoses managed at the MSIC may have been fatal had they occurred elsewhere;

"- the MSIC made referrals for drug treatment, especially among frequent attenders;

"- there was no increase in risk of blod borne virus transmission;

"- there was no overall loss of public amenity;

"- there was no increase of crime;

"- the majority of the community accepted the MSIC initiative;

"- the MSIC has afforded an opportunity to improve knowledge that can guide public health responses to drug injecting and its harms."

Source: MISC Evaluation Committee, "Final Report on the Sydney Medically Supervised Injecting Centre" (New South Wales, Australia: MISC Evaluation Committee, 2003), p. xiv.

Syringe/Needle Exchange Programs

1. "Syringe exchange programs (SEPs) provide sterile syringes in exchange for used syringes to reduce transmission of human immunodeficiency virus (HIV) and other bloodborne infections associated with reuse of contaminated syringes by injection-drug users (IDUs). . . . SEPs can help prevent bloodborne pathogen transmission by increasing access to sterile syringes among IDUs and enabling safe disposal of used syringes. Often, programs also provide other public health services, such as HIV testing, risk-reduction education, and referrals for substance-abuse treatment."

   Source: "Update: Syringe Exchange Programs — United States, 2002," Morbidity and Mortality Weekly Report, July 15, 2005, Vol. 54, No. 27 (Atlanta, GA: US Centers for Disease Control), p. 673.

2. "While it is not feasible to do a randomized controlled trial of the effectiveness of needle or syringe exchange programs (NEPs/SEPs) in reducing HIV incidence, the majority of studies have shown that NEPs/SEPs are strongly associated with reductions in the spread of HIV when used as a component of comprehensive approach to HIV prevention. NEPs/SEPs increase the availability of sterile syringes and other injection equipment, and for exchange participants, this decreases the fraction of needles in circulation that are contaminated. This lower fraction of contaminated needles reduces the risk of injection with a contaminated needle and lowers the risk of HIV transmission.

   "In addition to decreasing HIV infected needles in circulation through the physical exchange of syringes, most NEPs/SEPs are part of a comprehensive HIV prevention effort that may include education on risk reduction, and referral to drug addiction treatment, job or other social services, and these interventions may be responsible for a significant part of the overall effectiveness of NEPs/SEPs. NEPs/SEPs also provide an opportunity to reach out to populations that are often difficult to engage in treatment."

   Source: Volkow, Nora, Director, National Institute on Drug Abuse, correspondence with Allan Clear, Aug. 4, 2004, online at http://hepcproject.typepad.com/hep_c_project/2004/09/re_ souderzerhou.html last accessed Jan. 6, 2005.

3. "After reviewing all of the research to date, the senior scientists of the Department and I have unanimously agreed that there is conclusive scientific evidence that syringe exchange programs, as part of a comprehensive HIV prevention strategy, are an effective public health intervention that reduces the transmission of HIV and does not encourage the use of illegal drugs."

   Source: US Surgeon General Dr. David Satcher, Department of Health and Human Services, Evidence-Based Findings on the Efficacy of Syringe Exchange Programs: An Analysis from the Assistant Secretary for Health and Surgeon General of the Scientific Research Completed Since April 1998 (Washington, DC: Dept. of Health and Human Services, 2000), from the website of the Harm Reduction Coalition at **pp** *http://www.harmreduction.org/issues/surgeongenrev/surgreview.html, last accessed Feb. 6, 2004.*

Syringe/Needle Exchange Programs

4. According to Dr. Harold Varmus, then-Director of the National Institutes of Health, "An exhaustive review of the science in this area indicates that needle exchange programs can be an effective component in the global effort to end the epidemic of HIV disease."

   Source: Varmus, Harold, MD, Director of the National Institutes of Health, Press release from Department of Health and Human Services, (April 20, 1998).

5. "For injecting drug users who cannot gain access to treatment or are not ready to consider it, multi-component HIV prevention programs that include sterile needle and syringe access reduce drug-related HIV risk behavior, including self-reported sharing of needles and syringes, unsafe injecting and disposal practices, and frequency of injection. Sterile needle and syringe access may include needle and syringe exchange (NSE) or the legal, accessible, and economical sale of needles and syringes through pharmacies, voucher schemes, and physician prescription programs."

   Source: Committee on the Prevention of HIV Infection among Injecting Drug Users in High-Risk Countries, Institute of Medicine, National Academy of Sciences, "Preventing HIV Infection among Injecting Drug Users in High Risk Countries: An Assessment of the Evidence" (Washington, DC: National Academy Press, 2006), p. 142.

6. A literature review in 2004 by the European Union's drug monitoring agency, the European Monitoring Centre on Drugs and Drug Addiction, found that "Major reviews (summarised in Vlahov and Junge, 1998; Bastos and Strathdee, 2000; Ferrini, 2000) suggest that NSPs (Needle and Syringe Programs) may reduce rates of seroconversion to HIV and hepatitis by one third or more, without negative side effects on the number of IDUs (Vlahov and Junge, 1998). A landmark study from Hurley et al. combined HIV seroprevalence data from 81 cities with (n=52) or without (n=29) NSPs (Hurley et al., 1997). They showed that the average annual seroprevalence was 11% lower in cities with an NSP than in cities without an NSP, providing important evidence on the effectiveness of NSPs in reducing the spread of HIV."

   Source: de Wit, Ardine and Jasper Bos, "Cost-Effectiveness of Needle and Syringe Programmes: A Review of the Literature," in Hepatitis C and Injecting Drug Use: Impact, Costs and Policy Options, Johannes Jager, Wien Limburg, Mirjam Kretzschmar, Maarten Postma, Lucas Wiessing (eds.), European Monitoring Centre on Drugs and Drug Addiction, 2004.

7. "Access to sterile needles and syringes is an important, even vital, component of a comprehensive HIV prevention program for IDUs. The data on needle exchange in the United States are consistent with the conclusion that these programs do not encourage drug use and that needle exchanges can be effective in reducing HIV incidence. Other data show that NEPs help people stop drug use through referral to drug treatment programs. The studies outside of the United States are important for reminding us that unintended consequences can occur. While changes in needle prescription and possession laws and regulations have shown promise, the identification of organizational components that improve or hinder effectiveness of needle exchange and pharmacy-based access are needed."

Syringe/Needle Exchange Programs

Source: Vlahov, David, PhD, and Benjamin Junge, MHSc, "The Role of Needle Exchange Programs in HIV Prevention," Public Health Reports, Volume 113, Supplement 1, June 1998, pp. 75-80.

8. "Pediatricians should advocate for unencumbered access to sterile syringes and improved knowledge about decontamination of injection equipment. Physicians should be knowledgeable about their states' statutes regarding possession of syringes and needles and available mechanisms for procurement. These programs should be encouraged, expanded, and linked to drug treatment and other HIV-1 risk-reduction education. It is important that these programs be conducted within the context of continuing research to document effectiveness and clarify factors that seem linked to desired outcomes."

   Source: "Policy Statement: Reducing the Risk of HIV Infection Associated With Illicit Drug Use," Committee on Pediatric AIDS, Pediatrics, Vol. 117, No. 2, Feb. 2006 (Chicago, IL: American Academy of Pediatrics), p. 569.

9. Between 1991 and 1997, the U.S. Government funded seven reports on clean needle programs for persons who inject drugs. The reports are unanimous in their conclusions that clean needle programs reduce HIV transmission, and none find that clean needle programs cause rates of drug use to increase.

   Sources: National Commission on AIDS, The Twin Epidemics of Substance Abuse and HIV (Washington DC: National Commission on AIDS, 1991); General Accounting Office, Needle Exchange Programs: Research Suggests Promise as an AIDS Prevention Strategy (Washington DC: US Government Printing Office, 1993); Lurie, P. & Reingold, A.L., et al., The Public Health Impact of Needle Exchange Programs in the United States and Abroad (San Francisco, CA: University of California, 1993); Satcher, David, MD, (Note to Jo Ivey Bouffard), The Clinton Administration's Internal Reviews of Research on Needle Exchange Programs (Atlanta, GA: Centers for Disease Control, December 10, 1993); National Research Council and Institute of Medicine, Normand, J., Vlahov, D. & Moses, L. (eds.), Preventing HIV Transmission: The Role of Sterile Needles and Bleach (Washington DC: National Academy Press, 1995); Office of Technology Assessment of the U.S. Congress, The Effectiveness of AIDS Prevention Efforts (Springfield, VA: National Technology Information Service, 1995); National Institutes of Health Consensus Panel, Interventions to Prevent HIV Risk Behaviors (Kensington, MD: National Institutes of Health Consensus Program Information Center, February 1997).

10. Research published in the Journal of Urban Health estimated that in 1998, there were 1,364,874 injection drug users in the US.

    Source: Friedman, Samuel R., Barbara Tempalski, Hannah Cooper, Theresa Perlis, Marie Keem, Risa Friedman & Peter L. Flom, "Estimating Numbers of Injecting Drug Users in Metropolitan Areas for Structural Analyses of Community Vulnerability and for Assessing Relative Degrees of Service Provision for Injecting Drug Users," Journal of Urban Health (New York, NY: NY Academy of Medicine, 2004), Vol. 81, No. 3, p. 380.

11. "Estimates of the annual number of syringes required to meet the single-use standard run in the range of 1 billion. The most recent estimate of the number of syringes distributed by needle exchange programs in the United States (1997) was 17.5 million."

Syringe/Needle Exchange Programs

Source: Burris, Scott, JD, Lurie, Peter, MD, et al., "Physician Prescribing of Sterile Injection Equipment to Prevent HIV Infection: Time for Action", Annals of Internal Medicine (Philadelphia, PA: American College of Physicians, August 1, 2000), Vol. 133, No. 3, from the web at http://www.annals.org/issues/v133n3/full/200008010-00015.html, citing Lurie P, Jones TS, Foley J. A sterile syringe for every drug user injection: how many injections take place annually, and how might pharmacists contribute to syringe distribution? J Acquir Immune Defic Syndr Hum Retrovirol 1998;18(Suppl 1):S45-51, and Update: syringe exchange programs — United States, 1997. MMWR Morb Mortal Wkly Rep. 1998;47:652-55.

12. In 1997, Dr. Ernest Drucker wrote in The Lancet that if current U.S. policies limiting clean needle programs were not changed, an additional 5,150 to 11,329 preventable HIV infections could occur by the year 2000. In 1999 alone, the CDC reported there were at least 2,946 new injection-related HIV infections.

Source: Lurie, P. & Drucker, E., "An Opportunity Lost: HIV Infections Associated with Lack of a National Needle- Exchange Programme in the U.S.A.", Lancet, 349: 604-08 (1997); Centers for Disease Control, HIV/AIDS Surveillance Report (1999 Year-End Edition, December 1999), Vol. 11, No. 2, Table 6, p. 15, available online at http://www.cdc.gov/hiv/stats/hasr1102/table3.htm.

13. "Eastern Europe, the Commonwealth of Independent States, and significant parts of Asia are experiencing explosive growth in new HIV infections, driven largely by injecting drug use (UNAIDS, 2006). While the primary route of transmission in most of these areas is sharing of contaminated injecting equipment, sexual and perinatal transmission among IDUs and their partners also plays an important and growing role. In many highly affected countries, rapid growth in the number of IDUs infected with HIV has already created a public health crisis. Countries where the level of HIV infection is still relatively low have the chance — if they act now — to slow the spread of HIV."

Source: Committee on the Prevention of HIV Infection among Injecting Drug Users in High-Risk Countries, "Preventing HIV Infection among Injecting Drug Users in High Risk Countries: An Assessment of the Evidence" (Washington, DC: National Academy Press, 2006), p. 141.

14. In 2005 the US Centers for Disease Control published the results of a survey conducted by staff from Beth Israel Medical Center and the North American Syringe Exchange Network (NASEN) of 148 Syringe Exchange Program (SEP) directors around the country (of whom 126 completed the survey). According to the report: "These 126 SEPs reported operating in 102 cities in 31 states and the District of Columbia (DC). More than two-thirds (86) of SEPs were in seven states: California (25), Washington (15), New Mexico (14), New York (12), Wisconsin (eight), Massachusetts (six), and Oregon (six).

"SEP size was classified by the number of syringes exchanged (Table 1); 119 SEPs reported exchanging a total of 24,878,033 syringes; seven SEPs did not track the number of syringes exchanged. The 11 largest programs exchanged 49% of all syringes."

Syringe/Needle Exchange Programs

Source: "Update: Syringe Exchange Programs — United States, 2002," Morbidity and Mortality Weekly Report, July 15, 2005, Vol. 54, No. 27 (Atlanta, GA: US Centers for Disease Control), p. 673.

15. "SEPs provided other services in addition to syringe exchange. One hundred ten (87%) SEPs provided male condoms, 96 (76%) female condoms, 111 (88%) alcohol pads, and 86 (68%) bleach; 97 (77%) provided referrals for substance-abuse treatment; 91 (72%) offered voluntary on-site counseling and testing for HIV, 54 (43%) for hepatitis C, and 37 (29%) for hepatitis B; 42 (33%) provided vaccination for hepatitis A and 45 (36%) for hepatitis B; 39 (31%) offered sexually transmitted disease (STD) screening; 29 (23%) provided on-site medical care; and 28 (22%) provided tuberculosis screening. Most programs provided risk-reduction and risk-elimination education to IDUs. One hundred fifteen (91%) programs provided education on hepatitis A, B, and C; 114 (90%) on HIV/AIDS prevention; 111 (88%) on safer injection practices; 104 (83%) on abscess prevention and care; 100 (79%) on vein care; 110 (87%) on STD prevention; 110 (87%) on male condom use; and 94 (75%) on female condom use."

Source: "Update: Syringe Exchange Programs — United States, 2002," Morbidity and Mortality Weekly Report, July 15, 2005, Vol. 54, No. 27 (Atlanta, GA: US Centers for Disease Control), pp. 673-4.

16. "The purchase of syringes through pharmacies may be a major source of contact with the health service for some injectors, and the potential to exploit this contact point as a conduit to other services clearly exists. Work to motivate and support pharmacists to develop the services they offer to drug users could form an important part of extending the role of pharmacies, but to date only France, Portugal and the United Kingdom appear to be making significant investments in this direction."

Source: "Annual Report 2006: The State of the Drugs Problem in Europe," European Monitoring Centre for Drugs and Drug Addiction (Luxembourg: Office for Official Publications of the European Communities, 2006), p. 79.

17. "Studies on behalf of the US government conducted by the National Commission on AIDS, the University of California and the Centers for Disease Control and Prevention, the National Academy of Science, and the Office of Technology Assessment all concluded that syringe prescription and drug paraphernalia laws should be overturned or modified to allow IDUs to purchase, possess, and exchange sterile syringes."

Source: Diebert, Ryan J., MPH, Goldbaum, Gary, MD, MPH, Parker, Theodore R., MPH, Hagan, Holly, PhD, Marks, Robert, MEd, Hanrahan, Michael, BA, and Thiede, Hanne, DVM, MPH, "Increased Access to Unrestricted Pharmacy Sales of Syringe in Seattle-King County, Washington: Structural and Individual-Level Changes, 1996 Versus 2003," American Journal of Public Health, Vol. 96, No. 8, Aug. 2006, p. 1352.

Syringe/Needle Exchange Programs

18. "The data in this report offer no support for the idea that anti-OTC laws prevent illicit drug injection. However, the data do show associations between anti-OTC laws and HIV prevalence and incidence. In an ongoing epidemic of a fatal infectious disease, prudent public health policy suggests removing prescription requirements rather than awaiting definitive proof of causation. Such action has been taken by Connecticut, by Maine, and, recently, by New York. After Connecticut legalized OTC sales of syringes and the personal possession of syringes, syringe sharing by drug injectors decreased. Moreover, no evidence showed increased in drug use, drug-related arrests, or needlestick injuries to police officers."

    Source: Friedman, Samuel R. PhD, Theresa Perlis, PhD, and Don C. Des Jarlais, PhD, "Laws Prohibiting Over-the-Counter Syringe Sales to Injection Drug Users: Relations to Population Density, HIV Prevalence, and HIV Incidence," American Journal of Public Health (Washington, DC: American Public Health Association, May 2001), Vol. 91, No. 5, p. 793.

19. "Anti-OTC laws are not associated with lower population proportions of IDUs. Laws restricting syringe access are statistically associated with HIV transmission and should be repealed."

    Source: Friedman, Samuel R. PhD, Theresa Perlis, PhD, and Don C. Des Jarlais, PhD, "Laws Prohibiting Over-the-Counter Syringe Sales to Injection Drug Users: Relations to Population Density, HIV Prevalence, and HIV Incidence," American Journal of Public Health (Washington, DC: American Public Health Association, May 2001), Vol. 91, No. 5, p. 793.

20. "In multivariate analyses, we found that police contact was associated independently with residing in the area with no legal possession of syringes; among SEP users, those with access to SEPs without limits had lower syringe re-use but not lower syringe sharing; and that among non-SEP users, no significant differences in injection risk were observed among IDUs with and without pharmacy access to syringes.
    "Conclusion   We found that greater legal access to syringes, if accompanied by limits on the number of syringes that can be exchanged, purchased and possessed, may not have the intended impacts on injection-related infectious disease risk among IDUs."

    Source: Bluthenthal, Ricky N., Mohammed Rehan Malik, Lauretta E. Grau, Merrill Singer, Patricia Marshall & Robert Heimer for the Diffusion of Benefit through Syringe Exchange Study Team, "Sterile Syringe Access Conditions and Variations in HIV Risk Among Drug Injectors in Three Cities," Addiction Journal, Vol. 99, Issue 9, p. 1136, Sept. 2004, abstract online at http://www.blackwell-synergy.com/links/doi/10.1111/j.1360-0443.2004.00694.x/abs/ last accessed Jan. 6, 2005.

21. The US Office of National Drug Control Policy in 2005 was caught by the Washington Post misrepresenting the results of research on syringe exchange programs. According to the Post in its editorial, "Deadly Ignorance": "An official who requested anonymity directed us to a number of researchers who have allegedly cast doubt on the pro-exchange consensus. One of them is Steffanie A. Strathdee of the University of California at San Diego; when we contacted her, she

Syringe/Needle Exchange Programs

responded that her research 'supports the expansion of needle exchange programs, not the opposite.' Another researcher cited by the administration is Martin T. Schechter of the University of British Columbia; he wrote us that 'Our research here in Vancouver has been repeatedly used to cast doubt on needle exchange programs. I believe this is a clear misinterpretation of the facts.' Yet a third researcher cited by the administration is Julie Bruneau at the University of Montreal; she told us that 'in the vast majority of cases needle exchange programs drive HIV incidence lower.' We asked Dr. Bruneau whether she favored needle exchanges in countries such as Russia or Thailand. 'Yes, sure,' she responded.' The Post further noted: "The Bush administration attempted to bolster its case by providing us with three scientific articles. One, which has yet to be published in a peer-reviewed journal, was produced by an author unknown to leading experts in this field who is affiliated with a group called the Children's AIDS Fund. This group is more renowned for its ties to the Bush administration than for its public health rigor: As the Post's David Brown has reported, it recently received an administration grant despite the fact that an expert panel had deemed its application 'not suitable for funding.' The two other articles supplied by the administration had been published in the American Journal of Public Health. Although each raised questions about the certainty with which needle-exchange advocates state their case, neither opposed such programs."

Source: "Deadly Ignorance," The Washington Post, Feb. 27, 2005, from the web at http://www.mapinc.org/newscsdp/v05/n327/a08.html, last accessed March 18, 2005.

22. Former Drug Czar Barry McCaffrey misinterpreted results of two Canadian needle exchange studies when he suggested in testimony to Congress that the studies showed needle exchange efforts have failed to reduce the spread of HIV and may have worsened the problem. In a clarification published in The New York Times, the authors of the studies corrected him, pointing out that among other factors, in Canada syringes can be purchased legally while they could only be purchased with prescriptions in the United States. Therefore, unlike in the USA studies, the populations in the Canadian studies were less likely to include the more affluent and better functioning addicts who could purchase their own needles and who were less likely to engage in the riskiest activities. Thus, it was not surprising that participants in the study had higher rates of HIV than those who did not - they were in different risk categories.

Source: Bruneau, J. & Schechter, M.T., "Opinion: The Politics of Needles and AIDS," The New York Times (April 9, 1998); Federal Information Systems Corporation Federal News Service, "Hearing of the National Security, International Affairs and Criminal Justice Subcommittee of the House Government Reform and Oversight Committee subject: Office of National Drug Control Policy chaired by: Representative Dennis Hastert (R-IL) Barry R. Mccaffrey, Director, Office of National Drug Control Policy." (March 26, 1998)

The Netherlands and
the United States — A Comparison

1. "The sale of cannabis is illegal, yet coffee shops are tolerated in their sale of cannabis, if they adhere to certain criteria: no advertising, no sale of hard drugs, not selling to per-sons under the age of 18, not causing public nuisance and not selling more than 5 grams per transaction (AHOJ-G criteria). Three extra criteria are: no alcohol vendor, no more than 500 grams in stock and -in some cities- a minimum distance to a school or to the Dutch border. In recent years, government policy has aimed to reduce the number of coffee shops. However, the decision whether or not to tolerate a coffee shop lies with the local governments. At the end of 2005, the Netherlands had 729 officially tolerated cannabis outlets (coffee shops). This is a 1.0 percent overall decrease compared to the situation in 2004 (737 coffee shops, see paragraph 10.1). In 2005, the majority of the 467 municipalities in the Netherlands pursued a zero policy (72%) or a maximum policy (22%) with regard to the number of tolerated coffee shops."

Source: Trimbos Institute, "Drug Situation 2006 The Netherlands by the Reitox National Focal Point: Report to the EMCDDA" (Utrecht, Netherlands: Trimbos-Instuut, 2007), p. 18.

2. Comparing Important Drug and Violence Indicators

Social Indicator	Comparison Year	USA	Netherlands
Lifetime prevalence of marijuana use (ages 12+)	2001	36.9% #1	17.0% #2
Past month prevalence of marijuana use (ages 12+)	2001	5.4% #1	3.0% #2
Lifetime prevalence of heroin use (ages 12+)	2001	1.4% #1	0.4% #2
Incarceration Rate per 100,000 population	2002	704 #3	100 #4
Per capita spending on criminal justice system (in Euros)	1998	379 #5	223 #5
Homicide rate per 100,000 population	average 1999-2001	5.56 #6	1.52 #6

Source #1: US Department of Health and Human Services (HHS), Substance Abuse and Mental Health Services Administration, National Household Survey on Drug Abuse: Volume I. Summary of National Findings (Washington, DC: HHS, August 2002), p. 109, Table H.1.

Source #2: Trimbos Institute, "Report to the EMCDDA by the Reitox National Focal Point, The Netherlands Drug Situation 2002" (Lisboa, Portugal: European Monitoring Centre for Drugs and Drug Addiction, Nov. 2002), p. 28, Table 2.1.

Source #3: Walmsley, Roy, "World Prison Population List (fifth edition)" (London, England: Research, Development and Statistics Directorate of the Home Office), Dec. 2003, p. 3, Table 2.

Source #4: Walmsley, Roy, "World Prison Population List (fifth edition)" (London, England: Research, Development and Statistics Directorate of the Home Office), Dec. 2003, p. 5, Table 4.

The Netherlands and
the United States — A Comparison

Source #5: van Dijk, Frans & Jaap de Waard, "Legal infrastructure of the Netherlands in international perspective: Crime control" (Netherlands: Ministry of Justice, June 2000), p. 9, Table S.13.

Source #6: Barclay, Gordon, Cynthia Tavares, Sally Kenny, Arsalaan Siddique & Emma Wilby, "International comparisons of criminal justice statistics 2001," Issue 12/03 (London, England: Home Office Research, Development & Statistics Directorate, October 2003), p. 10, Table 1.1.

3. "There were 2.4 drug-related deaths per million inhabitants in the Netherlands in 1995. In France this figure was 9.5, in Germany 20, in Sweden 23.5 and in Spain 27.1. According to the 1995 report of the European Monitoring Centre for Drugs and Drug Addiction in Lisbon, the Dutch figures are the lowest in Europe. The Dutch AIDS prevention programme was equally successful. Europe-wide, an average of 39.2% of AIDS victims are intravenous drug-users. In the Netherlands, this percentage is as low as 10.5%."

   Source: Netherlands Ministry of Justice, Fact Sheet: Dutch Drugs Policy, (Utrecht: Trimbos Institute, Netherlands Institute of Mental Health and Addiction, 1999).

4. "The number of problem opiate/crack users seems to have remained relatively stable in the past ten years (3.1 per 1000 people aged 15-64 years). In the past decade, local field studies among traditional groups of problem opiate users have shown a strong in-crease in the co-use of crack cocaine, a reduction in injecting drug use, and an increase in psychiatric and somatic comorbidity."

   Source: Trimbos Institute, "Drug Situation 2006 The Netherlands by the Reitox National Focal Point: Report to the EMCDDA" (Utrecht, Netherlands: Trimbos-Instuut, 2007), p. 9.

5. "Cannabis use among young people has also increased in most Western European countries and in the US. The rate of (cannabis) use among young people in the US is much higher than in the Netherlands, and Great Britain and Ireland also have relatively larger numbers of school students who use cannabis."

   Source: Netherlands Ministry of Health, Welfare and Sport, Drug Policy in the Netherlands: Progress Report September 1997-September 1999, (The Hague: Ministry of Health, Welfare and Sport, November 1999), p. 7.

6. "The figures for cannabis use among the general population reveal the same pictures. The Netherlands does not differ greatly from other European countries. In contrast, a comparison with the US shows a striking difference in this area: 32.9% of Americans aged 12 and above have experience with cannabis and 5.1% have used in the past month. These figures are twice as high as those in the Netherlands."

   Source: Netherlands Ministry of Health, Welfare and Sport, Drug Policy in the Netherlands: Progress Report September 1997-September 1999, (The Hague: Ministry of Health, Welfare and Sport, November 1999), pp. 7-8.

qq

The Netherlands and the United States — A Comparison

7. "The prevalence figures for cocaine use in the Netherlands do not differ greatly from those for other European countries. However, the discrepancy with the United States is very large. The percentage of the general population who have used cocaine at some point is 10.5% in the US, five times higher than in the Netherlands. The percentage who have used cocaine in the past month is 0.7% in the US, compared with 0.2% in the Netherlands.*"

*Source: Netherlands Ministry of Health, Welfare and Sport, Drug Policy in the Netherlands: Progress Report September 1997-September 1999, (The Hague: Ministry of Health, Welfare and Sport, November 1999), p. 6. The report notes "*The figures quoted in this paragraph for drug use in the US are taken from the National Household Survey 1997, SAMSHA, Office of Applied Studies, Washington, DC".*

8. "The National Youth Health Surveys (in 1988, 1992, 1996, 1999) among pupils (12-18 years) showed that the increase in cannabis use since 1988 stabilised between 1996 and 1999 (De Zwart et al. 2000). According to the Health Behaviour in School-aged Children study, this trend continued in 2001 (Ter Bogt et al. 2003). Use of other drugs showed a similar trend or slightly drecreased (LTP of ecstasy and amphetamine)."

Source: Trimbos Institute, "Report to the EMCDDA by the Reitox National Focal Point, The Netherlands Drug Situation 2003" (Lisboa, Portugal: European Monitoring Centre for Drugs and Drug Addiction, Dec. 2003), p. 19.

Treatment

1. "Domestic enforcement costs 4 times as much as treatment for a given amount of user reduction, 7 times as much for consumption reduction, and 15 times as much for societal cost reduction."

   Source: Rydell, C.P. & Everingham, S.S., Controlling Cocaine, Prepared for the Office of National Drug Control Policy and the United States Army (Santa Monica, CA: Drug Policy Research Center, RAND Corporation, 1994), p. xvi.

2. "An additional cocaine-control dollar generates societal cost savings of 15 cents if used for source-country control, 32 cents if used for interdiction, and 52 cents if used for domestic enforcement. In contrast, the savings from treatment programs are larger than control costs: an additional cocaine-control dollar generates societal cost savings of $7.48 if used for treatment."

   Source: Rydell, C.P. & Everingham, S.S., Controlling Cocaine, Prepared for the Office of National Drug Control Policy and the United States Army (Santa Monica, CA: Drug Policy Research Center, RAND Corporation, 1994), p. 42.

3. The RAND Corporation found that the additional spending needed to achieve a 1% reduction in the number of cocaine users varies according to the sort of program used, and that treatment is the most cost-effective:

Control Program:	Additional Spending Needed to achieve a 1% reduction in number of cocaine users
Source Country Control	$2,062,000,000
Interdiction	$964,000,000
Domestic Enforcement	$675,000,000
Treatment	$155,000,000

   Source: Rydell, C.P. & Everingham, S.S., Controlling Cocaine, Prepared for the Office of National Drug Control Policy and the United States Army (Santa Monica, CA: Drug Policy Research Center, RAND Corporation, 1994), p. 36.

4. The US Office of National Drug Control Strategy estimated that the federal government spent $2.942 billion on treatment and treatment research in 2006 and an estimated $2.943 billion in 2007.

   Source: "National Drug Control Strategy: FY2008 Budget Summary," Office of National Drug Control Policy (ONDCP)(Washington, DC: Executive Office of the President, Feb. 2007), p. 9, Table 1.

5. In 2002, federal funding for drug treatment totaled $3,587,500,000, representing 19.1% of the $18,822,800,000 drug war budget. The FY2003 request for treatment funding was $3,811,700,000, which represents 19.9% of the $19,179,700,000 requested drug war budget. Combined, federal prevention and treatment funding — the demand-side — totaled $6,136,100,000 in FY2002, and a requested $6,285,100,000 for FY2003. Law enforcement and interdiction — the supply-side of the equation — ate up the remaining two-thirds of federal drug war spending, or $12,686,700,000 in FY2002, and $12,894,600,000 requested in FY2003.

rr

Treatment

Source: "National Drug Control Strategy: FY2003 Budget Summary," Office of National Drug Control Policy (ONDCP)(Washington, DC: Executive Office of the President, Feb. 2002), p. 6, Table 2.

6. "In 2005, an estimated 22.2 million persons aged 12 or older were classified with substance dependence or abuse in the past year (9.1 percent of the population aged 12 or older) (Figure 7.1). Of these, 3.3 million were classified with dependence on or abuse of both alcohol and illicit drugs, 3.6 million were dependent on or abused illicit drugs but not alcohol, and 15.4 million were dependent on or abused alcohol but not illicit drugs. "Between 2002 and 2005, there was no change in the number of persons with substance dependence or abuse (22.0 million in 2002, 21.6 million in 2003, 22.5 million in 2004, and 22.2 million in 2005). "There were 18.7 million persons aged 12 or older classified with dependence on or abuse of alcohol in 2005 (7.7 percent). This estimate has remained stable since 2002."

Source: Substance Abuse and Mental Health Services Administration, "Results from the 2005 National Survey on Drug Use and Health: National Findings," (Rockville, MD: Office of Applied Studies, SAMHSA, 2006), NSDUH Series H-30, DHHS Publication No. SMA 06-4194, p. 67.

7. "In 2005, the number of persons aged 12 or older needing treatment for an illicit drug or alcohol use problem was 23.2 million (9.5 percent of the population aged 12 or older) (Figure 7.6). Of these, 2.3 million (0.9 percent of persons aged 12 or older and 10.0 percent of those who needed treatment) received treatment at a specialty facility. Thus, there were 20.9 million persons (8.6 percent of the population aged 12 or older) who needed treatment for an illicit drug or alcohol use problem but did not receive treatment at a specialty substance abuse facility in the past year."

Source: Substance Abuse and Mental Health Services Administration, "Results from the 2005 National Survey on Drug Use and Health: National Findings," (Rockville, MD: Office of Applied Studies, SAMHSA, 2006), NSDUH Series H-30, DHHS Publication No. SMA 06-4194, p. 75.

8. According to the National Treatment Improvement Evaluation Study (NTIES), "The results show substantial reductions in criminal behavior and arrests after treatment: Selling drugs declined by 78 percent; Those who reported shoplifting declined by almost 82 percent; Before treatment, almost half the respondents reported 'beating someone up.' Following treatment that number declined to 11 percent; a 78 percent decrease; Changes in arrest rates were less striking than those in self-reported criminal behavior, but the 64 percent reduction in arrests for any crime was still dramatic; and The percentage who largely supported themselves through illegal activity dropped by nearly half - decreasing more than 48 percent."

Source: National Clearinghouse for Alcohol and Drug Information, US Dept. of Health and Human Services, "National Treatment Improvement Evaluation Study - Costs of Treatment," from the web at http://www.health.org/govstudy/f027/crime.aspx, last accessed Jan. 27, 2004.

rr

Treatment

9. "Treatment appears to be cost effective, particularly when compared to incarceration, which is often the alternative. Treatment costs ranged from a low of about $1,800 per client to a high of approximately $6,800 per client. While the cost of incarceration was not examined by NTIES, widely reported studies such as one reported by the American Correctional Association, gave an estimated 1994 cost of incarceration as $18,330 annually."

   Source: National Clearinghouse for Alcohol and Drug Information, US Dept. of Health and Human Services, "National Treatment Improvement Evaluation Study - Costs of Treatment," from the web at http://www.health.org/govstudy/f027/costs.aspx, last accessed Jan. 27, 2004.

10. "States report spending $2.5 billion a year on treatment. States did not distinguish whether the treatment was for alcohol, illicit drug abuse or nicotine addiction. Of the $2.5 billion total, $695 million is spent through the departments of health and $633 million through the state substance abuse agencies. We believe that virtually all of these funds are spent on alcohol and illegal drug treatment."

    Source: National Center on Addiction and Substance Abuse at Columbia University, Shoveling Up: The Impact of Substance Abuse on State Budgets (New York, NY: CASA, Jan. 2001), p. 24.

11. In January 2001, the National Center on Addiction and Substance Abuse at Columbia University published an analysis of costs to states from tobacco, alcohol and other drug addiction. According to the report, "The justice system spends $433 million on treatment: $149 million for state prison inmates; $103 million for those on probation and parole; $133 million for juvenile offenders; $46 million to help localities treat offenders; $1 million on drug courts. Treatment provided by mental health institutions for co-morbid patients totals $241 million. The remaining $492 million is for the substance abuse portion of state employee assistance programs ($97 million), treatment programs for adults involved in child welfare services ($4.5 million) and capital spending for the construction of treatment facilities ($391 million). (Figure 4.B)"

    Source: National Center on Addiction and Substance Abuse at Columbia University, Shoveling Up: The Impact of Substance Abuse on State Budgets (New York, NY: CASA, Jan. 2001), p. 24.

12. "The Panel anxiously awaits the time when the disease of addiction is no longer treated as a criminal justice issue, but as a public health problem. Moreover, the Panel embraces the notion of a society that enables any individual with a substance abuse problem, regardless of criminal history, to receive treatment in a safe and respectful environment. The Panel hopes to create a climate in which people who are at risk for, suffering from, or in recovery from alcohol or other drug addiction are valued and treated with dignity."

    Source: US Dept. of Health and Human Services, Substance Abuse and Mental Health Services Administration, "Changing the Conversation: Improving Substance Abuse Treatment: The National Treatment Plan Initiative; Panel Reports, Public Hearings, and Participant Acknowledgements" (Washington, DC: SAMHSA, November 2000), p. 41.

Treatment

13. "Regardless of the source, a conservative estimate of those in need of substance abuse treatment is between 13 and 16 million people. In contrast, both the 1997 Institute of Medicine (IOM) report, Managing Managed Care, and the 1998 National Household Survey conclude that approximately 3 million people receive care for alcohol or drugs in one year. Although, as previously stated, neither the estimates of need nor the estimates of those in treatment are all inclusive, the picture remains the same – more than 10 million people who need treatment each year are not receiving it."

   Source: US Dept. of Health and Human Services, Substance Abuse and Mental Health Services Administration, "Changing the Conversation: Improving Substance Abuse Treatment: The National Treatment Plan Initiative; Panel Reports, Public Hearings, and Participant Acknowledgements" (Washington, DC: SAMHSA, November 2000), p. 6.

14. Treatment decreased welfare use by 10.7% and increased employment by 18.7% after one year, according to the 1996 National Treatment Improvement Evaluation Study.

   Source: Center for Substance Abuse and Treatment, National Treatment Improvement Evaluation Study (Washington DC: US Government Printing Office, 1996), p. 11.

15. In 1996, voters in Arizona passed an initiative which mandated drug treatment instead of prison for non-violent drug offenders. At the end of the first year of implementation, Arizona's Supreme Court issued a report which found:
   A) Arizona taxpayers saved $2.6 million in one year;
   B) 77.5% of drug possession probationers tested negative for drug use after the program; The Court stated, "The Drug Medicalization, Prevention and Control Act of 1996 has allowed the judicial branch to build an effective probation model to treat and supervise substance abusing offenders... resulting in safer communities and more substance abusing probationers in recovery."

   Source: State of Arizona Supreme Court, Drug Treatment and Education Fund: Implementation Full Year Report: Fiscal Year 1997-1998, 1999

16. According to CASA (National Center on Addiction and Substance Abuse), the cost of proven treatment for inmates, accompanied by education, job training and health care, would average about $6,500 per inmate. For each inmate that becomes a law-abiding, tax-paying citizen, the economic benefit is $68,800. Even if only one in 10 inmates became a law-abiding citizen after this investment, there would still be a net social gain of $3,800.

   Source: National Center on Addiction and Substance Abuse at Columbia University, Behind Bars: Substance Abuse and America's Prison Population, (New York, NY: National Center on Addiction and Substance Abuse at Columbia University, January 8, 1998), Foreword by Joseph Califano.

17. "The percentage of recent drug users in State prison who reported participation in a variety of drug abuse programs rose from 34% in 1997 to 39% in 2004 (table 9). This increase was the result of the growing percentage of recent drug users who reported taking part in

Treatment

self-help groups, peer counseling and drug abuse education programs (up from 28% to 34%). Over the same period, the percentage of recent drug users taking part in drug treatment programs with a trained professional was almost unchanged (15% in 1997, 14% in 2004).

"Participation in drug abuse programs also increased among Federal inmates who had used drugs in the month before their offense, from 39% in 1997 to 45% in 2004. While there was no change in percentage of these inmates who had undergone drug treatment with a trained professional (15% in both years), the percentage taking part in other drug abuse programs rose from 32% in 1997 to 39% in 2004."

Source: Mumola, Christopher J., and Karberg, Jennifer C., "Drug Use and Dependence, State and Federal Prisoners, 2004," (Washington, DC: Bureau of Justice Statistics, Dept. of Justice, Oct. 2006) NCJ-213530, p. 8.

18. "In 2004, about 642,000 State prisoners were drug dependent or abusing in the year before their admission to prison. An estimated 258,900 of these inmates (or 40%) had taken part in some type of drug abuse program (table 10). These inmates were more than twice as likely to report participation in selfhelp or peer counseling groups and education programs (35%) than to receive drug treatment from a trained professional (15%).

"In Federal prison, a higher percentage of drug dependent or abusing inmates (49%) reported taking part in some type of drug abuse programs. Nearly 1 in 3 took part in drug abuse education classes, and 1 in 5 had participated in self-help or peer counseling groups. Overall, 17% took part in drug treatment programs with a trained professional, and 41% had participated in other drug abuse programs."

Source: Mumola, Christopher J., and Karberg, Jennifer C., "Drug Use and Dependence, State and Federal Prisoners, 2004," (Washington, DC: Bureau of Justice Statistics, Dept. of Justice, Oct. 2006) NCJ-213530, p. 9.

20. "One of the main reasons for the higher outlay in public spending is the frequently limited coverage of substance abuse treatment by private insurers. Although 70 percent of drug users are employed and most have private health insurance, 20 percent of public treatment funds were spent on people with private health insurance in 1993, due to limitations on their policy (ONDCP, 1996b). In the view of the Panel, private insurers should serve as the primary source of coverage, with public insurance serving as the safety net."

Source: US Dept. of Health and Human Services, Substance Abuse and Mental Health Services Administration, "Changing the Conversation: Improving Substance Abuse Treatment: The National Treatment Plan Initiative; Panel Reports, Public Hearings, and Participant Acknowledgements" (Washington, DC: SAMHSA, November 2000), p. 12.

21. "Public support and public policy are influenced by addiction stigma. Addiction stigma delays acknowledging the disease and inhibits prevention, care, treatment, and research. It diminishes the life opportunities of the stigmatized."

Source: US Dept. of Health and Human Services, Substance Abuse and Mental Health Services Administration, "Changing the Conversation: Improving Substance Abuse Treatment: The National Treatment Plan Initiative; Panel Reports, Public Hearings, and Participant Acknowledgements" (Washington, DC: SAMHSA, November 2000), p. 38-39.

rr

Women

1. The most serious offense for 65% of women in federal prisons and 29.1% of women in state prisons is violation of drug laws.

   Source: Bureau of Justice Statistics, Compendium of Federal Justice Statistics, 2003 (Washington, DC: US Dept. of Justice, Oct. 2005), p. 108, Table 7.10; Harrison, Paige M. & Allen J. Beck, PhD, Bureau of Justice Statistics, Prisoners in 2005 (Washington DC: US Department of Justice, Nov. 2006), p. 9, Table 13.

2. The number of women incarcerated in prisons and jails in the USA is approximately 10 times more than the number of women incarcerated in Western European countries, even though Western Europe's combined female population is about the same size as that of the USA.

   Source: Amnesty International, "Not Part of My Sentence: Violations of the Human Rights of Women in Custody" (Washington, DC: Amnesty International, March 1999), p. 15.

3. "During 2005 the number of females under the jurisdiction of State or Federal prison authorities increased by 2.6% (table 5). The number of males in prison rose 1.9%. At yearend 2005, 107,518 females and 1,418,406 males were in prison. Since 1995 the annual rate of growth in female prisoners averaged 4.6%, which was higher than the 3.0% increase in male prisoners. By yearend 2005 females accounted for 7.0% of all prisoners, up from 6.1% in 1995 and 5.7% in 1990."

   Source: Harrison, Paige M. & Allen J. Beck, PhD, Bureau of Justice Statistics, Prisoners in 2005 (Washington DC: US Department of Justice, Nov. 2006), p. 4.

4. "Since 1995 the total number of male prisoners has grown 34%; the number of female prisoners, 57%. At yearend 2005, 1 in every 1,538 women and 1 in every 108 men were incarcerated in a State or Federal prison."

   Source: Harrison, Paige M. & Allen J. Beck, PhD, Bureau of Justice Statistics, Prisoners in 2005 (Washington DC: US Department of Justice, Nov. 2006), p. 4.

5. "Relative to their number in the U.S. resident population, males were over 14 times more likely than females to be incarcerated in a State or Federal prison. At yearend 2005 there were 65 sentenced female inmates per 100,000 females in the resident population, compared to 929 sentenced male inmates per 100,000 males."

   Source: Harrison, Paige M. & Allen J. Beck, PhD, Bureau of Justice Statistics, Prisoners in 2005 (Washington DC: US Department of Justice, Nov. 2006), p. 4.

6. "Female incarceration rates, though substantially lower than male incarceration rates at every age, reveal similar racial and ethnic differences. Black females (with an incarceration rate of 156 per 100,000) were more than twice as likely as Hispanic females (76 per 100,000) and over 3 times more likely than white females (45 per 100,000) to have been in prison on December 31, 2005. These differences among white, black, and Hispanic females were consistent across all age groups."

   Source: Harrison, Paige M. & Allen J. Beck, PhD, Bureau of Justice Statistics, Prisoners in 2005 (Washington DC: US Department of Justice, Nov. 2006), p. 8.

Women

7. Women are the fastest growing and least violent segment of prison and jail populations. 85.1% of female jail inmates are behind bars for nonviolent offenses.

   Source: Irwin, John, PhD, Vincent Schiraldi, and Jason Ziedenberg, America's One Million Nonviolent Prisoners (Washington, DC: Justice Policy Institute, March 1999), pp. 6-7.

8. From 1986 (the year mandatory sentencing was enacted) to 1996, the number of women sentenced to state prison for drug crimes increased ten fold (from around 2,370 to 23,700) and has been the main element in the overall increase in the imprisonment of women.

   Source: Amnesty International, "Not Part of My Sentence: Violations of the Human Rights of Women in Custody" (Washington, DC: Amnesty International, March 1999), p. 26.

9. From 1985 to 1996, female drug arrests increased by 95%, while male drug arrests increased by 55.1%.

   Sources: Federal Bureau of Investigation, Uniform Crime Reports 1985 (Washington DC: US Government Printing Office, 1986), p. 181, Table 37; Federal Bureau of Investigation, 1997 Uniform Crime Report (Washington DC: US Government Printing Office, 1998), p. 231, Table 42.

10. In 2005, there were a reported 2,472,303 arrests of women, of which 259,362 (9.46%) were for drug offenses. (Note: This represents a portion of the total estimated arrests in 2005, covering 10,974 agencies comprising a total population of 217,722,329 Americans.)

    Source: Crime in the United States 2005, Uniform Crime Reports Washington, DC: Federal Bureau of Investigation, Oct. 2006), Table 40, from the web at http://www.fbi.gov/ucr/05cius/data/table_40.html.

11. Between 1990 and 1996, the number of women convicted of drug felonies increased by 37% (from 43,000 in 1990 to 59,536 in 1996). The number of convictions for simple possession increased 41% over that period, from 18,438 in 1990 to 26,022 in 1996.

    Source: Greenfield, Lawrence A., and Snell, Tracy L., Bureau of Justice Statistics, Women Offenders (Washington, DC: US Department of Justice, December 1999), p. 5, Table 11.

12. In 1997 a US Justice Department investigation of women's prisons in Arizona concluded that the authorities failed to protect women from sexual misconduct by correctional officers and other staff. The misconduct included rape, sexual relationships, sexual touching and fondling, and "without good reason, frequent, prolonged, close-up and prurient viewing during dressing, showing and use of toilet facilities." (CIV97-476, US District of Arizona).

    Source: Amnesty International, "Not Part of My Sentence: Violations of the Human Rights of Women in Custody" (Washington, DC: Amnesty International (March 1999), p. 39.

13. Retaliation for reports of abuse impedes women's access to protection of their human rights. One woman who won a lawsuit against the Federal Bureau of Prisons for sexual abuse reported that she was beaten, raped and sodomized by three men who in the course of the attack told her that they were attacking her in retaliation for providing a statement to investigators.

Women

Source: Amnesty International, "Not Part of My Sentence: Violations of the Human Rights of Women in Custody" (Washington, DC: Amnesty International, March 1999), p. 59.

14. Sick and pregnant women are routinely shackled during hospitalization and childbirth if they are inmates of prisons or jails in the USA.

Source: Amnesty International, "Not Part of My Sentence: Violations of the Human Rights of Women in Custody" (Washington, DC: Amnesty International, March 1999), p. 63.

15. Approximately 516,200 women on probation (72% of the total), 44,700 women in local jails (70% of the total), 49,200 women in State prisons (65% of the total), and 5,400 women in Federal prisons (59% of the total) have minor children.

Source: Greenfield, Lawrence A., and Snell, Tracy L., Bureau of Justice Statistics, Women Offenders (Washington, DC: US Department of Justice, December 1999), p. 7, Table 17.

16. Criminalizing substance abuse during pregnancy discourages substance-using or abusing women from seeking prenatal care, drug treatment, and other social services, and sometimes leads to unnecessary abortions.

Sources: Cole, H.M., "Legal Interventions During Pregnancy: Court-Ordered Medical Treatment and Legal Penalties for Potentially Harmful Behavior by Pregnant Women," Journal of the American Medical Association, 264: 2663-2670 (1990); Polan, M.L., Dombrowski, M.P., Ager, J.W., & Sokol, R.J., "Punishing Pregnant Drug Users: Enhancing the Flight from Care," Drug and Alcohol Dependence, 31: 199-203 (1993); Koren, G., Gladstone, D. Robeson, C. & Robieux, I., "The Perception of Teratogenic Risk of Cocaine," Teratology, 46: 567-571 (1992).

17. Forty-four percent of women under correctional authority, including 57% of the women in State prisons, reported that they were physically or sexually abused at some point in their lives. Sixty-nine percent of women reporting an assault said that it had occurred before age 18.

Source: Greenfield, Lawrence A., and Snell, Tracy L., Bureau of Justice Statistics, Women Offenders (Washington, DC: US Department of Justice, December 1999), p. 8, Table 20.

18. Many women in prisons and jails in the USA are victims of sexual abuse by staff, including male staff touching inmates' breasts and genitals when conducting searches; male staff watching inmates while they are naked; and rape.

Source: Amnesty International, "Not Part of My Sentence: Violations of the Human Rights of Women in Custody" (Washington, DC: Amnesty International, March 1999), p. 38.

19. "At the end of 2000, 86,000 women were living with injection-related AIDS or had already died from it. Many thousands more were infected with HIV. African American and Latina women are the hardest hit; they accounted for over 75 percent of all women with injection-related AIDS in 2001."

Source: Dawn Day, Ph.D., Health Emergency 2003: The Spread of Drug-Related AIDS and other Deadly Diseases Among African Americans and Latinos (New York, NY: Harm Reduction Coalition, 2002), p. 14.

Women

20. "The burden of HIV/AIDS falls most heavily on infants of color and their mothers. Some 80 percent of the infants born with HIV are African American or Latino."

   Source: Dawn Day, Ph.D., Health Emergency 2003: The Spread of Drug-Related AIDS and other Deadly Diseases Among African Americans and Latinos (New York, NY: Harm Reduction Coalition, 2002), p. 14.

21. "As women become infected and die of AIDS, they leave children behind. In 1998, there were 67,000 American children under the age of 18, mostly children of color, who had lost their mothers to the AIDS epidemic. More than half of these children were 12 or younger."

   Source: Dawn Day, Ph.D., Health Emergency 2003: The Spread of Drug-Related AIDS and other Deadly Diseases Among African Americans and Latinos (New York, NY: Harm Reduction Coalition, 2002), p. 14.

22. "Of the 13,573 treatment facilities that responded to the 2000 N-SSATS (National Survey of Substance Abuse Treatment Services), 60 percent reported that they provided at least one of the special programs or services for women. Almost one third of the facilities (33 percent) provided one program or service, 17 percent of the facilities provided two programs or services, 8 percent of the facilities provided three, and 3 percent provided four programs or services (data not shown). Of the facilities providing programs or services for women, 63 percent reported providing programs for women only, 56 percent reported services addressing domestic violence, 34 percent provided programs for pregnant or postpartum women, and 16 percent offered on-site child care services."

   Source: "Facilities Offering Special Programs or Services for Women," The Dasis Report (Washington, DC: Dept. of Health and Human Services, Substance Abuse and Mental Health Services Administration, Office of Applied Studies, Oct. 11, 2002), pp. 1-2.

23. "Facilities offering special programs or services for women were more likely to provide a variety of treatment services than facilities that did not offer such programs or services (Figure 1). These included transitional employment (with the largest difference, 42 percent vs. 25 percent), relapse prevention (83 percent vs. 67 percent), transportation assistance (42 percent vs. 26 percent), family counseling (83 percent vs. 69 percent), and pharmacotherapies (46 percent vs. 36 percent). Some 97 percent of facilities with women's programs or services offered individual therapy compared with 91 percent of facilities without special women's programs or services. In addition, 91 percent of facilities with women's programs or services offered group therapy compared with 84 percent of the other facilities."

   Source: "Facilities Offering Special Programs or Services for Women," The Dasis Report (Washington, DC: Dept. of Health and Human Services, Substance Abuse and Mental Health Services Administration, Office of Applied Studies, Oct. 11, 2002), p. 2.

SS

INDEX

INDEX

INDEX

Glossary

Agonist: Substance which mimics some of the physical effects of a drug (e.g. methadone, buprenorphine)

AIDS: Acquired Immune Deficiency Syndrome

AJPH: American Journal of Public Health

AMA: American Medical Association

Antagonist: Substance which blocks the effects of a drug (e.g. naltrexone, nalmefene) without producing tolerance, dependence, or psychological effects.

APHA: American Public Health Association

BJS: Bureau of Justice Statistics

BMJ: British Medical Journal

CDC: US Centers for Disease Control

CEWG: Community Epidemiology Working Group

CSAP: US Center for Substance Abuse Prevention (Division of SAMHSA)

CSAT: US Center for Substance Abuse Treatment (Division of SAMHSA)

DAWN: Drug Abuse Warning Network

DEA: US Drug Enforcement Administration

DOJ: US Dept. of Justice

EMCDDA: European Monitoring Centre on Drugs and Drug Addiction

ESPAD: European School Survey Project on Alcohol and Other Drugs

EU: European Union

FBI: US Federal Bureau of Investigation

FDA: US Food and Drug Administration

GAO: US Government Accountability Office (formerly General Accounting Office)

HCV: Hepatitis C Virus

HHS: US Dept. of Health and Human Services

HIV: Human Immunodeficiency Virus

HR: Harm Reduction

IDU: Injection Drug User

Jail: Incarceration facility typically used to hold inmates sentenced to terms of one year or less.

JAMA: Journal of the American Medical Association

MDMA: 3,4-methylenedioxymethamphetamine (Ecstasy)

MMT: Methadone Maintenance Treatment

NAS: US National Academy of Sciences

NEJM: New England Journal of Medicine

NEP: Needle Exchange Program

NHSDA: National Household Survey on Drug Abuse

NIDA: US National Institute on Drug Abuse

NIH: US National Institutes of Health

NSDUH: National Survey on Drug Use and Health

OBT: Office-Based Treatment

ONDCP: US Office of National Drug Control Policy

Opioid: Substance related to or derived from opium (e.g. heroin, methadone, oxycodone)

Parole: Period of conditional supervised release which sometimes follows a term of incarceration.

Prison: Incarceration facility typically used to hold more serious offenders, i.e. those sentenced to terms of more than a year.

Probation: Period of correctional supervision in the community to which criminal offenders are sentenced in lieu of incarceration.

SAMHSA: US Substance Abuse and Mental Health Services Administration, a part of the US Dept. of Health and Human Services

SEP: Syringe Exchange Program

SCF: Supervised Consumption Facility

SIF: Sanitary Injection Facility

UCR: Uniform Crime Report

UNODC: United Nations Office on Drugs and Crime, formerly the United Nations Drug Control Program.

WHO: United Nations World Health Organization

Notes

Notes